新托福
核心单词速记

蒋志榆 ◎ 著

北京理工大学出版社
BEIJING INSTITUTE OF TECHNOLOGY PRESS

使用说明
User's guide

1. 依字母顺序排列，方便搜寻查找

全书集结市面上托福书籍、考试题、英文新闻（CNN）、报纸杂志（The New York Times）中最专业的单词，电脑严格挑选出其中托福最爱考的2000单词，按照字母排列目编号，方便读者迅速查找，完全适用托福测验。

Aa 托福 TOEFL iBT

托福(TOEFL)的测验对象为母语为非英语的人
申请入学美加地区大学或研究所时，托福成绩单是必备文件之一。

1. **abandon** [ə'bændən] [a·ban·don] ★★★
   - v. 抛弃,放弃 — I truly believe that those who abandon themselves to despair can never succeed.
     我相信那些自暴自弃的人永远无法成功。
   - n. 放纵,沉溺 — The boy danced with wild abandon at his birthday party.
     这个男孩在他的生日舞会上狂放地跳舞。
   - 同义字词 ▲ relinquish

2. 托福单词分解拼读MP3，单词保证记得住

独家附赠保证记得住的"单词分解拼读法MP3"，全书单词采用三段式"完整／分解／中文"录制，先将单词清楚读出，接着以英文字母拼出单词，最后读出完整中文解释。例如："abnormal / a·b·n·o·r·m·a·l / 异常的"。不需随时随地捧着厚重的书本，也能轻轻松松背单词。托福单词走到哪，背到哪。

Aa 托福 TOEFL iBT

托福(TOEFL)的测验对象为母语为非英语的人
申请入学美加地区大学或研究所时，托福成绩单是必备文件之一。

1. **abandon** [ə'bændən] [a·ban·don] ★★★
   - v. 抛弃,放弃 — I truly believe that those who abandon themselves to despair can never succeed.
     我相信那些自暴自弃的人永远无法成功。
   - n. 放纵,沉溺 — The boy danced with wild abandon at his birthday party.
     这个男孩在他的生日舞会上狂放地跳舞。
   - 同义字词 ▲ relinquish
   - 反义字词 ▲ cherish, defend
   - 衍生字词 ▲ halt v. (使)停下来
   - 高分秘诀 ▲ troop n. 车队,部队

3. 最完整的"托福测验"学习方案

每个单词皆附有"KK音标"以及"字母拼读法"，搭配超神奇MP3，不论训练英文听力，还是加强地道英文腔调，保证双管齐下，再也不用为自己的英文听说能力发愁。

4. **abbreviate** [ə'brivɪ,et] [ab·bre·vi·ate] ★★★
   - v. 缩短,缩写 — We usually abbreviated "New York" to "NY".
     我们通常把"纽约New York"简写成"NY"。
   - 同义字词 ▲ shorten, cut, abridge
   - 反义字词 ▲ amplify, lengthen
   - 衍生字词 ▲ abbreviated adj. 简略的
     ▲ abbreviation n. 缩写,缩写词
   - 高分秘诀 ▲ New York 纽约
     ▲ usually adv. 通常,平常

5. **abdicate** ['æbdə,ket] [ab·di·cate] ★★★★
   - v. 退位,逊位 — We all known that the king was forced to abdicate and hand over power to others.
     我们都知道国王是被迫退位，交出政权的。

使用说明 User's guide

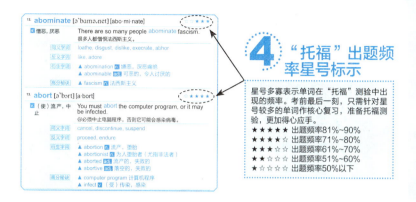

4 "托福"出题频率星号标示

星号多寡表示单词在"托福"测验中出现的频率。考前最后一刻,只需针对星号较多的单词作核心复习,准备托福测验,更加得心应手。
★★★★★ 出题频率81%～90%
★★★★☆ 出题频率71%～80%
★★★☆☆ 出题频率61%～70%
★★☆☆☆ 出题频率51%～60%
★☆☆☆☆ 出题频率50%以下

5 例句详尽,一个单词多种用法

市面上绝大多数的托福单词书中,每个单词通常只附单一例句,导致读者无法真正吸收并灵活运用在口说或写作测验中。本书单词针对不同词性,补充多个例句,增强读者对单词的理解力,彻底掌握托福测验。

6 高分秘诀,相关用法条列式补充

贴心的同反义字词、衍生字词补充以及精心设计的高分秘诀皆以条列式编排,方便读者一目了然,背单词的同时,也能吸收相关补充,以这种最有系统的方式准备托福测验,保证应考实力大增。

003

作者序
Preface

我和出版社曾合作出版了《英语单词7000分级背》,感谢各方读者的支持,出版至今广受好评且荣登各大书店、网络书店语言学习类畅销书籍排行榜第一名。通过出版社得知许多读者对于此书所提供的学习法非常认同且赞誉有加,并表示自己的分数也因此而受益良多。今年应许多考生要求,我又与出版社合作推出《新托福核心单词速记》,有鉴于此,编辑与我便开始讨论将托福考试套用这套"躺着背"学习法的可行性,希望借此能造福准备托福考试的考生,并让更多的英文学习者受益于此学习法。

已经实行四十年的托福测验(TOEFL,Test of English as a Foreign Language)的目的是测验考生的英语能力,测验对象则是母语为非英语的人,想要申请进入美加地区的大学或是研究所的申请人,非常有可能被要求考过并达到托福一定成绩。除了美国和加拿大地区之外,澳大利亚、英国、新西兰等英语系国家的学校也可能会要求申请者提供托福成绩。2000年,托福纸笔测验改制为电脑化测验(TOEFL CBT)。2006年5月20日起,再度将电脑化测验改制为现行的网络化测验,也就是所谓的TOEFL iBT。托福网络测验经由网际网络方式进行,测验项目包含"阅读(Reading)""听力(Listening)""口说(Speaking)"及"写作(Writing)"。

随着职场及商场竞争愈来愈激烈,出国深造逐渐变成投资自己最有效的方式,但若想挤进国外大学或是研究所的窄门,

作者序 Preface

不可避免地必须具备一张亮眼的托福成绩单。然而，对于母语为非英语的考生来说，托福测验的范围十分广泛，难度也比其他英语测验更高更复杂，因此，若能确实掌握托福出题老师偏爱的单词范围，对于想获得高分的考生来说无疑更加重要。

这本《新托福核心单词速记》集结市面上托福书籍、考试题、英文新闻（CNN，BBC，NBC）、报纸杂志（The New York Times，The Times，Times）最实用、最专业的单词，以电脑严格挑选"托福"最爱考的2 000单词，并对每个单词作最丰富完整的补充。不但如此，本书更独创保证记得住的"单词分解拼读法MP3"，采用三段式"完整／分解／中文"录制，先将单词清楚读出，接着以英文字母拼出单词，最后读出完整中文解释，例如"abnormal／a·b·n·o·r·m·a·l／异常的"。让读者不论是坐公车、乘地铁、逛街或运动都可以边听MP3边背单词。走到哪，背到哪，不需随时随地捧着厚重的书本，也能轻轻松松背托福单词。

此外，《新托福核心单词速记》更贴心地为考生做好了万全的考前准备工作，每个单词皆标示星号，星号愈多表示出题频率愈高，方便考生考前最后一刻对重点单词做总复习，加深记忆，保证单词一背就忘不了。想获得高分的考生千万不可错过我专为你们设计的高分秘诀，内容除了重点短语以及语法的补充外，还包括常用字词搭配。你会发现，准备托福考试，原来可以这么有效率，不需手忙脚乱。

作者序
Preface

　　出国留学是许多人的梦想,许多英文学习者因为害怕考试的难度及入学申请的高门槛而裹足不前,希望这本书能帮助所有想留学深造的读者实现自己的梦想,要记得,投资自己绝对是最明智的选择。

　　在此,预祝所有托福考生都能拿到梦寐以求的分数。

蒋志榆

2011年4月

目录 Contents

- **Aa** | abandon ~ awkward ... 010
- **Bb** | baboon ~ buzz ... 070
- **Cc** | cabin ~ cynic ... 110
- **Dd** | dagger ~ dynamic ... 172
- **Ee** | eager ~ eyewitness ... 214
- **Ff** | fable ~ fuse ... 252
- **Gg** | gallant ~ gyrate ... 282
- **Hh** | habitat ~ hypothesis ... 292
- **Ii** | icon ~ itinerary ... 306
- **Jj** | jar ~ juxtaposition ... 334
- **Kk** | keen ~ kinetic ... 338
- **Ll** | laborious ~ lyric ... 342
- **Mm** | magic ~ mythical ... 356

目录
Contents

- **Nn** | narcotic ~ nutritious ············ 372
- **Oo** | obligate ~ overwhelm ············ 378
- **Pp** | pack ~ purify ············ 388
- **Qq** | quaint ~ quota ············ 428
- **Rr** | radiate ~ rustic ············ 432
- **Ss** | sacred ~ synthesize ············ 472
- **Tt** | tableland ~ tyrannical ············ 508
- **Uu** | ultimate ~ utter ············ 524
- **Vv** | vacant ~ vulnerable ············ 532
- **Ww** | wade ~ wrinkle ············ 540
- **Yy** | yarn ~ yolk ············ 548
- **Zz** | zealous ~ zone ············ 550

Aa 托福 TOEFL iBT

托福(TOEFL)的测验对象为母语为非英语的人
申请入学美加地区大学或研究所时，托福成绩单是必备文件之一。

- n. 名词
- v. 动词
- adj. 形容词
- adv. 副词
- prep. 介词
- art. 冠词
- pron. 代词
- aux. 助词
- conj. 连词

Aa 托福 TOEFL iBT

托福(TOEFL)的测验对象为母语为非英语的人
申请入学美加地区大学或研究所时,托福成绩单是必备文件之一。

1. abandon [ə`bændən] [a·ban·don] ☆☆★★★

v. 抛弃,放弃	I truly believe that those who abandon themselves to despair can never succeed. 我相信那些自暴自弃的人永远无法成功。
n. 放纵,沉溺	The boy danced with wild abandon at his birthday party. 这个男孩在他的生日舞会上狂放地跳舞。
同义字词	▲ relinquish
反义字词	▲ cherish, defend
衍生字词	▲ halt v. (使)停下来
高分秘诀	▲ troop n. 军队,部队

2. abash [ə`bæʃ] [a·bash] ☆☆★★★

v. 使羞愧,使尴尬,使窘迫	My teacher's criticism left me feel rather abashed. 老师的指责让我感到好丢脸。
同义字词	shame, disconcert, embarrass
反义字词	embolden
衍生字词	abashed 羞愧的,尴尬的,困窘的
高分秘诀	▲ criticism n. 批评,批判,指责,评论(文章) ▲ rather adv. 在一定程度上,或多或少,有几分,相当

3. abate [ə`bet] [a·bate] ☆★★★★

v. 减少,减弱,减轻	It's necessary for the government to take measures to abate the smoke nuisance in the metropolises. 政府有必要采取手段消除大城市的烟尘污染。
同义字词	decrease, lessen, reduce
反义字词	increase, strengthen, raise, augment
衍生字词	abatement 减少,减轻,缓和

abandon ~ abhor

高分秘诀	▲ take measures 采取措施
	▲ nuisance n. 讨厌的东西（人、行为），损害，麻烦事

4. abbreviate [əˋbrivɪ͜et] [ab·bre·vi·ate]   ☆☆★★★

v. 缩短，缩写	We usually abbreviate "New York" to "NY".
	我们通常把"纽约New York"简写成"NY"。
同义字词	shorten, cut, abridge
反义字词	amplify, lengthen
衍生字词	▲ abbreviated adj. 简缩的
	▲ abbreviation n. 缩写，缩写词
高分秘诀	▲ New York 纽约
	▲ usually adv. 通常，平常

5. abdicate [ˋæbdə͵ket] [ab·di·cate]   ☆★★★★

v. 退位，逊位	We all knew that the king was forced to abdicate and hand over power to others.
	我们都知道国王是被迫退位、交出政权的。
同义字词	give up the throne, lay down the sceptre
衍生字词	▲ abdication n. 退位，让位
	▲ abdicator n. 退位者
	▲ abdicable adj. 可放弃的，可辞职的
高分秘诀	▲ hand over 交出，交付
	▲ power n. 权力，政权，职权，能力，天赋

6. abduct [æbˋdʌkt] [ab·duct]   ★★★★★

v. 诱拐，劫持	The merchant's mind reeled when he learned that his daughter had been abducted.
	得知女儿被人拐走，这个商人只觉得一阵晕眩。
同义字词	kidnap, hijack, highjack
衍生字词	▲ abduction n. 绑架，拐骗，劫持
	▲ abductor n. 诱拐者，劫持者，绑架者
	▲ abductive adj. 诱导的
高分秘诀	▲ merchant n. 商人
	▲ reel v. 发昏，发热，蹒跚地走路

7. abhor [əbˋhɔr] [ab·hor]   ☆☆★★★

v. 憎恶，嫌恶	I found I began to loathe and abhor my boss and utterly despise him.
	我发现我现在开始厌恶、憎恨我的老板，我彻底看不起他!

同义字词	hate, loathe, abominate, execrate, detest
反义字词	like
衍生字词	▲ abhorence n. 憎恨，厌恶 ▲ abhorrent adj. 讨厌的，可恶的
高分秘诀	▲ utterly adv. 全然，完全地，彻底地 ▲ despise v. 鄙视，看不起某人（某事）

8. abide [əˈbaɪd] [a·bide] ☆☆★★★

v. 遵守，忍受	We have no choice but to abide by the verdict. 我们除了服从裁决外别无选择。
同义字词	endure, bear, tolerate, follow
衍生字词	▲ abider n. 忍受者，遵守者 ▲ abiding adj. 持久的，永久的
高分秘诀	▲ abide by 遵守，信守 ▲ verdict n. （陪审团的）裁决，裁定

9. ablaze [əˈbleɪz] [a·blaze] ☆☆★★★

adj. 着火的，燃烧的	I don't know why my father was ablaze with anger. 我不知道父亲为何怒不可遏。
衍生字词	▲ burning adj. 燃烧的，着火的 ▲ radiant, bright, blazing adj. 发光的，闪耀的
高分秘诀	▲ ablaze with anger 怒火中烧

10. abnormal [æbˈnɔrml] [ab·nor·mal] ☆★★★★

adj. 反常的，异常的	There is something wrong with my grandmother. She seems mentally abnormal. 奶奶有些不对劲，似乎精神不正常。
同义字词	unnatural, odd, weird
反义字词	normal, usual, regular
衍生字词	▲ abnormality n. 异常，反常 ▲ abnormally adv. 反常地 ▲ paranormal adj. 超自然的 ▲ anomaly n. 异常，不规则，异常的人或物
高分秘诀	▲ mentally adv. 心理上，精神上；智力上

abide ~ abort

11. abolish [əˋbɑlɪʃ] [a·bol·ish] ☆★★★★

v. 废除，取消（法律、制度、习俗等）

It's Abraham Lincoln who abolished slavery in the United States.
亚伯拉罕·林肯废除了美国的奴隶制度。

同义字词　cancel, repeal

反义字词　establish, found, set

衍生字词
▲ abolishment **n.** 废除，取消
▲ abolishable **adj.** 可废除的，可取消的
▲ abolitionist **n.** 废除主义者
▲ abolition **n.** 废除，取消

高分秘诀
▲ Abraham Lincoln 亚伯拉罕·林肯
▲ slavery **n.** 奴隶身份，奴隶制度
▲ United States **n.** 美国

12. abominate [əˋbɑməˌnet] [abo·mi·nate] ☆☆★★★

v. 憎恶，厌恶

There are so many people abominate fascism.
很多人都憎恨法西斯主义。

同义字词　loathe, disgust, dislike, execrate, abhor

反义字词　like, adore

衍生字词
▲ abomination **n.** 嫌恶，深恶痛绝
▲ abominable **adj.** 可恶的，令人讨厌的

高分秘诀
▲ fascism **n.** 法西斯主义

13. abort [əˋbɔrt] [a·bort] ☆★★★★

v. （使）流产，中止

You must abort the computer program, or it may be infected.
你必须中止电脑程序，否则它可能会感染病毒。

同义字词　cancel, discontinue, suspend

反义字词　proceed, endure

衍生字词
▲ abortion **n.** 流产，堕胎
▲ abortionist **n.** 为人堕胎者（尤指非法者）
▲ aborted **adj.** 流产的，失败的
▲ abortive **adj.** 落空的，失败的

高分秘诀
▲ computer program 计算机程序
▲ infect **v.** （受）传染，感染

14. abrade [ə`bred] [a·brade] ☆☆★★★

v. 磨损，擦伤

The boy fell off the bike and most of the skin on his leg was abraded.
男孩从自行车上摔了下来，整只腿几乎都擦破了皮。

同义字词 abrase, rub off

衍生字词
▲ abrasive adj. 摩擦的
▲ abrasion n. 磨损，擦掉
▲ abradant n. 研磨材料，研磨剂
▲ abradability n. 耐磨性，耐磨度
▲ abrader n. 磨石，研磨器

高分秘诀 ▲ fall off 跌落，滚落下

15. abrupt [ə`brʌpt] [a·brupt] ☆☆★★★

adj. 突然的，意外的

I know this abrupt change of schedule would give us lots of trouble.
我知道突然改变这次行程会给我们造成许多麻烦。

同义字词 sudden, unforeseen, unexpected

反义字词 expected

衍生字词
▲ abruption n. 分裂，分离
▲ abruptness n. 突然，意外
▲ abruptly adv. 突然地，意外地

高分秘诀
▲ schedule n. 时间表，行程表
▲ trouble n. 麻烦，费事

16. absent [`æbsn̩t] [ab·sent] ☆★★★★

adj. 缺席的，缺乏的

The young lady became not only melancholy when alone, but dejected and absent in company.
这位年轻女士不但独处的时候闷闷不乐，就算是与他人在一起的时候也无精打采，心不在焉。

同义字词 absentminded, abstracted, distrait

反义字词 present

衍生字词
▲ absence n. 缺少，缺席
▲ absentee n. 缺席者

高分秘诀
▲ melancholy adj. 忧郁的，悲伤的
▲ dejected adj. 沮丧的，忧郁的，失望的

17. absorb [əbˈsɔrb] [ab·sorb] ☆☆★★

v. 吸收（液体、知识），吸引……的注意

Don't shout at him. He can't hear you, he's utterly absorbed in his comic strip.
别喊，他听不见，他正专注地看漫画。

同义字词	assimilate
反义字词	distract
衍生字词	▲ absorbing **adj.** 吸引人的，非常有趣的 ▲ absorbed **adj.** 全神贯注的 ▲ absorbent **adj.** 能吸收的
高分秘诀	▲ shout at 对……大声喊 ▲ be absorbed in... 全神贯注于 ▲ comic strip 连环漫画，连环图画

18. abstract [ˈæbstrækt] [ab·stract] ☆☆★★

n. 摘要，抽提（物）

Please make an abstract of the lecture when you listen to it.
在你听演讲时，请做个演讲的摘要。

v. 摘要

I think the speech is so long, you should abstract the most important point from it.
我认为这个演讲太冗长，你应该从中把重点提取出来。

adj. 抽象的

Do you agree the point that beauty itself is abstract?
美是很抽象的，你同意吗?

同义字词	extract, summary, nonrepresentational
反义字词	concrete
衍生字词	▲ abstraction **n.** 抽象，提取 ▲ abstractly **adv.** 抽象地 ▲ abstractionist **n.** 抽象派艺术家 ▲ abstractive **adj.** 具有抽象能力的，摘要式的
高分秘诀	▲ make an abstract of... 把……的要点摘录下来 ▲ lecture **n.** / **v.** 演讲，讲课 ▲ point **n.** 要点，论点，观点

19. absurd [əbˈsɝd] [ab·surd] ☆☆★★

adj. 荒谬的，可笑的

It's absurd to go camping in such a terrible weather.
在这种恶劣的天气出去露营简直荒谬。

同义字词	ridiculous, ludicrous, stupid
反义字词	reasonable, sensible
衍生字词	▲ absurdly adv. 荒谬地 ▲ absurdity n. 荒谬，愚蠢
高分秘诀	▲ go camping 露营 ▲ terrible adj. 可怕的，糟透了，令人恐惧的

20. abundant [əˈbʌndənt] [a·bun·dant] ☆★★★★

adj. 丰富的，充裕的，大量的

Don't worry; you have abundant proof of that gangster's guilt.
别担心，你有充分的证据证明那个歹徒有罪。

同义字词	fertile, rich, productive
反义字词	short, lacking, insufficient
衍生字词	▲ abound v. 充满，富于 ▲ abundance n. 大量，充足 ▲ abundantly adv. 丰富地，充裕地
高分秘诀	▲ proof n. 证明，证据，证物 ▲ gangster n. 匪徒，歹徒 ▲ guilt n. 有罪，对罪行有责任，使人内疚的责备

21. abuse [əˈbjuz] [a·buse] ☆☆★★★

v. 滥用，辱骂

It has been revealed that some officals abuse their authority and position to get illegal profits for themselves.
有些官员被揭露滥用职权，非法牟利。

n. 滥用，辱骂

I've never expected that my best friend attacked me with a stream of abuse.
没想到我最好的朋友竟然以一连串的谩骂攻击我。

同义字词	misuse, mistreat
衍生字词	▲ abuser n. 滥用者 ▲ abusive adj. 滥用的，辱骂的
高分秘诀	▲ official n. 行政官员 ▲ authority n. 权力，职权 ▲ illegal profit 非法利润 ▲ attack v. 攻击，进攻，抨击 ▲ a stream of 一连串，一系列

22. academic [ˌækəˈdɛmɪk] [ac·a·dem·ic] ★★★★★

adj. 学院的，理论的
It's impossible for you to be a historian; you know a good historian must have an academic mind.
你不可能成为一名历史学家；一个好的历史学家必须有学术头脑。

n. 大学老师，学者
Don't look down on that ugly old woman, she is an academic of Oxford Academy.
别小看那个丑老太婆，她可是牛津研究学院的学者。

同义字词	academician, learned
衍生字词	▲ academy **n.** 专科院校，学会 ▲ academe **n.** 研究院，学会，学术界 ▲ academia **n.** 学术界，学术环境
高分秘诀	▲ historian **n.** 历史学家 ▲ look down on 轻视，看不起 ▲ Oxford Academy 牛津研究学院

23. accelerate [ækˈsɛləˌret] [ac·ce·le·rate] ☆☆★★★

v. 加快，加速
You would lose ground as the rest of the rivals accelerate.
当其他竞争对手加速时，你就失去优势了。

同义字词	speed up, hasten, quicken
反义字词	decelerate, retard
衍生字词	▲ accelerated **adj.** 加速的，迅速的 ▲ accelerating **adj.** 加速的 ▲ acceleration **n.** 加速，加快，加速度 ▲ acceleratory **adj.** 加速的，催促的
高分秘诀	▲ lose ground 失利，败退，退却 ▲ rival **n.** 竞争对手

24. access [ˈæksɛs] [ac·cess] ☆★★★★

n. 接触，接近（的机会）
Susan is the general manager's private secretary that she has access to all his correspondence.
苏珊是总经理的私人秘书，所以能接触到他的所有信件。

同义字词	approach, entry, entrance
衍生字词	▲ accessible **adj.** 可接近的，可接触的 ▲ accessibility **n.** 易接近，可达到

高分秘诀	▲ general manager 总经理
	▲ private secretary 私人秘书
	▲ correspondence n. 信件，函件，通信，通信联络

25. accidental [ˌæksəˈdɛntl] [ac·ciden·tal] ★★★★★

adj. 意外的，偶然（发生）的	Breaking your vase was really accidental; you know I didn't meant to do it.
	打破你的花瓶纯属意外，我真的不是故意的。
同义字词	unexpected, casual, unforeseen, unanticipated
反义字词	intentional, deliberate
衍生字词	▲ accidentally adv. 偶然地，意外地
	▲ accident n. 意外事件，事故
高分秘诀	▲ vase n. 花瓶
	▲ mean to do 本意要做某事，打算做某事

26. acclaim [əˈklem] [ac·claim] ☆☆★★★

v. 喝彩，欢呼	The audience acclaimed this movie star as he appeared on the stage.
	当电影明星一上台，观众大声欢呼。
n. 赞誉，赞许	Despite the popular acclaim of my new project, the general manager harrumphed.
	尽管我的新方案颇受好评，总经理却对此嗤之以鼻。
同义字词	plaudit, applaud
反义字词	hiss, boo
衍生字词	▲ acclaimer n. 欢呼者
高分秘诀	▲ movie star 电影明星
	▲ appear v. 出现，显现
	▲ stage n. 舞台
	▲ despite prep. 不管，尽管
	▲ general manager 总经理
	▲ harrumph v. 发哼声

27. accommodate [əˈkɑməˌdet] [ac·com·mo·date] ☆★★★★

v. 为提供住宿，容纳	This hotel could accommodate eight hundred tourists.
	这家饭店可以容纳八百名观光客。
同义字词	contain, hold, fit, conform

accidental ~ account

衍生字词	▲ accommodation n. 住处
	▲ accommodating adj. 乐于助人的
	▲ accommodative adj. 乐于助人的，随和的
	▲ accommodator n. 调解
高分秘诀	▲ tourist n. 旅行者，观光客
	▲ accommodate oneself to 使自己适应于

28. accompany [əˈkʌmpənɪ] [ac·com·pa·ny] ☆☆★★★

v. 陪伴，伴随，伴奏

As we all know that the lightning usually accompanies thunder.
我们都知道闪电通常伴随雷声。

同义字词	go with, come with, follow
反义字词	leave
衍生字词	▲ accompanying adj. 陪伴的，伴随的
	▲ accompaniment n. 伴奏，伴随物
	▲ accompanist n. 伴奏者
高分秘诀	▲ as we all know 众所周知
	▲ lightning n. 闪电
	▲ thunder n. 雷声

29. accomplish [əˈkɑmplɪʃ] [ac·com·plish] ☆☆★★★

v. 完成，达到，实现

It's impossible for me to accomplish the mission successfully in one week.
我不可能在一个星期内成功完成任务。

同义字词	achieve, realize, finish, fulfill, complete
反义字词	fail
衍生字词	▲ accomplished adj. 精通的，熟练的
	▲ accomplishment n. 完成，实现
	▲ accomplishable adj. 可达成的，可完成的
高分秘诀	▲ it's impossible to do something 不可能做成某事
	▲ mission n. 使命，任务
	▲ successfully adv. 顺利地，成功地

30. account [əˈkaʊnt] [ac·count] ☆★★★★

n. 说明，户头

According to the account, I have spent more than I received.
账户表明我已经入不敷出。

v. 解释	Could you please account for your absence from work yesterday? 你能否解释昨天没有上班的原因呢?
同义字词	report, description, explain
衍生字词	▲ accountable adj. （对自己的行为等）应作解说，负责 ▲ accounting n. 会计学 ▲ accountant n. 会计，会计师
高分秘诀	▲ according to 根据，按照 ▲ account for 解释 ▲ absence n. 缺席，离开，不在场

31. accredit [əˋkrɛdɪt] [ac·cre·dit]   ☆☆★★

v. 任命，委派	It's said that the president will accredit Susan as his assistant. 据说董事长将任命苏珊为他的助理。
同义字词	authorize, commission
衍生字词	▲ accredited adj. 官方认可的 ▲ accreditation n. 任命，授权 ▲ accreditable adj. 可任命的，可授权的
高分秘诀	▲ it's said that 据说，听说 ▲ president n. 总统，董事长，总裁 ▲ assistant n. 助手，助理

32. accumulate [əˋkjumjəˌlet] [ac·cu·mu·late]   ☆☆★★

v. 堆积，累积	Accumulated energy must be released in one form or another, for example, an earthquake. 长期累积的能量必须以一种形式释放，例如（经由）地震。
同义字词	collect, pile up, amass
反义字词	scatter, dissipate
衍生字词	▲ accumulation n. 积聚 ▲ accumulated adj. 积聚的 ▲ accumulative adj. 累积的，聚积的
高分秘诀	▲ energy n. 能，能量，能源 ▲ release v. 释放，放开 ▲ for example 例如，譬如 ▲ earthquake n. 地震

accredit ~ accustom

33. accurate [ˈækjərɪt] [ac·cu·rate] ☆☆★★★

adj. 精确的，准确的	I think my description would enable you to form an accurate picture of what had happened last night. 我想我的描述会让你们对昨晚所发生的事如身临其境。
同义字词	correct, right, exact
反义字词	inaccurate, incorrect
衍生字词	▲ accurately adv. 准确地，正确无误地 ▲ accuracy n. 准确，精确度
高分秘诀	▲ description n. 描述，形容 ▲ enable v. 使能够，使可能

34. accuse [əˈkjuz] [ac·cuse] ☆☆★★★

v. 指责，归咎	The girl got fired, because she was accused of incompetence. 女孩被解雇，因为她被认为能力不足。
同义字词	blame, condemn, criminate
反义字词	defend
衍生字词	▲ accusation n. 谴责，控告 ▲ accuser n. 原告 ▲ accusingly adv. 用指责的态度
高分秘诀	▲ get fired 被解雇 ▲ be accused of 指责，控告 ▲ incompetence n. 无能力，不称职，不胜任

35. accustom [əˈkʌstəm] [ac·cus·tom] ☆★★★★

v. (使)习惯于	Though he is a newcomer, he soon gets accustomed to the new surroundings. 尽管他是新手，可是他很快就习惯了新环境。
同义字词	acclimate, condition
衍生字词	▲ accustomed adj. 惯常的，习惯于……的
高分秘诀	▲ though conj. 虽然，尽管 ▲ newcomer n. 新来的人，新手 ▲ get (be) accustomed to... 习惯于…… ▲ surroundings n. 环境，周遭的事物

36. achieve [əˋtʃiv] [a·chieve] ☆☆★★★

v. 完成，实现

If you are not diligent and intelligent, then it's impossible for you to achieve success.
如果你不够聪明勤奋，就不可能成功。

同义字词 accomplish, fulfill, realize

反义字词 fail

衍生字词
▲ achievement **n.** 完成，达到
▲ achievable **adj.** 可完成的，可达到的
▲ achiever **n.** 获得成功的人

高分秘诀
▲ intelligent **adj.** 聪明的，理解力强的
▲ diligent **adj.** 勤奋的，勤勉的
▲ impossible **adj.** 不可能的，办不到的

37. acknowledge [əkˋnɑlɪdʒ] [ac·know·ledge] ☆☆★★★

v. 承认，供认

Though I don't like him, I have to acknowledge his criticism is just.
虽然我不喜欢他，但我不得不承认他的批评是公正的。

同义字词 admit, recognize, express gratitude

反义字词 deny

衍生字词
▲ acknowledgement **n.** 承认，确认，致谢

高分秘诀
▲ though **conj.** 虽然，尽管
▲ criticism **n.** 批评，指责
▲ just **adj.** 公正的，公平的

38. acquaintance [əˋkwentəns] [ac·quain·tance] ☆★★★★

n. 熟人，了解

I remembered that I made the acquaintance of Robert at that small hotel.
我记得我是在那间小饭店认识罗伯特的。

同义字词 friend, familiarity

反义字词 stranger

衍生字词
▲ acquaint **v.** 使熟悉，使了解
▲ acquaintanceship **n.** 相识，相熟
▲ acquainted **adj.** 对某事熟悉

高分秘诀
▲ make one's acquaintance / make the acquaintance of sb. 结识某人
▲ Robert 罗伯特（男子名）

achieve ~ acute

39. acquire [ə`kwaɪr] [ac·quire] ☆☆★★★

v. 获得, 得到

Back once said: Be curious always! For knowledge will not acquire you; you must acquire it.
巴克曾经说过: "永远保持好奇心!"因为知识不会自己从天上掉下来, 你必须自己获得。

[同义字词] obtain, secure, gain

[反义字词] lose, miss

[衍生字词]
▲ acquirement **n.** 取得, 习得
▲ acquisition **n.** 获得物
▲ acquisitive **adj.** 可获得的

[高分秘诀]
▲ once **adv.** 曾经, 昔时
▲ curious **adj.** 好奇的, 好求知的
▲ knowledge **n.** 学问, 个人的知识

40. actuate [`æktʃuˌet] [ac·tu·ate] ☆☆★★★

v. 开动, 促使

Don't blame yourself so badly, I know you was just actuated solely by greed.
别过度责怪自己, 我知道你只是一时贪念。

[同义字词] motivate, activate, incite

[衍生字词]
▲ actuation **n.** 驱使, 激励, 行动
▲ actuated **adj.** 开动的

[高分秘诀]
▲ blame **v.** 指责, 责怪
▲ solely **adv.** 唯一地, 仅仅, 独一无二地
▲ greed **n.** 贪心, 贪婪

41. activate [`æktəˌvet] [ac·ti·vate] ☆★★★★

v. 刺激, 使活动

As is known to us all that your lofty spirit have greatly attracted and activated others.
众所皆知, 你的崇高精神大大地吸引并且激励他人。

[同义字词] encourage, motivate

[衍生字词]
▲ actively **adj.** 开动的, 活跃地, 积极地
▲ activator **n.** 触媒剂

[高分秘诀]
▲ as is known to us all... 众所皆知
▲ lofty **adj.** 高尚的, 崇高的

42. acute [ə`kjut] [a·cute] ☆☆★★★

adj. 灵敏的, 敏锐的, 急剧的

In the clinic, there is a patient who is complaining of acute earache.
在诊所中, 有个患者抱怨耳朵剧痛。

023

同义字词	keen, penetrating, severe
反义字词	obtuse, chronic
衍生字词	acumen n. 敏锐，聪明 acutely adv. 强烈意识到；极其，强烈地
高分秘诀	▲ clinic n. 诊所，医务室 ▲ patient n. 病患，患者， adj. 忍耐的，有耐心的 ▲ complain of 抱怨，诉苦 ▲ earache n. 耳朵痛

43. adapt [ə`dæpt] [a·dapt]   ☆☆★★

v. (使)适应,调整	I'm glad that you adapted yourself quickly to the new surrounding. 真高兴你这么快就适应了新环境。
同义字词	adjust, accommodate, modify
反义字词	unfit
衍生字词	▲ adaptable adj. 能适应的，适应能力强的 ▲ adaptation n. 改编，改写，适应环境 ▲ adaptive adj. 适应的，适合的
高分秘诀	▲ adapt oneself to 使自己适应或习惯于（某事） ▲ surrounding n. 环境，周遭的事物

44. addict [ə`dɪkt] [ad·dict]   ☆☆☆★★

v. 使上瘾,使沉溺	I'm very disappointed with my father; he was addicted to heroin. 我对父亲很失望，他吸食海洛因上瘾。
n. 上瘾的人	An addict will stop at nothing to get his drug. 瘾君子为了得到毒品什么事都做得出来。
同义字词	hook, junkie, junky
衍生字词	▲ addictive adj. （使人）上瘾的 ▲ addicted adj. 上瘾的 ▲ addiction n. 瘾，沉溺
高分秘诀	▲ be disappointed with sb. 对某人很失望 ▲ be addicted to 沉迷于，使上瘾 ▲ heroin n. 海洛因 ▲ stop at nothing 无所不为，肆无忌惮 ▲ drug n. 药剂，毒品

adapt ~ adhere

45. additional [əˋdɪʃənl] [ad·di·tion·al] ☆☆★★★

adj. 另外的，附加的，额外的

Don't worry, I will pay for the additional expenses.
别担心，额外的费用由我来付。

同义字词： further, extra

衍生字词：
▲ addition **n.** 加，加法，增加的人或事物
▲ additive **adj.** 添加的，附加的

高分秘诀：
▲ pay for... 为……付钱
▲ expenses **n.** 费用，开支

46. adept [əˋdɛpt] [a·dept] ☆★★★★

adj. 熟练的，擅长的

Wow, both of you are so great. You are adept in music and your brother is adept in drawing.
哇！你们两个真棒！你精通音乐，你弟弟擅长绘画。

同义字词： competent, skilled, skillful, proficient

反义字词： inept

衍生字词： ▲ adeptly **adv.** 熟练地，擅长地

高分秘诀：
▲ be adept in 擅长
▲ drawing **n.** 绘画，制图

47. adequate [ˋædəkwɪt] [a·de·quate] ★★★★★

adj. 足够的，充足的

If we could make adequate preparations, then the chance of success would be great.
如果我们准备充分，那么成功的机会就很大。

同义字词： sufficient, enough, plenty

反义字词： inadequate, deficient, insufficient

衍生字词：
▲ adequacy **n.** 足够，充分
▲ adequately **adv.** 足够地

高分秘诀： ▲ make preparations 做准备

48. adhere [ədˋhɪr] [ad·here] ☆☆★★★

v. 黏附，黏着

You have to chip the old paint from the walls, and then adhere from scratch.
首先你必须把旧的油漆全部刮掉，然后重新粉刷。

同义字词： cohere, stick, cling

衍生字词： adhesive **adj.** 黏着的

高分秘诀	▲ chip v. 剥落，刮去 ▲ paint n. 油漆，涂料 ▲ from scratch 从头开始

49. adjacent [ə`dʒesənt] [ad·ja·cent] ☆☆★★★

adj. 毗连的，邻近的	I know him very well, because my house is adjacent to his. 我和他很熟，因为我们毗邻而居。
同义字词	abutting, conterminous, neighboring, adjoining, nearby
衍生字词	▲ adjacency n. 邻接 ▲ adjacently adv. 毗连地，邻近地
高分秘诀	▲ be adjacent to 与……毗连，邻近

50. adjoin [ə`dʒɔɪn] [ad·join] ☆☆★★★

v. 毗连，邻近	The teacher told us that New Jersey adjoins New York. 老师告诉我们新泽西与纽约相邻。
同义字词	abut, be next to, border on
反义字词	disjoin
衍生字词	▲ adjoining adj. 毗邻的
高分秘诀	▲ New Jersey 新泽西 ▲ New York 纽约

51. adjust [ə`dʒʌst] [ad·just] ☆☆★★★

v. 调整，使适合于	You have no choice but to adjust yourself to the whirl of modern life in the metropolis. 你别无选择，只能让自己适应这个大都市现代忙碌的生活。
同义字词	adapt, regulate
反义字词	derange, disturb
衍生字词	▲ adjustment n. 调整 ▲ adjustable adj. 可调节的，可调整的
高分秘诀	▲ have no choice but to 别无他法，只好 ▲ adjust oneself to 使自己适应于 ▲ modern life 现代生活

52. administer [əd`mɪnəstə] [ad·mi·nis·ter] ☆★★★★

v. 管理，执行	It's hard for a woman to administer a large corporation. 一个女人管理大公司确实不容易。

adjacent ~ adopt

同义字词	administrate, govern, supervise, manage
衍生字词	▲ administration n. 管理，执行
	▲ administrant adj. 管理的
	▲ administrative adj. 行政的，管理的
	▲ administrator n. 管理人，行政人员
高分秘诀	▲ it's hard for somebody 对某人来说很难
	▲ corporation n. 公司

53. admire [əd`maɪr] [ad·mire] ☆★★★★

v. 钦佩，崇拜

I really admire your little sister's diplomatic tact.
我真的很佩服你妹妹的外交手腕。

同义字词	esteem, appreciate, look up to
反义字词	despise, look down on
衍生字词	▲ admiration n. 钦佩，赞美
	▲ admiring adj. 赞赏的，钦佩的
	▲ admirer n. 赞赏者，羡慕者
高分秘诀	▲ societal adj. 社会的
	▲ savoir-fair n. 机智手腕，才干

54. admit [əd`mɪt] [ad·mit] ☆☆★★★

v. 准许进入，承认

Only those who have tickets in hand were admitted.
只有持票者方可进入。

同义字词	acknowledge, accept
反义字词	deny, refuse, prohibit, forbid
衍生字词	▲ admittedly adv. 公认地，诚然，无可否认地
	▲ admittance n. 准入，入场许可
高分秘诀	▲ ticket n. 票，券，入场券
	▲ in hand 在手中

55. adopt [ə`dɑpt] [a·dopt] ☆☆☆★★

v. 采用，采纳

If you want to get more profit, you should adopt the consumers' suggestions.
如果你想赚更多利润，你应该接受消费者的建议。

同义字词	raise, foster, take on
反义字词	reject
衍生字词	▲ adoption n. 采用，收养
	▲ adoptive adj. 收养的，被采纳的

| 高分秘诀 | ▲ profit n. 利润，收益
▲ consumer n. 用户
▲ suggestion n. 建议，意见 |

56. adorn [ə`dɔrn] [a·dorn] ☆☆★★★

| v. 装饰 | Nowadays, more and more young ladies like to adorn themselves with jewels.
如今，越来越多的年轻女士喜欢佩戴珠宝。 |

同义字词	decorate, ornament, beautify, embellish
反义字词	disfigure
衍生字词	▲ adornment n. 装饰，装饰品 ▲ unadorned adj. 未装饰的，朴实的
高分秘诀	▲ nowadays adv. 现下，现时 ▲ more and more 越来越 ▲ adorn sb. with something 佩戴 ▲ jewel n. 宝石，珠宝

57. advance [əd`væns] [ad·vance] ☆☆★★★

| v. 前进, 发展 | It's the series of fortuitous circumstances that advanced my career.
这一连串的机遇使我的事业一帆风顺。 |
| n. 前进, 进步 | A snowstorm halted the advance of the enemy troops.
一场雪暴阻止了敌军的进攻。 |

同义字词	proceed, move forward
反义字词	back, retreat, fall back
衍生字词	▲ advanced adj. 进阶的，年老的，先进的 ▲ advancer n. 前进者
高分秘诀	▲ fortuitous adj. 偶然的，偶然发生的 ▲ circumstance n. 环境，条件，情况 ▲ career n. 职业，生涯 ▲ snowstorm n. 雪暴，雪崩 ▲ halt v. （使）停下来 ▲ troop n. 军队，部队

58. adventure [əd`vɛntʃə] [ad·ven·ture] ☆★★★★

| n. 冒险经历 | Thank God! My daughter got back safe from her adventure.
谢天谢地，我女儿有惊无险地从冒险旅程平安归来。 |

adorn ~ aesthetic

v. 冒险	I bet no man would adventure it. 我敢打赌没有人会冒这个险。
同义字词	risk, venture, hazard, gamble
衍生字词	▲ adventurous adj. 喜欢冒险的，敢作敢为的 ▲ adventurer n. 冒险家
高分秘诀	▲ thank God 谢天谢地 ▲ get back 回来，回家 ▲ bet n. / v. 打赌

59. adverse [æd`vɝs] [ad·verse] ☆★★★★

adj. 负面的，不利的	On our way home we encountered adverse weather condition. 在回家的路上，我们遇到了不利的气候条件。
同义字词	ill, disadvantageous, contrary, opposite
衍生字词	▲ adversely adv. 相反地，不利地 ▲ adversity n. 逆境，厄运
高分秘诀	▲ on the way 在途中，接近 ▲ encounter v. 遇到，遭遇 ▲ weather condition 气候条件，天气条件

60. advocate [`ædvəkɪt] [ad·vo·cate] ★★★★★

v. 拥护，主张	The mayor advocates to reform the economic system. 市长主张改良经济制度。
n. 提倡者，主张者	These people are advocates of free speech. 这些人是言论自由的倡导者。
同义字词	urge, preach, support
反义字词	oppose
衍生字词	▲ advocator n. 拥护者，提倡者 ▲ advocatory adj. 拥护者的，有关拥护者的
高分秘诀	▲ mayor n. 市长 ▲ reform v. 改革，改造，改善 ▲ economic system 经济体制 ▲ free speech 言论自由

61. aesthetic [ɛs`θɛtɪk] [aes·the·tic] ☆☆★★★

adj. 美学的，审美的	No one knows who advanced this aesthetic theory. 没有人知道是谁提出这个美学理论的。

同义字词	aesthetical, artistic, esthetic, esthetical
反义字词	inaesthetic, unaesthetic
衍生字词	▲ aesthetically adv. 美学地 ▲ aesthetics n. 美学，审美学，美术理论 ▲ aestheticism n. 唯美主义
高分秘诀	▲ aesthetic theory 美学理论

62. affect [ə`fɛkt] [af·fect] ☆☆☆★★

v. 影响，感动	The weather really affects us so directly—what we wear, what we do, and even how we feel. 天气对我们穿衣服、做事，甚至心情都有直接的影响。
同义字词	impact, influence
衍生字词	▲ affected adj. 装模作样的 ▲ affection n. 友爱，挚爱，情爱 ▲ affective adj. 感情的，表达感情的
高分秘诀	▲ directly adv. 直接地，径直地

63. affiliate [ə`fɪlɪ‚et] [af·fi·li·ate] ☆☆☆★★

v. 使隶属，接纳为成员	Both of us are affiliated with a local club. 我们两个都加入了当地的一个俱乐部。
同义字词	attach to, subject, receive back
衍生字词	▲ affiliation n. 加入，隶属 ▲ affiliation order 父子关系确认令（协助抚养非婚生子）
高分秘诀	▲ be affiliated with... 与……有关系，加入 ▲ local club 当地俱乐部

64. affirm [ə`fɝm] [af·firm] ☆☆★★★

v. 断言，确认	I dare affirm that the eggs will be very expensive during the Moon Festival. 我敢肯定中秋节期间鸡蛋一定会很贵。
同义字词	assert, declare, confirm, certify
反义字词	deny, negate
衍生字词	▲ affirmation n. 肯定，断言 ▲ affirmative adj. 表示同意的，肯定的
高分秘诀	▲ expensive adj. 昂贵的，花钱多的 ▲ Moon Festival 中秋节

affect ~ aggravate

65. afflict [əˋflɪkt] [af·flict] ☆☆★★★

| v. 折磨，使苦恼 | The old man was not afflicted with flatfoot.
这个老人并不因为扁平足而苦恼。 |

- 同义字词：plague, suffer, torment, disturb
- 反义字词：comfort, console, relieve, solace
- 衍生字词：
  - ▲ affliction n. 痛苦，苦恼
  - ▲ afflictive adj. 带给人痛苦的，苦恼的，难受的
- 高分秘诀：
  - ▲ be afflicted with 受折磨
  - ▲ flatfoot n. 扁平足

66. affluent [ˋæfluənt] [af·flu·ent] ☆★★★★

| adj. 富有的，丰富的 | My best friend Jennifer married a guy who is affluent in worldly goods.
我最好的朋友珍妮佛嫁给了一个很有钱的人。 |

- 同义字词：plentiful, bountiful, abundant, ample
- 反义字词：lacking, short
- 衍生字词：▲ affluence n. 富足，富裕
- 高分秘诀：
  - ▲ Jennifer 珍妮弗（女子名）
  - ▲ worldly adj. 世间的，世上的，世俗的

67. afford [əˋford] [af·ford] ☆☆★★★

| v. 付得起，提供 | Someone condemns television as a pestilence, but to a certain point it affords pleasure to us.
有人指责电视有害，但在某种程度上来说，它也给我们带来了娱乐。 |

- 同义字词：provide, give, offer, furnish, supply
- 衍生字词：▲ affordable adj. 负担得起的，便宜的
- 高分秘诀：
  - ▲ condemn v. 谴责，责备
  - ▲ pestilence n. 瘟疫
  - ▲ to a certain point 在某种程度上
  - ▲ pleasure n. 娱乐，消遣

68. aggravate [ˋægrə͵vet] [ag·gra·vate] ☆☆★★★

| v. 使恶化，使加重 | The old man told us that the lack of rain aggravated the already serious shortage of food.
老人告诉我们干旱少雨使原本很严重的粮食短缺问题更加严重。 |

同义字词	worsen, exacerbate
反义字词	ameliorate, improve, better
衍生字词	▲ aggravating adj. 恼人的，讨厌的 ▲ aggravation n. 加重，恶化，加剧
高分秘诀	▲ seriously adv. 严重地，危险地 ▲ shortage n. 不足（量），缺少

69. aggregate [ˈægrɪˌget] [ag·gre·gate] ☆☆☆★★

n. 总数	Could you tell us the complete aggregate of unemployment figures? 你可以告诉我们失业人口的总数是多少吗？
v. 总计, 收集	It turned out that the donation aggregated to $50,000. 结果表明捐款合计五万美元。
同义字词	total, sum, amount to
反义字词	segregate
衍生字词	▲ aggregation n. 集合，群体 ▲ aggregative adj. 集团的，集合的，集合性的 ▲ aggregator n. 聚合器
高分秘诀	▲ unemployment n. 失业，失业（人数），失业率 ▲ turn out 结果是 ▲ donation n. 捐赠，捐款

70. aggressive [əˈgrɛsɪv] [ag·gres·sive] ☆☆★★★

adj. 好斗的, 挑衅的	It's not good to train the dog to be aggressive. 把狗训练得有攻击性并不好。
同义字词	combative, offensive, belligerent, militant
反义字词	nonaggressive, unaggressive
衍生字词	▲ aggression n. 侵略，侵犯 ▲ aggressiveness n. 侵略，好斗 ▲ aggressor n. 侵略者，挑衅者，侵略国
高分秘诀	▲ train v. 训练，培养

71. agile [ˈædʒaɪl] [ag·ile] ☆★★★★

adj. 敏捷的, 活泼, 轻快的	John climbed the poplar tree, agile as a monkey. 约翰像猴子一样敏捷地爬上那棵杨树。

aggregate ~ akin

同义字词	nimble, quick, brisk
反义字词	dull, slow, torpid
衍生字词	▲ agility n. 敏捷，活泼
高分秘诀	▲ poplar tree 杨树 ▲ monkey n. 猴子，猿

72. agitate [ˈædʒəˌtet] [a·gi·tate] ☆☆★★★

v. 鼓动，煽动	You can sent agents to agitate the local people. 你可以派情报人员煽动当地的民众。
v. 使焦虑，搅动或摇动（液体）	I noticed that the girl became quite agitated when she was asked about her criminal past. 我发现当问到女孩过去的犯罪记录时，她变得十分焦虑不安。
同义字词	instigate, abet, foment, disturb
反义字词	calm, lull, quiet
衍生字词	▲ agitation n. 焦虑，不安，煽动 ▲ agitated adj. 焦虑的，激动的 ▲ agitator n. 鼓动者，煽动者
高分秘诀	▲ agent n. 间谍，特工，密探；代理人（商） ▲ local people 当地居民 ▲ criminal n. 罪犯，犯人

73. ailment [ˈelmənt] [ail·ment] ☆☆★★★

n. 疾病（尤指轻病、小病）	The girl got timely treatment for her ailment, and she is now released from the hospital. 女孩的疾病得到及时治疗，目前已经出院。
同义字词	complaint, illness, sickness, affliction
衍生字词	▲ ailing adj. 不舒服的，生病的
高分秘诀	▲ timely adj. 适时的，及时的 ▲ treatment n. 治疗，处理 ▲ be released from the hospital 出院

74. akin [əˈkɪn] [a·kin] ☆☆★★★

adj. 同族的，类似的	My mother always says that pity and love are closely akin. 妈妈常说"同情怜悯近乎爱"。
同义字词	kindred, consanguine, cognate

反义字词	alien
高分秘诀	▲ pity n. / v. 怜悯，同情 ▲ closely adv. 接近地，亲密地

75. alert [əˋlɝt] [a·lert] ☆☆★★★

adj. 警惕的，警觉的	From the telescope, I saw an alert leopard went up to an antelope quietly. 从望远镜里，我看到一只警觉的美洲豹静悄悄地靠近一只羚羊。
v. 向……发警报，使警惕	It's the Doctor Smith who alerted me to the danger of a heart attack. 史密斯医生提醒我注意心脏病发的危险。
n. 警戒，警报	Police warned the public to be on the alert for suspected terrorist. 警方警告群众对涉嫌的恐怖分子要有警觉心。
同义字词	vigilant, watchful, switched-on
反义字词	unalert
衍生字词	▲ alertness n. 警戒，机敏 ▲ alertly adv. 提升警觉地，留意地
高分秘诀	▲ telescope n. 望远镜 ▲ leopard n. 美洲豹 ▲ antelope n. 羚羊 ▲ heart attack 心脏病发作 ▲ on the alert against/ for 警惕，提防…… ▲ suspect adj. 可疑的，n. 嫌疑犯 ▲ terrorist n. 恐怖主义者，恐怖分子

76. alien [ˋeljən] [a·lien] ☆☆★★★

adj. 外国的，外国人的	It's great to run into an old friend in the alien land. 他乡遇故知真是太好了。
n. 外国人，外星人	According to the unwritten law, the immigrant workers were classed as resident aliens. 依照不成文规定，移民来的工人被归入外侨。
同义字词	foreign, exotic, strange
反义字词	citizen
衍生字词	▲ alienate v. 使疏远，使不友好 ▲ alienation n. 疏远，离间

alert ~ allude

| 高分秘诀 | ▲ run into 偶然遇见
▲ according to 根据，依照
▲ unwritten law 不成文规定
▲ immigrant **n.** 移民
▲ resident **adj.** 定居的，常驻的； **n.** 居民，住宿者 |

77. allege [əˈlɛdʒ] [al·lege]   ☆☆★★★

v. 断言,宣称	Though the police alleged that the girl was murdered, they couldn't give enough proof. 虽然警方声称女孩是被谋杀的，但并无法提供充分的证据。
同义字词	declare, state, aver
衍生字词	▲ allegation **n.** 宣称，主张，断言 ▲ allegement **n.** 断言，宣称 ▲ alleged **adj.** 声称的，所谓的
高分秘诀	▲ murder **n.** / **v.** 谋杀 ▲ proof **n.** 证明，证据

78. allocate [ˈæləˌket] [al·lo·cate]   ☆☆☆★★

v. 分发,分配	Unfortunately, man can't allocate his own death. 遗憾的是，人无法控制自己的死期。
同义字词	allot, assign, apportion
衍生字词	▲ allocation **n.** 配给，分发，拨出 ▲ allocator **n.** 分发 ▲ allocatable **adj.** 可分发的，能分派的 ▲ allocatee **n.** 分发者，受分发者
高分秘诀	▲ unfortunately **adv.** 遗憾地，不幸地 ▲ death **n.** 死，死亡

79. allude [əˈlud] [al·lude]   ☆☆★★★

v. 暗指,影射	Don't allude to Susan about her ex-boyfriend's engagement to Mary. 别向苏珊提及她前男友与玛丽订婚的事。
同义字词	hint, imply, intimate
衍生字词	▲ allusion **n.** 暗指，间接提到 ▲ illusive **adj.** 暗指的，含暗示的
高分秘诀	▲ ex-boyfriend 前男友 ▲ engagement **n.** 订婚，婚约，约会，约定

80. ally [əˋlaɪ] [al·ly] ☆☆☆★★

n. 联盟，同盟者	England and Russia were allies in the Second World War. 英国和俄国在第二次世界大战时是盟国。	
v. 结盟	How about we ally against our boss? 我们联合起来反对老板如何？	
同义字词	confederate, partner, collaborator	
反义字词	enemy, foe	
衍生字词	▲ allied **adj.** 有关联的，类似的 ▲ the Allies （第一次世界大战中的）协约国，（第二次世界大战中的）同盟国	
高分秘诀	▲ England **n.** 英格兰，英国 ▲ Russia **n.** 俄国，俄罗斯 ▲ Second World War 第二次世界大战 ▲ how about... ……怎么样 ▲ ally against 结盟，联合	

81. aloof [əˋluːf] [a·loof] ☆☆★★

adj. 远离的，冷淡的	I didn't know why he had held himself aloof from his best friends. 我不知道他为什么不和自己的好朋友在一起。	
同义字词	separate, remote, distant, indifferent, standoffish	
衍生字词	▲ aloofness **n.** 冷漠，超然离群 ▲ aloofly **adv.** 远离地，冷淡地，漠不关心地	
高分秘诀	▲ hold oneself from someone 对某人无友好表示	

82. alter [ˋɔltə] [al·ter] ☆★★★★

v. 改变，更改	I know it's the manager who altered the mistake on the price tag. 我知道是经理更正价格标签上的错误的。	
同义字词	change, modify, vary	
反义字词	preserve, conserve	
衍生字词	▲ alteration **n.** 变更，改造 ▲ alterable **adj.** 可改变的，可修改的	
高分秘诀	▲ manager **n.** 经理，管理人 ▲ price tag 价格标签	

83. alternate [`ɔltənɪt] [al·ter·nate] ☆★★★★

adj. 交替的，轮流的
The weather forecast says that there will be a week of alternate rain and sunshine.
天气预报说，下星期时雨时晴。

v. 交替，轮流
After got bitten by a dog, the rabies things stuck in my mind, and I alternated between hope and fear.
被狗咬后，我脑子里想的都是狂犬病，时而满怀希望，时而充满恐惧。

同义字词 intermittent, alternating, alternative

衍生字词
▲ alternation **n.** 交替，轮流
▲ alternative **adj.** 另一可选的，另外的
▲ alternator **n.** 交流发电机
▲ alternating current 交流电，交变电流

高分秘诀
▲ sunshine **n.** 阳光，日光
▲ rabies **n.** 狂犬病，恐水症

84. amateur [`æməˌtʃur] [a·ma·teur] ☆★★★★

adj. 业余的
Can you imagine that these pictures were taken by an amateur photographer?
你相信这些照片是一位业余摄影师拍的吗？

n. 业余爱好者
Maybe you don't know our actors are all enthusiastic amateurs.
或许你不知道我们的演员都是热情的业余爱好者。

同义字词 nonprofessional, inexpert

反义字词 expert, specialist, professional

衍生字词 ▲ amateurism **n.** 业余性

高分秘诀
▲ imagine **v.** 想象，猜想
▲ photographer **n.** 摄影者，摄影师
▲ enthusiastic **adj.** 热心的，极感兴趣的

85. amaze [ə`mez] [a·maze] ☆☆★★★

v. 使吃惊，使惊叹
Sometimes women have strengths that amaze men.
有时候女人有着令男人惊叹的力量。

同义字词 stun, astonish, shock, astound

衍生字词
▲ amazement **n.** 惊愕，惊异
▲ amazing **adj.** 令人惊异的
▲ amazingly **adv.** 令人惊奇地

| 高分秘诀 | ▲ sometimes adv. 有时，间或 |
| | ▲ strength n. 力，力量；优点，长处 |

86. ambience [ˈæmbɪəns] [am·bi·ence] ☆☆★★★

n. 周遭环境,气氛	I like this little town; you know the ambience delighted me. 我喜欢这个小镇，幽雅的环境让我心旷神怡。
同义字词	environment, surrounding
衍生字词	▲ ambient adj. 周遭的，包围着的 ▲ ambiance n. 气氛，周遭，环境
高分秘诀	▲ town n. 镇，市镇 ▲ delight v. 使高兴，使欣喜

87. ambitious [æmˈbɪʃəs] [ambi·tious] ☆☆★★★

adj. 有雄心的，有野心的	I can tell you that my younger brother is an ambitious self-starter. 我可以告诉你，我弟弟是一位雄心勃勃并富有主动精神的人。
同义字词	aspiring, enterprising
衍生字词	▲ ambition n. 雄心，抱负 ▲ ambitiously adv. 雄心勃勃地
高分秘诀	▲ self-starter n. 做事主动的人，有主动精神的人

88. amble [ˈæmbl] [am·ble] ☆★★★★

v. 漫步,溜达	Under the shine of the setting sun, there are a young couple ambled along the path. 夕阳下，一对年轻夫妇悠闲地在小径上漫步。
同义字词	ramble, roam, mosey, stroll, saunter
高分秘诀	▲ shine n. 光亮，光泽 ▲ setting sun 夕阳 ▲ couple n. 夫妻，情侣 ▲ path n. 小路，小径

89. amenable [əˈminəbl] [a·me·na·ble] ☆☆★★★

| adj. 经得起检验的，应服从的 | Though he has a quick temper, he is amenable to counsel.
虽然他性情暴躁，但他这人听劝。 |
| 同义字词 | submissive, tractable, obedient, compliant |

ambience ~ amplify

衍生字词 ▲ amenability n. 顺从
高分秘诀 ▲ tempter n. 性情

90. amend [əˈmɛnd] [a·mend] ☆☆☆★★

| v. 改善，改良 | I beg my elder sister to amend the spelling in my composition.
我求姐姐帮我修改作文的拼写错误。 |

同义字词 revise, change, modify
反义字词 exacerbate, worsen, aggravate
衍生字词 ▲ Amendment n. 宪法修正案
▲ amendment n. 改正，修正
高分秘诀 ▲ elder sister 姐姐
▲ spelling n. 拼写，拼法
▲ composition n. 作文，写作

91. ample [ˈæmpl] [am·ple] ☆☆★★

| adj. 富足的，充足的 | As is known to us all, the ample sunshine and rainfall can bring the crops on nicely.
众所皆知，充足的阳光和雨水可以使农作物茁壮生长。 |

同义字词 abundant, plentiful, sufficient, enough, copious, plenteous
反义字词 scrimpy, meagre, meager, insufficient, scanty
衍生字词 ▲ amply adv. 充足地，详细地
高分秘诀 ▲ as is known to us all 众所周知
▲ sunshine n. 阳光，日光
▲ rainfall n. 下雨，雨量

92. amplify [ˈæmpləˌfaɪ] [am·pli·fy] ☆☆★★

| v. 放大，增强 | It's my father who told me that a tube or a transistor can amplify an incoming signal.
我父亲告诉我电子管或晶体管可以放大输入的信号。 |

同义字词 enlarge, expand, exaggerate, magnify, strengthen
衍生字词 ▲ application n. 扩大
▲ amplifier n. 放大器，扩大器
高分秘诀 ▲ tube n. 管，软管
▲ transistor n. 晶体管
▲ incoming adj. 进来的，新任的
▲ signal n. 信号，讯号

93. analogy [əˋnælədʒɪ] [a·nal·o·gy] ☆★★★★

n. 类似，相似

I don't think there is analogy between my position and yours.
我认为我的见解与你的并无相似之处。

同义字词	comparison, parallel, similarity
衍生字词	▲ analogous adj. 类似的
高分秘诀	▲ position n. 态度，立场

94. analyze [ˋænəˌlaɪz] [ana·lyze] ☆☆★★★

v. 分析，分解

The boss said a good accountant could analyze the unprofitable operation quickly.
老板说一名优秀的会计师可以迅速分析出亏损的环节。

同义字词	analyse, diagnose, examine, dissect
反义字词	synthesize, synthesise
衍生字词	▲ analysis n. 分析，分析报告 ▲ analyzable adj. 可被分析的，可以分解的 ▲ psychoanalysis n. 心理分析
高分秘诀	▲ accountant n. 会计人员，会计师 ▲ unprofitable adj. 无利益的，不赚钱的 ▲ operation n. 操作，运转，经营

95. anarchist [ˋænəˌkɪst] [an·arch·ist] ☆☆★★★

n. 无政府主义者

The middle-aged man is an anarchist and a terrorist as well.
这个中年人是一名无政府主义者，也是恐怖分子。

同义字词	nihilism, syndicalist
衍生字词	▲ anarchy n. 无政府状态，混乱 ▲ anarchic adj. 无政府状态的，无秩序的，混乱的 ▲ anarchism n. 无政府主义
高分秘诀	▲ middle-aged adj. 中年的 ▲ terrorist n. 恐怖主义者，恐怖分子 ▲ as well 也，还有

96. anatomy [əˋnætəmɪ] [a·nat·o·my] ☆☆★★★

n. 解剖，解剖学

It's said that a knowledge to anatomy helps to the appreciation of works of art.
据说解剖学知识有助于提升对艺术作品的鉴赏力。

analogy ~ animate

同义字词	dissection
衍生字词	▲ anatomic adj. 解剖的，解剖学上的 ▲ anatomical adj. 架构（上）的；解剖的
高分秘诀	▲ knowledge n. 知识，学问 ▲ appreciation n. 欣赏，鉴赏 ▲ work of art 艺术作品

97. ancestor [ˈænsɛstə] [an·ces·tor] ☆☆★★★

n. 祖先，祖宗	What you did just soiled the very name the ancestors have bequeathed us. 你的所作所为真是愧对祖先，有辱家风。
同义字词	forefather, forebear
反义字词	descendant, descendent
衍生字词	▲ ancestral adj. 祖先的，祖传的 ▲ ancestry n. 家系，血统
高分秘诀	▲ soil v. 弄脏，污辱 ▲ bequeath v. 将……遗赠给

98. anesthetic [ˌænəsˈθɛtɪk] [a·nes·the·tic] ☆☆☆★★

n. 麻醉剂，麻醉药	Even now my great grandfather is still groggy from the anesthetic. 直到现在曾祖父仍因为麻药而虚弱无力。
同义字词	anesthetic agent
衍生字词	▲ anesthesis n. 麻醉，麻木 ▲ anesthetist n. 麻醉师 ▲ anesthetize v. 使麻醉，使麻木
高分秘诀	▲ great grandfather n. 曾祖父 ▲ groggy adj. 不稳的，摇摆的

99. animate [ˈænəˌmet] [a·ni·mate] ☆★★★★

adj. 有生命的，有生气的	The cat lay so still, it scarcely seemed animate. 那只猫趴着一动也不动，简直不像活的。
v. 使有生命，使有活力	I had to admit that Johnson's arrival served to animate the whole party. 我不得不承认詹森的到来使聚会的整个气氛活跃起来。
同义字词	give life to, make lively, invigorate, enliven, living
反义字词	inanimate, lifeless

衍生字词	▲ animated adj. 活生生的，活泼的，生动的 ▲ animacy n. 生命性，生命度 ▲ animation n. 生气，活力
高分秘诀	▲ still adj. 不动的，静止的 ▲ scarcely adv. 仅仅，几乎不，绝不 ▲ arrival n. 到达，抵达

100. annihilate [əˈnaɪəˌlet] [an·ni·hi·late] ☆☆★★

v. （完全）消灭，歼灭	How I wish to annihilate the tedious intervening days! 我多希望那些无聊的时光快点消逝！
同义字词	destroy, decimate, eliminate, eradicate
衍生字词	▲ annihilation n. 全部毁灭，灭绝 ▲ annihilable adj. 可消灭的，可毁灭的 ▲ annihilator n. 歼灭者，消灭者
高分秘诀	▲ tedious adj. 单调的，乏味的 ▲ intervening adj. 发生于其间的

101. announce [əˈnaʊns] [an·no·unce] ☆★★★★

v. 宣布，发表	The surprised-looking secretary came running up to announce an official. 满脸惊诧的秘书跑上来通报，有位官员来访。
同义字词	declare, proclaim, give out, notify
反义字词	conceal
高分秘诀	▲ surprised-looking 满脸惊诧的 ▲ secretary n. 秘书 ▲ run up to 跑到，达到 ▲ official n. 行政官员

102. annoy [əˈnɔɪ] [an·noy] ☆☆★★★

v. 使恼怒，打扰	I can't fall asleep; these mosquitoes are annoying me. 这些蚊子一直打扰我，使我不能入睡。
同义字词	disturb, irritate, vex, disturb, bother
反义字词	gratify, please
衍生字词	▲ annoying adj. 恼人的，讨厌的，使人愤怒的
高分秘诀	▲ fall asleep 入睡 ▲ mosquito n. 蚊子

annihilate ~ antibiotic

103. anonymous [ə`nɑnəməs] [a·no·ny·mous] ☆☆★★★

adj. 匿名的

If the author chooses to remain anonymous, just let him be.
如果作者不愿署名，就随他吧。

同义字词	unknown, nameless
反义字词	onymous
衍生字词	▲ anonym n. 假名，匿名，无名氏 ▲ anonymously adv. 不具名地，化名地 ▲ anonymity n. 无名，匿名，作者不明
高分秘诀	▲ author n. 著作者，作者 ▲ let sb. be 随某人去，任某人那样

104. anthropology [͵ænθrə`pɑlədʒɪ] [an·thro·pol·o·gy] ☆☆☆★★

n. 人类学

I recommend you to read up anthropology.
我建议你攻读人类学。

同义字词	humanics, anthrop
衍生字词	▲ anthropologic adj. 人类学的 ▲ anthropological adj. 人类学的 ▲ anthropologist n. 人类学者，人类学家
高分秘诀	▲ recommend v. 推荐，介绍，建议 ▲ read up 攻读，钻研

105. antibiotic [͵æntɪbaɪ`ɑtɪk] [an·ti·bi·o·tic] ☆☆★★★

n. 抗菌素, 抗生素

I don't know whether I'm allergic to antibiotics or not.
我不知道我是否对抗生素过敏。

同义字词	antibacterial
衍生字词	▲ antibiotics n. 抗生素 ▲ antibiosis n. 抗生 ▲ antibody n. 抗体（血液中形成的抵抗并杀死病菌的物质）
高分秘诀	▲ amazing adj. 令人惊异的 ▲ earthworm n. 蚯蚓 ▲ substance n. 物质 ▲ allergic adj. 过敏的

106. anticipate [ænˈtɪsəˌpet] [an·ti·ci·pate] ☆★★★★

v. 预期，预料

My boss anticipated that some people would meet a certain amount of resistance to our plan.
老板预料我们的计划会遭到一些人的反对。

同义字词: expect, predict, forebode, foreknow, forecast

衍生字词:
▲ anticipation **n.** 期望，预料
▲ anticipant **n.** 预期者，预言者

高分秘诀:
▲ a amount of 一定量的
▲ resistance **n.** 抵抗，反抗，阻力

107. antiquated [ˈæntəˌkwetɪd] [an·ti·quat·ed] ☆☆★★★

adj. 陈旧的，过时的

I saw a train of antiquated coaches was waiting for us at the siding.
我看见一列陈旧的火车在侧边等着我们。

同义字词: old-fashioned, obsolete, archaic, antediluvian

反义字词: in fashion, fashionable

衍生字词:
▲ antiquate **v.** 使古旧，废弃
▲ antiquary **n.** 古文研究者
▲ antiquarian **n.** 古文物研究者，收集古文物者

高分秘诀:
▲ train **n.** 火车，列车
▲ coach **n.** （铁路）旅客车厢
▲ siding **n.** 铁路的侧线，侧轨

108. anxious [ˈæŋkʃəs] [an·xious] ☆☆★★★

adj. 渴望的，担忧的

I'm anxious to go abroad.
我非常渴望出国。

同义字词: concerned, worried, agitated, eager, keen

反义字词: easy, reassuring

衍生字词:
▲ anxiously **adv.** 忧虑地
▲ anxiety **n.** 焦虑，担心，渴望，热望

高分秘诀:
▲ be anxious to 急于，渴望
▲ go abroad 出国

109. apologize [əˈpɑləˌdʒaɪz] [a·po·lo·gize] ☆☆★★★

v. 道歉

The old man had already apologized for his transgressions. I think we should forgive him.
老人已经为自己所犯的错误道歉，我认为我们应该原谅他。

anticipate ~ apply

同义字词	beg pardon, apologise
衍生字词	▲ apologetic adj. 认错的，道歉的 ▲ apology n. 道歉，歉意 ▲ apologia n. 辩解文，辩解书
高分秘诀	▲ apologize for 为……道歉，替……道歉 ▲ transgression n. 违反，违法，罪过 ▲ forgive v. 原谅，宽恕

110. appeal [əˋpil] [ap·peal] ☆☆★★

n. 吸引力	The subject have lost its appeal for most students gradually. 对多数学生来说，这门学科逐渐失去了吸引力。
v. 吸引，恳求，上诉	The young lady appealed against the six-year sentence she had been given. 这个年轻女士对被判六年徒刑提出上诉。
同义字词	attraction, charm, beg, entreat, implore
反义字词	repel
衍生字词	▲ appealing adj. 动人的，媚人的
高分秘诀	▲ subject n. 学科，科目，课程 ▲ gradually adv. 逐渐地，渐渐地 ▲ appeal against 提起上诉 ▲ sentence n. / v. 宣判，判决

111. appetite [ˋæpəˌtaɪt] [ap·pe·tite] ☆★★★

n. 胃口，食欲	I'd like something which could whet my appetite, for these days I'm having a dull appetite. 我想要一些可以让我开胃的东西，因为最近我的胃口不好。
同义字词	desire, hunger, craving, appetence, appetency
衍生字词	▲ appetizer n. 开胃品；促进食欲的活动 ▲ appetizing adj. 促进食欲的，开胃的
高分秘诀	▲ whet v. 引起，刺激（食欲、欲望、兴趣等） ▲ dull adj. 枯燥无味的

112. apply [əˋplaɪ] [ap·ply] ☆☆★★

| v. 应用，适用 | The old man advised us to apply advanced experience according to local conditions, instead of applying it mechanically.
老人建议我们对先进的经验应该因地制宜地应用，而不是盲目套用。 |

同义字词	exert, employ, exercise, make use
衍生字词	▲ application n. 申请，施用 ▲ applicant n. 申请人 ▲ applied adj. 应用的，实用的
高分秘诀	▲ advanced adj. 进阶的，先进的 ▲ local conditions 当地情况（条件） ▲ mechanically adv. 机械地，盲目地；呆板地

113. appoint [əˋpɔɪnt] [ap·point] ☆☆★★★

v. 任命, 选派	As a top leader of a company, you should appoint none but people on their merit. 作为公司的高层领导，你应该任人唯贤。
同义字词	designate, nominate, constitute, assign
衍生字词	▲ appointment n. 任命，委派 ▲ appointments n. 设备，家具 ▲ appointee n. 被任命者，被委派者
高分秘诀	▲ top leader 进阶领导人 ▲ merit n. 功勋，功劳；价值，长处，优点

114. appreciate [əˋpriʃɪet] [ap·pre·ci·ate] ☆☆★★★

v. 赏识, 感激	You know appreciate self is better than appreciate the pointless man. 欣赏没有用的男人不如多爱自己。
同义字词	admire , value
反义字词	depreciate, despise
衍生字词	▲ appreciation n. 欣赏，兴趣 ▲ appreciable adj. （数量或变化）很大的，值得重视的 ▲ appreciatory adj. 欣赏力的，感激的
高分秘诀	▲ self n. 自己，自我，自身 ▲ pointless adj. 无意义的，无用的，无益的

115. apprentice [əˋprɛntɪs] [ap·pren·tice] ☆☆☆★★

n. 学徒, 徒弟	My younger brother had formerly been an blacksmith's apprentice in New York. 我弟弟曾在纽约当过铁匠学徒。
v. 使……当学徒	The old man apprenticed his little son to an engineer. 老人让他的小儿子跟一个工程师当学徒。

appoint ~ appropriate

同义字词	learner, beginner, novice, prentice
衍生字词	▲ apprenticeship n. 学徒身份
高分秘诀	▲ formerly adv. 以前，从前 ▲ blacksmith n. 铁匠，锻工 ▲ engineer n. 工程师，机械师

116. approach [əˋprotʃ] [ap·proach] ☆☆★★★

n. 方法，入口	I saw some guys cautiously approached the house. 我看到有人小心翼翼地走近那座房子。
n. 方法，入口	I don't think you have chance to get to the Palace, all the approaches to it are guarded by troops. 我觉得你不可能进入宫殿，通往宫殿的道路都有部队把守。
同义字词	access, inlet, method
高分秘诀	▲ approaching adj. 接近的，逼近的 ▲ approachable adj. 可亲近的，可接近的
高分秘诀	▲ cautiously adv. 小心地，谨慎地 ▲ get to 到达，抵达 ▲ palace n. 宫，宫殿 ▲ guard v. 保护，控制 ▲ troop n. 军队，部队

117. appropriate [əˋproprɪet] [ap·pro·pri·ate] ☆★★★★

adj. 适当的，恰当的	Read the paragraph first, then fill in each of the blanks with an appropriate word. 先阅读整个段落，然后在每个空白处填入一个合适的字。
v. 拨出（款项）	The government will appropriate funds for the new airport 政府将拨款建造新机场。
同义字词	apt, proper, suitable, allot, apportion, budget
反义字词	inappropriate, unsuitable
衍生字词	▲ appropriable adj. 可供专用的 ▲ appropriately adv. 适当地 ▲ appropriation n. 拨款
高分秘诀	▲ paragraph n. 段落 ▲ fill in 填写 ▲ blank adj. 空白的，空着的 ▲ government n. 政府 ▲ fund n. 资金，基金 ▲ airport n. 机场

118. approval [əˋpruvl] [ap·pro·val]

n. 赞成，正式批准

The general manager nodded his approval.
总经理点头表示同意。

- 同义字词: sanction, endorsement
- 反义字词: disapproval
- 衍生字词:
  - ▲ approve **v.** 赞成，同意，批准，透过
  - ▲ approving **adj.** 满意的
  - ▲ approver **n.** 批准者
- 高分秘诀:
  - ▲ nod one's approval 点头同意

119. approximate [əˋprɑksəmɪt] [ap·pro·xi·mate]

v. 接近，近似

You have to approximate the time to finish the task.
你必须先估计一下做完这项工作要花多少时间。

adj. 大约的，估计的

The plane's approximate time of arrival is 12:00.
飞机到达的时间大约是十二点。

- 同义字词: approach, near, estimated, rough, close
- 衍生字词:
  - ▲ approximately **adv.** 近似地，大约
  - ▲ approximative **adj.** 近似的，接近的
- 高分秘诀:
  - ▲ finish **v.** 结束，完成
  - ▲ task **n.** 工作，任务
  - ▲ arrival **n.** 到达，抵达

120. aquatic [əˋkwætɪk] [a·qua·tic]

adj. 水生的，水栖的

There are so many aquatic animals inhabit ponds.
有很多水生动植物栖居在池塘里。

- 同义字词: waterborne
- 衍生字词:
  - ▲ aquarium **n.** 水族馆
  - ▲ semiaquatic **adj.** 半水生的，半水栖的
  - ▲ terrestrial **adj.** 陆地的，陆上的，陆栖的，陆生的
- 高分秘诀:
  - ▲ inhabit **v.** 居住于，栖居于
  - ▲ pond **n.** 池塘

approval ~ architecture

121. arbitrary [ˈɑrbəˌtrɛrɪ] [ar·bi·tra·ry] ☆☆★★★

adj. 专横的，专制的	In Brazil, the phenomenon of arbitrary collection of charges, unchecked apportionment are still rampant. 在巴西乱收费和乱摊派的现象依然很严重。
同义字词	dictatorial, autocratic
反义字词	unarbitrary, nonarbitrary
衍生字词	▲ arbitrarily adv. 专横地，武断地 ▲ arbitrable adj. 可调停的，可仲裁的
高分秘诀	▲ phenomenon n. 现象 ▲ collection of charges 收取费用 ▲ unchecked adj. 未受制止的，未遏制的 ▲ apportionment n. 土地分发 ▲ rampant adj. 猖獗的，无法控制的

122. archaeology [ˌɑrkɪˈɑlədʒɪ] [ar·chae·o·lo·gy] ☆☆★★★

n. 考古学	I remember it's an article that waked my interest in archaeology. 我记得是一篇文章引起了我对考古学的兴趣。
同义字词	archeology, archaeo
衍生字词	▲ archaeologist n. 考古学家 ▲ archaeologic adj. 考古学的 ▲ archaic adj. 古代的，陈旧的
高分秘诀	▲ article n. 文章 ▲ interest n. 兴趣，爱好，嗜好

123. architecture [ˈɑrkəˌtɛktʃə] [ˈar·chi·tec·ture] ☆☆★★★

n. 建筑（学），建筑式样	I've never seen such an impressive architecture in my life. 我从来没有见过如此令人难忘的建筑。
同义字词	building, construction, structure
衍生字词	▲ architect n. 建筑师 ▲ architectural adj. 建筑上的，建筑学的
高分秘诀	▲ impressive adj. 给人印象深刻的

124. ardent [ˈɑrdənt] [ar·dent] ★★★★

adj. 热烈投入的，极热心的	You know your parents were held ardent expectations for your college career. 你父母对你的大学求学抱着殷切的期望。
同义字词	passionate, zealous, enthusiastic, earnest
反义字词	indifferent
衍生字词	▲ ardency n. 热心，热烈 ▲ ardently adv. 热心地，热烈地
高分秘诀	▲ expectation n. 预料，期望 ▲ college n. 大学，学院 ▲ career n. 生涯

125. arduous [ˈɑrdʒuəs] [ar·du·ous] ★★★★

adj. 费力的，艰难的	The girl didn't give up, instead she braced up for the arduous task. 女孩并没有退缩，相反地，她鼓起勇气从事那个艰巨的任务。
同义字词	difficult, strenuous, hard, toilsome
反义字词	easy, effortless
衍生字词	▲ arduously adv. 费力地，严酷地 ▲ arduousness n. 费力，艰难
高分秘诀	▲ give up 放弃，认输 ▲ brace up 振奋精神

126. arid [ˈærɪd] [a·rid] ★★★★

adj. 干旱的，贫瘠的	It hasn't rained for several months, so the villagers have to irrigate the arid land. 几个月没有下雨，村民们不得不灌溉干燥的土地。
同义字词	dry, waterless, barren, infertile
反义字词	fertile, interesting
衍生字词	▲ aridity n. 干旱，乏味 ▲ aridness n. 干旱，乏味 ▲ semiarid adj. 雨量非常少的，半干旱的
高分秘诀	▲ irrigate v. 灌溉 ▲ arid land 旱地，贫瘠地

ardent ~ arrange

127. armour [`ɑrmə] [ar·mour] ☆☆★★★

n. 盔甲，装甲车

I couldn't hurt him; his body was protected by armour fore and aft.
我无法伤害他，他的身体前前后后都有盔甲保护。

同义字词	armor
衍生字词	▲ armored **adj.** 披甲的，装甲的 ▲ arms **n.** 武器，军火 ▲ armory **n.** 兵工厂，军械库
高分秘诀	▲ protect **v.** 保护，保卫 ▲ fore and aft 从船头到船尾的，纵向的

128. aroma [ə`romə] [a·ro·ma] ☆★★★★

n. 香气，芬芳，芳香

The aroma of fine coffee penetrated the whole room.
满屋子都是咖啡的香味。

同义字词	fragrance, perfume, scent
衍生字词	aromatic **adj.** 芬芳的
高分秘诀	▲ coffee **n.** 咖啡 ▲ penetrate **v.** 穿过，渗入

129. arouse [ə`raʊz] [a·rouse] ☆★★★★

v. 刺激，激起

It took me some time to arouse from a hypnotic state.
过了好一会儿，我才从催眠状态苏醒过来。

同义字词	excite, stimulate, awake, rouse
反义字词	doze off, dope off
衍生字词	▲ arousal **n.** 觉醒，激励
高分秘诀	▲ hypnotic state 催眠状态

130. arrange [ə`rendʒ] [a·rrange] ☆☆★★★

v. 安排，准备

Don't worry! I've arranged to meet John at the train station.
别担心，我已安排好去火车站接约翰。

| 同义字词 | schedule, set up, put together, organize |
| 反义字词 | disarrange, derange |

衍生字词	▲ arrangement n. 排列，安排
	▲ arranger n. 传动装置
高分秘诀	▲ meet v. 迎接
	▲ train station 火车站

131. arthritis [ɑrˋθraɪtɪs] [ar·thri·tis] ☆☆★★★

n. 关节炎	We all know that arthritis is a common complaint among the elderly.
	大家都知道关节炎是老年人常患的一种疾病。
衍生字词	▲ arthritic adj. 关节炎的
	▲ arthritically adv. 患关节炎
	▲ sacroiliitis n. 骼关节炎
	▲ coxitis n. 髋关节炎
高分秘诀	▲ common adj. 普遍的，常见的
	▲ complaint n. 疾病
	▲ the elderly n. 老年人，年长者

132. articulate [ɑrˋtɪkjəlɪt] [ar·ti·cu·late] ☆☆★★★

v. 清楚地讲话，清晰地发音	If you want people understand you totally, you have to articulate your words first.
	如果想要大家完全听懂你说的话，你必须说话清晰。
adj. 善于言辞的，表达清晰的	Sometimes the child cannot use articulate speech.
	这孩子有时说话口齿不清。
同义字词	enunciate, pronounce
反义字词	inarticulate, unarticulated
衍生字词	▲ articulately adv. 善于表达地
	▲ articulation n. 发音；连接，关节
	▲ articulacy n. 口齿清楚的说话能力
	▲ articulated vehicle 拖车
高分秘诀	▲ totally adv. 完全地，全部地
	▲ speech n. 说话，言语，说话能力

133. artificial [ˌɑrtəˋfɪʃəl] [ar·ti·fi·cial] ☆☆★★★

adj. 人造的，人工的	I found her eyebrows are artificial in a glance.
	我一眼就看出她的眉毛是假的。
同义字词	synthetic, man-made, unreal
反义字词	natural

arthritis ~ aspiration

衍生字词
▲ artificially adv. 人工地
▲ artificiality n. 人工，不自然，人造物
▲ artifact n. 人工制品，手工艺品，加工品

高分秘诀
▲ eyebrows n. 眉毛
▲ in a glance 向……瞟一眼

134. ascend [əˋsɛnd] [as·cend] ☆★★★★

v. （渐渐）上升，升高

According to the newspaper, there is a small party planning to ascend Mount Everest.
据报道，有一群人正计划攀登圣母峰。

同义字词
climb, mount, rise

反义字词
descend, come down

衍生字词
▲ ascending adj. 上升的，向上的
▲ ascent n. 攀登，上升
▲ ascendancy/ascendance n. 优势；支配地位
▲ ascendant adj. 上升的

高分秘诀
▲ newspaper n. 报纸
▲ Mount Everest 圣母峰

135. ascribe [əˋskraɪb] [as·cribe] ☆☆★★★

v. 把……归于

You shouldn't ascribe vice to me, it's unfair.
你不应该把过错怪在我身上，这不公平。

同义字词
attribute, impute, assign

衍生字词
▲ ascribable adj. 可归于……的，起因于……的
▲ ascription n. 归因，归咎

高分秘诀
▲ vice n. 不道德行为，恶习，恶行
▲ unfair adj. 不公平的，不公正的

136. aspiration [͵æspəˋreʃən] [as·pi·ra·tion] ☆☆★★★

n. 雄心，抱负

The soldier nurses an aspiration to be a general.
这个士兵怀有当将军的梦想。

同义字词
ambition, longing

衍生字词
▲ aspire v. 渴望，追求
▲ aspiring adj. 有抱负的，有理想的，积极向上的

高分秘诀
▲ soldier n. 士兵，军人
▲ nurse n. 怀有……想法，梦想
▲ general n. 将军

137. assault [əˈsɔlt] [as·sault]

n. (武力)袭击，(口头)攻击

The fierce enemies made a strong assault on the town.
凶猛的敌人对城市进行猛烈的袭击。

同义字词: attack, onslaught, offense

衍生字词:
▲ assaulter n. 攻击者，殴打者
▲ assault and battery 殴打，人身攻击
▲ assault craft 突击艇

高分秘诀:
▲ fierce adj. 凶猛的，激烈的
▲ enemy n. 敌人，敌军

138. assemble [əˈsɛmbl] [as·sem·ble]

v. 集合，装配

All the staff was assembled at the hall to honor the President's visit.
所有员工都聚集在礼堂欢迎董事长的来访。

同义字词: put together, gather, congregate, convene

反义字词: disassemble, dismantle, disperse

衍生字词:
▲ assembly n. 集会，参加集会的人们
▲ assembly line n. 装配线，流水线
▲ assemblage n. 集合，组合

高分秘诀:
▲ staff n. 全体职员
▲ hall n. 礼堂，会堂，大厅
▲ honor v. 尊敬，给以荣誉
▲ visit n. 访问，参观

139. assert [əˈsɜt] [as·sert]

v. 声称，断言

The young man most positively asserted the charge to be incorrect.
这个年轻人斩钉截铁地声称这一指控是错误的。

同义字词: declare, affirm, asseverate, insist

衍生字词:
▲ assertion n. 言明，断言
▲ assertable adj. 可断言的
▲ asserted adj. 宣称的

高分秘诀:
▲ positively adv. 极其，十分肯定地，坚定地
▲ charge n. 控告
▲ incorrect adj. 不正确的，错误的

140. assess [əˈsɛs] [as·sess] ☆★★★★

v. 估计，分析

It's too early to assess the achievement of the new manager.
现在就评价新经理的成就还为时过早。

同义字词	estimate, judge, appraise, evaluate, valuate
衍生字词	▲ assessment **n.** 估价，评估 ▲ assessable **adj.** 可估价的，可征收的
高分秘诀	▲ early **adj.** 早的，提早的 ▲ achievement **n.** 成就，成绩，功绩

141. asset [ˈæsɛt] [as·set] ☆☆★★★

n. 财产，资产；优势；重要的品性

The company has assets of over eight million dollars.
这家公司有八百万美元以上的资产。

同义字词	property, wealth, advantage
衍生字词	▲ asset-stripping 资产炒卖，资产剥除
高分秘诀	▲ company **n.** 公司 ▲ million **n.** 百万 ▲ dollar **n.** 美元

142. assimilate [əˈsɪməˌlet] [as·sim·i·late] ☆★★★★

v. 吸收，消化

It's not easy to assimilate a lot of information in such a short time.
要在短的时间内吸收这么多资讯不是件容易的事。

同义字词	absorb, imbibe, ingest, digest
反义字词	dissimilate
衍生字词	▲ assimilable **adj.** 可同化的，可吸收的 ▲ assimilation **n.** （被）吸收或同化的过程
高分秘诀	▲ a lot of 很多，许多 ▲ information **n.** 信息，资料

143. assist [əˈsɪst] [as·sist] ☆☆★★★

v. 援助，帮助

Take these tablets, they would assist digestion.
吃些药吧，它们有助消化。

同义字词	help, aid
反义字词	oppose, resist

衍生字词	▲ assistance n. 协助，帮助 ▲ assistant n. 助手，助理 ▲ assistantship n. 研究生助教奖学金
高分秘诀	▲ tablet n. 药片 ▲ digestion n. 消化（能力）

144. associate [əˈsoʃɪet] [as·so·ci·ate] ☆★★★★

v. 关联，联合	We always associate turkey with Thanksgiving. 我们总把火鸡与感恩节联想在一起。
n. 伙伴	Susan and I are associates in business. 苏珊和我是生意伙伴。
adj. 副的（比正职低一级）	Your salary is the highest among the associate manager. 你的薪水在副经理中算最高的。
同义字词	ally, combine, connect, join, unite
衍生字词	▲ association n. 关联，联合，协会
高分秘诀	▲ turkey n. 火鸡 ▲ Thanksgiving n. 感恩节 ▲ in business 在做买卖 ▲ salary n. 工资，薪水

145. assorted [əˈsɔrtɪd] [as·sort·ed] ☆☆★★★

adj. 各式各样的，综合的	I'm fond of the assorted chocolate. 我喜欢综合巧克力。
同义字词	varied, miscellaneous, various, different
反义字词	uniform
衍生字词	▲ assortment n. 各类物品的聚集，混合物 ▲ assorter n. 服装配件工
高分秘诀	▲ be fond of 喜爱，爱好 ▲ assorted chocolate 综合巧克力

146. assume [əˈsjum] [as·sume] ☆☆★★★

v. 假定，设想	During the term of your office, you should not concurrently assume other public or private posts. 任职期间，你不能兼任其他公职或任何私人职务。
同义字词	suppose, presume, take on, bear

associate ~ astronomy

衍生字词	▲ assumable adj. 可假定的 ▲ assumption n. 假设，就职 ▲ assumedly adv. 多半，大概
高分秘诀	▲ term of office 任期 ▲ concurrently adv. 同时地 ▲ private adj. 私人的，私营的

147. assure [ə`ʃʊr] [as·sure] ☆☆★★★

v. 确保，保证	I assure you that I would take care of the children. 我向你保证我会好好照顾孩子们的。
同义字词	solidify, guarantee, ensure, convince, reassure
反义字词	worry, vex
衍生字词	▲ assurance n. 确信，保证，保险 ▲ assurable adj. 可保证的 ▲ assuror n. 保证人，保险业者 ▲ assuredly adv. 确实地，确信地
高分秘诀	▲ take care of 照顾

148. astonish [ə`stɑnɪʃ] [as·to·nish] ☆☆★★★

v. 使惊讶，使大为吃惊	I was so astonished at the news of my grandpa's sudden death. 听到外公突然去世的消息，我非常震惊。
同义字词	surprise, shock, astound
衍生字词	▲ astonished adj. 惊讶的 ▲ astonishing adj. 惊人的，奇迹的 ▲ astonishment n. 惊讶，惊奇
高分秘诀	▲ sudden death 暴死，突然死亡

149. astronomy [əs`trɑnəmɪ] [as·tro·no·my] ☆☆★★★

n. 天文学	It's said that astronomy inherits from astrology. 据说天文学的前身是占星术。
同义字词	uranology 天文学
衍生字词	▲ astronomical adj. 天文学的 ▲ astronomer n. 天文学家
高分秘诀	▲ inherit from 从……继承……，从……得到 ▲ astrology n. 占星术 ▲ astrologer n. 占星家

150. astute [ə'stjut] [as·tute]

adj. 机敏的，精明的

Mr. Smith is an astute and politic statesman.
史密斯先生是位老谋深算的政治家。

同义字词	shrewd, judicious, sharp
反义字词	half-witted, stupid, goofy
衍生字词	▲ astutely **adv.** 机敏地，精明地 ▲ astuteness **n.** 机敏，精明
高分秘诀	▲ politic **adj.** 考虑周到的，有见识的，有洞察力的 ▲ statesman **n.** 政治家

151. asymmetric [ˌæsɪ'mɛtrɪk] [a·sym·me·tric]

adj. 不均匀的，不对称的

I'm interested in this fanciful asymmetric ornamentation.
我对这种奇怪又不对称的装饰风格很感兴趣。

同义字词	asymmetrical, unbalanced, uneven
反义字词	symmetric, symmetrical
衍生字词	▲ asymmetrically **adv.** 不均匀地，不对称地
高分秘诀	▲ be interested in 对……感兴趣 ▲ fanciful ornamentation 奇形装饰

152. atheist ['eθɪɪst] [a·the·ist]

n. 无神主义者

How dare you openly declare yourself as atheist.
你竟敢公开宣布自己是无神主义者。

同义字词	antitheist
反义字词	theist
衍生字词	▲ atheism **n.** 无神主义
高分秘诀	▲ how dare you ……胆子真大 ▲ openly **adv.** 公开地，公然地 ▲ declare **v.** 宣布，宣称

153. atmosphere ['ætməsˌfɪr] [at·mos·phere]

n. 大气，大气层

From the book, I know that most meteors burn up when they enter the earth's atmosphere.
这本书告诉我大多数流星在进入地球大气层时就已经被燃烧殆尽了。

| 同义字词 | air, ambiance, ambience, aura |

astute ~ attach

| 衍生字词 | ▲ atmospheric adj. 大气的，大气层的 |
| 高分秘诀 | ▲ meteor n. 流星
▲ earth atmosphere 地球大气 |

154. atom [ˈætəm] [a·tom]   ☆☆★★

n. 原子，微量	An atom bomb is the offspring of the 20th century physics. 原子弹是二十世纪物理学的产物。
同义字词	particle, speck
衍生字词	▲ atomic adj. 原子的，微小的 ▲ atomization n. 原子化，雾化 ▲ molecule n. 分子 ▲ neutron n. 中子 ▲ proton n. 质子 ▲ nucleus n. （原子）核
高分秘诀	▲ atom bomb 原子弹 ▲ offspring n. 后代，子孙 ▲ century n. 一世纪，一百年 ▲ physics n. 物理学

155. atrophy [ˈætrəfɪ] [at·ro·phy]   ☆☆★★

n. 萎缩，萎缩症	If there are no writers and artists out there, the cultural life of the country will sink into atrophy. 如果没有作家和艺术家，一个国家的文化生活将衰落。
v. （使）萎缩，（使）衰退	You have to work out frequently, you know muscles that are not used will atrophy. 你必须经常锻炼，要知道肌肉经常不用就会萎缩。
同义字词	shrinkage, wither
衍生字词	▲ atrophic adj. 萎缩的
高分秘诀	▲ writer n. 作者，作家 ▲ artist n. 艺术家，美术家 ▲ cultural adj. 文化的，与文化有关的 ▲ sink into 陷入，进入，沉入

156. attach [əˈtætʃ] [at·tach]   ☆☆★★

| v. 系，贴上，使……附属 | The No.3 hospital is attached to the medical college nearby.
第三医院是附近的那所医学院的附属医院。 |

同义字词	fix, fasten, affix
反义字词	detach
衍生字词	▲ attachable adj. 可附上的，可连接的 ▲ attachment n. 依恋，喜欢 ▲ attached adj. 附加的，附属的 ▲ attache n. 大使随员，大使馆专员
高分秘诀	▲ hospital n. 医院 ▲ be attached to 附属于 ▲ medical college 医学院 ▲ nearby adj. / adv. 附近的/地

157. attain [əˈten] [at·tain]   ☆★★★★

v. 实现，达到　　It's a long way for China to attain a high civilization.
对中国来说，要达到高度文明还有很长一段路要走。

同义字词	accomplish, achieve, fulfill, realize
反义字词	fail
衍生字词	▲ attainment n. 成就 ▲ attainable adj. 可获得的，可达到的，可实现的 ▲ attainability n. 可达到，所及
高分秘诀	▲ civilization n. 衣冠文物，文化

158. attempt [əˈtɛmpt] [at·tempt]   ☆★★★★

v. 试图，尝试　　The prisoner attempted to escape last night, but failed.
那个囚犯昨晚企图逃跑，但未成功。

n. 试图，尝试　　You know my attempts at learning driving were successful.
你知道我试图学开车而且成功了。

同义字词	try, endeavor
衍生字词	▲ attempted adj. 企图的，未遂的
高分秘诀	▲ prisoner n. 囚徒，俘虏 ▲ escape v. 逃脱，逃跑 ▲ successful adj. 成功的，如愿以偿的

159. attend [əˈtɛnd] [at·tend]   ☆★★★★

v. 参加，照顾　　Please try to attend the lecture. It's very important for your examination.
请尽量参加课程，这对你们的考试很重要。

attain ~ attract

同义字词	be present at, present, participate
衍生字词	▲ attendant n. 侍者，护理人员 ▲ attendance n. 出席，出席的人数
高分秘诀	▲ lecture n. 演讲，讲课 ▲ examination n. 考试

160. attire [ə`taɪr] [at·tire] ☆☆★★★

n. 穿着，服饰（正规服装的总称）	You have to have formal attire on such an occasion. 在这种场合，你必须着正式服装。
v. 使穿衣，打扮	The bride was attired in white on the wedding. 在婚礼上，新娘穿着白色礼服。
同义字词	clothing, dress, array, deck up, dress up
高分秘诀	▲ formal adj. 正式的 ▲ occasion n. 场合，时机 ▲ bride n. 新娘 ▲ wedding n. 婚礼

161. attorney [ə`tɝnɪ] [at·tor·ney]   ☆☆★★★

n. 代理人，辩护律师	The boy wants to be a prominent attorney when he grows up. 男孩长大后想当一名著名律师。
同义字词	lawyer, counselor
衍生字词	▲ attorneyship n. 代理人的职务 ▲ barrister n. 大律师 ▲ solicitor n. 初级律师
高分秘诀	▲ prominent adj. 杰出的，著名的，卓越的 ▲ grow up 长大，成熟

162. attract [ə`trækt] [at·tract] ☆★★★★

v. 吸引，引起注意	It's normal that pretty girls attracted men's attention. 美丽的女孩吸引男人的目光，这是很正常的。
同义字词	lure, allure, appeal, draw
反义字词	distract
衍生字词	▲ attraction n. 吸引，吸引人的事物 ▲ attractive adj. 吸引人的，有魅力的 ▲ attractively adv. 动人地，迷人地

163. attribute [əˈtrɪbjut] [at·tri·bute] ☆☆★★★

v. 把……归于，归因于	I have no secrets, and I attribute my success to hard work. 我没有什么秘密，我的成功归因于艰苦努力。	
n. 属性，品性	Kindness is one of my grandmother's attributes. 仁慈是外婆的特色之一。	
同义字词	ascribe, identify as, characteristic, trait, feature	
衍生字词	▲ attributable **adj.** 可归因于……的，可归属的 ▲ attribution **n.** 归属，归因，属性，归属物 ▲ attributive **adj.** 归属的，用作定语的	
高分秘诀	▲ secret **n.** 秘密，机密 **adj.** 秘密的，机密的 ▲ success **n.** 成功，成就 ▲ hard work 繁重的工作	

164. audit [ˈɔdɪt] [au·dit] ☆☆★★★

n. 稽核，审查	The audit of the official's property revealed unpaid taxes. 这位官员的财产在审计中被发现漏税。	
同义字词	scrutinise, inspect, scrutinize	
衍生字词	▲ auditable **adj.** 可查证的，可审计的 ▲ auditor **n.** 审计员 ▲ auditorial **adj.** 查账的，稽查的	
高分秘诀	▲ property **n.** 财产，资产，所有物 ▲ official **n.** 行政官员 ▲ reveal **v.** 显示，露出 ▲ unpaid **adj.** 未付的，（债等）未还的，未缴纳的 ▲ taxes **n.** 税捐	

165. auditorium [ˌɔdəˈtorɪəm] [au·di·to·ri·um] ☆☆★★★

n. 观众席，大礼堂	The auditorium is hot; there was not a breath of air in it. 大礼堂里很闷热；一点儿风都没有。	
同义字词	spectator seats, audience seats	
衍生字词	▲ audience **n.** 观众 ▲ audition **n.** 试听，试音	
高分秘诀	▲ hot **adj.** 闷热的 ▲ not a breath of 一点儿没有	

attribute ~ authority

166. augment [ɔgˋmɛnt] [aug·ment]

v. 增加，增大

Maybe you can augment your income by doing some part-time job.
或许你可以做些兼职工作增加收入。

同义字词　increase, enlarge, expand, extend, magnify

反义字词　abate

衍生字词
▲ augmentation **n.** 增加，增多，增大
▲ augmentable **adj.** 可扩张的，可增大的
▲ augmentor **n.** 起扩大作用的人，推力增强装置

高分秘诀
▲ income **n.** 收入，所得
▲ part-time job 兼职工作

167. authentic [ɔˋθɛntɪk] [au·then·tic]　☆☆★★★

adj. 真的，真正的

I've heard that restaurant engaged an authentic Sichuan chef to serve authentic Sichuan-flavor dishes to customers.
我听说那家餐饮店为了提供给顾客正宗川味菜肴，聘请了一位正宗川菜主厨。

同义字词　genuine, real, valid, trustworthy

反义字词　false, fictitious, spurious

衍生字词
▲ authenticate **v.** 证明……为真
▲ authenticity **n.** 真实性，可靠性，确实性
▲ authentication **n.** 确证，证实，证明
▲ authentically **adv.** 真正地，确实地，可靠地

高分秘诀
▲ restaurant **n.** 饭店，餐馆
▲ engage **v.** 雇，聘
▲ Sichuan. 四川
▲ chef **n.** 厨师，主厨
▲ flavor **n.** 味，味道，风味，特色
▲ customer **n.** 顾客，主顾

168. authority [əˋθɔrətɪ] [au·tho·ri·ty]　☆☆★★★

n. 权力，权限，当权者

My grandfather is an authority on international law.
我外公是一位国际法权威。

同义字词　jurisdiction, power

063

| 衍生字词 | ▲ authoritarian n. 权力主义者，独裁者
▲ authorization n. 授权，批准
▲ authoritative adj. 有权力的，有威权的，官方的，当局的
▲ authoritarianism n. 权力主义，独裁主义 |
| --- | --- |
| 高分秘诀 | ▲ international law 国际法 |

169. autobiography [ˌɔtəbaɪˈɑgrəfɪ] [au·to·bio·gra·phy] ☆☆★★★

n. 自传	Mark Twain's autobiography was once acknowledged to be number one on the best-seller list. 马克·吐温的自传曾被公认为是最畅销的一本书。
同义字词	memoir 自传
衍生字词	▲ autobiographical adj. 自传的，自传体的 ▲ autobiographer n. 自传作者 ▲ autobiographic adj. 自传的
高分秘诀	▲ Mark Twain 马克·吐温 ▲ once adv. 曾经，昔时 ▲ acknowledge v. 承认，供认 ▲ best-seller n. 畅销书或唱片 ▲ list n. 一览表，目录，名单，清单

170. automatic [ˌɔtəˈmætɪk] [au·to·ma·tic] ☆☆★★★

adj. 自动（化）的，机械的	I've never seen a real automatic rifle in my life. 我还从来没有见过真正的自动步枪长什么样子。
同义字词	automated, self-acting, mechanize, machinelike
反义字词	manual
衍生字词	▲ automatically adv. 自动地 ▲ automation n. 自动化（技术），自动操作
高分秘诀	▲ automatic rifle 自动步枪

171. autonomy [ɔˈtɑnəmɪ] [au·to·no·my] ☆☆★★★

n. 自治，自治权	Some people in China advocate practicing the regional autonomy for it ensures the rights of the ethnic minorities. 在中国，有些人提倡实行民族区域自治，因为这样能够确保少数民族的权利。
同义字词	independence, liberty, self-reliance, self-direct

autobiography ~ avalanche

衍生字词	▲ autonomous adj. 自治的，独立的 ▲ autonomic adj. 自发的，自治的，自律的 ▲ autonomist n. 主张自治者，自治论者
高分秘诀	▲ advocate v. 提倡，主张 ▲ regional autonomy 区域自治，地区自治 ▲ ethnic minority 少数民族 ▲ uphold v. 维持，保持 ▲ unification n. 统一，联合，一致

172. auxiliary [ɔgˋzɪljərɪ] [au·xi·lia·ry] ☆☆★★★

adj. 辅助的，补充的	Several auxiliary medical service were sent to the earthquake-stricken district to save the dying and help the wounded. 几支医疗辅助队被派往地震灾区协助搜寻灾民。
同义字词	aiding, accessory
衍生字词	auxiliary
高分秘诀	▲ medical service 医疗服务 ▲ earthquake n. 地震 ▲ district n. 区域 ▲ the dying 快要死的人 ▲ the wounded 受伤的人

173. available [əˋveləbl] [a·vai·la·ble] ☆☆★★★

adj. 自由的，有空的	All sorts of furniture are available in that furniture center. 在那个家具城可以买到各式各样的家具。
同义字词	free, obtainable, accessible
反义字词	unavailable
衍生字词	▲ availability n. 有效，可利用性
高分秘诀	▲ all sorts of 各种各样的 ▲ furniture n. 家具 ▲ furniture centre 家具城

174. avalanche [ˋævəˌlæntʃ] [av·a·lanche] ☆☆★★★

n. 雪崩	The climber was buried by an avalanche, and so far, he has not been rescued. 那位登山者遇雪崩被埋住，目前仍生死未卜。
同义字词	snowslide, snowslip, snow crash
衍生字词	▲ snowshed n. 防雪崩的建筑物

高分秘诀
▲ climber n. 攀登者，攀登物
▲ so far 迄今为止
▲ rescue n. / v. 营救，援救

175. aversion [əˋvɝʃən] [a·ver·sion] ☆☆★★★

| n. 厌恶，憎恨 | I know that cats have a natural aversion to water from that accident.
通过那次事件，我才知道原来猫天生怕水。 |

同义字词　dislike, loathing, hatred, distaste, antipathy

衍生字词　▲ averse adj. 反对的，不愿意的

高分秘诀
▲ natural adj. 天生的，生来的
▲ accident n. 意外遭遇，事故

176. avert [əˋvɝt] [a·vert] ☆★★★★

| v. 转移，避免 | Thank God, they discovered the danger at the last moment, and made shift to avert it.
谢天谢地，他们在最后一刻发现了这个危机，连忙设法挽救。 |

同义字词　prevent, avoid, deflect, turn away

衍生字词
▲ avertible adj. 可防止的，可避开的
▲ avertable adj. 可避开的，可防止的

高分秘诀
▲ Thank God 谢天谢地
▲ discover v. 发现
▲ at the last moment 最后一刻，刚刚赶上
▲ make shift 尽力／设法

177. aviation [ˌevɪˋeʃən] [a·vi·a·tion] ☆☆★★★

| n. 航空，航空学 | As is known to us all that The Wright brothers pioneered in early aviation.
大家都知道莱特兄弟是早期航空的先驱。 |

同义字词　flying, flight, airmanship, aeronautics

衍生字词　▲ aviator n. 飞行员，飞行家

高分秘诀
▲ Wright brothers 莱特兄弟
▲ pioneer v. 开拓，开发，创始

178. avid [ˋævɪd] [av·id] ☆☆★★★

| adj. 渴望的，热心的 | I'm an exception, but most of girls are avid for costumes and cosmetics.
大多数女孩热衷于服装以及化妆品，但我是个例外。 |

aversion ~ aware

同义字词	eager, greedy, enthusiastic
衍生字词	▲ avidity n. 渴望，贪婪 ▲ avidly adv. 渴望地，热望地，热烈地
高分秘诀	▲ exception n. 例外 ▲ avid for 渴望 ▲ costume n. 服装，女装 ▲ cosmetic n. 化妆品

179. avocation [ˌævəˈkeʃən] [av·o·ca·tion] ☆☆★★★

n. 副业, 业余爱好	My best friend is a doctor by profession and a rock singer by avocation. 我最好的朋友正职是名医生，副业则是摇滚歌手。
同义字词	sideline, byline, side occupation, parergon
衍生字词	avocational adj. 副业的，嗜好的
高分秘诀	▲ profession n. 专业 ▲ rock singer 摇滚歌手

180. avoid [əˈvɔɪd] [a·void] ☆★★★★

v. 躲避, 回避	My husband was braking to avoid hitting that truck. 我丈夫刹住车避免了撞到那辆货车。
同义字词	shun, evade, keep away from, escape
反义字词	face, confront
衍生字词	▲ avoidable adj. 可避免的 ▲ avoidance n. 避免 ▲ avoider n. 回避者，逃避者
高分秘诀	▲ brake v. 刹车 ▲ hit v. 碰撞 ▲ truck n. 货车，卡车，载重汽车

181. aware [əˈwɛr] [a·ware] ☆★★★★

adj. 意识到的, 知道的	The boy was not aware of having done something wrong. 那个男孩没有意识到自己做错了什么事。
同义字词	cognizant, conscious, knowing
反义字词	unaware, incognizant
衍生字词	awareness n. 意识

高分秘诀	▲ be aware of 知道
	▲ wrong adj. 错误的，不正确的

182. awkward [ˈɔkwəd] [awk·ward]　☆☆★★★

adj. 笨拙的，不灵活的	I was in such an awkward situation, please put in a good word for me. 我陷入尴尬的情况，请替我说说好话。
同义字词	clumsy, inept, ungainly
反义字词	dexterous, deft, skillful
衍生字词	▲ awkwardly adv. （见到生人）局促不安地，笨拙地
	▲ awkwardness n. 笨拙，不雅观
高分秘诀	▲ situation n. 情势，情况
	▲ put in a good word for 为……说好话，为……说情

Bb 托福 TOEFL iBT

托福(TOEFL)的测验对象为母语为非英语的人
申请入学美加地区大学或研究所时，托福成绩单是必备文件之一。

- n. 名词
- v. 动词
- adj. 形容词
- adv. 副词
- prep. 介词
- art. 冠词
- pron. 代词
- aux. 助词
- conj. 连词

Bb 托福 TOEFL iBT

托福(TOEFL)的测验对象为母语为非英语的人
申请入学美加地区大学或研究所时，托福成绩单是必备文件之一。

183. baboon [bæˋbun] [ba·boon]   ☆☆★★★

n. 狒狒	That brown baboon is very angry. 那只褐色的狒狒很愤怒。
同义字词	gelada, hamadryas, chacma
衍生字词	▲ baboonery **n.** 笨拙，粗鲁的行为或态度 ▲ monkey **n.** 猴 ▲ orangutan **n.** 猩猩 ▲ pongo **n.** （非洲）类人猿；（俚）黑猩猩
高分秘诀	▲ brown **adj.** 棕色的，褐色的 ▲ ugly **adj.** 难看的，丑陋的

184. bachelor [ˋbætʃələ] [ba·che·lor]   ☆☆★★★

n. 学士（学位），单身汉	Can you imagine that nowadays all the married men live like bachelors, while all the bachelors live like married men? 你能想象当今所有已婚男人都过得像单身汉，所有单身汉又都过着像已婚男人的生活吗？
同义字词	unmarried man
衍生字词	▲ master **n.** 硕士 ▲ doctor **n.** 博士
高分秘诀	▲ imagine **v.** 想象，设想 ▲ nowadays **adv.** 现在，现时

185. balance [ˋbæləns] [ba·lance]   ☆★★★★

n. 平衡	The boy couldn't keep his balance on his new bike and fell over. 男孩骑在他的新自行车上不能保持平衡，因此摔了下来。
v. 使平衡，使均衡	In order to balance the trade, we would have to buy less goods in Japan. 为了平衡贸易，我们必须减少在日本购货。
同义字词	equilibrium, symmetry, stability

baboon ~ ban

反义字词	unbalance
衍生字词	▲ balanced adj. 均衡的 ▲ imbalance n. 不平衡，不均衡
高分秘诀	▲ keep one's balance 保持平衡 ▲ fall over 从……上跌落，掉下来 ▲ in order to 为了……

186. bald [bɔld] [bald] ☆☆★★★

adj. 秃头的，光秃的	Do you believe the theory that wearing hats could make men go bald? 你相信男人戴帽子就会秃顶的理论吗？
同义字词	hairless, bare, uncovered
衍生字词	▲ balding adj. 变秃的 ▲ baldly adv. 坦率地 ▲ baldness n. 光秃，枯燥，率真
高分秘诀	▲ theory n. 学说，理论 ▲ go bald 变秃顶

187. balmy [ˋbamɪ] [ˋbal·my] ☆★★★★

adj. 芳香的，（空气）温和的	I think it's quite often that a balmy morning passes into a chilly afternoon. 一个温暖的上午到了下午就变得寒冷，这种事经常发生。
同义字词	fragrant, gentle, soft
反义字词	noisome, nidorous, stinky
衍生字词	▲ balm n. 香脂，香膏 ▲ balmily adv. 芳香地，温和地
高分秘诀	▲ quite often 经常，常常 ▲ pass into 逐渐变成 ▲ chilly adj. 寒冷的，冷得难受的

188. ban [bæn] [ban] ☆☆★★★

v. 禁止，查禁	I've heard that the indecent film was banned by the government. 我听说政府禁止那部伤风败俗的影片上映。
同义字词	prohibit, proscribe, forbid
反义字词	approve, consent, permit
衍生字词	banner

| 高分秘诀 | ▲ indecent adj. 下流的，猥亵的，粗鄙的 |

189. band [bænd] [band] ☆☆★★★

| n. 乐队，队，带 | Stop stretch your rubber band.
不可拉长你的橡皮筋。 |
| v. 联合，集合 | We should band together to oppose the plan.
我们应该联合起来反对这个计划。 |

同义字词	orchestra, team, strip, ribbon, belt
衍生字词	▲ bandleader n. 乐队指挥 ▲ bandmaster n. 乐队指挥 ▲ bandeau n. 束发带，细丝带
高分秘诀	▲ stretch v. 伸展，拉紧，延伸 ▲ rubber band 橡皮圈 ▲ band together （使）联合起来 ▲ oppose v. 反对，使相对

190. bankrupt [ˈbæŋkrʌpt] [bank·rupt] ☆☆★★★

v. （使）破产	Though the businessman has spent so much money on the venture that it will bankrupt him. 尽管这个商人花很多钱从事冒险买卖，最终依然会破产。
adj. 破产的	A beggar can never be bankrupt. 乞丐永远不会破产。
n. 破产者	It's said that the bankrupt had made over all his property to his daughter. 据说这个破产的人已经把所有财产转让给他的女儿了。

同义字词	insolvent, ruin
衍生字词	▲ bankruptcy n. 破产
高分秘诀	▲ businessman n. 商人 ▲ venture n. 冒险，风险，投机 ▲ beggar n. 乞丐 ▲ it's said that, 据说 ▲ make over 转让，移交 ▲ property n. 财产，资产，所有物

191. banquet [ˈbæŋkwɪt] [ban·quet] ☆☆★★★

| n. 宴会，盛宴 | Red wine has been assigned for state banquets in that country.
红酒在这个国家被指定为国宴饮料。 |

band ~ bargain

| v. 宴请，参加宴会 | The villager banqueted the stranger like a king.
村民们犹如对待国王般设盛宴款待这个陌生人。 |

同义字词	feast, dinner, junket
衍生字词	▲ lucullian banquet 豪华的酒宴 ▲ banquet room/ hall 宴会室（厅）
高分秘诀	▲ liquor n. 酒，烈酒 ▲ assign for 指定，选定 ▲ villager n. 村民

192. bare [bɛr] [bare] ☆☆★★★

| adj. 无遮蔽的，赤裸的 | The boy's family is so poor that the rooms are bare of furniture.
男孩家里很穷，房间里家具很少。 |
| v. 使赤裸；使暴露 | I saw a yellow dog bared its gums at me.
我看见一只黄色的狗龇牙咧嘴冲着我叫。 |

同义字词	naked, nude, denudate
反义字词	covered, sheathed
衍生字词	▲ barely adv. 仅仅，几乎不能 ▲ bareness n. 赤裸，裸露 ▲ barefoot adj. 赤脚的 ▲ barefaced adj. 厚颜无耻的，露骨的
高分秘诀	▲ poor adj. 贫困的，贫穷的 ▲ furniture n. 家具 ▲ gum n. 牙龈

193. bargain [ˈbɑrgɪn] [bar·gain] ☆☆★★★
02-02

| n. 协议，交易 | Okay, you win! You really drive a hard bargain.
好吧，你赢了！你真的很会杀价。 |
| v. 讨价还价，商谈 | My brother-in-law is bargaining with the street vendor over the price.
我姐夫正在和摊贩讨价还价。 |

| 同义字词 | agreement, deal, contract |
| 衍生字词 | ▲ bargaining n. 计价，商讨
▲ bargaining counter 特殊的、足以压倒对方的优势
▲ bargaining position 讨价还价的地位
▲ bargain-hunter n. 专拣便宜货的人 |

高分秘诀	▲ drive a hard bargain 极力讨价还价，杀价 ▲ brother-in-law n. 姐夫，妹夫 ▲ vendor n. 摊贩，小贩

194. barge [bɑrdʒ] [barge] ☆☆★★★

n. 驳船，平底船	The barge was broken and we had to send a launch to tug it. 驳船坏了，我们不得不派一艘汽艇拖拽。
v. 猛撞，冲，闯	Don't barge in the conversation when people talking. 别人在讲话的时候不要插嘴。
同义字词	flatboat, hoy, thrust ahead, push forward
衍生字词	▲ barge-pole n. 驳船撑竿
高分秘诀	▲ launch n. 汽艇，游艇 ▲ tug v. 用力拉，使劲拉，猛扯 ▲ barge in 闯入，干涉 ▲ conversation n. 交谈，谈话，会话

195. bark [bɑrk] [bark] ☆★★★★

n. 树皮、犬吠声	The black dog gave several fierce barks then ran away. 那只黑狗汪汪叫几声后就跑开了。
v. 狗吠，咆哮	Go and see what the dogs are barking at. 去看看狗狗在叫什么。
同义字词	skin, outer covering
衍生字词	▲ barker n. 大声叫卖的摊贩
高分秘诀	▲ fierce adj. 凶猛的，激烈的 ▲ run away 逃跑，跑开，走掉

196. barren [ˈbærən] [bar·ren] ☆☆★★★

adj. 贫瘠的；荒凉的	It turned out that the barren land has been turned into fertile fields. 结果这块贫瘠的土地变成了良田。
同义字词	infertile, sterile, unfertile, desolate
反义字词	fertile, rich
衍生字词	▲ barrenness n. 荒凉

barge ~ bashful

高分秘诀	▲ turn out 结果是，原来是 ▲ barren land 荒地 ▲ turn into （使）变成 ▲ fertile adj. 多产的，富饶的

197. barrier [ˈbærɪr] [bar·ri·er]   ☆★★★★

n. 屏障，障碍	You should take care of yourself, you know poor health is the barrier to success. 你应该好好照顾自己，不健康的身体是通往成功大道的路障。
同义字词	obstacle, hurdle, hindrance, obstruction
衍生字词	▲ barricade v. 设置障于，以障碍物阻塞 ▲ barrier cream 护肤霜 ▲ barrier reef 堡礁，堤礁
高分秘诀	▲ take care of 照顾 ▲ success n. 成功，成就

198. barter [ˈbɑrtə] [bar·ter]   ☆☆★★★

n. 物品交换，易货贸易	In some areas, the system of barter is still used. 某些地区仍然实行以物换物的制度。
v. 物品交换，易货贸易	Those peasants barter grains for cloth and fruits. 那些农民用谷物换布和水果等。
同义字词	trade, exchange, deal, swap
衍生字词	▲ barterer n. 交易商
高分秘诀	▲ system n. 系统，体系，制度，体制 ▲ peasant n. 农民，农夫 ▲ grain n. 谷粒，谷物，谷类 ▲ fruit n. 水果，果实

199. bashful [ˈbæʃfəl] [bash·ful]   ☆★★★★

adj. 羞怯的，腼腆的	I don't know how to improve the situation that my daughter is bashful in doing anything. 我女儿不管做什么事都害羞，我不知道怎么改善这个状况。
同义字词	shy, timid
反义字词	bashfully

高分秘诀	▲ improve v. 改善，改进，提升 ▲ situation n. 情势，情况 ▲ daughter n. 女儿

200. batter [ˋbætə] [bat·ter] ☆☆★★★

v. 连续猛击	From the photo, you can see the victim's face was battered to a pulp. 从照片来看，被害者的脸被打得血肉模糊。
n. （为烹调而将面粉、蛋、奶等搅拌成的）糊状物	Hand me the pancake batter, please. 请把煎饼面糊递给我。
同义字词	baste, beat, buffet, knock about, pound
衍生字词	▲ battered adj. 打扁的，憔悴的 ▲ battering-ram n. 攻城槌（古代用来撞破城墙的木制或铁制的槌）
高分秘诀	▲ photo n. 照片，相片 ▲ victim n. 受害者 ▲ pulp n. 果肉，纸浆 ▲ pancake n. 煎饼

201. bead [bid] [bead] ☆☆★★★

n. 珠子，（液体）小滴	Your mission is to thread the bead. 你的任务是用线把这些珠子穿起来。
同义字词	pearl, drops, droplet
衍生字词	▲ beaded adj. 以珠装饰的，珠状的 ▲ beading n. 小珠饰，串珠饰，串珠状缘饰
高分秘诀	▲ mission n. 任务，使命 ▲ thread v. 将（针、线等）穿过……

202. beam [bim] [beam] ☆☆★★★

n. 大梁，（光线的）束，柱	The beam from the flashlight showed a hedgehog was eating the vegetables in the kitchen. 手电筒的光照到一只在厨房里偷吃蔬菜的刺猬。
同义字词	rafter, brace
衍生字词	▲ beam-ends n. 船梁末端 ▲ girder n. 钢架构大梁

高分秘诀
- ▲ flashlight n. 手电筒
- ▲ hedgehog n. 刺猬
- ▲ vegetable n. 蔬菜
- ▲ kitchen n. 厨房

203. bear [bɛr] [bear] 　☆★★★★

v. 负担, 容忍

She couldn't bear that her husband should laugh at her.
她受不了她的丈夫竟然也嘲笑她。

n. 熊

Have you ever seen a polar bear in your life?
你一生中见过真正的北极熊吗？

同义字词　support, sustain, endure, hold

衍生字词
- ▲ bearable adj. 可忍受的, 可容忍的
- ▲ unbearable adj. 无法忍受的, 承受不住的
- ▲ bearish adj. （尤指脾气）像熊一样的, 粗暴的, （股）行情下跌的
- ▲ bearskin n. 熊皮, （英国卫兵戴的）黑皮高帽
- ▲ bear-hug n. 熊抱（喻：热情的拥抱）

高分秘诀
- ▲ husband n. 丈夫
- ▲ laugh at 嘲笑
- ▲ polar bear 北极熊

204. beard [bɪrd] [beard]　☆☆★★★

n. 胡须

His false beard fell off, which made him felt so embarrassed.
他的假胡须掉了下来，这让他很尴尬。

同义字词　whisker, face fungus

衍生字词
- ▲ bearded adj. 有胡须的, 蓄胡的
- ▲ beardless adj. 无须的, 年轻的

高分秘诀
- ▲ fall off 跌落, 滚落下
- ▲ embarrassed adj. 局促不安的, 为难的, 尴尬的

205. beat [bit] [beat]　☆☆★★★

v. 打击, 敲击

The boy had a strong desire to beat his opponent.
男孩有强烈击败对手的欲望。

adj. 疲倦的

I'm dead beat and don't want to go anywhere.
我已经精疲力竭，不想去任何地方。

n. (音乐)拍子	I found there are five beats in the measure. 我发现这一小节有五拍。
同义字词	whip, strike, defeat, tired, worn out
衍生字词	▲ beating n. 狠打，揍，笞打 ▲ beat-up adj. 破旧的 ▲ beater n. 敲打者，搅拌器
高分秘诀	▲ opponent n. 对手，敌手，反对者 ▲ anywhere adv. 任何地方，无论何处

206. begrudge [bɪˋgrʌdʒ] [be·grudge] ☆★★★★

v. 嫉妒, 不舍得	I begrudge it very much that Susan is going to Paris. 苏珊要去巴黎，对此我感到很嫉妒。
同义字词	envy, be jealous of
衍生字词	▲ begrudgingly adv. 小气地，吝啬地
高分秘诀	▲ Paris n. 巴黎

207. beguile [bɪˋgaɪl] [be·guile] ☆★★★★

v. 欺骗, 哄骗	My ex-girlfriend beguiled me into lending her most of my savings. 我前女友哄骗我把大部分的积蓄都借给了她。
同义字词	coax, bamboozle, hoodwink, deceive
衍生字词	beguiler n. 欺骗者，消遣者
高分秘诀	▲ ex-girlfriend n. 前女友 ▲ saving n. 储蓄金，存款

208. behalf [bɪˋhæf] [be·half] ☆☆★★★

n. 代表……, 利益	On behalf of my government I have the honour to make to you're the following communications. 我荣幸地代表我国政府向您转达如下内容。
同义字词	benefit, interest
衍生字词	▲ behave v. 举止，表现 ▲ behavior n. 举止，行为 ▲ behaviourism n. 行为主义 ▲ behavioural adj. 行为的
高分秘诀	▲ on behalf of sb. 代表某人 ▲ honour n. 名节，荣誉 ▲ communication n. 信息，消息

begrudge ~ benefit

209. belie [bɪˋlaɪ] [be·lie] ☆☆★★

v. 给人错觉，掩饰

You don't know her sorrow, because her cheerful manner belied her real feelings.
你不了解她的忧伤，因为她开心的样子掩饰了她的真实感情。

同义字词： misrepresent, disguise

衍生字词：
▲ belief n. 相信，信仰，信念

高分秘诀：
▲ sorrow n. 悲痛，悲伤
▲ cheerful adj. 欢乐的，高兴的
▲ manner n. 模式，方法；态度

210. belittle [bɪˋlɪtl] [be·lit·tle] ☆☆★★

v. 贬低，轻视

If you belittle yourself, then no one would value you.
如果你自己都小看自己，那么就没有人会看重你了。

同义字词： disparage, depreciate, underestimate, underrate

衍生字词：
▲ belittling adj. 轻视某人的，小看某人的
▲ belittlement n. 贬低，轻视

高分秘诀：
▲ value v. 重视，尊重

211. beneath [bɪˋniθ] [be·neath] ☆☆★★

prep. 在……下面

The body buried beneath the plastic bags really scared the shit out of me.
塑料袋下面的尸体真的把我吓得魂不守舍。

adv. 在……下面

You will never guess how old she is, for her careful make-up hid the signs of age beneath.
你永远也猜不到她的年纪，因为她的精心装扮掩饰了岁月刻下的痕迹。

同义字词： below, under, underneath

反义字词： on, above

高分秘诀：
▲ plastic bag 塑料袋
▲ scare the shit out of me 把我吓得要死
▲ careful adj. 仔细的，小心的
▲ make-up n. 化装，打扮

212. benefit [ˋbɛnəfɪt] [be·ne·fit] ☆★★★

n. 利益，好处

I don't think our government brought tangible benefit to the citizens.
我认为政府没有为市民带来实际好处。

v. 有益于，有助于	I've benefited a lot from the extensive reading. 大量的阅读使我受益匪浅。
同义字词	welfare, gain, profit, advantage
反义字词	damage, loss
衍生字词	▲ beneficial adj. 有益的，有利的 ▲ beneficiary n. 受益者，受惠者
高分秘诀	▲ tangible adj. 明确的，可触摸的 ▲ citizen n. 市民，平民 ▲ extensive reading 泛读

213. benign [bɪˈnaɪn] [be·nign]   ☆☆★★★

adj. （病）良性的，亲切和蔼的	Don't worry. This benign tumour will not cause your mother any fatal harm. 别担心，这个良性肿瘤对你母亲不会有任何致命伤害。
同义字词	innocuous, nonmalignant, gentle, benignant
反义字词	malignant, malign
衍生字词	benignly adv. 仁慈地，亲切地
高分秘诀	▲ tumour n. 肿瘤 ▲ fatal adj. 致命的，灾难性的 ▲ harm n. / v. 损害，伤害

214. bequest [bɪˈkwɛst] [be·quest] ☆☆★★★

n. 遗产, 遗赠	The old man was so kind that he left bequest of money to all his relatives. 老人很和善，遗赠所有的亲人一笔金钱。
同义字词	inheritance, legacy, endowment
衍生字词	▲ bequeath v. 遗赠，遗留 ▲ bequeather n. 遗赠者
高分秘诀	▲ relative n. 亲属，亲戚

215. bereave [bəˈriv] [be·reave] ☆☆★★★

v. 剥夺，使丧失（亲友）	The car accident bereaved her of her brother. 车祸夺走了她弟弟的生命。
同义字词	deprive, strip
衍生字词	▲ bereaved adj. 丧失亲友的 ▲ bereavement n. 丧失亲人，丧亲之痛

benign ~ beverage

| 高分秘诀 | ▲ car accident 车祸 |

216. besiege [bɪˋsidʒ] [be·siege] ☆☆★★★

v. 围攻, 包围	The movie star was besieged by his fans. 电影明星被粉丝们围在中间。
同义字词	siege, surround
反义字词	release
衍生字词	besieger n. 包围者，围攻者
高分秘诀	▲ movie star 电影明星 ▲ fan n. 狂热爱好者，迷

217. bestow [bɪˋsto] [be·stow] ☆☆★★★

v. 给予, 赐赠	I don't think I deserve the praises that were bestowed upon me. 我认为我担当不起这样的赞美。
同义字词	endow, confer, present, give
衍生字词	▲ bestowal n. 赠予，给予 ▲ bestowable adj. 可给予的，可赠予的
高分秘诀	▲ deserve v. 应得，应受 ▲ praise n. / v. 称扬，赞赏

218. betray [bɪˋtre] [be·tray] ☆☆★★★

v. 背叛, 显露	The soldier would suffer death rather than betray his country. 这位士兵宁死也不背叛自己的国家。
同义字词	be disloyal to, be unfaithful to, sell
反义字词	be loyal to, be faithful to
衍生字词	▲ betrayal n. 背叛或被出卖 ▲ betrayer n. 叛徒，背叛者
高分秘诀	▲ suffer v. 受痛苦，受损害 ▲ rather than （要）……而不……

219. beverage [ˋbɛvərɪdʒ] [be·ve·rage] ☆☆★★★

n. （除水之外的）饮料	Beverages are not allowed in this hotel. 这家酒店禁止自带酒水。
同义字词	drinks, refreshment, potable

衍生字词	▲ soda water 苏打水 ▲ soft drink 不含酒精的饮料 ▲ aerated water 碳酸水，汽水
高分秘诀	▲ allow in 准许进入 ▲ hotel n. 酒店，饭店

220. bewilder [bɪˋwɪldə] [be·wil·der] ☆★★★★

v. 使迷惑, 使昏乱	The crossword puzzle totally bewildered me. 这个填字游戏完全把我弄糊涂了。
同义字词	bemuse, flummox, discombobulate, puzzle, perplex
衍生字词	▲ bewildering adj. （情况）让人困惑的，令人费解的 ▲ bewilderment n. 迷惘，困惑，迷乱 ▲ bewilderingly adv. 令人困惑地，使人迷乱地
高分秘诀	▲ crossword puzzle 纵横字谜 ▲ totally adv. 完全地，整个地，全部地

221. bias [ˋbaɪəs] [bi·as] ☆★★★★

n. 偏见, 成见	My grandparents have a bias against China products. 我外公外婆对中国的产品有偏见。
同义字词	prejudice, preconception, preference
衍生字词	unbiased adj. 没有偏见的；bias binding 斜开料
高分秘诀	▲ grandparent n. （外）祖父（母） ▲ against prep. （表示态度）反对，反抗 ▲ product n. 产品，产物

222. bigoted [ˋbɪgətɪd] [big·ot·ed] ☆☆★★★

adj. 偏执的, 顽固的	I found the old man is so bigoted that it is impossible to argue with him. 我发现这位老人固执得不可理喻。
同义字词	intolerant, narrow-minded
反义字词	tolerant
衍生字词	▲ bigot n. 偏执的人，顽固者 ▲ bigotry n. 固执的态度或行为 ▲ bigotedly adv. 偏执地，胸怀狭窄地

223. bicameral [baɪˋkæmərəl] [bi·cam·er·al] ☆☆★★★

adj. 两院制的, 有两个议院的	The United States Congress is a bicameral body. 美国国会由两个议院组成。

bewilder ~ biography

同义字词	two-chambered
衍生字词	▲ bicamera n. 双镜头摄影机 ▲ parliament n. 议会，国会 ▲ chamber n. 议院 ▲ legislative assembly n. 议院
高分秘诀	▲ congress n. 国会，议会 ▲ body n. 团契，机构，群体

224. bilateral [baɪˈlætərəl] [bi·la·te·ral] ☆★★★★

adj. 两边的，双边的	The boss said a contract is either bilateral or unilateral. 老板说合约可以是双边的，也可以是单方的。
同义字词	two-sided, mutual
衍生字词	▲ bilateralism n. 两侧对称 ▲ bilaterally adv. 两边地，双边地
高分秘诀	▲ contract n. 契约，合约 ▲ unilateral adj. 单方面的，单边的

225. bill [bɪl] [bill] ☆★★★★

n. 账单，钞票，纸币	It's my parents who footed the bill for the wedding. 是我父母支付婚礼的费用。
同义字词	invoice, act, proposal, bank paper
衍生字词	▲ billboard n. 广告牌 ▲ billfold n. 皮夹子，钱包 ▲ bill of rights 权利法案，人权法案
高分秘诀	▲ foot the bill 付账 ▲ wedding n. 婚礼

226. biography [baɪˈɑgrəfɪ] [bio·gra·phy] ☆☆★★★

n. 传记	A few years ago I watched Dr. Smith's biography on the Biography Channel. 几年前我在传记频道收看了史密斯博士的传记。
同义字词	life story, lift history
衍生字词	▲ biograph n. 初期之电影放映机或录音机 ▲ biographer n. 传记作家 ▲ autobiography n. 自传
高分秘诀	▲ Biography Channel 传记频道

227. biologist [baɪ`ɑlədʒɪst] [bio·lo·gist] ☆☆★★★

| n. 生物学家 | The biologist is so great that he advanced a new theory of life.
这个生物学家真的很了不起,他提出了有关生命的新理论。 |

同义字词	life scientist
衍生字词	▲ biologic adj. 生物的,生物学的 ▲ biological adj. 生物的,生物学的 ▲ biological diversity n. 生物多样性
高分秘诀	▲ great adj. 伟大的,杰出的 ▲ advance v. 提出 ▲ theory n. 理论,学说

228. bison [`baɪsn̩] [bi·son] ☆☆★★★

| n. 美洲或欧洲的野牛 | As a zoologist, you should know the characteristics of bison.
作为一个动物学家,你应该了解欧洲野牛的特点。 |

同义字词	wild ox
衍生字词	▲ buffalo n. 水牛 ▲ antelope n. 羚羊
高分秘诀	▲ zoologist n. 动物学家 ▲ characteristic n. 特性,特色

229. bitter [`bɪtɚ] [bit·ter] ☆☆★★★

| adj. 苦(味)的;(令人)痛苦的 | As is known to us all that bitter pills may have blessed effects.
大家都知道良药苦口利于病。 |

同义字词	painful, acerb, acrid, acrimonious
反义字词	sweet, 甜(味)的
衍生字词	▲ bitterness n. 苦味,苦难 ▲ bitterly adv. 苦苦地,惨痛地
高分秘诀	▲ pill n. 药丸,药片 ▲ blessed adj. 快乐的,喜悦的 ▲ effect n. 结果,效果,影响

230. bizarre [bɪ`zɑr] [bi·zarre] ☆☆★★★

| adj. 奇异的,古怪的 | That night a bizarre thought leaped into my mind.
那天晚上,一个怪异的念头闪过我脑海中。 |

biologist ~ blast

同义字词	eccentric, flakey, grotesque, odd, strange, fantastic, weird
衍生字词	▲ bizarrely adv. 奇异地，古怪地
高分秘诀	▲ leap into 跳入，突然进入

231. blame [blem] [blame] ☆★★★★

v. 谴责, 责备	They blame the rise in oil price for big increase in inflation. 他们把通货膨胀的原因归咎于油价上涨。
n. 过失, 责备	I had to admit that the blame rested entirely with me. 我不得不承认，这件事全怪我。
同义字词	condemn, rebuke, censure, accuse
反义字词	praise
衍生字词	▲ blameless adj. 无罪的，无可指责的，清白的 ▲ blameworthy adj. 应受责备的 ▲ blamer n. 责备者
高分秘诀	▲ increase v. 增加 ▲ inflation n. 通货膨胀 ▲ admit v. 承认，供认 ▲ rest with 在于，取决于 ▲ entirely adv. 全部地，完全地

232. bland [blænd] [bland] ☆☆★★★

adj. 清淡的, 无味的	My grandfahter was stricken by ulcer, and can only eat the bland food. 我外公患有溃疡，只能吃清淡的食物。
同义字词	mild, gentle, soft
衍生字词	▲ blandly adv. 温和地，殷勤地 ▲ blandness n. 温柔，爽快
高分秘诀	▲ stricken adj. 经受或不堪……之苦的 ▲ ulcer n. （医）溃疡

233. blast [blæst] [blast] ☆☆★★★

v. 爆破	The city wall was blasted open with a cannon. 城墙被大炮轰开了。
n. 一阵, 爆炸	A blast of wind blew my sheet away. 一阵风把我的床单刮走了。

同义字词	explode, burst, gale, gust
衍生字词	▲ blaster n. 爆破人员 ▲ blasted adj. 枯萎的，被害的 ▲ blasting n. 爆破（作业）
高分秘诀	▲ city wall 城墙 ▲ cannon n. 大炮，火焰 ▲ a blast of 一阵 ▲ sheet n. 床单 ▲ blow away （使）吹掉

234. blaze [blez] [blaze] ☆☆★★★

v. 燃烧，照耀	A fierce fire was blazing on the hearth. 火在壁炉里熊熊燃烧。
n. 火焰，光辉	Before the blaze was put out, there are seven buildings had been burnt to the ground. 大火扑灭前，有七所大厦被夷成平地。
同义字词	fire, flame, flare, burn, kindle
衍生字词	▲ blazing adj. 炽烧的，闪耀的 ▲ ablaze adj. 着火的，闪耀的
高分秘诀	▲ fierce adj. 强烈的，激烈的，剧烈的 ▲ hearth n. 壁炉 ▲ put out 扑灭，熄灭 ▲ burn to the ground 烧塌

235. bleach [blitʃ] [bleach] ☆☆★★★

v. 去色，漂白	As I see it, the only way to get out the stain is to bleach it out. 在我看来，去污的唯一方法是漂白。
n. 漂白剂	I think the strong bleach might rot the fibers. 我认为强力漂白剂可能会破坏衣物的纤维。
同义字词	whiten, blanch, declourize, eliminate
衍生字词	▲ bleaching powder 漂白粉 ▲ bleachers n. （运动场内票价低廉的）露天座位
高分秘诀	▲ as I see it 在我看来 ▲ stain n. 污点 ▲ bleach out 漂白，褪色 ▲ rot v. 腐烂，腐朽 ▲ fiber n. （动植物的）纤维，纤维质

236. bleak [blik] [bleak] ☆☆★★★

adj. 荒凉的，凄凉的	The future looked bleak after the man got fired. 这个男人被炒鱿鱼后，前途渺茫。

同义字词	desolate, barren, dismal
衍生字词	▲ bleakness n. 无望，苍凉，阴郁 ▲ bleakly adv. 无望地，苍凉地，阴郁地
高分秘诀	▲ future n. 前途，未来 ▲ get fired 被解雇后

237. blemish [ˈblɛmɪʃ] [ble·mish] ☆★★★★

v. 有损……的完美，玷污	Your reputation would be blemished if you take bribes. 你若收贿，你的名声就会留下污点。
n. 瑕疵，污点	It's not a good jade, and there are blemishes in it. 这不是一块上好的玉，它有瑕疵。

同义字词	defect, flaw, stain, tarnish, sully
衍生字词	▲ blemished adj. 有瑕疵的，有污点的 ▲ blemished leaf 残叶 ▲ blemished skin 暗疮皮肤
高分秘诀	▲ reputation n. 名声，名节 ▲ take bribe 受贿 ▲ jade n. 翡翠，玉

238. blend [blɛnd] [blend] ☆☆★★★

v. 混合，掺混	First, you have to blend the butter and sugar together. 首先，你必须把奶油和糖混合在一起。
n. 混合(物)	Excuse me, which blend of coffee would you like to drink? 请问你要喝哪种混合咖啡？

同义字词	mix, combine
衍生字词	▲ blended adj. 混合的，混杂的 ▲ blender n. 搅拌机，果汁机
高分秘诀	▲ butter n. 奶油 ▲ sugar n. 糖

239. blessing [`blɛsɪŋ] [bless·ing]

n. 祝福，恩赐

His unemployment was a blessing in disguise, because he afterwards got another better job.
他失业可以说是塞翁失马，因为后来他又找到一份更好的工作。

同义字词	boon, benediction
反义字词	curse
衍生字词	▲ bliss **n.** 快乐，至上福祉 ▲ blessed **adj.** 神圣的，圣洁的，有福的 ▲ the Blessed 与上帝同在天堂中的圣徒们
高分秘诀	▲ unemployment **n.** 失业 ▲ a blessing in disguise 塞翁失马之福（初看似乎不幸，然后过后看却是幸运的事） ▲ afterwards **adv.** 然后，后来

240. blink [`blɪŋk] [blink]

v. 眨眼，闪烁

He smiled at me and asked how long I can stare without blinking my eyes.
他微笑着看着我，问我能瞪着看多长时间不眨眼。

同义字词	wink, flash, twinkle
衍生字词	▲ blinker **n.** 眨眼睛者，闪光警戒灯 ▲ blinkers **n.** 有色眼镜，马眼罩，护目镜 ▲ blinking **adj.** 闪光的，一眨眼的
高分秘诀	▲ smile at 对……微笑

241. blizzard [`blɪzəd] [bliz·zard]

n. 暴风雪

All aircraft at Beijing Airport is grounded by blizzard today.
今天的暴风雪让北京机场的所有飞机被迫停飞。

同义字词	snowstorm, tempest, storm
衍生字词	▲ rainstorm **n.** 暴风雨 ▲ cyclone **n.** 飓风 ▲ tornado **n.** 龙卷风
高分秘诀	▲ aircraft **n.** 飞机，航空器 ▲ airport **n.** 机场，航空站

blessing ~ bluff

242. block [blɑk] [block] ☆☆★★★

n. 一块，街区
The supermarket is only two blocks away.
那家超市只有两条街的距离。

v. 阻塞，阻止
Those street vendors always block up the path.
那些摊贩们经常堵塞道路。

- 同义字词: chunk, mass
- 衍生字词:
  - ▲ blocker **n.** 阻挡之物或人
  - ▲ blockage **n.** 堵塞物
  - ▲ block letter **n.** 木板字，印刷体字母
  - ▲ block vote 集团投票
- 高分秘诀:
  - ▲ supermarket **n.** 超市
  - ▲ street vendor 摊贩
  - ▲ block up 封闭，堵塞
  - ▲ path **n.** 小路，路径

243. bloom [blum] [bloom] ☆☆★★★

n. 花
I like rose best, because they have beautiful blooms.
我最喜欢玫瑰，因为玫瑰花很美丽。

v. 开花
Most of the flowers, such as daffodils, crocuses, bloom in the spring.
大部分花都在春季盛开，比如水仙花和番红花。

- 同义字词: flower, blossom
- 反义字词: wither, fade
- 衍生字词:
  - ▲ bloomer **n.** 挫折，失败，完全成熟的人
  - ▲ bloomers **n.** 灯笼裤
  - ▲ blooming **adj.** 开着花的，旺盛的
  - ▲ bloomy **adj.** 多花的，盛开的
- 高分秘诀:
  - ▲ rose **n.** 玫瑰
  - ▲ daffodil **n.** 水仙花，黄水仙
  - ▲ crocus **n.** 番红花
  - ▲ spring **n.** 春，春天

244. bluff [blʌf] [bluff] ☆☆★★★

n. 悬崖，绝壁
I saw a girl standing at the edge of the bluff.
我看到一个女孩站在悬崖边。

v. 虚张声势	I really admired you for the way you bluffed your way through all these difficulties. 我真的很佩服你招摇撞骗闯过难关的方法。
同义字词	cliff, precipice, delude, trick
衍生字词	bluffer n. 虚张声势者，吓唬别人的人
高分秘诀	▲ edge n. 边，边缘 ▲ difficulty n. 困难，难事，麻烦

245. blunt [blʌnt] [blunt] ☆☆★★★

adj. 直言不讳的，钝的	My pencil is blunt, but I don't have a knife to sharpen it. 我的铅笔很钝，但是我没有刀可以削。
v. 弄钝	Don't cut the hard thing, or you'll blunt the scissors. 别剪硬物，否则你会把剪刀弄钝。
同义字词	outspoken, candid, direct, straightforward, frank 不锋利的
反义字词	acute, sharp
衍生字词	▲ bluntly adv. 钝地，率直地 ▲ bluntness n. 率直，迟钝
高分秘诀	▲ pencil n. 铅笔 ▲ sharpen v. （使）变锋利，削尖 ▲ scissor n. 剪刀

246. blush [blʌʃ] [blush] ☆★★★★

v. 脸红，羞愧	The boy blushed when his teacher scolded him. 老师责备他时，男孩的脸红了起来。
n. 脸红	The young girl murmured her secret with a blush. 那个年轻女孩脸红着脸说出自己的秘密。
同义字词	flush, redden
衍生字词	▲ blushingly adv. 红着脸地，羞愧地
高分秘诀	▲ scold v. 责骂，斥责 ▲ murmur v. 小声说 ▲ secret n. 秘密，机密

blunt ~ boil

247. board [bɔːrd] [board] ☆☆★★★

n. 木板，委员会	If you have time, please come to the editorial board meeting. 如果你有时间，请来参加编委会议。
v. 上（船、飞机等）	All the passengers must board the ship before 8 a.m. 所有的乘客必须在早上八点前登船。
同义字词	lumber, plank, wood
衍生字词	▲ boarder **n.** 寄宿者，登机登船者 ▲ boarding **n.** 寄膳（宿） ▲ board 木板（建造之物） ▲ boarding house **n.** 寄宿公寓
高分秘诀	▲ editorial **adj.** 编辑的，主笔的 ▲ passenger **n.** 乘客，旅客

248. boast [bost] [boast] ☆★★★★

v. 自夸，以有……而自豪	Don't believe what she said; she is just boasting. 别相信她说的话，她只是在吹嘘罢了。
n. 自夸	Ernest Hemingway was the boast of American literature. 恩尼斯特·海明威是美国文学引以为傲的文学家。
同义字词	brag, vaunt
反义字词	belittle, depreciate
衍生字词	▲ boaster **n.** 自夸者 ▲ boastful **adj.** 吹嘘的，自负的
高分秘诀	▲ Ernest Hemingway 恩尼斯特·海明威 ▲ literature **n.** 文学，文学作品

249. boil [bɔɪl] [boil] ☆☆★★★

v. 沸腾，开	Please help me turn off the gas, the milk will boil over. 请帮我把煤气关掉，牛奶快溢出来了。
n. 煮沸	Wait a minute. The water has nearly come to the boil. 等一下，水快烧开了。
同义字词	seethe, scald

反义字词	freeze
衍生字词	▲ boilable adj. 可蒸煮的 ▲ boiler n. 锅炉，烧水器 ▲ boiling adj. 沸腾的，激昂的
高分秘诀	▲ turn off （把……）关掉 ▲ gas n. 气，煤气 ▲ boil over 沸溢 ▲ wait a minute 等一下 ▲ come to 到达，达成

250. bold [bold] [bold] ☆☆★★★

adj. 勇敢的，大胆的	I've heard that James is bold enough to tilt at social injustices. 我听说詹姆斯敢于抨击社会上的不公正现象。
同义字词	courageous, bold, gallant, valiant
反义字词	cowardly, faint-hearted, timid
衍生字词	▲ boldness n. 勇敢，大胆 ▲ boldly adv. 大胆地，显眼地
高分秘诀	▲ social adj. 社会的，交际的，社交的 ▲ injustice n. 不公平，非正义

251. bombastic [bɑmˋbæstɪk] [bom·bas·tic] ☆☆★★★

adj. 夸夸其谈的，空洞的	I don't like the orator; he always spoke in a bombastic manner. 我不喜欢这个演说家，他讲话总是言过其实。
同义字词	orotund, tumid, turgid
衍生字词	▲ bombastically adv. 夸夸其谈地，空洞地 ▲ bombast n. 浮夸的言语，高调
高分秘诀	▲ orator n. 演说者，演讲家 ▲ manner n. 模式，方法

252. bolster [ˋbolstə] [bol·ster] ☆☆★★★

n. 垫子，枕垫	The bed is empty, only a bolster across the head of the bed. 床上没有人，只有一个长枕垫在床头上。

bold ~ boom

| v. 支援 | I couldn't help you if you can't offer statistics to bolster your arguments.
如果你不能拿出统计数字支持你的论点，我就帮不了你。 |

同义字词　pad, mat, cushion
反义字词　oppose, fight against
高分秘诀
▲ empty adj. 空的
▲ offer v. 提供，提出
▲ statistic n. 统计量
▲ argument n. 论点，论据

253. bonanza [boˋnænzə] [bo·nan·za] ☆☆★★★

| n. 富矿带，意想不到的幸运 | You won the lottery, what a heaven-sent bonanza!
你中了彩票，真是一笔天上掉下来的横财！ |

同义字词　godsend, manna, windfall
高分秘诀
▲ lottery n. 奖券，运气，彩票
▲ heaven-sent adj. 天赋的，天赐的

254. bond [bɑnd] [bond]　☆★★★★

| n. 联结，联系 | I would buy government bonds instead of stock.
我会买政府公债而不是股票。 |
| v. 使黏结，使结合 | I need a strong adhesive to bond wood to metal.
我需要强力胶才能把木料黏在金属上。 |

同义字词　adhesion, link, tie, connection
衍生字词
▲ bonder n. 连接器，接合器，黏合器
▲ bondage n. 奴役，束缚
高分秘诀
▲ government bond 政府公债
▲ stock n. 股票
▲ strong adhesive 强力胶
▲ metal n. 金属

255. boom [bum] [boom]　☆☆★★★

| n. 激增，繁荣 | The businessman made his pile during the cosmetic boom.
这个商人在化妆品生意兴隆期间发了大财。 |
| v. 激增，繁荣 | As we all know Alaska boomed with the discovery of oil.
正如我们所知，阿拉斯加因发现石油而突然繁荣。 |

同义字词	flourish, thrive
反义字词	slump
衍生字词	▲ baby boom n. 生育高峰 ▲ boom town 新兴城市 ▲ microphone boom 送话器架，传声器架
高分秘诀	▲ make one's pile 挣大钱，发财 ▲ cosmetic n. 化妆品 ▲ Alaska n. 美国阿拉斯加州 ▲ discovery n. 发现；被发现的事物 ▲ oil n. 油，石油

256. boon [bun] [boon] ☆☆★★★

n. 恩赐, 恩惠	May I ask a boon of you both? 我能请你们俩人帮个忙吗？
同义字词	blessing, benefit, godsend
反义字词	boon companion
高分秘诀	▲ ask a boon (of sb.) 请求（某人）

257. boost [bust] [boost] ☆★★★★

v. 增加, 提升	I accomplished the task ahead of schedule, which boost my confidence. 提前完成任务，大大增强了我的信心。
同义字词	advance, increase, hike up
反义字词	lower, drop, reduce
衍生字词	▲ booster n. 令人鼓舞的事物，增加动力或电压的装置 ▲ booster rocket 助推火箭
高分秘诀	▲ accomplish v. 完成，实现 ▲ ahead of schedule 提前 ▲ confidence n. 信心，自信

258. bore [bor] [bore] ☆☆★★★

v. 令人厌烦, 钻孔	That man bored us all by talking for hours about his new girlfriend. 这家伙连续几个小时讲他的新女友，我们大家都快被烦死了。
n. 令人讨厌的人或事物, 麻烦	I don't like you, you are such a dreadful bore. 我不喜欢你，你是个麻烦人物。

boon ~ bound

同义字词	drill, puncture, pierce, disgust, bother, nuisance
反义字词	interest
衍生字词	▲ boredom n. 烦恼，无聊 ▲ boring adj. 令人厌烦的
高分秘诀	▲ girlfriend n. 女友 ▲ dreadful adj. 可怕的，极端的，糟糕的，讨厌的

259. bounce [bauns] [bounce] ☆★★★★

| v. 跳起，弹回 | My grandmother's had many misfortune in her life but she always bounces back.
我外婆一生中经历过许多挫折，她却总是能振作起来。 |

同义字词	bound, rebound, spring
衍生字词	▲ bouncer n. 巨大的东西，跳跃的人 ▲ bouncing adj. 健壮的，强健的 ▲ bouncy adj. 有弹性的，快活的，精神的
高分秘诀	▲ misfortune n. 不幸，厄运，逆境 ▲ bounce back 受挫后恢复原状

260. bound [baund] [bound] ☆☆★★★

adj. 被束缚的，有义务的	My father felt bound to help the old lady. 父亲觉得有义务帮助那个老妇人。
n. 范围，限制	When he heard his son failed the test again, his anger knew no bounds. 当他听说儿子考试又不及格时，怒不可遏。
v. 给……划界，限制，弹回	Everybody knows that we should bound our desire by reason, but seldom make it. 每个人都知道我们应该理智限制欲望，却很少做到。

同义字词	tied, held
反义字词	unbound
衍生字词	▲ boundless adj. 无限的，无边无际的 ▲ boundary n. 分界线，边界
高分秘诀	▲ old lady 老妇人，母亲 ▲ know no bounds 不知限量，无限 ▲ desire n. 愿望，欲望 ▲ seldom adv. 很少，罕见，难得

261. boycott [ˈbɔɪˌkɑt] [boy·cott] ☆☆★★★

| v. 抵制, 拒绝参加 | My grandparents are boycotting the shop because all their goods are overpriced.
我外公外婆拒绝购买那家商店的货物，因为他们的货物价格过高。 |

同义字词 reject, refuse

衍生字词 ▲ boycotter n. 抵制者

高分秘诀 ▲ grandparent n. （外）祖父，（外）祖母
▲ made in Japan 日本制造

262. braid [bred] [braid] ☆☆★★★

| v. 编织
n. 辫子 | My hands are full, see I'm braiding the rugs.
我忙着呢，看我正在编织地毯呢。 |
| n. 辫子, 穗带 | Your dress is so beautiful, and it was trimmed with gold braid.
你的礼服真漂亮，镶着金黄色的穗带。 |

同义字词 weave, plait, pleach

反义字词 unbraid

衍生字词 ▲ braiding n. 编织物
▲ braider n. 编穗带的人，缝辫机

高分秘诀 ▲ rug n. 地垫
▲ dress n. 衣服，服装；连衣裙
▲ trim v. 装饰

263. brawl [brɔl] [brawl] ☆★★★★

| n. 争吵, 打架 | I really don't want to see you two engaged in a brawl.
我真的不想看到你们两个吵得不可开交。 |
| v. 争吵, 打架 | You are such a timid girl; it's impossible for you to brawl with that hoodlum.
你那么胆小，不可能和那个流氓吵架。 |

同义字词 quarrel, wrangle, fight

衍生字词 ▲ brawling n. 争吵, 喧嚷
▲ brawler n. 争吵者，打架者

高分秘诀 ▲ engage in 参加，从事，忙于
▲ timid adj. 胆小的，羞怯的
▲ hoodlum n. 流氓，暴徒

264. brazen [ˈbrezən] [bra·zen] ☆☆★★★

adj. 黄铜制的，黄铜色的
David gifted her a brazen vase.
大卫送了她一个黄铜做的花瓶。

v. 使变得无耻，厚着脸皮做
I hate the kind of person who prefer to brazen a thing out rather than admit defeat.
我讨厌这种人，他们不愿意承认失败，而是厚着脸皮做下去。

同义字词 audacious, barefaced, insolent, shameless

衍生字词
▲ brazenly **adv.** 无耻地，无礼地
▲ brazenness **n.** 厚颜无耻

高分秘诀
▲ prefer to 较喜欢，宁愿
▲ brazen out 厚着脸对待
▲ defeat **n.** / **v.** 战败，失败

265. breach [britʃ] [breach] ☆★★★★

v. 违反，违背
Don't breach the contract, or you would be in a position of weakness.
别违反合约，否则你会处于劣势状态。

n. 违背，破坏
It's obvious that your behavior is a breach of our agreement.
很明显你的行为违反我们的协议。

同义字词 break, violate

反义字词 abide by, observe

衍生字词
▲ breach of promise （旧时）悔婚
▲ breach of the peace 扰乱治安罪（街上斗殴等）

高分秘诀
▲ contract **n.** 契约，合约
▲ position **n.** 状态，境况
▲ obvious **adj.** 明显的，显而易见的
▲ behavior **n.** 行为，举止
▲ agreement **n.** 协定，协议，契约

266. break [brek] [break] ☆☆★★★

v. 打破，折断
The old man fell off the roof of the house and broke his ankle.
老人从屋顶摔了下来，跌断了脚踝。

同义字词 crack, fracture

反义字词 mend, repair

衍生字词	▲ break apart 分开,分裂 ▲ break all ties with 与……断绝一切关系 ▲ break out 爆发,发生
高分秘诀	▲ fall off 跌落,滚落下 ▲ roof n. 屋顶,顶部 ▲ ankle n. 踝,踝关节

267. breathe [brið] [breathe] ☆★★★★

v. 呼吸	Mother told me to breathe in deeply and then breathe out. 妈妈叫我先深深吸一口气,然后再把气吐出来。
同义字词	respire, inhale
反义字词	choke, smother, suffocate
衍生字词	▲ breath n. 呼吸,气息 ▲ breathing n. 呼吸 ▲ breathless adj. 无声息的,喘不过气来的 ▲ breather n. 短暂的休息时间
高分秘诀	▲ breathe in 吸气 ▲ breathe out 呼气,呼出

268. breathtaking [ˋbrɛθˌtekɪŋ] [breath·tak·ing]

adj. 令人激动的,惊人的	The prospect from the mountain top is breathtaking. 从山顶上看去景色美极了。
同义字词	stunning, awesome
衍生字词	▲ breathtakingly adv. 令人激动地,惊人地
高分秘诀	▲ prospect n. 景色,景象 ▲ mountain n. 山,山岳,山脉

269. breed [brid] [breed] ☆☆★★★

v. 养育,繁殖	The boys were bred up as acrobats. 这些男孩子从小被当作杂技艺人培养。
n. 种类,品种	I know spaniel is a breed of dog with large ears, but I haven't seen it. 我知道西班牙猎狗是一种长着大耳朵的猎狗,但没有亲眼见过。
同义字词	raise, bring up

breathe ~ brilliant

衍生字词	▲ breeder n. 饲养员，产仔的动物 ▲ breeder reactor n. 增殖回应堆 ▲ breeding n. （动物的）生育，繁殖，生殖 ▲ breeding-ground （野生动物的）繁殖地
高分秘诀	▲ breed up 养育，教育，养成 ▲ acrobat n. 杂技演员 ▲ spaniel n. 西班牙猎狗

270. breeze [briz] [breeze] ☆☆★★★

n. 微风，轻风	I saw the wheat rippled in the breeze. 我看到小麦在微风吹拂下起伏波动。
v. 飘然而行，轻松地得胜或进步	I really envy her, you know she breezes through life, never worrying about anything. 我真的很羡慕她，她生活一帆风顺，什么事也不用操心。
衍生字词	▲ breezy adj. 有微风的，微风吹过的 ▲ breezeway n. 有屋顶的通路 ▲ breeze-block n. 轻型建筑用砖
高分秘诀	▲ wheat n. 小麦 ▲ ripple v. （使）泛起涟漪，在……上形成波痕 ▲ envy v. 妒忌，羡慕 ▲ breeze through life 快乐生活，生活一帆风顺

271. brighten [`braɪtn̩] [bright·en] ☆★★★★

v. （使）发亮，（使）发光	The movie star's presence greatly brightened up the whole party. 这个电影明星的出席使整个晚会令人眼睛为之一亮。
同义字词	light up, lighten, cheer, encourage
反义字词	darken, dim
衍生字词	▲ bright adj. 光亮的，闪光的，前途光明的
高分秘诀	▲ movie star 电影明星 ▲ brighten up 发亮 ▲ party n. 聚会

272. brilliant [`brɪljənt] [bril·liant] ☆★★★★

adj. 光辉的，灿烂的	Don't look down on that disabled girl, she is brilliant at English. 可别小看那个残疾女孩，她英语特别棒。

同义字词	bright, shinning, prominent, excellent
反义字词	dismal, gloomy, mediocre, common
衍生字词	▲ brilliantly adv. 辉煌地，灿烂地 ▲ brilliance n. 聪明，辉煌
高分秘诀	▲ look down on sb. 看不起（某人） ▲ disabled adj. 残废的，有缺陷的

273. brim [brɪm] [brim] ☆☆★★★

n. 边, 边缘	The young lady wears a large bonnet with a projecting brim. 那个年轻女士戴着一顶宽边女帽。
v. 注满	We can do nothing but watch the river brimmed over its banks. 河水溢出堤岸，对此我们无能为力。

同义字词	lip, rim, edge, border
衍生字词	▲ brimful adj. 装满……的，充盈的
高分秘诀	▲ bonnet n. 童帽，女帽 ▲ projecting adj. 突出的，伸出的 ▲ brim over 满而溢出 ▲ bank n. （河的）岸，堤

274. briny [ˈbraɪnɪ] [brin·y] ☆☆★★★

adj. 盐水的, 咸的	The skilled fisherman knows that the briny air gives a foretaste of the nearby sea. 有经验的渔民知道咸空气是靠近海洋的前兆。

同义字词	saline, salty, brackish
反义字词	bland, mild
衍生字词	▲ brine n. 海，海水，咸水，浓盐水
高分秘诀	▲ skilled adj. 熟练的，有技能的 ▲ foretaste n. 预示 ▲ nearby adj./adv. 附近的（地），不远的（地）

275. brisk [brɪsk] [brisk] ☆★★★★

adj. 活泼的, 轻快的	The doctor told me a brisk massage could restore the body's vigour. 医生告诉我轻快的按摩能恢复体力。

同义字词	active, breezy, jolly, lively

brim ~ brochure

反义字词	inactive, slack, sluggish
衍生字词	▲ briskness n. 敏捷，活泼 ▲ briskly adv. 轻快地，活泼地，迅速地
高分秘诀	▲ massage n. 按摩，推拿 ▲ restore v. 使恢复，修复 ▲ vigour n. 精力，元气

276. brittle [`brɪtl] [brit·tle]   ☆☆★★★

adj. 易碎的，易损坏的	Save your breath, we all know that brittle things break easily. 省省力气吧，大家都知道脆的东西容易破碎。
同义字词	breakable, fragile, frail
反义字词	firm, solid, hard
衍生字词	▲ brittlely adv. 易碎地，易损坏地 ▲ brittleness n. 脆性，脆度，脆弱性
高分秘诀	▲ save your breath 省点力气别开口 ▲ easily adv. 容易地，不费力地

277. broaden [`brɔdn̩] [broad·en]   ☆☆★★★

v. 放宽，变宽，扩大	I recommend you to broaden your experience by travelling more. 我建议你应该多到各地走走以增长见识。
同义字词	widen, expand, extend, branch out
反义字词	narrow, narrow down
衍生字词	▲ broad adj. 宽的，阔的，广的 ▲ broadly adv. 宽广地，明白地，清楚地 ▲ broad bean 蚕豆
高分秘诀	▲ recommend v. 推荐，建议 ▲ experience n. 经验，体验，经历，阅历

278. brochure [bro`ʃʊr] [bro·chure]   ☆☆★★★

n. 小册子	You can check out our brochure to know more about our new laptop. 你可以检查我们的简介，以便了解我们的新笔记本电脑。
同义字词	booklet, pamphlet

衍生字词	▲ leaflet n. 传单，散页印刷品 ▲ handbook n. 手册，便览 ▲ guidebook n. 旅行指南
高分秘诀	▲ check out 检视，检查，核实 ▲ laptop n. 便携式电脑，笔记本电脑

279. bronze [brɑnz] [bronze]   ☆☆★★★

n. 青铜,铜像	From its appearance we could tell that the statue is made of bronze. 从外表看，这座雕像是青铜铸成的。
同义字词	gunmetal
衍生字词	▲ bronzer n. 古铜色化妆品 ▲ bronzy adj. 青铜色的，仿青铜的 ▲ sun-bronzed adj. 被太阳晒成古铜色的 ▲ the Bronze Age 青铜器时代 ▲ bronze medal 铜牌，铜质奖章
高分秘诀	▲ appearance n. 外观，外表 ▲ statue n. 雕像，塑像 ▲ be made of 用……造成

280. bruise [bruz] [bruise]   ☆☆★★★

n. 瘀伤,擦伤	I can see there is a dilly of bruise on his leg. 我看见他腿上有一块显眼的伤痕。
v. (使)碰伤,擦伤	The young boy fell off from the shelf and bruised his knee. 男孩从架子上摔下来，膝盖瘀青。
同义字词	wound, hurt, injure, contuse
衍生字词	▲ bruiser n. 彪形大汉，粗壮的人
高分秘诀	▲ dilly n. 突出的事物 ▲ fall off 跌落，滚落下 ▲ shelf n. 架，棚 ▲ knee n. 膝，膝盖

281. bubble [ˈbʌbl] [bub·ble]   ☆★★★★

n. 气泡,泡影	As is known to us all that a bubble would burst at the slightest touch. 大家都知道气泡稍微一碰就破。

bronze ~ budget

| v. 起泡,冒泡 | When I entered the room, I saw a pot of water was bubbling on the range.
一进屋，我就看见一壶水在炉上沸腾着。 |

同义字词	foam
衍生字词	▲ bubbly adj. 充满泡沫的，生气勃勃的 ▲ bubble bath 泡沫液，泡沫粉 ▲ bubble gum 泡泡糖
高分秘诀	▲ burst v. 爆炸，爆裂 ▲ slight adj. 微小的，轻微的，微不足道的 ▲ pot n. 罐，锅，壶 ▲ range n. 多炉炉灶

282. buckle [ˈbʌkl] [buc·kle]   ☆☆★★★

| v. 扣紧,（使）变弯曲 | Before the old general buckle his armours on, he fell down.
还没有来得及穿上他的盔甲，老将军就倒下了。 |
| n. 搭扣,扣环 | Mother asked me to undo the buckles of my hat.
妈妈叫我把帽子上的扣环解开。 |

同义字词	fasten, clap, distort
反义字词	unbuckle, undo
衍生字词	▲ buckler n. 小圆盾，防御物，防卫
高分秘诀	▲ general n. 将军 ▲ armour n. 盔甲，铁甲 ▲ fall down 倒塌，跌倒 ▲ undo v. 松开，解开

283. budget [ˈbʌdʒɪt] [bud·get]   ☆★★★★

| n. 预算 | I think it's essential to balance one's budget.
我认为量入为出是很重要的。 |
| v. 编制预算,安排开支 | The university budgeted three million yuan for a new classroom building.
那所大学安排三百万元预算建筑新教学楼。 |

| 同义字词 | estimate |
| 衍生字词 | ▲ budget for ……的预算
▲ budget airline 廉价航空公司，低成本航空公司
▲ budget deficit 预算赤字 |

- ▲ account for 说明，对……负有责任
- ▲ account to 对……作出解释
- ▲ call someone to account 要求某人作出解释，责问
- ▲ from all accounts 根据各种流传的说法
- ▲ give a good account of oneself 表现出色
- ▲ give a poor account of oneself 表现拙劣
- ▲ on account 作为部分付款
- ▲ on account of 因为，由于
- ▲ on no account 绝不
- ▲ on someone's own account 为自身利益，依靠自己
- ▲ take account of 考虑到，体谅
- ▲ take into account 考虑到，体谅

- ▲ essential adj. 绝对必要的，必不可少的
- ▲ university n. 大学
- ▲ million n. 百万
- ▲ classroom building 教学楼

284. bump [bʌmp] [bump] ☆☆★★★

v. 碰撞，颠簸着前进	We have no choice but to ditch the car and bump up and down along the gravel path. 我们除了弃车沿砾石小路颠簸而行外，别无选择。
n. 肿块，突起	The lad fell heavily to the ground and got a bump on his head. 那个家伙扑通一声摔倒了，头上肿起一个包。
同义字词	lump, bulge, collide, hit
衍生字词	▲ bumper n. （汽车上的）保险杠，缓冲器 ▲ bumpy adj. 崎岖的，不平的，颠簸的 ▲ bumper-to-bumper adj. （指车辆）首尾相接的
高分秘诀	▲ ditch v. 摆脱，抛弃 ▲ up and down 上上下下 ▲ gravel path 砾石小径 ▲ lad n. 男孩，小伙子

285. bunch [bʌntʃ] [bunch] ☆☆★★★

n. 串，束，群	I saw a handsome man taking a big bunch of flowers done up in white tissue waiting for you downstairs. 我看到一个帅哥拿着一大束白色薄纱包装的花，在楼下等你。

bump ~ burdensome

v. 捆成一束，聚集

"Don't bunch up! Cross the road one at a time!" yelled the traffic policeman.

"不要都挤在一起！一个一个地过马路！"交警大声喊道。

同义字词　batch, clump, cluster, gathering, caboodle

高分秘诀
- ▲ handsome **adj.** 英俊的
- ▲ do up 包扎，捆
- ▲ tissue **n.** 薄纸，棉纸
- ▲ downstairs **adv.** 在楼下　**adj.** 楼下的
- ▲ bunch up 束在一起，挤在一起
- ▲ cross **v.** 穿过，越过，
- ▲ yell **v.** 叫喊，叫着说
- ▲ traffic policeman 交通警察

286. bundle [`bʌndl] [bun·dle]　☆☆★★★

v. 捆

I spent the whole morning to bundle the back numbers.

我花了一个上午的时间把那些旧杂志扎成一捆。

n. 捆，束，包

Yesterday afternoon I got a large bundle from my niece.

昨天下午我收到侄女寄来的一个大包裹。

同义字词　bale, packet, parcel

衍生字词　bundler **n.** 打包机，捆束机

高分秘诀
- ▲ back number 过期刊物
- ▲ niece **n.** 侄女

287. burdensome [`bɝdnsəm] [bur·den·some]　☆★★★★

adj. 繁重的，劳累的

Sometimes we have to take some burdensome responsibilities, such as raise children, look after aged parents, etc.

有些时候我们必须承担一些沉重的责任，比如抚养孩子以及照顾年迈的双亲等。

同义字词　onerous, taxing

反义字词　relaxed, light

衍生字词
- ▲ burden **n.** 重负，负担
- ▲ the burden of proof 举证责任

高分秘诀
- ▲ responsibility **n.** 责任，职责，所负责任的事
- ▲ look after 照顾，照看（某人或某物）
- ▲ aged parents 年迈的父母

288. burgeon [ˈbɝdʒən] [bur·geon] ☆★★★★

v. 迅速成长, 发展	I really wish the festivals would burgeon out slowly but steadily. 我真的希望这些欢乐的日子能够逐步稳定地发展下去。
同义字词	thrive, mushroom, flourish
反义字词	decay, decline
高分秘诀	▲ festival n. 节日，喜庆日 ▲ steadily adv. 稳定地，不断地

289. burrow [ˈbɝroʊ] [bur·row]

n. 洞穴	Some animals store many food in their burrows during autumn. 有些动物在秋天会在洞穴里贮存大量食物。
v. 挖地洞	My daughter refused to sleep but burrowed under the bedclothes. 我女儿拒绝睡觉，而且在被窝里钻来钻去。
同义字词	tunnel, den, excavate
高分秘诀	▲ store v. 储藏，存放 ▲ autumn n. 秋天，秋季 ▲ bedclothes n. 寝具，铺盖

290. bust [bʌst] [bust] ☆☆★★★

n. 半身雕像, 胸围	The sculptor made a cast of a bust for the old general. 雕刻家为老将军雕铸了一座半身像。
v. 打破, 打碎	The couple busted up two years ago for no reason. 这对夫妇两年前无缘无故分居。
同义字词	break, fall apart, rupture
衍生字词	▲ statue n. 全身雕像 ▲ sculpture n. 雕刻，雕塑 ▲ bust-up n. 分离，分手
高分秘诀	▲ sculptor n. 雕刻家 ▲ cast n. 铸造物，塑件 ▲ couple n. 夫妻，情侣 ▲ bust up （尤指夫妻之间）争吵而离异，使终止，破坏 ▲ for no reason 无缘无故，没有理由

burgeon ~ buzz

291. bustle [`bʌsl] [bus·tle] ☆☆★★★

n. 喧闹, 忙乱	The old man was unwilling to be transplanted from his home in the country to the noise and bustle of life in the city. 老人不想从乡间的居所迁到喧闹的城市里。
v. 催促, 闹哄哄地忙乱	Being a housewife, you have to bustle about the house. 作为一个家庭主妇, 你不得不为家务忙个没完。

同义字词　commotion, noise, to-do, fuss

反义字词　compose, quiet, soothe

高分秘诀
▲ unwilling adj. 不愿意的, 不情愿的, 勉强的
▲ transplant v. 移居, 迁移
▲ housewife n. 家庭主妇
▲ bustle about 忙碌

292. buzz [bʌz] [buzz] ☆☆★★★

n. 嗡嗡声	I heard a sight buzz of conversation sprang up, but didn't know who were talking. 我听见一阵嗡嗡的谈话声响起, 但不知道是谁在说话。
v. 发出嗡嗡声	Suddenly the hall buzzed with excitement. 突然间, 大厅发出一阵兴奋的叫喊声。

同义字词　bombilation

衍生字词
▲ buzzer n. 蜂鸣器
▲ buzz word 行话, 术语
▲ buzzard n. 秃鹰

高分秘诀
▲ a sight of 非常, 很多
▲ conversation n. 交谈, 谈话, 会话
▲ spring up 突然开始, 突然产生
▲ suddenly adv. 意外地, 忽然, 冷不防
▲ hall n. 礼堂, 大厅
▲ excitement n. 兴奋, 激动, 令人兴奋的事

Cc 托福 TOEFL iBT

托福(TOEFL)的测验对象为母语为非英语的人
申请入学美加地区大学或研究所时，托福成绩单是必备文件之一。

- n. 名词
- v. 动词
- adj. 形容词
- adv. 副词
- prep. 介词
- art. 冠词
- pron. 代词
- aux. 助词
- conj. 连词

Cc 托福 TOEFL iBT

托福(TOEFL)的测验对象为母语为非英语的人
申请入学美加地区大学或研究所时，托福成绩单是必备文件之一。

293. cabin [ˈkæbɪn] [ca·bin] ☆☆★★

n. 小屋，船舱

Last night the old man's cabin caught fire and burnt to ashes.
昨晚老人的小木屋失火了，屋子被烧成灰烬。

同义字词	cottage, hut, shed
衍生字词	▲ log cabin **n.** 小木屋 ▲ cabin boy 船上侍者 ▲ cabin class （轮船）二等舱
高分秘诀	▲ catch fire 着火 ▲ burn to ashes 把……化为灰烬

294. cadence [ˈkedn̩s] [ca·dence] ☆☆★★

n. （语调的）抑扬顿挫，节奏

In the dictionary, cadence means that the rise and fall of the voice in reading with rhythm.
在字典里，"Cadence"是形容朗读时声音高低曲折和谐的节奏。

同义字词	beat, rhyme, metre
衍生字词	▲ cadency **n.** 有节奏的调子 ▲ tone **n.** 音，音调，腔调，语气
高分秘诀	▲ dictionary **n.** 词典，字典 ▲ rise and fall 起落 ▲ rhythm **n.** 节奏，韵律

295. calculate [ˈkælkjəˌlet] [cal·cu·late] ☆★★★

v. 计算，估计

It's amazing that the astronomers can calculate when there will be eclipses of the sun and moon.
天文学家可以算出何时发生月食及日食，真是非常神奇。

| 同义字词 | compute, count, determine |
| 衍生字词 | ▲ calculation **n.** 计算，考虑
▲ calculator **n.** 电子计算机
▲ calculating **adj.** 精明的，有心计的 |

cabin ~ campaign

高分秘诀
▲ amazing adj. 令人惊异的
▲ astronomer n. 天文学家
▲ eclipse n. 日食或月食

296. calendar [ˈkæləndə] [ca·len·dar] ☆☆★★★

n. 日历, 日程表
Make sure to mark the appointment on your calendar.
一定要在你的日历上记下约会的时间。

同义字词: agenda, schedule

衍生字词:
▲ calendar month 历月（日历中十二个月份中的任何一个月）
▲ calendar year 历年

高分秘诀:
▲ make sure 设法确保出现某事物
▲ appointment n. 约会，约定

297. camouflage [ˈkæməˌflɑʒ] [ca·mou·flage] ☆★★★★

n. 掩饰, 伪装
My mother said that the polar bear's white fur is a natural camouflage, which could protect them from being found.
妈妈说北极熊的白色毛皮是天然的保护色，可以保护自己不被发现。

v. 掩饰, 伪装
We have to take action to camouflage the operation from the public.
为了瞒过众人耳目，我们必须采取行动。

同义字词: cover, disguise, masquerade
反义字词: reveal, disclose

高分秘诀:
▲ polar bear 北极熊
▲ fur n. 毛皮
▲ natural adj. 自然的，天然的
▲ take action 采取行动，行动起来

298. campaign [kæmˈpen] [cam·paign] ☆☆★★★

n. 战役, 竞选活动
It turned out that the campaign to seize the old city was a failure.
攻占这座老城的战役最终失败了。

v. 参加（发起）运动, 参加竞选
I recommend you not to campaign for the senate. 我建议你不要参加参议员的竞选。

同义字词: battle, activity, event

111

衍生字词 ▲ campaigner n. 从军者，出征者，竞选者

高分秘诀 ▲ turn out 结果是，原来是
▲ seize v. 夺取，占领
▲ failure n. 失败，不成功，失败的人（或事）
▲ recommend v. 劝告，建议
▲ campaign for 争取……的运动，为……而斗争
▲ senate n. 参议院，上院

299. cancel [ˈkænsl] [can·cel] ☆★★★★

v. 取消，废除

I have to say your weakness cancel out your virtues.
我不得不说你的缺点抵消了你的优点。

同义字词 revoke, repeal, call off

衍生字词 ▲ cancellation n. 取消
▲ cancelled adj. 取消的
▲ canceller n. 消除器
▲ cancelable adj. 可取消的

高分秘诀 ▲ weakness n. 弱点，缺点
▲ cancel out （使）平衡／抵消
▲ virtue n. 美德，优点

300. candidate [ˈkændədet] [can·di·date] ☆☆★★★

n. 候选人，求职者

I can say your past achievements weighed in your favour as a candidate.
我敢说你过去的成就对于身为候选人很有利。

同义字词 applicant, nominee, prospect

衍生字词 ▲ candidature n. 候选人身份，候选人资格

高分秘诀 ▲ achievement n. 成就，成绩，功绩
▲ in one's favour 对某人有利

301. capacity [kəˈpæsətɪ] [ca·pa·ci·ty] ☆☆★★★

n. 容量，能力

Housewives who don't go out to work feel they are not working to their full capacity.
没有外出工作的家庭妇女往往觉得自己的才能没有得到充分的发挥。

同义字词 content, volume, ability, capability

衍生字词 ▲ capacious adj. 宽敞的
▲ capaciousness n. 宽敞

cancel ~ cardinal

高分秘诀
▲ housewife n. 家庭主妇
▲ to one's full capacity 充分施展其才华

302. captivity [kæp`tɪvətɪ] [cap·ti·vi·ty] ☆★★★★

n. 囚禁, 拘留

Those refugee prayed for an early deliverance from captivity.
难民们为早日获释而祈祷。

同义字词
prison, confinement, imprisonment, incarcerate

衍生字词
▲ captive adj. 被俘的, 被捕获的
▲ captive audience 被动听众, 被动观众

高分秘诀
▲ refugee n. 避难者, 难民
▲ pray for 为……而祈祷, 祷告
▲ deliverance n. 解救, 解脱

303. carbohydrate [`kɑrbə`haɪdret] [car·bo·hy·drate] ☆☆☆★★

n. 碳水化合物, 糖类

To human being, carbohydrate, fat and protein are the basic nutrition.
对人类来讲, 碳水化合物、脂肪与蛋白质是基本营养成分。

同义字词
saccharide, sugar

衍生字词
▲ fat n. 脂肪
▲ protein n. 蛋白质
▲ mineral salt 无机盐
▲ vitamin n. 维生素

高分秘诀
▲ human being 人类
▲ nutrition n. 营养

304. cardinal [`kɑrdɪnəl] [car·di·nal] ☆★★★★

adj. 首要的, 主要的

In the speech, he emphasized the cardinal importance of building up good habits to lead to the success.
在演讲中, 他强调养成好习惯的重要性：好习惯是成功之母。

n. 北美红雀, 红衣凤头鸟

Have you ever seen a cardinal?
你见过北美红雀吗？

同义字词
central, chief, fundamental, primal

反义字词
common, ordinary. adj. 普通的

衍生字词
▲ cardinalship n. 红衣主教之职位或任期
▲ cardinal points 基本方位
▲ cardinal number 基数

高分秘诀	▲ speech n. 演讲，演说
	▲ emphasize v. 强调，加强语气
	▲ build up 建立，增强
	▲ lead to 导致，引起

305. career [kəˋrɪr] [ca·reer] ☆☆★★★

n. 生涯，职业	I have to admit that a series of fortuitous circumstances advanced my career. 我不得不承认一连串的好运使我的事业一帆风顺。
同义字词	vacation, occupation, calling, profession
高分秘诀	▲ a series of 一系列
	▲ fortuitous adj. 偶然发生的，偶然的
	▲ circumstance n. 境遇，情况

306. carnivore [ˋkɑrnəˌvɔr] [car·ni·vore] ☆☆☆★★

n. 肉食性动物, 动物	My aunt is an ecologist, who engaged in the study of carnivore ecology. 我阿姨是一位生物学者，她从事肉食性动物生态学的研究。
同义字词	carnivora
高分秘诀	▲ ecologist n. 生态学者
	▲ engage in 参加，从事，忙于
	▲ carnivore ecology 肉食性动物生态学

307. carpenter [ˋkɑrpəntɚ] [car·pen·ter] ☆☆☆★★

n. 木工, 木匠	In the back yard, there is a carpenter planing away at a plank. 有一个木工在后院正使劲地刨一块木板。
同义字词	woodworker, cabinetmaker, joiner
高分秘诀	▲ back yard 后院
	▲ plane away 刨掉
	▲ plank n. （厚）木板

308. carve [kɑrv] [carve] ☆☆★★★

| v. 切开, 雕刻 | The sculptor carved an angel on the wall with his knife.
雕刻家用刀子在墙上雕刻出一个天使。 |
| 同义字词 | cut, chip, slice |

career ~ catastrophe

高分秘诀	▲ sculptor n. 雕刻家
	▲ angel n. 天使
	▲ knife n. 刀

309. cast [kæst] [cast] ☆☆★★★

v. 浇铸, 抛	The narrator told us that the statue was cast in bronze.
	解说员告诉我们这座雕像是用青铜铸成的。
n. 铸造物, 塑件	In his dream, he imagined himself to be a macho cast.
	在梦中, 他想象自己是个强壮的男子。
同义字词	shape, mold, project, throw, toss

310. casual [ˈkæʒuəl] [ca·sual] ☆☆★★★

adj. 非正式的, 随便的, 偶然的	My car had stalled on my way to work. I had no choice but to seek help from casual passers-by.
	我的车在上班的路上无法发动, 我除了向路过的人求助外, 别无选择。
同义字词	informal, accidental, unexpected
反义字词	formal, planned, purposed
高分秘诀	▲ stall v. （使）熄火, （使）停止转动
	▲ seek help 求助
	▲ passer-by 过路人, 经过者

311. catalyst [ˈkætəlɪst] [ca·ta·lyst] ☆☆★★★

n. 催化剂	Of course to the catalyst producer, the most important thing is the catalyst manufacturing cost.
	当然对催化剂制造商来说, 催化剂的生产成本是最重要的事。
同义字词	enzyme, accelerator, stimulus
反义字词	anticatalyst 抗化剂, 反激活剂
高分秘诀	▲ producer n. 生产者, 制造者
	▲ manufacturing cost 工厂成本, 生产成本, 造价

312. catastrophe [kəˈtæstrəfɪ] [ca·tas·tro·phe] ☆☆★★★

n. 大灾难, 浩劫	Japan catastrophe highlights contrasts of high technology and ancient culture.
	日本浩劫震出高科技发展与古明文保存的矛盾。
同义字词	calamity, disaster, cataclysm, tragedy, misfortune
反义字词	fortune

高分秘诀 ▲ contrast n. 对比, 对照（悬殊差别）

313. cater [`ketə] [ca·ter] ★★★★

| v. 满足需要, 迎合 | Those magazines cater to the lowest tastes.
那些杂志迎合最低俗的趣味。 |

同义字词　provide, supply, serve

高分秘诀　▲ magazine n. 杂志, 期刊
　　　　　▲ cater to 迎合, 供应伙食
　　　　　▲ taste n. 爱好, 嗜好

314. cautious [`kɔʃəs] [cau·tious] ★★★★

| adj. 小心的, 谨慎的 | I can say Mr. Smith's nephew is a cautious investor.
我认为史密斯先生的侄子是一个小心谨慎的投资者。 |

同义字词　conservative, careful, prudent

反义字词　careless, incautious, rash

高分秘诀　▲ nephew n. 侄子
　　　　　▲ investor n. 投资者, 出资者

315. cease [sis] [cease] ★★★★

| v. 停止, 终止 | I'm sorry that our company has ceased making heavy products.
对不起, 我们公司已经停止制造重型产品。 |

同义字词　halt, stop, discontinue, end, terminate

反义字词　begin, start

高分秘诀　▲ heavy good vehicle 重型车辆, 重型货车

316. celebrate [`sɛlə͵bret] [ce·le·brate] ★★★

| v. 庆祝, 祝贺, 赞美 | How about we crack open a bottle of champagne to celebrate?
我们开瓶红酒庆祝一下如何？ |

同义字词　commemorate, praise, acclaim, commend

反义字词　blame

高分秘诀　▲ crack open "啪"的一声打开
　　　　　▲ champagne n. 香槟酒

317. celestial [sɪˈlɛstʃəl] [ce·les·ti·al] ☆☆★★★

adj. 天的，天空的	I wonder whether the celestial world is heavily guarded or not. 我在想天上的世界是否也是戒备森严。
同义字词	heavenly, angelic
反义字词	earthly, terrestrial
高分秘诀	▲ wonder **v.** 对……感到疑惑，想知道，问自己 ▲ heavily **adv.** 严重地，大量地 ▲ guard **v.** 保护，控制

318. census [ˈsɛnsəs] [cen·sus] ☆☆☆★★

n. 人口调查，人口普查	According to the latest census, Chile's population has increased. 根据最近人口调查，智利的人口有所增加。
同义字词	nose count
高分秘诀	▲ according to 根据，按照 ▲ latest **adj.** 最近的，最新的 ▲ Chile **n.** 智利（南美洲南部的一个国家） ▲ population **n.** 人口

319. centennial [sɛnˈtɛnɪəl] [cen·ten·ni·al] ☆☆☆★★

n. 百年纪念	It's my honor to take part in the celebration of the school's centennial. 参加本校百年校庆是我的荣幸。
同义字词	centenary, hundredth anniversary
高分秘诀	▲ honor **n.** 荣誉，光荣 ▲ take part in 参加，参与……活动

320. ceremonial [ˌsɛrəˈmonɪəl] [ce·re·mo·ni·al] ☆★★★★

n. 仪式	Tonight there will be a ceremonial to mark my brother's birth. 今晚有一项庆典，庆祝我弟弟的出生。
adj. 正式的；仪式的	My colleague told me that the ceremonial opening of the Olympic Games was a fine spectacle. 同事告诉我奥运开幕典礼的场面隆重。
同义字词	observance, ritual, ceremony

反义字词	informal adj. 非正式的
高分秘诀	▲ mark v. 标志，纪念
	▲ birth n. 出生
	▲ colleague n. 同事
	▲ opening n. 开幕
	▲ Olympic Games 奥运

321. certificate [sə'tɪfəkɪt] [cer·ti·fi·cate] ☆☆★★★

n. 证明书，执照	I even didn't know you. Since you've won the certificate, you are proud as a peacock.
	我都快不认识你了。自从赢得证书后，你就变得非常骄傲。
同义字词	credentials, certification
高分秘诀	▲ proud adj. 骄傲的，傲慢的
	▲ peacock n. 孔雀

322. chafe [tʃef] [chafe] ☆☆☆★★

v.（将皮肤等）擦热，擦破；使恼火	I recommend you this shirt, for a stiff collar may chafe your neck.
	我向你推荐这件衬衫，因为过硬的领子可能会磨损脖子。
同义字词	scratch, abrade, irritate, vex, anger, annoy
反义字词	comfort, gratify, please
高分秘诀	▲ shirt n. 衬衫，衬衣
	▲ stiff adj. 僵硬的
	▲ collar n. 衣领，领子

323. characteristic [ˌkærəktə'rɪstɪk] [cha·ra·cte·ris·tic] ☆☆★★★

adj. 典型的，表现特征的	It's characteristic of you to talk nonsense.
	胡说八道就是典型的你。
n. 特征，特性	As I told you before ambition is a characteristic of all successful people.
	正如我以前告诉你的，雄心勃勃是所有成功人士的共同特点。
同义字词	typical, distinctive, feature, peculiarity, character
反义字词	uncharacteristic

certificate ~ check

高分秘诀
▲ talk nonsense 胡说八道
▲ ambition n. 抱负，雄心，野心
▲ successful adj. 成功的

324. charitable [ˈtʃærətəbl] [cha·ri·ta·ble] ☆☆☆★★

adj. 慈善事业的，慈善的

The old man embarked in a lordly and charitable enterprise.
老人从事一项高贵并且慈善的事业。

同义字词　benevolent, kind, humane

反义字词　uncharitable adj. 无情的

高分秘诀
▲ embark in 从事
▲ lordly adj. 高贵的，宏伟的
▲ enterprise n. 事业，计划

325. charter [ˈtʃɑrtə] [char·ter] ☆☆★★★

v. 包租，特许

They are rich enough that they chartered a helicopter for the trip.
他们有钱到可以租一架直升机去旅行。

n. 宪章，章程

Have you ever read the charter of the United Nations?
你读过《联合国宪章》吗？

同义字词　lease, rent, license

高分秘诀
▲ helicopter n. 直升机
▲ trip n. 旅行，旅游
▲ the United Nations 联合国

326. check [tʃɛk] [check] ☆★★★★

v. 检查，核对

Where can I check in?
我在哪里办理登记手续？

n. 支票

Show me your check book.
让我看看你们的支票簿。

同义字词　prove, verify, contain, control

高分秘诀
▲ check in 登记，签到
▲ check book 支票簿

327. cherish [ˋtʃɛrɪʃ] [che·rish] ☆☆★★★

v. 怀抱（希望），珍视

It's not right to cherish possessions more than friends.
喜爱财物胜于朋友是不对的。

[同义字词] treasure, value, adore

[反义字词] ignore, neglect, disregard

[高分秘诀] ▲ possession **n.** 个人财产，私人财物
▲ more than 超过

328. chill [tʃɪl] [chill] ☆☆★★★

v. 使冷，变冷

I don't want to go anywhere. You know the freezing weather chilled me to the bone.
我哪里也不去，这寒冷的天气令我感到冰冷刺骨。

n. 寒意，寒颤

Winter is coming; the chill of it is in the air.
冬天来临，寒意到处感觉得到。

[同义字词] cool, freeze, coolness, coldness

[反义字词] heat, warm, hot up

[高分秘诀] ▲ freezing **adj.** 严寒的
▲ to the bone 到极点
▲ winter **n.** 冬天，冬季

329. chisel [ˋtʃɪzl] [chi·sel] ☆☆☆★★

v. 凿，欺骗

It's not easy for you to chisel a figure out of a stone.
把石头刻成雕像不是那么容易的事。

n. 凿子

Finally I borrowed a chisel, and prise off the lid.
最后我借来一个凿子，把盖子凿开了。

[同义字词] cut, carve, sculpt, engrave, inscribe

[高分秘诀] ▲ figure **n.** 画像，肖像
▲ out of 用……材料
▲ prise **v.** 强行打开或移去

330. chivalry [ˋʃɪvḷrɪ] [chi·val·ry]   ☆☆☆★★

n. 骑士精神

You can feel a sort of instinctive chivalry in him.
从他身上你能感觉到一种天生的骑士精神。

[同义字词] gallantry, knightliness

cherish ~ chorus

高分秘诀
▲ a sort of 一种
▲ instinctive adj. 天生的，直觉的

331. choke [tʃok] [choke] ☆☆★★★

| v. 使窒息，填塞 | It's my first time to face so large audience; I choked up and didn't know what to do.
这是我第一次面对如此多的观众，我说不出话来，不知道如何是好。 |

同义字词　smother, asphyxiate, suffocate, strangle
反义字词　breathe
高分秘诀
▲ audience n. 观众，听众
▲ choke up （因激动等）说不出话

332. chop [tʃɑp] [chop] ☆★★★★

| v. 砍，伐，劈 | I think it's better to chop the meat into cubes before frying it.
我认为先把肉切成方块再炸比较好。 |
| n. 带骨的肉块 | How about we have pork chops for dinner tonight?
今晚我们吃猪排如何？ |

同义字词　cut, hew, hack, cleave, sever
高分秘诀
▲ cube n. 立方形的东西，立方体
▲ fry v. 油炸，油煎
▲ pork n. 猪肉

333. choreography [ˌkɔrɪˈɑgrəfɪ] [cho·re·og·ra·phy] ☆☆★★★

| n. 舞蹈编排，舞蹈设计 | The middle-aged man is more interested in the balletic choreography.
这个中年人对芭蕾舞的动作设计比较感兴趣。 |

高分秘诀
▲ middle-aged adj. 中年的
▲ be interested in... 对……感兴趣
▲ balletic adj. 像芭蕾舞的

334. chorus [ˈkɔrəs] [cho·rus]

| n. 合唱，合唱团 | Be quiet! The chorus is about to sing.
安静！合唱团要开始唱了。 |
| v. 合唱，齐声背诵 | Every morning before I open my eyes, I can hear the birds are chorusing in the tree.
每天早上我还没有睁开眼，就听见鸟儿们在树上齐鸣。 |

同义字词	ensemble, unison, choir v. 合唱
高分秘诀	▲ quiet adj. 轻声的，安静的
	▲ be about to 将要，正打算

335. chronic [`krɑnɪk] [chron·ic] ☆★★★★

adj. 长期的，慢性的	My old grandpa has chronic bronchitis. 我年迈的爷爷患有慢性支气管炎。
同义字词	persistent, habitual, long-term
反义字词	acute
高分秘诀	bronchitis n. 支气管炎

336. chronology [krə`nɑlədʒɪ] [chro·nol·o·gy] ☆☆★★★

n. 年表，年代学	I know nothing about the relative chronology. 对于相对年代学，我一窍不通。
同义字词	time sequence
高分秘诀	▲ relative chronology 相对年代学

337. chubby [`tʃʌbɪ] [chub·by] ☆★★★★

adj. 丰满的，圆胖的	The baby, with a cute chubby face, is falling asleep. 那个有着可爱胖嘟嘟脸蛋的婴儿睡着了。
同义字词	plump, fat, round, stout
反义字词	slim, svelte, slender
高分秘诀	▲ cute adj. 漂亮的，可爱的
	▲ fall asleep 入睡

338. circulate [`sɝkjə‚let] [cir·cu·late] ☆☆★★★

v. (使)循环，(使)流通；(使)传播，(使)流传	As we all know that blood circulate through the body. 大家都知道血液在体内循环。
同义字词	circle, broadcast
高分秘诀	▲ blood n. 血，血液
	▲ through prep. 透过，经过

chronic ~ civil

339. circumscribe [ˈsɝkəmˌskraɪb] [cir·cum·scribe] ☆★★★★

v. 限制，约束；画……的外接圆

When you get into the prison, all your activities would be circumscribed.
如果被关进监狱，你所有的行动都受到限制。

同义字词 confine, limit, restrict

高分秘诀
▲ get into 进入
▲ prison **n.** 监狱，看守所
▲ activity **n.** 活动

340. circumstance [ˈsɝkəmˌstæns] [cir·cum·stance] ☆★★★★

n. 环境，情况

I have only a dim memory and couldn't recall the exact circumstances.
我记忆模糊，回想不起确切的情况。

同义字词 situation, condition, environment, surrounding

高分秘诀
▲ dim **adj.** 隐约的，模糊不清的
▲ memory **n.** 记忆，记性
▲ recall **v.** 回忆起，回想
▲ exact **adj.** 准确的，确切的，精确的

341. cite [saɪt] [cite] ☆☆★★★

v. 引用，举例，表扬

I guess you could be cited for contempt of court.
我猜你会因藐视法庭而受到传讯。

同义字词 refer to, quote, summon

反义字词 criticise, stricture

高分秘诀
▲ cite for 因……传讯
▲ contempt of court 藐视法庭

342. civil [ˈsɪvl] [ci·vil] ☆☆★★★

adj. 公民的，市民的

As is known to us all, Martin Luther King was the leader of the civil rights movement.
大家都知道，马丁·路德·金是民权运动的领袖。

同义字词 civic, courteous, polite, ceremonious

反义字词 impolite, rude, uncivil

高分秘诀
▲ leader **n.** 领袖，领导人
▲ civil right 民事权利

343. claim [klem] [claim] ☆★★★★

n. 主张，断言
I wonder what claim he has to the property.
我在想他有何权利要求得到这笔财产。

v. 声称，主张
The lady claimed that her diamond was stolen, not lost.
那位女士声称她的钻石是被偷了，不是掉了。

同义字词 demand, require, right, title

高分秘诀
▲ property **n.** 财产，资产
▲ diamond **n.** 钻石

344. clamor [ˈklæmə] [clam·or] ☆☆★★★

n. 叫嚣
The workers went on a strike and made a clamor for reform.
工人罢工，并强烈要求改革。

v. 叫嚣，喧哗
Every day she does nothing just clamor his demand.
她每天什么也不做，只是吵闹地提出自己的要求。

同义字词 outcry, uproar, commotion, din, hue and cry

高分秘诀
▲ go on 进行，发生
▲ strike **n.** 罢工
▲ reform **n.** 改革，改良

345. clap [klæp] [clap] ☆★★★★

n. 拍手掌；霹雳声
I can't help giving the speaker a clap.
我忍不住向演讲者鼓掌。

v. 鼓掌；轻拍
The audience clapped their hands and expressed their admiration.
观众们鼓掌表达他们的赞美之情。

同义字词 applaud, slap

反义字词 boo, hiss

高分秘诀
▲ can't help doing 忍不住做……
▲ speaker **n.** 演讲者
▲ audience **n.** 观众
▲ express **v.** 表达，表示

346. clarify [ˈklærəˌfaɪ] [cla·ri·fy]

v. 澄清, 阐明

Maybe some examples would help to clarify what you mean.
或许举一些例子会有助于厘清你的想法。

同义字词 　explain, make clear, clear up, illuminate, elucidate

高分秘诀 　▲ example **n.** 例子，实例

347. classify [ˈklæsəˌfaɪ] [clas·si·fy]

v. 把……分类, 分等级

Do you know how to classify the information?
你知道如何把信息分类吗?

同义字词 　categorize, sort, group

反义字词 　classified advertisements 分类广告

高分秘诀 　▲ information **n.** 信息，资料，情报

348. clergy [ˈklɝdʒɪ] [cler·gy]

n. 牧师

On that day all the local clergy would attend the ceremony.
那天当地的所有牧师都出席了仪式。

同义字词 　priest, cleric

反义字词 　laity

高分秘诀 　▲ local **adj.** 地方性的，当地的，本地的
　　　　　▲ ceremony **n.** 典礼，仪式

349. cling [klɪŋ] [cling]

v. 黏紧, 附着

In the marriage, don't let your partner cling to you or allow him or she to cling to you.
在婚姻生活中，不要黏着你的另一半，也别让对方黏着你。

同义字词 　stick, adhere to, hold

高分秘诀 　▲ marriage **n.** 婚姻
　　　　　▲ cling to 紧抓，紧附

350. clinic [ˈklɪnɪk] [cli·nic]

n. 诊所

Nowadays the mobile clinic would visit this remote village every week.
现在巡回医疗队每周都会来这个偏僻的村庄一次。

同义字词 　dispensary, infirmary

| 高分秘诀 | ▲ mobile clinic 汽车诊所，巡回医疗队
▲ remote adj. 遥远的，偏僻的
▲ village n. 村庄 |

351. clip [klɪp] [clip] ☆☆☆★★

v. 修剪，用别针别在某物上	First sort out the documents, then clip them together. 首先整理这些档案，然后用回形针把它们夹起来。
n. 夹子，回形针	Fasten those papers with a clip, please. 用回形针夹住这些纸张。
同义字词	trim, cut off, crop
反义字词	unclip
高分秘诀	▲ sort out 分类，整理 ▲ document n. 公文，档案 ▲ fasten v. 系紧

352. clumsy [ˈklʌmzɪ] [clum·sy] ☆★★★★

adj. 笨拙的；愚笨的	Though that youngster is clumsy and untidy, he's always willing to help. 虽然那个年轻人笨手笨脚又邋遢，但他总是乐于助人。
同义字词	awkward, cumbersome, ungainly, inept, gawky
反义字词	clever, dexterous, skillful
高分秘诀	▲ youngster n. 青年 ▲ untidy adj. 不整洁的，凌乱的

353. cluster [ˈklʌstɚ] [clus·ter] ☆★★★★

v. 丛生，聚集	From the top of the building, you can see the square was clustered with people. 你可以从屋顶上看到广场上聚集着成群的人。
n. 簇，串，群	There is no need to ask whether the grapefruit grow in clusters or not. 根本就没有必要问葡萄柚是不是成串生长。
高分秘诀	▲ building n. 建筑物，楼房 ▲ grapefruit n. 葡萄柚

354. coalesce [ˌkoʊəˈlɛs] [co·a·lesce] ☆☆★★★

| v. 联合，合并 | The views of board of directors coalesced to form a coherent policy.
董事会的各种观点已统一成为一致的政策。 |

clip ~ cognitive

同义字词	associate, combine, conflate, meld, merge
反义字词	separate, part
高分秘诀	▲ view n. 看法，意见，观点
	▲ coherent adj. 条理清楚的，前后一致的

355. coarse [kɔ:rs] [coarse] ☆☆★★★

adj. 粗糙的，粗野的

Stop using that kind of coarse language.
不要用那种粗俗的语言。

同义字词	rough, harsh, crude
反义字词	delicate, fine
高分秘诀	▲ language n. 语言

356. coax [koks] [coax] ☆☆★★★

v. 哄诱，巧言诱哄

His wife coaxed him out of his bad temper.
他老婆循循善诱劝他改掉坏脾气。

| 同义字词 | persuade, cajole |
| 高分秘诀 | ▲ temper n. 脾气，性情 |

357. coexist [ˋkoɪgˋzɪst] [co·ex·ist] ☆★★★★

v. 同时存在，共存

I don't think that you can get along well with her. You know a violent temper can never coexist with a love of peace.
我认为你和她不会相处得来，暴躁的脾气与爱好平静从来无法共存。

同义字词	coincide
高分秘诀	▲ get along with 和……和睦相处
	▲ violent adj. 粗暴的，剧烈的

358. cognitive [ˋkɑgnətɪv] [cog·ni·tive] ☆★★★★

adj. 认知的，感知的

I recommend all of the parents in the world to pay much attention to the development of the children's cognitive.
我建议世界上的父母都重视孩子认知能力的发展。

同义字词	perceptive, sentient
高分秘诀	▲ recommend v. 劝告，建议
	▲ in the world 世界上
	▲ pay attention to 注意

359. coherent [ko`hɪrənt] [co·he·rent] ☆☆★★★

adj. 黏的，思路清晰有条理的

Maybe some coherent explanation would help you to know this theory well.
或许用一些有条理的说明能帮助你更好地理解这个理论。

同义字词　adhesive, cohesive, tenacious
反义字词　incoherent
高分秘诀　▲ explanation **n.** 解释，说明
　　　　　▲ theory **n.** 理论，学说

360. cohesion [ko`hiʒən] [co·he·sion] ☆★★★★

n. 附着（力），凝聚力

The only way to save your company is to bring cohesion and unity into it.
挽救你公司的唯一方法就是加强公司的团结和统一。

同义字词　unity, solidarity, cohesiveness
反义字词　incohesion, incoherence
高分秘诀　▲ company **n.** 公司
　　　　　▲ unity **n.** 一致，同心协力

361. coincide [ˌkoɪn`saɪd] [co·in·cide] ☆★★★★

v. 同时发生，相巧合

My religious beliefs coincide with those of yours.
我的宗教信仰与你的恰巧一样。

同义字词　correspond, cooccur, concur
高分秘诀　▲ religious **adj.** 宗教的
　　　　　▲ belief **n.** 信念，信仰

362. collaborate [kə`læbəˌret] [col·lab·o·rate] ★★★★★

v. 协作，合作

Everything seemed to be going in my favor. You know the time, the incidents had to collaborate with me.
一切看来都在朝对我有利的方向发展，时间和各种事件仿佛都在配合我似的。

同义字词　cooperate, work together
高分秘诀　▲ in my favor 对某人有利
　　　　　▲ incident **n.** 发生的事
　　　　　▲ collaborate with 合作

coherent ~ colonize

363. collapse [kəˈlæps] [col·lapse] ☆☆★★★

n. 倒塌，崩溃
It's lucky that the collapse of the building caused no casualties.
幸运的是建筑物倒塌没有造成伤亡。

v. 倒塌，失败
Finally their project which had been prepared for a long time, collapsed for lack of money.
最后，他们准备良久的计划还是因为缺钱而宣告失败。

同义字词: breakdown, failure, break down

反义字词: success

高分秘诀:
▲ casualty **n.** 伤亡者，受害者，牺牲品
▲ prepare for （使）为……作准备
▲ for lack of 因……而没有

364. collide [kəˈlaɪd] [col·lide] ☆☆★★★

v. 碰撞，冲突
As the taxi turned the corner, it collided with a lorry.
出租车转过街角时与货车相撞了。

同义字词: bump, hit, clash, conflict

365. colloquial [kəˈlokwɪəl] [col·lo·qui·al] ☆★★★★

adj. 口语的，通俗语的
Though your English is fluent, it is not colloquial.
虽然你的英语讲得很流利，但不够口语化。

同义字词: conversational, informal

反义字词: literary, written

高分秘诀:
▲ though **conj.** 虽然，尽管
▲ fluent **adj.** 流利的

366. colonize [ˈkɑləˌnaɪz] [co·lo·nize] ☆☆☆★★

v. 建立殖民地，拓殖
According to the history, we know that around 700 Arabs began to colonize East Africa.
根据历史，我们知道在公元700年阿拉伯人开始把东非变成殖民地。

同义字词: colonise

反义字词: decolonize, decolonise

367. colossal [kəˈlɑsl] [co·los·sal]

adj. 巨大的

If it reaches the agreement, then the government would spend on a colossal scale.
如果达成协议，政府就会付出巨额开支。

同义字词　huge, gigantic, enormous, immense, mammoth
反义字词　very small, diminutive
高分秘诀
▲ agreement n. 协议，契约
▲ scale n. 规模，范围，程度

368. combine [kəmˈbaɪn] [com·bine]

v. 联合，结合

It's marvelous that elements can combine in many different ways to form thousands of compounds.
真神奇，元素以多种形式结合成数千种化合物。

同义字词　blend, fuse, merge
反义字词　depart
高分秘诀
▲ marvelous adj. 不可思议的，非凡的，引起惊异的
▲ element n. （化学）元素，成分，原件
▲ thousands of 数千的

369. combustible [kəmˈbʌstəbl] [com·bus·ti·ble]

adj. 易燃的

We all know that the petrol is highly combustible.
众所皆知，汽油极易燃。

同义字词　flammable, burnable, inflamable, fiery
反义字词　noncombustible, incombustible
高分秘诀
▲ petrol n. 汽油
▲ highly adv. 高度地，极，非常

370. comet [ˈkɑmɪt] [com·et]

n. 彗星

How I wish I could have a binoculars to see the comet!
我真希望我能有个望远镜看那颗彗星！

高分秘诀
▲ binoculars n. 双筒望远镜

371. comic [ˈkɑmɪk] [com·ic]

adj. 滑稽的，好笑的

I don't like that movie, as the comic scenes were overdone.
我不喜欢那部电影，电影的滑稽场面演得太过夸张。

colossal ~ commerce

同义字词	funny, ridiculous, comical, amusing, laughable
反义字词	tragic
高分秘诀	▲ scene n. 场景，现象
	▲ overdone 做得过分，夸张，过度，过火

372. commemorate [kəˋmɛməˌret] [com·me·mo·rate] ☆★★★★

v. 纪念，庆祝

Do you know that Christmas commemorates the birth of Christ?
你知道圣诞节是为了纪念耶稣的诞生吗？

同义字词	remember, memorialize
高分秘诀	▲ Christmas n. 圣诞节
	▲ Christ n. 耶稣，基督，救世主

373. comment [ˋkamɛnt] [com·ment] ☆☆★★★

v. 谈及，评论

I don't know what's in his mind, for he didn't comment on what I said.
我不知道他是怎么想的，因为他对我的话未作评论。

n. 注释，评论

A: Could you let us know your true feeling about the event?
A：关于这件事你能告诉我们你的真实想法吗？
B: No comment!
B：无可奉告！

同义字词	remark, judgment, mention, note, annotate
高分秘诀	▲ comment on 就……发表看法（评论）
	▲ no comment 无可奉告，拒绝评论

374. commerce [ˋkamɝs] [com·merce] ☆☆★★★

n. 商业

I remembered that my uncle majored in international commerce in college.
我记得我叔叔大学时主修的是国际贸易。

同义字词	trade, business
衍生字词	commercial adj. 商业的，贸易的
	commercialize v. 使商业化，使商品化
	commercialism n. 重商主义，营利主义
	commercial traveller 旅行推销员

高分秘诀	▲ major in 主修
	▲ international commerce 国际商务
	▲ college n. 大学，学院，高等专科学校

375. commission [kəˈmɪʃən] [com·mis·sion] ☆★★★★

v. 委任,任命	My grandfather was commissioned a general at the age of 60.
	我外公在六十岁时被任命为将军。
n. 佣金,授权	No one knows why he resigned his position as chairman of the commission.
	没有人知道他为什么辞去委员会主席的职务。
同义字词	authorize
反义字词	commissioner, commissioned officer（持有委任状的）军
高分秘诀	▲ resign v. 辞职，放弃
	▲ position n. 职位，职务
	▲ chairman n. 主席，委员长，董事长

376. commit [kəˈmɪt] [com·mit] ☆☆★★★

v. 犯（错误），交付	No one can help you, you know you committed a fatal mistake.
	没有人能帮你，你犯了一个无可挽回的错误。
同义字词	entrust, perpetrate
高分秘诀	▲ commit a mistake 犯错误
	▲ fatal adj. 致命的，灾难性的

377. commodity [kəˈmɑdətɪ] [com·mo·di·ty] ☆☆★★★

n. 商品,日用品	Generally speaking, Taiwan is heavily dependent on its exports of agricultural commodities.
	通常来说，台湾十分依靠农产品的出口贸易。
同义字词	goods, article of trade, product, ware
高分秘诀	▲ generally speaking 一般而言，总的来说
	▲ be dependent on 依靠，倚赖
	▲ agricultural commodity 农产品

378. communal [ˈkɑmjunl] [com·mu·nal] ☆★★★★

adj. 社会的,公有的	I recommend you to take part in some kind of communal recreations.
	我建议你参加一些集体的康乐活动。

commission ~ comparable

衍生字词
▲ communally adv. 公有地，社区地
▲ communality n. 集体性，社区

高分秘诀
▲ take part in 参加，参与……活动
▲ recreation n. 娱乐（模式），消遣（模式）

379. communicate [kə`mjunə͵ket] [com·mu·ni·cate] ☆★★★★

v. 传达，沟通
Sometimes I found it's difficult to communicate with you.
有时候我觉得你很难沟通。

同义字词
convey, inform, correspond

反义字词
▲ communicable adj. 可以传授的，会传染的
▲ communication n. 沟通

高分秘诀
▲ difficult adj. 困难的
▲ communicate with 与……沟通

380. commute [kə`mjut] [com·mute] ☆☆★★★

v. 通勤，交换
Susan has to commute between New York to Chicago every day.
苏珊每天往返于纽约和芝加哥。

同义字词
exchange

高分秘诀
▲ New York 纽约
▲ Chicago n. 芝加哥（美国城市名）

381. compact [kəm`pækt] [com·pact] ☆★★★★

v. 压缩，使密集
The next day, I found the old snow has compacted into the hard ice.
隔天我发现雪堆已经凝固成冰。

adj. 紧凑的，紧密的
Though my father is in his sixties, he still has a compact build.
尽管父亲已经六十多岁了，但身体依然结实。

同义字词
compressed, condensed, dense

反义字词
decompress, uncompress

高分秘诀
▲ compact into 把……压实
▲ build n. 体形，架构

382. comparable [`kɑmpərəbl] [com·pa·ra·ble] ☆☆★★★

adj. 可比的，比得上的
This kind of comparable and reliable date is often lacking, which can only be built up gradually.
这种可比较而又可靠的资料常不足，它们只能靠逐渐累积获得。

同义字词	equivalent, corresponding
反义字词	uncomparable, incomparable
衍生字词	comparative **adj.** 比较的 comparatively **adv.** 相当地，比较地 comparability **n.** 可比较，相似 comparison **n.** 比较，对照，比拟，比喻
高分秘诀	▲ reliable **adj.** 可靠的，可倚赖的 ▲ lacking **adj.** 缺乏的，不足的 ▲ gradually **adv.** 逐步地，渐渐地

383. compatible [kəmˋpætəbl] [com·pa·ti·ble] ☆★★★★

adj. 相容的，协调的	I dare say it's not him. See those actions are not compatible with his character. 我敢说不是他。看这些行为与他的性格不一致。
同义字词	agreeable, congenial, harmonious
反义字词	incompatible
高分秘诀	▲ action **n.** 行动，活动 ▲ character **n.** 品性，特色，特性

384. compel [kəmˋpɛl] [com·pel] ☆☆★★★

v. 强迫，使不得不	I have no right to compel them to work overtime. 我没有权利要求他们加班。
同义字词	force, coerce, oblige
高分秘诀	▲ right **n.** 权利 ▲ work overtime 加班

385. compensate [ˋkɑmpənˌset] [com·pen·sate] ☆☆★★★

v. 补偿，赔偿	You have to keep in mind that nothing can compensate for the loss of one's health. 你必须牢记，失去身体健康是没有东西能弥补的。
同义字词	make up for, reimburse, recompense
高分秘诀	▲ keep in mind 记住 ▲ compensate for 赔偿，补偿损失 ▲ loss **n.** 丧失，遗失，损失

386. compete [kəmˋpit] [com·pete] ☆★★★★

compatible ~ complex

| v. 竞争, 竞赛 | The catering trade competes intensely in this city.
这个城市的餐饮业竞争十分激烈。 |

同义字词　vie, contest, fight, rival

高分秘诀
▲ catering trade 餐饮行业
▲ intensely adv. 强烈地，极度

387. compile [kəmˋpaɪl] [com·pile] ☆☆★★★

| v. 汇集, 编辑 | It would take much time and toil to compile an encyclopedia.
汇编一本百科全书是花费时间和精力的事。 |

同义字词　gather, collect, accumulate

高分秘诀
▲ toil n. 辛苦，劳累
▲ encyclopedia n. 百科全书

388. complain [kəmˋplen] [com·plain] ☆★★★★

| v. 抱怨, 诉苦 | Julia is such a nag that she always complains about things.
茱丽亚很唠叨，她终日牢骚满腹。 |

同义字词　grumble, gripe, grouse, squawk

高分秘诀
▲ nag n. 好唠叨的人
▲ complain about 抱怨，投诉

389. complement [ˋkɑmpləmənt] [com·ple·ment] ☆☆★★

| v. 补充, 使完善 | It would be better to have a bottle of wine to complement the food.
如果有瓶酒配这些菜肴将会更相得益彰。 |
| n. 补足物, 补充物 | Almost every one think the homework is a necessary complement to classroom study, but sometimes it's a burden for the student.
几乎每个人都认为家庭作业是课堂教学的必要补充，但是有些时候它却是学生的负担。 |

同义字词　supplement, complete

高分秘诀
▲ necessary adj. 必要的，必然的
▲ burden n. 重担

390. complex [ˋkɑmplɛks] [com·plex] ☆★★★★

| adj. 复杂的, 费解的 | The question is so complex that I don't know how to answer it.
这个问题太复杂了，我不知道如何回答。 |

135

| n. 综合体，复合 | An iron and steel complex is to be built here.
这里将会建造一个钢铁联合企业。 |

同义字词	intricate, compound, complicated
反义字词	brief, plain, simple
高分秘诀	▲ iron and steel complex 钢铁联合企业

391. compliment [ˈkɑmpləmənt] [com·pli·ment] ☆☆★★★

| n. 恭维，赞扬 | My boss paid me a compliment because of my diligence.
我的勤劳受到老板的赞美。 |
| v. 恭维，赞扬 | I complimented the girl on her skillful performance.
我称赞那个女孩的娴熟技艺。 |

| 高分秘诀 | ▲ pay a compliment to 恭维，夸奖，称赞
▲ diligence n. 勤勉，勤奋
▲ skillful adj. 灵巧的，熟练的 |

392. comply [kəmˈplaɪ] [com·ply] ☆☆★★★

| v. 遵从，依从 | When you work for her, you have to comply with her request.
如果你为她工作，你必须服从她。 |

同义字词	conform, obey
反义字词	reject, refuse, deny
高分秘诀	▲ work for 受雇于，为……而工作 ▲ comply with 遵从，符合

393. compose [kəmˈpoz] [com·pose] ☆☆★★★

| v. 作曲，写作 | We all know that water is composed of hydrogen and oxygen.
众所周知，水是由氢和氧组成的。 |

| 同义字词 | write, create, construct, make up |
| 高分秘诀 | ▲ be composed of 由……组成
▲ hydrogen n. 氢 |

394. comprehend [ˌkɑmprɪˈhɛnd] [com·pre·hend] ☆☆★★★

| v. 领悟，理解 | I really cannot comprehend how you could have been so stupid.
我真不明白你怎么那么笨。 |

compliment ~ compulsory

| 同义字词 | understand, grasp |
| 高分秘诀 | ▲ stupid adj. 蠢的，傻的 |

395. compress [kəmˋprɛs] [com·press] ☆★★★★

v. 压缩，浓缩

How about you compress your speech into fifteen minutes?
能否把你的演讲压缩至十五分钟？

同义字词	compact, concentrate, condense
反义字词	decompress, uncompress
高分秘诀	▲ compress into 将……压缩成
	▲ speech n. 演讲，讲话

396. comprise [kəmˋpraɪz] [com·prise] ☆★★★★

v. 包含；由……组成

This medical team comprises eight doctors and three nurses.
这支医疗队由八名医生和三名护士组成。

同义字词	contain, consist of, include, involve
高分秘诀	▲ medical team 医疗队
	▲ nurse n. 护士

397. compromise [ˋkɑmprəˌmaɪz] [com·pro·mise] ☆☆★★★

n. 妥协，折中

I think the good way to solve this problem is to arrive at a compromise.
我认为解决这个问题的好方法就是达成妥协。

v. 妥协，折中

You are wise to compromise with that old lady.
向那个老太太妥协是明智的。

同义字词	concession, yield, give in, temporize
高分秘诀	▲ arrive at 达成，获得
	▲ wise adj. 聪明的，明智的
	▲ compromise with 向（某人）妥协

398. compulsory [kəmˋpʌlsərɪ] [com·pul·so·ry] ☆☆★★★

adj. 必须做的，被强制的

I wonder whether the military service is compulsory in your country.
我在想你们国家是否实行义务兵役制度。

| 同义字词 | mandatory, obligatory |
| 反义字词 | optional, voluntary |

399. compute [kəmˋpjut] [com·pute] ☆☆★★★

v. 计算

Who can give us a more accurate method to compute the average?
谁能给我们一个更精确的求平均数方法?

同义字词 calculate, reckon

高分秘诀
▲ accurate adj. 精确的,准确的
▲ method n. 方法,办法
▲ average n. 平均数

400. concave [ˋkɑnkev] [con·cave] ☆☆☆★★

adj. 凹的

The contour of the lung can be straight, slightly concave or slightly convex.
肺的形状可以是直的、轻微凹下或稍微突出。

高分秘诀
▲ contour n. 外形,轮廓
▲ straight adj. 直的,笔直的
▲ slightly adv. 轻微地,稍微

401. conceal [kənˋsil] [con·ceal] ☆☆★★★

v. 隐蔽,隐瞒

It's said that it's easy to conceal the wealth but difficult to conceal the poverty.
藏富容易,掩饰贫穷则困难。

同义字词 hide, secrete

反义字词 disclose, reveal

高分秘诀
▲ wealth n. 财产,财富
▲ poverty n. 贫穷,贫困

402. concede [kənˋsid] [con·cede] ☆★★★★

v. 承认

After investigation, people have to concede the president's incorruptible honesty.
经过调查,人们不得不承认总统的清白与诚实。

同义字词 acknowledge, admit, confess, grant

高分秘诀
▲ investigation n. 调查,侦查
▲ president n. 总统,主席
▲ incorruptible adj. 不腐败的,清廉的

compute ~ concert

403. conceive [kən`siv] [con·ceive] ☆☆★★★

v. 构思, 怀孕

We have to admit that the plot of the novel is ingeniously conceived.
我们不得不承认小说情节的构思相当巧妙。

同义字词 design, consider, gestate

高分秘诀
▲ plot **n.** 故事情节
▲ ingeniously **adv.** 有才能地, 巧妙地

404. concentrate [`kɑnsɛnˌtret] [con·cen·trate] ☆★★★★

v. 专心于, 注意

I concentrated on the lecture and didn't notice what happened outside.
我专心听课, 没有注意到外面发生了什么事。

同义字词 focus, pay attention on

反义字词 distract, deconcentrate

高分秘诀
▲ concentrate on 专心于, 把思想集中于
▲ lecture **n.** 演讲, 讲课
▲ outside **adv.** 在外面

405. concept [`kɑnsɛpt] [con·cept] ☆★★★★

n. 概念, 理念

The concept of the earth is flat is turned out to be erroneous.
地球是平的这个理念被证明是错的。

同义字词 notion, idea, conception, opinion

高分秘诀
▲ flat **adj.** 平的, 扁平的
▲ erroneous **adj.** 错误的, 不正确的

406. concern [kən`sɝn] [con·cern] ☆★★★★

v. 有关于, 使烦恼

The old man's poor health concerned his children.
那位老先生的健康不佳, 令儿女们深感担忧。

n. 忧虑, 担心

I think how much money I have is none of your concern.
我认为我有多少钱与你无关。

高分秘诀
▲ poor **adj.** (身体) 衰弱的
▲ health **n.** 健康 (状况)

407. concert [`kɑnsɝt] [con·cert] ☆☆★★★

n. 音乐会, 一致

Do you have any tickets for the concert?
还有那场音乐会的票吗?

| 同义字词 | philharmonic, harmony, accord, unison |
| 高分秘诀 | ▲ ticket n. 票 |

408. concise [kənˈsaɪs] [con·cise] ☆★★★★

adj. 简洁的，简明的	When you write something, be sure to make it clear and concise and avoid long-windedness. 当你写东西时，注意要简明扼要，避免长篇大论。
同义字词	succinct, terse, brief, curt
反义字词	diffuse, redundant, prolix
高分秘诀	▲ clear adj. 清楚的，明白的 ▲ long-windedness n. 冗长，啰唆

409. conclude [kənˈklud] [con·clude] ☆☆★★★

v. 推断；作出结论	The speaker concluded his speech with a famous proverb. 演说者以一句有名的谚语结束自己的演讲。
同义字词	deduce, infer, finalize, wind up
反义字词	begin, commence, star
高分秘诀	▲ famous adj. 著名的 ▲ proverb n. 谚语，格言

410. concomitant [kɑnˈkɑmətənt] [con·co·mi·tant] ☆☆★★★

adj. 伴随的，同时发生或出现的	In order to arrive at those multiple purposes which requires the concomitant use of three drugs. 为了达到这些目的，需要同时应用三种药物。
n. 伴随物，共存	We can say that the infirmities are the concomitants of old age. 我们认为虚弱伴随着老年。
同义字词	accompanying, happening together, attendant
高分秘诀	▲ multiple adj. 多重的，多种多样的 ▲ drug n. 药物，药剂，药材 ▲ infirmity n. 体弱，虚弱 ▲ old age 晚年

411. concrete [ˈkɑnkrit] [con·crete] ☆☆★★★

| n. 水泥 | The builders reinforced the concrete wall with steel rods.
建筑工人们用钢筋加固水泥墙。 |

concise ~ condition

| adj. 具体的，实体的 | The word "pineapple" is a concrete noun.
"凤梨"是个具体名词。 |

同义字词　cement, tangible, solid

高分秘诀
▲ reinforce v. 增强，加强
▲ steel rod 钢条，钢棍
▲ concrete noun 具体名词

412. condemn [kənˋdɛm] [con·demn]　☆★★★★

| v. 谴责；判罪，处刑 | The judge condemned the robber to three years of community service.
法官判这个抢劫犯三年社区服务。 |

同义字词　blame, denounce, criticize, reproach, decry

反义字词　praise

高分秘诀
▲ judge n. 法官
▲ robber n. 抢劫者，盗贼
▲ community service 社区服务

413. condense [kənˋdɛns] [con·dense]　☆☆★★★

| v. 使浓缩，精简 | As is known to us all that steam condenses into water when cooling down.
大家都知道蒸汽冷却时凝结成水。 |

同义字词　compress, concentrate

反义字词　rarefy

高分秘诀
▲ steam n. 蒸汽
▲ condense into （使）凝结成
▲ cool down （使）变凉，冷静下来

414. condiment [ˋkɑndəmənt] [con·di·ment]　☆☆★★★

| n. 调味品 | I think what they sold is the best quality condiment.
我认为他们卖的是最好的调味品。 |

同义字词　seasoning, spice, flavouring, food additive

高分秘诀
▲ best quality 最好的品性

415. condition [kənˋdɪʃən] [con·di·tion]　☆★★★★

| n. 条件，状况 | I'm hoping against hope for a change in my grandmother's condition.
我希望外婆的病情有一丝转机。 |

同义字词	situation, state
高分秘诀	▲ hope against hope 抱一线希望

416. conduct [kənˋdʌkt] [con·duct] ☆★★★★

v. 控制, 管理	It's said that copper conducts electricity better than iron does. 据说铜的导电性比铁强。
n. 举止, 行为	The lawyer was accused of unprofessional conduct. 这位律师被控违反职业道德。
同义字词	direct, guide, lead
高分秘诀	▲ accuse of 指责，控告 ▲ unprofessional adj. 违反职业道德标准的

417. confederate [kənˋfɛdərɪt] [con·fed·er·ate] ☆☆★★★

n. 同盟者, 盟友	You have to be careful, you know though the gangster was arrested, his confederate escaped. 你必须小心，虽然那个坏人被逮捕了，但他的同伙却逃逸了。
v. 联合, 结盟	The little kingdom tried to confederate itself with others for mutual safety. 这个小国为了共同安全，曾试图与其他的国家结盟。
adj. 联盟的, 同盟的	My grandfather was once a Confederate soldiers in the Civil War. 在南北战争期间，我外公曾经是南方联邦的士兵。
同义字词	band together, ally, collaborator, alliance
高分秘诀	▲ kingdom n. 王国 ▲ mutual adj. 相互的，彼此的 ▲ the Civil War 南北战争（美国内战）

418. confer [kənˋfɝ] [con·fer] ☆☆★★★

v. 颁给, 赋予	The old man was once conferred the dignity of a peerage by the queen. 老人曾经被女王授予贵族身份。
同义字词	bestow, discuss, consult, talk over
高分秘诀	▲ dignity n. 庄严，尊贵 ▲ peerage n. 贵族 ▲ queen n. 女王

conduct ~ confirm

419. confess [kənˋfɛs] [con·fess] ☆☆★★★

v. 坦白承认

The convict finally confessed his crime.
这个罪犯最后终于承认了自己的罪行。

- 同义字词: acknowledge, admit
- 反义字词: conceal
- 高分秘诀:
  - ▲ convict **n.** 已决犯
  - ▲ crime **n.** 罪，罪行，犯罪

420. confide [kənˋfaɪd] [con·fide] ☆☆★★★

v. 吐露（心事），倾诉

I have to confide my trouble to my friends, or I'll go mad.
我必须向朋友倾诉我的烦恼，不然我会发疯。

- 同义字词: disclose, reveal, tell
- 高分秘诀:
  - ▲ trouble **n.** 困难，麻烦
  - ▲ go mad 发疯

421. confident [ˋkɑnfədənt] [con·fi·dent] ☆★★★★

adj. 有信心的，自信的

It's my grandmother's encouragement that made me more confident of my future.
外婆的鼓励使我对未来更有信心。

- 同义字词: assured, sure, convinced, certain
- 反义字词: diffident
- 高分秘诀:
  - ▲ encouragement **n.** 鼓励
  - ▲ future **n.** 未来，将来

422. confine [kənˋfaɪn] [con·fine] ☆☆★★★

v. 限制

I has been confined to bed half a month by gout.
我因痛风而卧床半个月。

- 同义字词: limit, circumscribe, enclose, restrain
- 反义字词: free, liberate, release
- 高分秘诀:
  - ▲ confined to bed 卧病不起的
  - ▲ gout **n.** 痛风

423. confirm [kənˋfɝm] [con·firm] ☆☆★★★

v. 证实，使……更坚定

I'm calling to confirm my flight reservation.
我打电话是想确认我预订的班机。

同义字词	verify, corroborate, affirm, substantiate
反义字词	contradict, negate, deny
高分秘诀	▲ reservation n. 保留的座位等，预订

424. conflict [ˋkɑnflɪkt] [con·flict] ☆★★★★

n. 战斗, 斗争	You have to know that there has always been some conflict between the sexes. 你必须知道两性之间一直都有矛盾。
v. 抵触, 冲突	The hours of the two interviews conflict, so I don't know how to do with it. 两场面试的时间有冲突，我不知道如何是好。
同义字词	fight, struggle, battle, clash, run afoul
高分秘诀	▲ interview n. 面谈，面试

425. conform [kənˋfɔrm] [con·form] ☆☆★★★

v. 遵守, 符合	You have no choice but to conform your plans to the new specifications. 你除了使自己的计划符合新的详细说明外，别无选择。
同义字词	comply with, follow, fit, meet
高分秘诀	▲ specification n. 说明书，详述，说明

426. confront [kənˋfrʌnt] [con·front] ☆☆★★★

| v. 面对, 正视 | The judge don't know how to do with it, just confronted the accused with his accuser.
法官不知如何是好，只好让被告和原告对质。 |
| 高分秘诀 | ▲ the accused n. 被告
▲ accuser n. 原告 |

427. confuse [kənˋfjuz] [con·fuse] ☆☆★★★

v. 搞乱, 使糊涂	I was confused by your conflicting advice. 我被你相互矛盾的建议搞糊涂了。
同义字词	disorient, mix up, jumble, muddle, bewilder
高分秘诀	▲ conflicting adj. 相互矛盾的，冲突的

428. congenial [kənˋdʒinjəl] [con·gen·ial] ☆☆★★★

| adj. 同性质的, 趣味相同的 | It's hard for me to find congenial companionship in this big city.
在这个大城市很难找到志同道合的朋友。 |

conflict ~ congress

同义字词	agreeable, compatible
反义字词	incompatible, uncongenial
高分秘诀	▲ companionship n. 友情，友谊

429. congenital [kənˋdʒɛnətl] [con·ge·ni·tal] ☆☆★★★

adj. 先天的，天生的

That birth mark on my bum is congenital.
我臀部上的胎记是天生的。

| 同义字词 | inborn, innate |
| 高分秘诀 | ▲ birth mark 胎记 |

430. congestion [kənˋdʒɛstʃən] [con·ges·tion] ☆☆★★★

n. 拥挤，拥塞

How to relieve the traffic congestion?
如何缓解交通拥挤？

| 高分秘诀 | ▲ relieve v. 缓解，消除，减少
▲ traffic congestion 交通拥挤 |

431. congregate [ˋkɑŋgrɪˏget] [con·gre·gate] ☆★★★★

v. 集合，聚集

The crowds congregated in the hall to hear the president speak.
群众聚集在大厅听总统演讲。

| 同义字词 | assemble, convene, crowd, gather |
| 高分秘诀 | ▲ crowd n. 人群
▲ hall n. 礼堂，会堂，大厅 |

432. conglomerate [kənˋglɑmərɪt] [con·glo·me·rate] ☆☆★★★

n. 聚集物，集团

An unknown conglomerate holds a major share in the company.
一家不知名的集团企业持有该公司的大部分股份。

| 高分秘诀 | ▲ unknown adj. 未知的，不出名的
▲ hold v. 持有
▲ share n. 股，股份，股票 |

433. congress [ˋkɑŋgrəs] [con·gress] ☆☆★★★

n. 国会，议会

It turned out that his proposal has raised squawks of protest in congress.
结果他的建议在国会里引起大声抗议。

| 同义字词 | parliament |
| 高分秘诀 | ▲ proposal n. 提议，建议
▲ squawk n. 叫声，抗议
▲ protest n. 抗议，反对 |

434. conjectural [kənˋdʒɛktʃərəl] [con·jec·tur·al] ☆☆★★

adj. 推测的	All the estimates are so conjectural as to be almost worthless. 所有这些估计全凭猜测，因此没有任何价值。
同义字词	hypothetical, supposed, hypothetic
高分秘诀	▲ estimate n. 估计 ▲ worthless adj. 无价值的，没有用处的

435. connect [kəˋnɛkt] [con·nect] ☆☆★★

v. 连接，联合	Make sure the machine's connected properly before you use it. 使用前注意机器要接好电源。
同义字词	join, attach, relate, combine
高分秘诀	▲ make sure 设法确保 ▲ machine n. 机器 ▲ properly adv. 适当地，正确地

436. conscience [ˋkɑnʃəns] [con·science] ☆☆★★

n. 良心，良知	I found sometimes conscience can be overruled by passion. 我发现有时良知容易受感情的支配。
同义字词	moral sense
高分秘诀	▲ sometimes adv. 有时，间或 ▲ overrule v. 推翻 ▲ passion n. 激情，热情

437. conscious [ˋkɑnʃəs] [con·scious] ☆★★★

adj. 有意识的，神志清醒的	Though the girl was badly hurt, she still remained conscious. 虽然女孩受了重伤，但意识仍清楚。
同义字词	awake, aware, cognizant
高分秘诀	▲ badly adv. 非常，在很大程度上 ▲ remain v. 保持

conjectural ~ considerate

438. consecutive [kən`sɛkjutɪv] [con·sec·u·tive] ☆☆★★★

adj. 连续的

Our team won three consecutive games on the road.
我们队伍一路连赢三局。

同义字词 successive, sequential, continuous, straight

高分秘诀 ▲ on the road 在途中，一路上

439. consequence [`kɑnsəˌkwɛns] [con·se·quence] ☆☆★★★

n. 结果，后果

He worked hard, and in consequence he got promoted to manager.
他工作努力，因此被提拔为经理。

同义字词 result, aftermath, outcome

反义字词 cause, reason

高分秘诀 ▲ in consequence 结果
▲ promote **v.** 提升，提拔

440. conservative [kən`sɝvətɪv] [con·ser·va·tive] ☆☆★★★

adj. 保守的，谨慎的

I think it's your conservative views that made you unpopular.
我认为是你保守的观点使你不受欢迎。

同义字词 traditional, conventional, cautious

高分秘诀 ▲ view **n.** 观点，看法
▲ unpopular **adj.** 不受欢迎的，不流行的

441. considerable [kən`sɪdərəbl] [con·si·de·rable] ☆☆★★★

adj. 相当大（多）的，值得考虑的

These business made a considerable sum of money in real estate.
这位商人做房地产生意赚了大钱。

同义字词 much, great, significant

高分秘诀 ▲ sum of money 款项
▲ real estate 房地产

442. considerate [kən`sɪdərɪt] [con·si·de·rate] ☆☆★★★

adj. 考虑周到的，体贴的

It is considerate of you to call on your relatives quiet often.
你真体贴，常常拜访你的亲友。

高分秘诀 ▲ call on 拜访（某人）
▲ relative **n.** 亲属，亲戚

443. consistent [kənˈsɪstənt] [con·sis·tent] ☆★★★★

adj. 一致的，变化少的	I just don't understand why you remained consistent in your opposition to anything new. 我不明白你为什么始终反对一切新事物。
同义字词	uniform, coherent, consonant
高分秘诀	▲ opposition n. 反对，敌对

444. consort [ˈkɑnsɔrt] [con·sort] ☆☆★★★

v. 陪伴，结交	I think you should consort with those whom you can learn from. 我认为你应该结交能与之学习之人。
同义字词	associate, join
高分秘诀	▲ consort with 结交 ▲ learn from 向……学习，从……获得（吸取）

445. conspicuous [kənˈspɪkjuəs] [con·spi·cu·ous] ☆★★★★

adj. 显著的，引人注目的	We must admit that Lincoln is a conspicuous example of a poor boy who succeed. 我们必须承认林肯是一个穷苦孩子到最后却功成名就的最好例子。
同义字词	noticeable, prominent
反义字词	inconspicuous, plain
高分秘诀	▲ example n. 例子 ▲ succeed v. 成功

446. conspiracy [kənˈspɪrəsɪ] [con·spi·ra·cy] ☆☆★★★

n. 阴谋，共谋	That stupid guy just let out their conspiracy to overthrow the government. 那个愚蠢的家伙泄露了他们推翻政府的阴谋。
同义字词	plot, intrigue, cabal
高分秘诀	▲ stupid adj. 笨的，蠢的 ▲ let out 泄露秘密 ▲ overthrow v. 推翻，打倒

447. constant [ˈkɑnstənt] [con·stant] ☆☆★★★

adj. 不变的，持续的	My mother's constant nagging really annoyed me. 我妈不停地唠叨，让我觉得很烦。

consistent ~ constrain

同义字词	invariable, unchanging, fixed, unvarying
反义字词	changeable, inconstant
高分秘诀	▲ nagging adj. 唠叨的，挑剔的 ▲ annoy v. 使烦恼，使恼怒

448. constellation [ˌkɑnstəˈlɛʃən] [con·stel·la·tion] ☆☆★★★

n. 星座，灿烂的一群

The teacher told us that a constellation is a pattern of stars as seen from the earth.
老师告诉我们一个星座就是从地球上看到某些恒星的样子。

| 同义字词 | group of stars, asterism |

449. consternation [ˌkɑnstəˈneʃən] [con·ster·na·tion] ☆☆★★★

n. 惊愕，惊慌失措

Their behaviours threw me into consternation.
他们的行为让我惊慌失措。

| 同义字词 | dismay, shock, surprise, astonishment |
| 高分秘诀 | ▲ behaviour n. 行为，举止，表现
▲ throw sb. into consternation 使某人惊慌失措 |

450. constitute [ˈkɑnstəˌtjut] [con·sti·tute] ☆★★★★

v. 建立（政府），组成

After consultation, a committee was constituted to investigate rising prices.
经过协商后，成立了一个委员会调查价格上涨的问题。

| 同义字词 | make up, form, compose, establish |
| 高分秘诀 | ▲ consultation n. 磋商，协商
▲ committee n. 委员会
▲ price n. 价格，价钱 |

451. constrain [kənˈstren] [con·strain] ☆☆★★★

v. 限制，约束

One of the scientists told me that their research had been constrained by lack of money.
一位科学家告诉我他们的研究工作因缺少资金而受到限制。

| 同义字词 | restrain, hold back, compel, force |
| 高分秘诀 | ▲ scientist n. 科学家
▲ research n. 研究，探讨 |

452. constrict [kənˈstrɪkt] [con·strict] ☆☆★★★

v. 约束，使收缩

The bastard constrict my throat and keep me from breathing.
那个坏蛋掐住了我的喉部，使我不能呼吸。

同义字词　limit, restrict, shrink, contract

高分秘诀　▲ bastard **n.** 坏蛋，混蛋
▲ throat **n.** 咽喉
▲ breathing **n.** 呼吸

453. construct [kənˈstrʌkt] [con·struct] ☆☆★★★

v. 建造，创立

It took the builders three years to construct this skyscraper.
建筑工人们花费三年的时间修建了这座摩天大楼。

同义字词　build, erect, form, make
反义字词　demolish, destroy, ruin
高分秘诀　▲ builder **n.** 建筑工人
▲ skyscraper **n.** 摩天大楼

454. consult [kənˈsʌlt] [con·sult] ☆☆★★★

v. 咨询，请教

Before I make a decision I must consult with my wife.
我必须与妻子商量，才能做出决定。

同义字词　confer, advice
高分秘诀　▲ make a decision 决定下来，作出决定
▲ consult with 与……协商

455. consume [kənˈsjum] [con·sume] ☆☆★★★

v. 消费，消耗

I consumed most of my time in playing computer games.
我大部分时间都花在了玩电子游戏上。

高分秘诀　▲ play computer games 玩电子游戏

456. contact [ˈkɑntækt] [con·tact] ☆☆★★★

v. 使接触，与……联系

Wait a minute! I will contact him by cellphone.
等一下，我用手机与他联系。

同义字词　get in touch with, reach

constrict ~ contemporary

高分秘诀 ▲ wait a minute 等一下，稍等
▲ cellphone v. 手机

457. contagious [kən`tedʒəs] [con·ta·gious] ☆☆★★★

| adj. 传染性的，有感染力的 | Be careful, measles is a contagious disease.
小心，麻疹是一种接触性传染性疾病。 |

同义字词　infectious, infective, catching
反义字词　noncommunicable
高分秘诀　▲ measles n. 麻疹
　　　　　▲ contagious disease 接触性传染病

458. contain [kən`ten] [con·tain] ☆★★★★

| v. 包含，容纳 | The vegetables contain so many vitamins, which is good for your health.
这些蔬菜含有多种维生素，对你的身体很有好处。 |

同义字词　comprise, include, incorporate, hold
高分秘诀　▲ vegetable n. 蔬菜
　　　　　▲ vitamin n. 维生素，维他命
　　　　　▲ health n. 健康（状况）

459. contaminate [kən`tæmə,net] [con·tam·i·nate] ☆☆★★★

| v. 弄脏，污染 | Flies are pest; they contaminated food.
苍蝇是害虫，它们污染食物。 |

同义字词　taint, pollute, defile
高分秘诀　▲ fly n. 苍蝇
　　　　　▲ pest n. 有害的人或物，令人讨厌的人或物

460. contemplate [`kɑntɛm,plet] [con·tem·plate] ☆☆★★★

| v. 沉思，对……作周密思考 | I have to contemplate it before making a final decision.
做最后决定前，我必须仔细考虑清楚。 |

同义字词　ponder, meditate, deliberate
高分秘诀　▲ final adj. 最终的，最后的

461. contemporary [kən`tɛmpə,rɛrɪ] [con·tem·po·ra·ry] ☆☆★★★

| adj. 当代的，同时代的 | I don't know whether Dickens and Byron were contemporary or not.
我不知道狄更斯和拜伦是不是同时代的人。 |

| n. 当代人，同龄人 | My uncle was always looked down upon by his contemporaries.
我叔叔总被他同龄的人瞧不起。 |

| 同义字词 | contemporaneous, modern-day, coeval |
| 高分秘诀 | ▲ Dickens 狄更斯（英国著名现实主义小说家）
▲ Byron 拜伦（英国浪漫主义文学的杰出代表作家）
▲ look down upon 蔑视，瞧不起 |

462. content [kənˋtɛnt] [con·tent]   ☆★★★★

| n. 内容, 容量 | I think the play lacks content.
我认为这部剧本缺乏内容。 |
| adj. 满足的，满意的 | That lady in blue seemed content with her life as a rich man's plaything.
那位穿蓝色衣服的女孩似乎满足于做有钱男子的玩物。 |

同义字词	volume, capacity, gratified, satisfied
反义字词	discontent, discontented
高分秘诀	▲ play n. 戏剧，剧本 ▲ plaything n. 玩物，供消遣的东西

463. contiguous [kənˋtɪgjʊəs] [con·tig·u·ous]   ☆☆★★★

| adj. 接近的，接壤的 | It's James who told me that California and Mexico are contiguous.
詹姆斯告诉我加利福尼亚州和墨西哥相邻。 |

| 同义字词 | abutting, adjacent, adjoining, conterminous |
| 高分秘诀 | ▲ California n. 美国加利福尼亚州
▲ Mexico n. 墨西哥 |

464. continent [ˋkɑntənənt] [con·ti·nent]   ☆☆★★★

| n. 大陆，洲 | As is known to us all that Asia is the largest continent.
众所皆知，亚洲是最大的洲。 |

| 反义字词 | island, isle |
| 高分秘诀 | ▲ Asia n. 亚洲 |

465. continuity [ˌkɑntəˋnjuətɪ] [con·ti·nu·i·ty]   ☆★★★★

| n. （时间或空间的）连续性 | We found out that the article lacks continuity, you just keeps jumping from one subject to another.
我们发现这篇文章缺乏连贯性，你只是一味地东扯西扯。 |

content ~ contrary

高分秘诀
▲ find out 发现
▲ article **n.** 文章
▲ subject **n.** 话题，主题

466. contract [`kɑntrækt] [con·tract]   ☆☆★★★

v. 收缩，订立合同

My company contracted with an electronics factory for the purchase of their electronic instruments.
我们公司与一家电子厂签约购买他们的电子仪器。

n. 契约，合约

The contract expressly forbids sale to the Japan.
此合约明确禁止对日本销售。

同义字词　shrink, constrict, compress, compact, agreement

反义字词　dilate, expand

高分秘诀
▲ contract with 与……订立（某种协议或合约）
▲ electronics factory 电子厂
▲ electronic instruments 电子仪器

467. contradict [ˌkɑntrə`dɪkt] [con·tra·dict]   ☆☆★★★

v.（陈述或证据等）相抵触，驳斥

The two statements contradict each other; I don't know which one is right.
这两种说法相互抵触；我不知道哪个是对的。

同义字词　confront, oppose, deny

反义字词　acknowledge, admit, recognize

高分秘诀　▲ statement **n.** 声明，陈述

468. contrast [`kɑnˌtræst] [con·trast]   ☆★★★★

v. 对比，对照

Compare and contrast English with Chinese carefully, you will find some difference.
把英语和中文仔细进行比较和对比，你就会发现差别。

n. 大不相同的人（或物）

I think you are an amusing contrast to your father.
我认为你和你父亲形成有趣的对比。

同义字词　compare, liken

高分秘诀　▲ difference **n.** 差别，差异

469. contrary [`kɑntrɛrɪ] [con·tra·ry]   ☆☆★★★

adj. 相反的，对抗的

Sometimes we should hear opinions contrary to ours.
有时候我们应该听取相反的意见。

| n. 相反，对立面 | Hate is the contrary of love.
爱和恨是一体两面的东西。 |

同义字词　opposite, adverse, converse, in conflict with

高分秘诀
▲ opinion n. 意见，看法，主张
▲ contrary to... 和……相反，违反
▲ hate n. 憎恨，厌恶

470. contribute [kən'trɪbjut] [con·tri·bute]　☆☆★★★

| v. 捐赠，捐献 | The youngster lives on contributing to some local magazines.
这个年轻人靠为一些地方杂志撰稿为生。 |

高分秘诀
▲ youngster n. 年轻人
▲ live on 以……为食，靠……为生
▲ local adj. 当地的，本地的

471. controversy ['kɑntrə,vɜsɪ] [con·tro·ver·sy]　☆★★★★

| n. 争论，辩论 | I've never thought that my remark touched off a heated controversy.
我没有料到我的一句话引起了激烈的争论。 |

同义字词　contention, argument, dispute

高分秘诀
▲ remark n. 话语，评论
▲ touch off 引起，触发某事
▲ heated adj. 热烈的，激烈的

472. convene [kən'vin] [con·vene]　☆☆★★★

| v. 召开，召集 | He decided to convene a meeting of the members of the club.
他决定召集俱乐部成员开会。 |

同义字词　convoke, assemble, gather

高分秘诀
▲ member n. 成员，会员
▲ club n. 社团，俱乐部

473. convenient [kən'vinjənt] [con·ve·ni·ent]　☆★★★★

| adj. 方便的，近便的 | Nowadays everyday lives are easier and more convenient.
现在日常生活越来越便利。 |

同义字词　handy, suitable, near, accessible

反义字词　inconvenient, unhandy, incommodious

contribute ~ convert

高分秘诀 ▲ everyday life 日常生活

474. convention [kən'vɛnʃən] [con·ven·tion] ☆☆★★

n. 会议,惯例

"Lady first!" is a social convention in most of western countries.
在西方国家,"女士优先!"是一种社会习俗。

同义字词 conference, norm, custom, rule

高分秘诀 ▲ lady first 女士优先
▲ social convention 社会约定
▲ western **adj.** 西方的,西部的

475. converge [kən'vɝdʒ] [con·verge] ☆☆★★

v. 聚合,集中于一点

Gradually their previously opposed views are beginning to converge.
渐渐地,他们原来相互对立的观点开始趋于一致。

同义字词 meet, come together

高分秘诀 ▲ gradually **adv.** 逐步地,渐渐地
▲ previously **adv.** 事先,以前
▲ opposed **adj.** 反对的,对抗的

476. conversation [ˌkɑnvɚ'seʃən] [con·ver·sa·tion] ☆☆★★

n. 会话,非正式会谈

It's impolite to break in on other's conversations.
打断别人的谈话是不礼貌的。

同义字词 dialogue, talk

高分秘诀 ▲ impolite **adj.** 不礼貌的,失礼的,粗鲁的
▲ break in on 打断,打扰

477. convert [kən'vɝt] [con·vert] ☆★★★

v. 转换,转变信仰

All donations received will be converted into Yen and forwarded to the Japanese Red Cross Society.
所有收到的善款将兑换为日币并转交给日本红十字会。

同义字词 alter, change, transform

高分秘诀 ▲ Yen **n.** 日元
▲ forward to **ph.** 转交
▲ convert into (使)转而变成……

478. convict [kənˈvɪkt] [con·vict] ☆☆★★★

v. 证明……有罪
The judge convicted the middle-aged woman of murder.
法官判这位中年妇女谋杀有罪。

n. 囚犯
The convict finally confessed his crime.
这个罪犯最后供认了自己的罪行。

同义字词 condemn, sentence, prisoner, gaolbird, inmate, jail bird

反义字词 acquit, absolve, exculpate, exonerate

高分秘诀
▲ judge **n.** 法官
▲ middle-aged **adj.** 中年的
▲ convicted of 宣判（某人）犯有（某罪）

479. convince [kənˈvɪns] [con·vince] ☆☆★★★

v. 使相信，使明白
If you contact with me for some time, then you will be convinced of my honesty.
如果你和我认识一段时间，你就会相信我是个诚实的人。

同义字词 assure, make certain

高分秘诀
▲ contact with 与……有交往（联系）
▲ for some time 一段时间
▲ be convinced of 确信，承认

480. convivial [kənˈvɪvɪəl] [con·vi·vi·al] ☆☆★★★

adj. 好交际的，欢乐的
Last night I was invited out to a convivial party.
昨晚我应邀参加一个社交宴会。

同义字词 sociable, festival, good-time

反义字词 segregative, unsocial

高分秘诀 ▲ invite out 请（某人）出去

481. cooperate [koˈɑpəˌret] [co·op·er·ate] ☆☆★★★

v. 合作，配合
You'd better not to cooperate with that deceitful businessman.
你最好不要与那个不诚实的商人合作。

高分秘诀
▲ you'd better... 你最好……
▲ cooperate with 与（某人）合作
▲ deceitful **adj.** 不诚实的，骗人的

convict ~ corrosion

482. coordinate [ko`ɔrdnet] [co·or·di·nate] ☆☆★★★

v. 使……协调，相配合
It's not easy for a baby to coordinate his movement.
对婴儿来说，协调自己的动作不容易。

adj. 同等的，并列的
The army, navy and air force are coordinate branches.
陆、海、空三军是三个平等并列的军种。

同义字词 harmonize, integrate, regulate, adjust

高分秘诀
▲ army **n.** 陆军
▲ navy **n.** 海军
▲ air force **n.** 空军

483. cordial [`kɔrdʒəl] [cor·di·al] ☆☆★★★

adj. 热诚的，热情友好的
My uncle is so handsome and always got cordial greeting from young ladies.
我叔叔很英俊，总能得到年轻女士的热忱问候。

同义字词 friendly, hearty, genial

高分秘诀
▲ handsome **adj.** 英俊的
▲ greeting **n.** 招呼，问候

484. correlate [`kɔrə‚let] [cor·re·late] ☆☆★★★

v. 使相互关联，使相互影响
I found the results of this experiment do not correlate with the results of the former ones.
我发现这次与上次实验的结果毫不相干。

同义字词 relate, associate

高分秘诀
▲ result **n.** 结果，后果
▲ experiment **n.** 实验，试验
▲ correlate with 把……联系起来
▲ former **adj.** 过去的，以前的

485. corrosion [kə`roʒən] [cor·ro·sion] ☆★★★★

n. 腐蚀，侵蚀
Before applying the paint, you'd better clean off the corrosion on it.
你上油漆前，最好先把上面的锈迹全部除去。

同义字词 decay, erosion, corroding

高分秘诀
▲ apply **v.** 敷，涂
▲ clean off 除去

486. corruption [kəˈrʌpʃən] [corrup·tion] ☆☆★★★

n. 堕落, 腐化 | We know that corruption and crime go hand in hand.
我们知道腐败与犯罪携手并行。

同义字词 | bribery, corruptness, degeneracy, putrescence
高分秘诀 | ▲ hand in hand 手拉手，密切合作

487. cosmetic [kɑzˈmɛtɪk] [cos·me·tic] ☆☆★★★

n. 化妆品 | I think that lipstick and hair conditioner are cosmetics.
我认为口红和护发素都是化妆品。

adj. 化妆用的，美容的 | Would you buy some a cosmetic cream for me when you go shopping?
你去逛街时能否帮我买一瓶美容霜？

高分秘诀 | ▲ hair conditioner 护发素
▲ go shopping 购物，去买东西

488. cosmopolitan [ˌkɑzməˈpɑlətṇ] [cos·mo·pol·i·tan] ☆★★★★

adj. 世界性的，全球的 | London is a cosmopolitan city; it is the capital of UK.
伦敦是一个国际都市，同时它也是英国的首都。

n. 四海为家者；世界主义者 | The old man is a rootless cosmopolitan.
老人是一个四海漂泊的人。

同义字词 | worldwide, universal
高分秘诀 | ▲ capital **n.** 首都，首府
▲ rootless **adj.** 无根的

489. costume [ˈkɑstjum] [cos·tume] ☆☆★★★

n. 服装 | I don't think a man's costume can say something about his intelligence.
我不认为一个人的服装可以说明他的智力。

同义字词 | dress, attire, garment, outfit, suit
高分秘诀 | ▲ intelligence **n.** 智力，智慧

490. counsel [ˈkaʊnsl] [coun·sel] ☆☆★★★

n. 忠告，辩护律师 | Mr. White is the counsel of the prosecution.
怀特先生是原告的律师。

corruption ~ couple

v. 劝告，建议	My sister's job is to counsel students on how to choose a career. 我姐姐的工作是辅导学生就业。
同义字词	advise, suggest, recommend, rede
高分秘诀	▲ prosecution n. 原告 ▲ career n. 职业，职涯

491. counteract [ˌkaʊntəˈækt] [coun·ter·act] ☆☆★★★

v. 消除，抵消	It's amazing that our bodies can produce antibodies to counteract disease. 真神奇，我们的身体能自动产生抗体抵制疾病。
同义字词	neutralize, offset, act against, balance, counterbalance
高分秘诀	▲ amazing adj. 令人惊异的 ▲ disease n. 疾病，病害

492. counterfeit [ˈkaʊntəˌfɪt] [coun·ter·feit] ☆☆★★★

v. 伪造，仿造	They know it's a crime to counterfeit money, but they still do it. 他们知道伪造货币是违法的，但依然去做。
adj. 伪造的，假冒的	Damn it! I got a counterfeit bill. 可恶！我收到一张假钞。
同义字词	forge, bogus, fake, imitative, artificial
反义字词	genuine, real
高分秘诀	▲ damn adj. 该死的 ▲ counterfeit money 假币，伪钞

493. couple [ˈkʌpl] [cou·ple]

n. (一)对，情侣	You are a happy couple; I really admire you. 你们真是美满的一对，我真羡慕你们。
v. 联合，结合	The government send some workers to couple the carriages of the train together. 政府派工人把火车的车厢连接好了。
高分秘诀	▲ admire v. 羡慕，钦佩 ▲ government n. 政府 ▲ carriage n. 车厢

494. courageous [kəˋredʒəs] [cou·ra·geous] ☆★★★★

adj. 勇敢的，无畏的	It's courageous of you to oppose the authority. 你敢反对权威，真是勇敢。
同义字词	brave, bold, valiant, valorous
反义字词	cowardly, fearful, timid
高分秘诀	▲ oppose **v.** 反对 ▲ authority **n.** 威权，专家

495. court [kort] [court] ☆☆★★★

n. 法庭，球场	The court found her guilty, for there are no evidences go in her favor. 因为没有对她有利的证据，所以法庭判她有罪。
v. 追求；设法获得	My friend courted that pretty girl by bring her flowers every day. 我朋友每天送花给那位漂亮女孩向她求爱。
同义字词	woo, pursue
高分秘诀	▲ guilty **adj.** 有罪的 ▲ evidence **n.** 证据，证词，迹象 ▲ pretty **adj.** 漂亮的

496. courteous [ˋkɝtjəs] [cour·te·ous] ☆★★★★

adj. 彬彬有礼的，客气的	I like to visit that hotel, for the stall of it are particularly courteous. 我喜欢入住那家饭店，因为那里的员工特别客气有礼。
同义字词	polite, gracious, respectful
反义字词	discourteous, impolite
高分秘诀	▲ staff **n.** 全体职员 ▲ particularly **adv.** 特别，尤其

497. cover [ˋkʌvə] [co·ver] ☆☆★★★

v. 覆盖，报道	Even he tried to cover up his nervousness, but we still saw it on his face. 尽管他尽力掩饰紧张，但我们还是可以从他脸上看出来。
同义字词	include, incorporate, contain, report, detail
反义字词	uncover, expose

court ~ cramped

高分秘诀	▲ cover up 掩盖，掩饰
	▲ nervousness n. 焦躁，紧张

498. cozy [ˋkozɪ] [cozy]   ☆★★★★

adj. 舒适的, 惬意的	It's cold outside, but I felt all cozy tucked up in bed. 外面很冷，但我钻进被窝里，感觉暖和舒服极了。
同义字词	comfortable, relaxing, homey, cosy
高分秘诀	▲ outside adv. 在外面，在户外
	▲ tuck up 折起，塞进

499. crack [kræk] [crack]   ☆☆★★★

n. 裂缝, 裂纹	Don't worry, there is only a crack in the glass. 不用担心，玻璃上只有一条裂缝。
v. (使)爆裂, 裂开	Be careful! When the hot water pours into the glass it will crack. 小心点，当热水倒进玻璃杯时，它会裂开。
高分秘诀	▲ hot water 热水
	▲ pour into 不断地流进

500. craft [kræft] [craft]   ☆☆★★★

n. 手艺, 容器	I learned the craft from a wood carver. 我是从一位木雕师那里学来的手艺。
同义字词	art, skill, trade, handicraft
高分秘诀	▲ wood n. 木，木头
	▲ carver n. 雕刻师，雕工

501. cram [kræm] [cram]   ☆★★★★

v. 塞入, 填塞	We can't cram into that doll's house. 我们挤不下那间小房子。
同义字词	pack, stuff, fill
高分秘诀	▲ cram into 勉强塞入，填满
	▲ doll's house 小房子

502. cramped [ˋkræmpt] [cramped]   ☆☆★★★

adj. (空间)狭小的, 受限制的	Their accommodation is rather cramped. 他们住的地方很挤。
同义字词	jammed, stuffed, narrow, restricted

| 高分秘诀 | ▲ accommodation n. 住处 |
| | ▲ rather adv. 在一定程度上，颇 |

503. crash [kræʃ] [crash] ☆★★★★

n. 碰撞，垮台	The little girl is so lucky; she is the sole survivor of the crash.
	这个小女孩真的很幸运，她是坠机事件的唯一生还者。
v. 碰撞，坠毁	The driver was drunk; he crashed his car into a wall.
	司机喝醉了，把汽车撞到墙上。
高分秘诀	▲ lucky adj. 幸运的，侥幸的
	▲ sole adj. 单独的，唯一的
	▲ survivor n. 幸存者，生还者
	▲ drunk adj. 醉的

504. crawl [krɔl] [crawl] ☆☆★★

v. 爬，爬行	The baby couldn't walk; he had to crawls on all fours.
	婴儿不会走路；他只会爬行。
高分秘诀	▲ on all fours 四脚着地的

505. crazy [ˈkrezɪ] [cra·zy] ☆☆★★

adj. 发疯的，疯狂的	He's a workaholic, and always works like crazy.
	他是个工作狂，总是疯狂工作。
同义字词	insane, deranged, demented
高分秘诀	▲ workaholic n. 工作狂
	▲ like crazy 疯狂地，拼命地

506. credentials [krɪˈdɛnʃəlz] [cre·den·tials] ☆★★★★

n. 凭证，证书	I've already send all my credentials to you. They would reach you shortly.
	我已经把所有证书寄给你了，你不久就可以收到。
同义字词	certificate, certification, credential
高分秘诀	▲ send v. 送，寄
	▲ shortly adv. 不久，很快

507. credit [ˈkrɛdɪt] [cre·dit] ☆☆★★

| n. 学分，信用 | Don't worry, their company's international credit is excellent. |
| | 不用担心，他们公司的国际信誉极好。 |

crawl ~ crimson

v. 认定……，归于 | After investigation, we know that the accident was credited to carelessness on the part of the driver.
经过调查，我们知道这起事故是由于驾车人不小心所引起的。

同义字词 | reputation, prestige, recognize, ascribe

高分秘诀 |
▲ international credit 国际信用
▲ excellent adj. 优秀的，卓越的，杰出的
▲ accident n. 事故
▲ carelessness n. 粗心大意
▲ on the part of 在……方面

508. creep [krip] [creep] ☆☆★★★

v. 慢慢行进，爬行 | The snail crept along at an agonizingly slow speed.
蜗牛以极缓慢的速度爬行。

高分秘诀 |
▲ snail n. 蜗牛
▲ agonizingly adv. 使人烦恼地，苦闷地

509. crew [kru] [crew] ☆★★★★

n. 全体从业人员，同事们 | It's great that the lifeboat brought off all the crew from the ship.
太棒了，救生船把所有船员都救走了。

同义字词 | staff, work party, gang

高分秘诀 |
▲ lifeboat n. 救生艇，救生船
▲ bring off 使脱离险境

510. criminal [ˈkrɪmənl] [cri·mi·nal] ☆☆★★★

n. 罪犯，犯人 | Stay away from that man, he is a wanted criminal.
离那个男人远点，他是通缉犯。

adj. 犯罪的，刑事的 | You know every country has its own criminal law.
每个国家都有自己的刑法。

高分秘诀 |
▲ keep away from 使不接近，避开
▲ wanted adj. 受通缉的
▲ criminal law 刑法

511. crimson [ˈkrɪmzn̩] [crim·son] ☆☆★★★

n. 深红色 | The evening sky was suffused with crimson. It's so beautiful.
黄昏时分天空红霞灿烂，美极了。

| adj. 深红色的 | When she heard what I said, she got embarrassed and turned crimson.
听到我说的话，她十分尴尬，脸变得通红。 |

| 同义字词 | blood-red, carmine, scarlet |
| 高分秘诀 | ▲ suffuse v. （指颜色、水气等）弥漫于，布满
▲ embarrassed adj. 尴尬的，为难的 |

512. cripple [ˈkrɪpl] [crip·ple]   ☆☆★★★

| v. 削弱，使残废 | What a pity! The accident crippled the athlete for life.
真可惜，这次意外使这位运动员终身残疾。 |

| 同义字词 | handicap, maim, disable |
| 高分秘诀 | ▲ what a pity 真可惜，真遗憾
▲ for life 终生，终身 |

513. crisis [ˈkraɪsɪs] [cri·sis]   ☆★★★★

| n. 危机，危急关头 | It's quite lucky for our company not suffered huge losses in the financial crisis.
我们公司在经济危机时没有遭受巨大损失，真是幸运。 |

| 高分秘诀 | ▲ suffer v. 遭受；受损害
▲ loss n. 损失
▲ financial crisis 金融（财政）危机 |

514. critical [ˈkrɪtɪkl] [cri·ti·cal]   ☆☆★★★

| adj. 批评的，批判的 | We have to be careful, for we have come to the critical moment.
我们必须小心点，因为现在是紧要关头。 |

| 同义字词 | captious, essential, acute, crucial, decisive |
| 反义字词 | approbatory, complimentary, noncritical, noncrucial |
| 高分秘诀 | ▲ come to 到达，达成
▲ critical moment 决定性时刻 |

515. crooked [ˈkrukɪd] [crooked]   ☆☆★★★

| adj. 不诚实的，欺诈的 | I think you'd better not deal with crooked people.
我认为你最好不要与不正派的人打交道。 |

| 同义字词 | falsehearted, deceitful |
| 高分秘诀 | ▲ deal with 和……交易，和……做买卖 |

cripple ~ cruelty

516. crowd [kraʊd] [crowd] ☆☆★★★

n. 人群，群众

It turned out that the crowd were swayed by the man's eloquence.
结果，那个男人的能言善道打动了群众的心。

v. 群集，拥挤

I couldn't find you, you know there are so many passengers crowded the platform.
我找不到你，月台上挤满了乘客。

同义字词 group, mass, throng

高分秘诀
▲ sway **v.** 影响、改变……的观点（行动）
▲ eloquence **n.** 口才，雄辩
▲ passenger **n.** 乘客，旅客

517. crucial [ˈkruʃəl] [cru·cial] ☆☆★★★

adj. 决定性的，至关紧要的

First read the book carefully, and then distill the crucial points from it.
首先，认真阅读这本书，然后从书中摘要关键的重点。

同义字词 critical, very important, decisive

反义字词 noncrucial, noncritical

高分秘诀 ▲ distill **v.** 蒸馏，提取

518. crude [krud] [cru·de] ☆☆★★★

adj. 粗糙的，粗鲁的

To tell the truth, I condemn such crude manner.
老实说，我痛恨这种粗鲁的态度。

高分秘诀
▲ to tell the truth 说实话
▲ condemn **v.** 谴责，责备
▲ manner **n.** 模式，方法，态度

519. cruelty [ˈkruəltɪ] [cru·el·ty] ☆★★★★

n. 残忍

As I see it, it is cruelty to the innocent not to punish the guilty.
在我看来，不惩罚罪犯就是对无辜者的残忍。

同义字词 cruelness, merciless, pitilessness, ruthlessness

高分秘诀
▲ as I see it 在我看来
▲ the innocent 无辜者
▲ punish **v.** 处罚，惩罚

520. crumple [ˈkrʌmpl] [crum·ple] ☆☆★★★

v. 把……弄皱；起皱

It's quite common that some material crumple more easily than others.
有些衣服的质料比其他布料容易起皱褶，这很正常。

[同义字词] wrinkle, rumple, ripple, crinkle, crease

[高分秘诀] ▲ material **n.** 材料，原料，衣料

521. crumble [ˈkrʌmbl] [crum·ble] ☆☆★★★

v. 粉碎，崩溃

In the earthquake, many houses crumbled into cinders.
在这次地震中，许多房子化为灰烬。

[同义字词] fall apart, disintegrate, break up

[高分秘诀] ▲ earthquake **n.** 地震
▲ cinder **n.** 煤渣，炭渣

522. crush [krʌʃ] [crush] ☆☆★★★

v. 压碎，碾碎

Let me teach how to crush juice from a grape.
让我教你怎样从葡萄中榨出汁。

[同义字词] squash, smash, press

[高分秘诀] ▲ juice **n.** 汁，液
▲ grape **n.** 葡萄

523. crust [krʌst] [crust] ☆★★★★

n. 外壳，面包皮，地壳

Do you know that the crust of the moon is almost four times thicker than the earth's?
你知道月球地壳几乎是地球地壳硬度的四倍吗？

[高分秘诀] ▲ thick **adj.** 厚的；浓的

524. crystal [ˈkrɪstl] [crys·tal] ☆☆★★★

n. 水晶，晶体

I can tell you that each crystals of the mineral have a particular shape.
我可以告诉你每种矿物的晶体都有其特殊的形状。

adj. 清澈的，结晶状的

I know what you want just to make it crystal clear that you don't agree with me.
我知道你想清楚地表明你不同意我的意见。

[高分秘诀] ▲ particular **adj.** 特殊的，特别的，特有的
▲ crystal clear 完全透明的，极其明白
▲ agree with 与……相符，与……一致

crumble ~ cultivate

525. cube [kjub] [cube] ☆☆★★★

n. 立方体，立方

Please fetch me some ice-cube from the fridge.
请从冰箱里帮我拿些冰块。

高分秘诀
▲ fetch **v.** 接来（某人），取来（某物）
▲ ice-cube **n.** 小冰块，方形冰块

526. cue [kju] [cue] ☆☆★★★

n. 提示，暗示

When I cough, that's your cue to interrupt the conversation.
我一咳嗽，就是暗示你打断谈话。

v. 提示，暗示

I'll cue you in by shaking my head.
我一摇头，你就开始。

同义字词
clue, clew, hint

高分秘诀
▲ interrupt **v.** 打断
▲ conversation **n.** 交谈，谈话
▲ shake one's head 摇头

527. culinary [ˈkʌlɪˌnɛrɪ] [cul·i·nar·y] ☆☆★★★

adj. 厨房的，烹调的

My aunt is a mistress of the culinary art.
我姑姑是烹调高手。

高分秘诀
▲ aunt **n.** 姑母，姨母，婶母，舅母
▲ mistress **n.** 主妇，女主人

528. culminate [ˈkʌlməˌnet] [cul·mi·nate] ☆☆★★★

v. 达到高峰

My career culminated in my appointment as chief executive.
我一生事业的高峰是当上行政总裁。

同义字词
climax, reach a climax

高分秘诀
▲ career **n.** 职业生涯，履历
▲ culminate in 达到顶峰
▲ chief executive 行政总裁

529. cultivate [ˈkʌltəˌvet] [cul·ti·vate] ☆☆★★★

v. 耕种，培养

Nowadays that the land can be cultivated is becoming rare.
如今可以耕种的土地越来越少。

高分秘诀
▲ rare **adj.** 稀少的，罕见的

530. culture [ˈkʌltʃə] [cul·ture]

n. 文化 — In my opinion, universities should be centres of culture.
我认为大学应该是文化的中心。

同义字词: civilization, civilisation, foster

高分秘诀:
▲ in my opinion... 我认为……
▲ university **n.** 大学
▲ centre **n.** 中心，中央，中枢

531. cumbersome [ˈkʌmbəsəm] [cum·ber·some]

adj. 笨重的，难处理的 — No one wants to take this cumbersome parcel.
没有人愿意拿这个笨重的包裹。

同义字词: burdensome, unwieldy, bulky, clumsy

高分秘诀: ▲ parcel **n.** 包裹

532. cunning [ˈkʌnɪŋ] [cun·ning]

adj. 狡猾的，狡诈的 — The little girl just played a cunning trick, and got all what she wanted.
这个小女孩只是略施心计，就得到了她想要的所有东西。

n. 狡猾，狡诈 — Human always believe that the fox has a great deal of cunning.
人们总是认为狐狸十分狡猾。

同义字词: crafty, scheming, sly

高分秘诀:
▲ trick **n.** 计谋，诡计，花招
▲ fox **n.** 狐狸
▲ a great deal 大量

533. curative [ˈkjurətɪv] [cur·a·tive]

adj. 有疗效的，能治病的 — It turned out that the curative effect far exceeded all expectations.
结果，疗效出人意料的好。

同义字词: healing, sanative, therapeutic

高分秘诀:
▲ curative effect 疗效
▲ exceed **v.** 超出，超越
▲ expectation **n.** 预料，期望

cumbersome ~ cushion

534. curious [ˈkjʊrɪəs] [cu·ri·ous] ☆★★★★

| adj. (令人)好奇的 | I'm very curious of this locked trunk.
我对这个锁着的箱子充满好奇。 |

高分秘诀
▲ be curious of... 对……好奇
▲ trunk n. 衣箱

535. current [ˈkɝrənt] [cur·rent] ☆☆★★★

| n. (液体、气体)流, 趋势 | Don't swim in the middle of the river, for the current is strongest in it.
不要在河中央游泳，因为那里的水流最湍急。 |
| adj. 现在的, 现行的 | I don't know, because the word is no longer in current use.
我不知道，因为这个字现在已经不再使用了。 |

同义字词 stream, flow, up-to-date, present

高分秘诀
▲ in the middle of 在……的中间
▲ no longer 不再

536. curriculum [kəˈrɪkjələm] [cur·ri·cu·lum] ☆☆★★★

| n. 学校的全部课程 | My brother is very knowledgeable because he also studies things not in the curriculum.
我哥哥知识丰富，因为除了学校课程，他还学习别的东西。 |

同义字词 course, program

高分秘诀 ▲ knowledgeable adj. 博学的，知识渊博的

537. cursory [ˈkɝsərɪ] [cur·so·ry] ☆☆★★★

| adj. 粗略的, 草率的 | He didn't pay much attention to the report, just gave it a cursory glance.
他对报告不关心，只是粗略地看了一下。 |

同义字词 passing, perfunctory

高分秘诀
▲ pay attention to 注意
▲ report n. 报告, 报道
▲ glance n. 一瞥, 瞥视

538. cushion [ˈkʊʃən] [cush·ion] ☆☆★★★

| n. 垫子, 软垫 | When I entered, I saw the old man knelt on cushion to pray.
我进去的时候，看到这个老人跪在垫子上祈祷。 |

| v. 缓和……的冲力 | I don't think this training program would cushion the effect of unemployment.
我不认为这项训练计划可以缓和失业造成的影响。 |

高分秘诀
▲ pray v. 祈祷，祷告
▲ training program 训练议案
▲ unemployment n. 失业

539. custodian [kʌsˈtodɪən] [cus·to·di·an] ☆☆★★★

| n. 看守人，管理人 | A custodian must be appointed to oversee the child's estate.
必须指定一个监护人监管这个孩子的财产。 |

同义字词　curator, guardian, keeper

高分秘诀
▲ appointed adj. 指定的，约定的
▲ oversee v. 监督，监视
▲ estate n. 地产，财产

540. customary [ˈkʌstəmɛrɪ] [cus·tom·ar·y] ☆★★★★

| adj. 习惯上的，惯常的 | In western countries, it's customary to tip the waiter.
在西方国家，给侍者小费是一种习俗。 |

同义字词　accustomed, habitual, wonted

高分秘诀
▲ tip v. 给小费
▲ waiter n. 侍者，服务生

541. cylinder [ˈsɪlɪndə] [cyl·in·der] ☆☆★★★

| n. 圆筒，圆柱体 | You can coil the string onto a cardboard cylinder.
你可以把线缠绕在纸筒上。 |

高分秘诀
▲ coil v. 将……卷成圆或螺旋形
▲ cardboard n. 硬纸板

542. cynic [ˈsɪnɪk] [cy·nic] ☆☆★★★

| n. 愤世嫉俗者 | It's said that a cynic is a man who looks at the world with a monocle in his mind's eyes.
据说愤世嫉俗的人，就是在心目中戴上单片眼镜看世界的人。 |

高分秘诀　▲ monocle n. 单片眼镜

Dd 托福 TOEFL iBT

托福(TOEFL)的测验对象为母语为非英语的人
申请入学美加地区大学或研究所时,托福成绩单是必备文件之一。

- n. 名词
- v. 动词
- adj. 形容词
- adv. 副词
- prep. 介词
- art. 冠词
- pron. 代词
- aux. 助词
- conj. 连词

Dd 托福 TOEFL iBT

托福(TOEFL)的测验对象为母语为非英语的人
申请入学美加地区大学或研究所时，托福成绩单是必备文件之一。

543. dagger [`dægə] [dag·ger]
☆☆★★★

n. 短剑，匕首

We went to Chris' apartment last week. He showed us his dagger collections.
我们上星期去克里斯的公寓，他向我们展示他收藏的匕首。

[同义字词] stylet, cutlass, creese, dirk, poniard

[高分秘诀] ▲ weep **v.** （伤口）流血，渗出水汽

544. damp [dæmp] [damp]
☆★★★★

adj. 潮湿的，有湿气的

Don't stay outside; it's damp and cold.
别待在外面，外面又冷又湿。

v. 使潮湿

Damp the dishclout before you clean the desk.
在擦桌子前，先把抹布弄湿。

[同义字词] dampen, moisten, humid, moist, wet

[高分秘诀] ▲ dishclout **n.** 抹布

545. dangerous [`dendʒərəs] [dan·ger·ous]
☆★★★★

adj. 危险的

You'd better tear down that dangerous wall.
你最好拆掉那堵危墙。

[同义字词] harmful, risky, hazardous, perilous, unsafe

[高分秘诀] ▲ tear down 拆毁，拆卸

546. dangle [`dæŋgl] [dan·gle]
☆☆★★★

v. 悬吊着，摆动不定

I dangle the balloon in front of the baby to cheer him up.
为了逗婴儿高兴，我在他面前摇晃气球。

[高分秘诀] ▲ balloon **n.** 气球
▲ cheer up 使高兴起来

547. daring [ˈdɛrɪŋ] [dar·ing] ☆☆★★★

adj. 大胆的，勇敢的

I really admired those daring exploits of the parachutists.
我真的很钦佩那些跳伞者大胆的冒险动作。

高分秘诀
▲ exploit **n.** 英勇行为
▲ parachutist **n.** 跳伞者

548. dart [dɑrt] [dart] ☆☆★★★

v. 飞奔，投掷

The thief darted away at the sight of the policeman.
小偷一看到警察就飞奔而逃。

n. 标枪，镖，箭

Wow, the dart you threw just landed plunk in the center of the target.
哇，你投的标枪正中靶心。

同义字词 rush, dash, flit, cast, fling

高分秘诀
▲ dart away 飞奔而逃
▲ at the sight of 看见……时
▲ policeman **n.** 警察
▲ in the center of 在中间，在中央

549. dash [dæʃ] [dash] ☆☆★★★

v. 猛冲，飞奔

In order to tell me the good news, the boy dashed in breathlessly.
为了告诉我这个好消息，这个男孩上气不接下气地冲进来。

高分秘诀
▲ in order to 为了……
▲ dash in 猛冲进来
▲ breathlessly **adv.** 气喘地，屏息地

550. date [det] [date] ☆★★★★

v. 注明……的日期，相约

I can't date that fossil exactly, but it must be very old.
我不能确切地说出这化石的年代，但它一定很古老。

n. 日期，年份

They hold a meeting to stipulate a date of payment and a price.
他们举行一个会议规定偿付日和赔偿的金额。

同义字词 appointment, engagement, go out

高分秘诀
▲ exactly **adv.** 精确地，准确地，确切的
▲ stipulate **v.** 规定，讲明
▲ payment **n.** 支付，付款

551. daunting [`dɔntɪŋ] [daun·ting]

adj. 使人畏缩的

The prospect of meeting my future parents-in-law is quite daunting.
一想到要见未来的岳父岳母就令人胆怯。

同义字词: intimidating, discouraging

高分秘诀:
▲ prospect n. 景象，景色
▲ parents-in-law n. 岳父、岳母

552. dawn [dɔn] [dawn]

n. 黎明, 拂晓

Our commandos attacked the enemy's outpost at dawn.
我军的突击队员在黎明时分袭击了敌军的前哨基地。

同义字词: dawning, sunrise, beginning, start

反义字词: dusk, twilight, sunset

高分秘诀:
▲ commando n. 突击队，突击队员
▲ outpost n. 前哨，哨站

553. dazzling [`dæzlɪŋ] [daz·zling]

adj. 眼花缭乱的, 耀眼的

Suddenly a dazzling streak lit up the whole sky.
突然一道耀眼的强光照亮了整个天空。

同义字词: bright, brilliant, fulgent, fulgurant

高分秘诀:
▲ suddenly adv. 意外地，忽然，冷不防
▲ streak n. 条纹，痕迹
▲ light up 照亮，亮起来

554. deal [dil] [deal]

n. 交易, 分量

I recommend you to give this question a great deal of thought.
我建议你对这个问题多加考虑。

v. 分给, 分发

To tell the truth, I hate to deal with those impersonal companies.
老实说，我讨厌与那些没有人情味的公司打交道。

高分秘诀:
▲ a great deal 丰富，大量
▲ deal with 与……交易，与……打交道
▲ impersonal adj. 冷淡的，没有人情味的

daunting ~ decelerate

555. debate [dɪˈbet] [de·bate] ☆★★★★

n. 争论, 辩论
I've never thought that my resignation caused much public debate.
我从来没有想到我的辞职竟然引得大家议论纷纷。

v. 争论, 辩论
How about we hold a meeting to debate the question openly?
我们开个会议公开辩论这个问题如何？

高分秘诀
▲ resignation **n.** 辞职
▲ public debate 讨论
▲ openly **adv.** 公开地, 公然地

556. decadent [ˈdɛkədn̩t] [dec·a·dent] ☆☆★★★

adj. 堕落的, 颓废的
My husband went back with decadent sentiments.
我丈夫垂头丧气地回来了。

高分秘诀
▲ go back 回来
▲ sentiment **n.** 感情, 情绪

557. decay [dɪˈke] [de·cay] ☆☆★★★

n. 腐败、衰退的状态
My grandmother told me that salt can preserve food from decay.
我外婆告诉我盐能防止食物腐烂。

v. 腐烂, 腐朽
Our powers could decay in old age, but we can do nothing about it.
我们的体力精力会在老年时期衰退, 对此我们无能为力。

高分秘诀
▲ preserve from 防止, 保护……不……
▲ power **n.** 体力
▲ old age 晚年

558. deceive [dɪˈsiv] [de·ceive] ☆☆★★★

v. 欺骗, 行骗
It's not honorable to deceive the old guy.
欺骗这个老头是不光彩的。

同义字词
fool, beguile dupe

高分秘诀
▲ honorable **adj.** 光荣的, 荣誉的

559. decelerate [diˈsɛləˌret] [de·ce·le·rate] ☆☆★★★

v. 减速
Every time when I near the corner, I would decelerate the car.
每当到转弯处, 我开车就会减速。

| 同义字词 | retard, slow down, slow up |
| 高分秘诀 | ▲ near v. 接近，靠近
▲ corner n. 角落，拐角 |

560. decent ['disn̩t] [de·cent] ☆★★★★

adj. 适当的，可接受的	The village is very beautiful, but the lack of decent public transport is a great disadvantage. 这个小村庄很美，但是没有适当的大众运输工具很不方便。
同义字词	suitable, fitting, honorable
高分秘诀	▲ public transport 公共交通工具 ▲ disadvantage n. 不利，劣势，短处

561. deceptive [dɪ'sɛptɪv] [de·cep·tive] ☆☆★★★

adj. 欺骗的，导致误解的	I think it's the deceptive advertising that have damaged our company's image among the consumer. 我认为不实的广告损坏了我们公司在消费者心中的形象。
同义字词	misleading, fraudulent
高分秘诀	▲ advertising n. 广告，广告宣传 ▲ damage v. 损害，毁坏 ▲ consumer n. 消费者，顾客

562. decipher [dɪ'saɪfə] [de·ci·pher] ☆☆★★★

v. 破译（密码），辨认	You know it's quite a headache to decipher his scrawl. 辨认他的潦草的字迹真叫人头疼。
反义字词	code, encipher, encode
高分秘诀	▲ headache n. 头痛；令人头痛的事 ▲ scrawl n. 潦草的笔迹

563. declare [dɪ'klɛr] [de·clare] ☆★★★★

v. 宣布，声明	The president declared his intention in the speech. 总统在谈话中声明自己的想法。
同义字词	announce, pronounce, state
高分秘诀	▲ intention n. 意图，目的，打算

decent ~ decorum

564. decline [dɪˋklaɪn] [de·cline] ☆☆★★★

n. 衰退，下降
Though I got promoted, there was a decline in real wages.
虽然我升官了，但实际薪水有所减少。

v. 衰退，下降
I declined to have dinner with that man, saying that I wasn't feeling well.
我说身体不舒服，婉拒了那个男士的晚餐邀约。

同义字词　deterioration, wane, descent, refuse, reject

高分秘诀
▲ promote **v.** 提升，提拔
▲ real wages 实际收入

565. decompose [ˌdikəmˋpoz] [de·com·pose] ☆☆★★★

v. 分解，（使）腐烂
No one clean those fallen leaves on the ground, and they gradually decompose.
没有人清扫这些落叶，它们逐渐开始腐烂。

同义字词　disintegrate, break up, decay, rot

高分秘诀
▲ clean **v.** （使）清洁，变干净
▲ gradually **adv.** 逐步地，渐渐地

566. decorate [ˋdɛkəˌret] [de·co·rate] ☆☆★★★

v. 装饰，装潢
They decorated the house for the Spring Festival.
他们装饰屋子过春节。

同义字词　adorn, embellish, ornament, beautify

高分秘诀
▲ braid **n.** 穗带，镶边
▲ ribbon **n.** 缎带，丝带

567. decorum [dɪˋkorəm] [de·co·rum] ☆★★★★

n. 端庄得体，礼节
I really wish you could behave with decorum at the wedding.
我真的希望你在婚礼上能表现得有礼得体。

同义字词　decency, decorousness, etiquette, manners

反义字词　indecorousness, indecorum

高分秘诀
▲ behave **v.** （行为或举止）表现
▲ wedding **n.** 婚礼

568. decry [dɪˈkraɪ] [de·cry] ☆☆★★★

v. 公开反对，谴责

On the meeting the headmaster decry gambling in all its form.
在会议上，校长谴责赌博。

同义字词: condemn, excoriate, objurgate

衍生字词: decrier **n.** 责难的人

高分秘诀:
▲ headmaster **n.** 校长
▲ gambling **n.** 赌博

569. decrease [dɪˈkris] [de·crease] ☆★★★★

v. 缩减，减小，减少

The manager offered some measures which could help decrease the cost of production.
经理提出一些措施有助于降低生产成本。

同义字词: lessen, reduce, abate

高分秘诀:
▲ measure **n.** 措施，办法
▲ cost **n.** 价格，成本，费用
▲ production **n.** 生产，制作

570. dedicate [ˈdɛdəˌket] [de·di·cate] ☆☆★★★

v. 奉献，贡献

The old man never got married; he dedicated his life to science.
那个老人没有结婚，他将毕生奉献于科学。

同义字词: devote, consecrate

高分秘诀:
▲ science **n.** 科学，科学研究

571. defecate [ˈdɛfəˌket] [de·fe·cate] ☆☆★★★

v. 澄清，排粪

You'd better to train your Labrador to urinate and defecate outside or in a special place.
你最好训练你的拉布拉多（狗名）出去或在指定的地方方便。

同义字词: crap, shit

高分秘诀:
▲ Labrador **n.** 拉布拉多狗
▲ urinate **n.** / **v.** 排尿，撒尿

572. defect [dɪˈfɛkt] [de·fect] ☆★★★★

n. 缺点，瑕疵

I think we should improve the defects in system of education.
我认为我们应该改善教育制度上的缺陷。

decry ~ deficient

v. 变节，叛变	He finally defected from the Liberals and joined the Socialists. 他最后脱离了自由党，加入了社会党。

同义字词	flaw, fault, failing, deficiency, blemish
反义字词	merit, advantage, virtue
高分秘诀	▲ defect from 背叛，叛离 ▲ the Liberals 自由党 ▲ the Socialists 社会党

573. defend [dɪˋfɛnd] [de·fend] ☆☆★★★

v. 防护，辩护	I don't think the fort can be defended against an air attack. 我认为这个要塞无法抵挡来自空中的袭击。

同义字词	protect, safeguard, shield, guard
高分秘诀	▲ fort n. 堡垒，城堡，要塞 ▲ defend against... 保护……不受…… ▲ air attack 空袭

574. defer [dɪˋfɝ] [de·fer] ☆☆★★★

v. 遵从，听从	It's important for youth to defer to age. 青年对老年恭顺是很重要的。

同义字词	yield, submit, delay, postpone
高分秘诀	▲ out of date 过时的，陈旧的 ▲ defer to 顺从，听从

575. defiant [dɪˋfaɪənt] [de·fi·ant] ☆★★★★

adj. 公然违抗的，反抗的	If I were really innocent, I would jumped to my feet in my defiant way. 如果我真是无辜的，我会一跃而起公然表示抗议。

高分秘诀	▲ innocent adj. 清白的，无辜的 ▲ jump to one's feet 一跃而起，突然站起

576. deficient [dɪˋfɪʃənt] [de·fi·cient] ☆☆★★★

adj. 缺乏的，不足的	We should give those who are physically or mentally deficient much help and attention. 我们应该给予那些身心不健全的人多一些帮助和关心。

同义字词	inadequate, lacking, wanting

反义字词	enough, sufficient, plenty, ample
高分秘诀	▲ physically adv. 身体上，体格上
	▲ mentally adv. 心理上，精神上；智力上

577. definite ['dɛfənɪt] [de·fi·nite] ☆★★★★

adj. 一定的，肯定的	It's definite that he would bad mouth me. 他肯定又会在背后说我坏话。
高分秘诀	▲ definitely adv. 肯定地
	▲ absolutely adv. 绝对地，完全地

578. deform [dɪ'fɔrm] [de·form] ☆☆★★★

v. 使变形；使变丑	The girl is pretty, but her leg was deformed in an accident. 她很漂亮，但她的腿在一次意外中变形了。
同义字词	distort, disfigure, spoil
反义字词	embellish
高分秘诀	▲ pretty adj. 漂亮的
	▲ accident n. 事故

579. defraud [dɪ'frɔd] [de·fraud] ☆☆★★★

v. 诈取，骗取	The middle-aged woman was defrauded of her money by a dishonest accountant. 这个中年女子的钱被一个奸诈的会计骗走了。
高分秘诀	▲ dishonest adj. 不诚实的，不老实的
	▲ accountant n. 会计人员，会计师

580. deft [dɛft] [deft] ☆☆★★★

adj. 灵巧的，熟练的	The man untangled the wire with his deft fingers. 男人用灵巧的手指解开金属线。
同义字词	skilled, skillful, dexterous, handy
反义字词	clumsy, unskillful, awkward
高分秘诀	▲ untangle v. 解开（某物的）结，使不再打结

581. degenerate [dɪ'dʒɛnəˌret] [de·ge·ne·rate] ☆☆★★★

| v. 衰退，堕落 | I worried so much about her, you know her health is degenerating rapidly.
我很担心，她的健康状况迅速恶化。 |

definite ~ delay

adj. 衰退的,堕落的	Don't let the riches and luxury make you degenerate. 不要因财富和奢华而自甘堕落。
高分秘诀	▲ rapidly adv. 很快地，立即，迅速地 ▲ luxury n. 奢侈，豪华

582. degrade [dɪˋgred] [de·grade]

v. 使降低,贬低	What you've done would only ruin your daughter's happiness, and degrade her in the public estimation. 你所做的一切只会破坏你女儿的幸福，降低她在社交界的声望。
同义字词	humiliate, debase, demote, downgrade
高分秘诀	▲ happiness n. 幸福 ▲ public estimation 社会声望

583. dehydrate [diˋhaɪˌdret] [de·hy·drate]

v. 使……脱水	Don't drink spirits, as the alcohol in it would dehydrate you. 不要喝酒，因为酒精会使你脱水。
同义字词	dry, desiccate, exsiccate
高分秘诀	▲ spirits n. 烈酒 ▲ alcohol n. 酒，酒精

584. deign [den] [deign]

v. 降低身份屈尊俯就	I hate him, you know when he passed by without even deigning to look at me. 我恨他，你知道吗，他从我身边经过时，竟然不屑看我一眼。
同义字词	condescend, stoop
高分秘诀	▲ pass by 经过，过去

585. delay [dɪˋle] [de·lay]

v. 延迟,耽搁	I have to tell you that all flights are delayed by a heavy snowfall. 我必须告诉你所有的飞机都因大雪而延误了。
n. 延迟,耽搁	After much delay, I finally finished my task. 拖了那么久，我终于完成了任务。
同义字词	defer, put off, postpone
反义字词	hasten, hurry

| 高分秘诀 | ▲ flight n. 飞机 |
| | ▲ snowfall n. 下雪，降雪 |

586. delegate [ˈdɛləgɪt] [de·le·gate] ☆★★★★

n. 代表	Susan was an official delegate. 苏珊是一名官方代表。
v. 委派, 授权	You'd better to delegate the task to an assistant. 你最好把这项工作授权给助手去做。
同义字词	representative, deputy, authorize, empower
高分秘诀	▲ official adj. 官方的，正式的

587. deliberate [dɪˈlɪbərɪt] [de·li·be·rate] ☆★★★★

adj. 故意的, 早有准备的	I think it's a deliberate crime not an accident. 我认为这是蓄意的罪行，并非意外事故。
v. 仔细考虑	You have to deliberated on the case. 你必须认真考虑那件事。
同义字词	intentional, planned, careful, prudent
高分秘诀	▲ crime n. 罪，罪行，犯罪 ▲ deliberate on 就……仔细考虑

588. delicate [ˈdɛləkət] [de·li·cate] ☆☆★★★

adj. 易碎的, 易损的	Don't interrupt him; the surgeon is performing a delicate operation. 别打扰他，这个外科医生正在做一个很精细的手术。
同义字词	fragile, vulnerable, feeble
高分秘诀	▲ interrupt v. 打断 ▲ surgeon n. 外科医生 ▲ operation n. 手术

589. delicious [dɪˈlɪʃəs] [de·li·cious] ☆★★★★

adj. 美味的, 可口的	The eel you roasted is absolutely delicious. 你烤的鳝鱼真是美味极了。
同义字词	tasty, delectable, luscious, savory
高分秘诀	▲ eel n. 鳝，鳗 ▲ roast v. 烤，烘，焙 ▲ absolutely adv. 完全地，绝对地

delegate ~ democracy

590. delineate [dɪˈlɪnɪˌet] [de·lin·e·ate] ☆☆★★★

v. 勾画，描述

He seemed very confident when he delineated his plans.
他在描述自己的计划时，显得相当自信。

同义字词　portray, describe, draw

高分秘诀　▲ confident **adj.** 有信心的，自信的

591. delirium [dɪˈlɪrɪəm] [de·lir·i·um] ☆★★★★

n. 精神错乱，发狂

The patient was in a state of delirium when he was sent to hospital.
病人在送入医院的时候已处于神智昏迷状态。

同义字词　insanity, madness

高分秘诀　▲ patient **n.** 患者，病人
　　　　　▲ in a state 处于激动（焦躁）的情绪中
　　　　　▲ hospital **n.** 医院

592. demise [dɪˈmaɪz] [de·mise] ☆☆★★★

n. 死，终止

It's the loss which led to the demise of the business.
这次的损失导致公司倒闭。

同义字词　death, dying

高分秘诀　▲ loss **n.** 损失，亏损
　　　　　▲ lead to 导致，引起

593. demobilize [diˈmoblaɪz] [de·mo·bi·lize] ☆☆★★★

v. 遣散，使复原

I don't think it's a good way to demobilize all our troops.
我认为把我们的军队全部撤掉并不是个好办法。

高分秘诀　▲ troop **n.** 军队，部队

594. democracy [dɪˈmɑkrəsɪ] [de·mo·cra·cy] ☆☆★★★

n. 民主政治，民主主义

The leader has reaffirmed his faith in democracy in public.
领导人物再次当众重申自己的民主信仰。

同义字词　democratic politics

高分秘诀　▲ reaffirm **v.** 重申，再确认
　　　　　▲ faith **n.** 信任，信仰，宗教信仰

595. demolish [dɪˋmɑlɪʃ] [de·mol·ish] ☆☆★★★

v. 破坏，摧毁

Unfortunately, there are so many buildings were demolished by a hurricane.
不幸的是，许多房屋被飓风吹毁了。

同义字词: raze, destroy, devastate, dismantle, wreck

高分秘诀:
▲ unfortunately **adv.** 不幸地，遗憾地
▲ hurricane **n.** 飓风，旋风

596. demonstrate [ˋdɛmənˌstret] [de·mon·strate] ☆☆★★★

v. 演示，示范

In the center hall, one salesperson is demonstrating the functions of a new washing machine.
在大厅中心，一位推销员正在当众示范新式洗衣机的功能。

同义字词: show, illustrate, confirm, prove

高分秘诀:
▲ salesperson **n.** 售货员，推销员
▲ function **n.** 功能，作用
▲ washing machine 洗衣机

597. denote [dɪˋnot] [de·note] ☆☆★★★

v. 指示，表示

As we all know that a smile usually denotes pleasure and friendship.
我们都知道微笑通常表示高兴和友善。

同义字词: signify, indicate, show

高分秘诀:
▲ pleasure **n.** 愉快，快乐
▲ friendship **n.** 友谊

598. denounce [dɪˋnaʊns] [de·nounce] ☆★★★★

v. (公开)谴责，斥责

He is so brave that he denounced the offenders to the authorities.
他很勇敢，向当局告发那些罪犯。

同义字词: accuse, condemn, censure, reproach

高分秘诀:
▲ offender **n.** 罪犯
▲ authority **n.** 当局，官方

599. dense [dɛns] [dense] ☆☆★★★

adj. 密集的，浓浓的

I can see nothing but the dense palls of smoke hung over the site.
除了浓浓的烟雾，我什么也看不见。

demolish ~ dependent

同义字词	thick, compact
反义字词	sparse, thin
高分秘诀	▲ a pall of smoke 烟雾 ▲ hang over 挂在……之上，悬浮在……之上

600. dentistry [ˈdɛntɪstrɪ] [den·tis·try] ☆★★★★

| n. 牙科 | The girl has only practised dentistry for five months.
这个女孩只当过五个月的牙医。 |
| 高分秘诀 | ▲ practise v. 练习，实习，积极从事 |

601. deny [dɪˈnaɪ] [de·ny] ☆★★★★

v. 否认, 否定	How dare you stoutly denied your guilt! 你怎么敢断然否定自己有罪。
同义字词	disagree with, disavow
反义字词	acknowledge, affirm, concede, confirm
高分秘诀	▲ stoutly adv. 刚强地，坚决地 ▲ guilt n. 有罪，对罪行有责任

602. depart [dɪˈpɑrt] [de·part] ☆☆★★★

v. 离开, 出发	Misfortunes come on wings and depart on foot. 祸来如飞，祸去如步行。
同义字词	take off, leave, set out
高分秘诀	▲ misfortune n. 不幸，厄运，灾祸 ▲ on wings 像飞一样地 ▲ on foot 步行

603. dependent [dɪˈpɛndənt] [de·pend·ent] ☆☆★★★

adj. 倚赖的, 由……而定的	As is known to us all that success is dependent on your efforts and ability. 众所周知，成功与否得看你的努力和能力。
同义字词	relying; conditional
高分秘诀	▲ be dependent on 依靠，倚赖 ▲ effort n. 努力，努力的结果 ▲ ability n. 才智，天资；能力

604. depict [dɪˋpɪkt] [de·pict] ☆☆★★★

v. 描绘, 描述

In the book, the character of the heroine is depicted to a nicety.
在这本书里，主角的性格刻画得非常细腻。

同义字词　portray, picture, describe, characterize, represent

高分秘诀
▲ character **n.** 品性，特性，特色，特征
▲ heroine **n.** 女英雄，女主角
▲ to a nicety 准确地，恰到好处地

605. deplete [dɪˋplit] [de·plete] ☆☆★★★

v. 耗尽, 使衰竭

Our stock of food is greatly depleted, what we are going to do next?
我们的食物储备已经消耗殆尽，下一步该怎么做？

同义字词　exhaust, consume, use up, eat up

高分秘诀
▲ stock **n.** 储备品，供应物，现货，存货
▲ greatly **adv.** 大大地，非常

606. deposit [dɪˋpɑzɪt] [de·po·sit] ☆☆★★★

v. 堆积, 沉淀

It's a good habit to deposit a sum of money in the bank each month.
每月在银行存一笔钱是个好习惯。

n. 堆积物, 沉淀

When will the house purchaser pay the deposit?
买房者什么时候付订金？

高分秘诀
▲ a sum of 一笔
▲ purchaser **n.** 买方，购买者

607. depreciation [dɪˏpriʃɪˋeʃən] [de·pre·ci·a·tion] ☆★★★★

n. 贬值, 跌价

Chinese currency suffered a sharp depreciation these days.
近来中国货币遭受巨大贬值损失。

高分秘诀　▲ currency **n.** 货币，通货

608. depredation [ˏdɛprɪˋdeʃən] [dep·re·da·tion] ☆★★★★

n. 劫掠, 毁坏

This city has suffered from the reckless depredation of the armed gangsters.
这个城市遭受了武装歹徒的野蛮掠夺。

同义字词　pillage, predation, ravage

depict ~ desalinate

| 高分秘诀 | ▲ reckless adj. 鲁莽的，不顾危险的
▲ armed adj. 武装的，带枪的
▲ gangster n. 匪徒，歹徒 |

609. depress [dɪˋprɛs] [de·press] ☆☆★★★

v. 压下，压低	Don't take so many medicines. Some of them would depress the action of the heart. 不要吃太多药，有些药会减弱心脏的功能。
同义字词	lower, press down, dishearten, discourage
反义字词	encourage, inspire
高分秘诀	▲ medicine n. 药 ▲ action n. 作用，功能

610. deprive [dɪˋpraɪv] [de·prive] ☆☆★★★

v. 剥夺，使失去	The man was deprived of schooling when he was a boy. 这个男人自小就失学。
同义字词	divest, take away, strip
高分秘诀	▲ deprive of 剥夺某人的…… ▲ schooling n. 教育，学校教育

611. derive [dɪˋraɪv] [de·rive] ☆☆★★★

v. 得到，获取	The old man derives great pleasure from his Kung Fu practice. 老人从练武中获得很大乐趣。
同义字词	obtain, get, gain
高分秘诀	▲ Kung Fu 中国功夫 ▲ practice n. 练习，实践

612. desalinate [͵diˋsæləͺnet] [de·sal·i·nate] ☆☆★★★

v. 除去盐分，淡化海水	According to the newspaper, this system can desalinate up to 300 liters of brackish water a day. 根据报纸上说，这个系统一天可以将高于三百公升的盐水去盐。
高分秘诀	▲ up to 多达；直到 ▲ liter n. 公升 ▲ brackish water 苦盐水，淡盐味水

613. descend [dɪˈsɛnd] [de·scend]   ☆★★★★

v. 传下，遗传，下降

The poor guy claimed that he was descended from Royalty.
那个穷小子竟然声称自己是皇室后裔。

同义字词   drop, fall, decline

高分秘诀
▲ claim **v.** 声称
▲ be descended from 是……的后代
▲ royalty **n.** 王族（成员）

614. deserve [dɪˈzɝv] [de·serve]   ☆☆★★★

v. 应得

What he had done deserved to be punished with the full rigour of the law.
他的所作所为应受到法律最严厉的惩罚。

同义字词   be worthy of, have a right to, merit

高分秘诀   ▲ rigour **n.** 严格，严厉

615. designate [ˈdɛzɪɡˌnet] [de·sig·nate]   ☆☆★★★

v. 指定，任命

I was designated to manage the sales department.
我被指派管理营业部门。

同义字词   nominate, assign, name, destine

高分秘诀   ▲ sales department 营业部

616. desire [dɪˈzaɪr] [de·sire]   ☆☆★★★

n. 欲望，要求

As some students' desires, we started the cram school.
应某些学生的要求，我们开办这个补习班。

v. 想要

The young lady desired badly to marry a millionaire.
这个年轻女士非常想嫁给百万富翁。

同义字词   aspiration, wish, hope, want, wish

高分秘诀
▲ as sb.'s desire 应某人的要求
▲ cram school **n.** 补习班
▲ millionaire **n.** 百万富翁

617. desolate [ˈdɛslɪt] [de·so·late]   ☆☆★★★

adj. 荒凉的，无人烟的

It's so pitiful for the old man to end his life in this desolate place, and in this desolate manner.
老人在这个孤零零的地方和情况下度过他的余生，真是可怜。

同义字词   bleak, barren, uninhabited

detect ~ detect

高分秘诀
▲ pitiful adj. 可怜的，值得同情的
▲ manner n. 模式，方法

618. desperate [ˈdɛspərɪt] [des·pe·rate] ☆☆★★★

adj. 绝望的，罔顾一切的

I have no choice but to invoke help in such a desperate situation.
在这种走投无路的情况下，我除了恳求援助外别无他法。

同义字词 hopeless, despairing, reckless

高分秘诀
▲ invoke v. 祈求求助，恳求，乞求
▲ situation n. 情势，情况；环境，位置

619. despoil [dɪˈspɔɪl] [de·spoil] ☆☆★★★

v. 夺取，掠夺

The invaders had despoiled China of many priceless treasures.
侵略者从中国掠夺了许多无价之宝。

同义字词 plunder, pillage, loot

高分秘诀
▲ invader n. 入侵者，侵略者
▲ priceless adj. 无价的，贵重的
▲ treasure n. 金银财宝，宝藏

620. destine [ˈdɛstɪn] [des·tine] ☆☆★★★

v. 命运注定，预定

The little girl is destine for a career on the stage, for she comes from a theatrical family.
小女孩生于戏剧工作者之家，注定了她的舞台生涯。

同义字词 predestine, fate, doom

高分秘诀
▲ stage n. 舞台，舞台生涯
▲ theatrical adj. 戏剧的，剧场的

621. destruction [dɪˈstrʌkʃən] [des·truc·tion] ☆★★★★

n. 破坏，毁灭

The earthquake left a trail of destruction behind it.
地震过后满目疮痍。

同义字词 havoc, demolition, devastation

高分秘诀
▲ earthquake n. 地震
▲ trail n. 痕迹，踪迹

622. detect [dɪˈtɛkt] [de·tect] ☆★★★★

| v. 察觉, 发觉 | Though he didn't say anything, I can detect sadness from his expression.
虽然他一句话也没有说，但我能从他的表情中看出他的忧伤。|

| 同义字词 | feel, discern, sense, perceive, discover |
| 高分秘诀 | ▲ sadness n. 悲哀，忧伤
▲ expression n. 表情，感情 |

623. deter [dɪ`tɝ] [de·ter] ☆★★★★

| v. 阻碍, 制止 | I think maybe death penalty could deter the corruption.
我想死刑或许能阻止人性腐败。|

| 同义字词 | inhibit, keep from, stop |
| 高分秘诀 | ▲ death penalty 死刑
▲ corruption n. 腐败，贿赂 |

624. deteriorate [dɪ`tɪrɪə͵ret] [de·te·ri·o·rate] ☆☆★★★

| v. 使恶化, 质量下降 | It's true that food is apt to deteriorate in summer.
食物在夏天容易变质是事实。|

| 同义字词 | become worse |
| 反义字词 | improve, ameliorate |
| 高分秘诀 | ▲ be apt to 倾向于
▲ summer n. 夏天，夏季 |

625. determine [dɪ`tɝmɪn] [de·ter·mine] ☆★★★★

| v. 确定, 下决心 | British novelist Eliot once said that our deeds determine us, much as we determine our deeds.
英国小说家艾略特曾经说过："什么样的人决定做什么样的事；同样，做什么样的事也决定一个人是什么样的人。" |

| 同义字词 | decide, resolve, settle |
| 高分秘诀 | ▲ British adj. 英国的，英国人的
▲ novelist n. 小说家
▲ deed n. 行为，行动 |

626. detest [dɪ`tɛst] [de·test] ☆☆★★★

| v. 深恶, 憎恶 | In fact, we all detest our boss' overbearing manner.
事实上我们都讨厌老板那种盛气凌人的态度。|

| 同义字词 | abhor, loathe, hate |
| 反义字词 | adore, love, worship |

detect ~ devoid

高分秘诀　▲ in fact 实际上，其实
　　　　　▲ overbearing adj. 专横的，傲慢的；难忍的

627. detriment [ˈdɛtrəmənt] [de·tri·ment]　☆★★★★

n. 伤害，危害

He reads on the bus, to the detriment of his eyes.
他在公交车上看书，对眼睛有害。

同义字词　harm, damage, injury

高分秘诀　▲ to the detriment of sb./sth. 对某人有害；对某事物有害

628. devastate [ˈdɛvəsˌtet] [de·vas·tate]　☆☆★★★

v. 毁坏

The enemy intended to devastate the town at one stroke.
敌军企图一举摧毁整个城镇。

同义字词　ruin, destroy, wreck

高分秘诀　▲ at one stroke 一举

629. deviate [ˈdiviˌet] [de·vi·ate]　☆☆★★★

v. 偏离，越轨

Just believe in me, I would never deviate from our rules.
请相信我，我决不会背离我们的规则。

高分秘诀　▲ believe in 相信，信任
　　　　　▲ deviate from 背离，偏离……

630. devise [dɪˈvaɪz] [de·vise]　☆☆★★★

v. 设计，发明

The professor devised a new method of teaching oral English.
教授设计一种新的教英语口语的方法。

同义字词　create, invent, contrive, excogitate

高分秘诀　▲ professor n. 教授
　　　　　▲ oral adj. 口头的，口述的
　　　　　▲ oral English 英语口语

631. devoid [dɪˈvɔɪd] [de·void]　☆★★★★

adj. 全无的，缺乏的

He is such a man devoid of courage and enthusiasm.
他是一个缺乏勇气和热情的男人。

高分秘诀　▲ devoid of 缺乏
　　　　　▲ enthusiasm n. 热情，热心

632. devote [dɪˈvot] [de·vote]

v. 投身于，献身

The scientist devoted the entirety of his life to medical research.
这位科学家把毕生精力贡献给了医学研究工作。

同义字词　dedicate, contribute, consecrate

高分秘诀
▲ entirety **n.** 整体，全面
▲ medical **adj.** 医学的，医疗的，医术的

633. devour [dɪˈvaʊr] [de·vour]

v. 贪婪地吃，吞食

I regretted very much, but have to devour my repentance and disgust in secret.
我很后悔，但只能默默吞下我的后悔和憎恨。

同义字词　consume, gorge, gobble

高分秘诀
▲ repentance **n.** 后悔，告解
▲ disgust **n.** 厌恶，反感

634. diagnose [ˈdaɪəgnoz] [di·ag·nose]

v. 诊断

After a thorough examination, the doctor diagnosed his illness as influenza.
经过一番彻底检查，医生诊断出他得的是流行性感冒。

高分秘诀
▲ thorough **adj.** 彻底的，十足的，考虑周到的
▲ influenza **n.** 流行性感冒

635. dictate [ˈdɪktet] [dic·tate]

v. 大声讲或读，口授

The boss dictated a letter to his assistant.
老板向助理口述了一封信。

高分秘诀
▲ assitant **n.** 助理

636. didactic [dɪˈdæktɪk] [di·dac·tic]

adj. 教导的，教诲性的，说教的

Before I start, there is necessary for me to announce that my book was not intended to be neither didactic nor aggressive.
在开始之前，我有必要先声明一点，这本书的本意既不想教训人，也不想攻击人。

devote ~ digest

| 高分秘诀 | ▲ be necessary for 有……的必要
▲ intended adj. 有意的，故意的
▲ aggressive adj. 挑衅的，侵略性的 |

637. diet [ˈdaɪət] [di·et] ☆☆★★★

n. 饮食，食物	Nowadays tofu is now regarded as a healthful diet. 现在豆腐被认为是有益健康的食物。
v. 节食，忌食	I'm getting fatter, and have to diet to lose weight. 我变胖了，必须节食减肥。
同义字词	nutritional plan, nourishment
高分秘诀	▲ tofu 豆腐 ▲ regard as 把……认作 ▲ healthful adj. 有益于健康的 ▲ lose weight 体重减轻

638. differentiate [ˌdɪfəˈrɛnʃɪet] [dif·fer·en·ti·ate] ☆☆★★★

v. 区分，区别	To be a botanist, you can differentiate varieties of plants. 作为一个植物学家，你必须会区分不同种类的植物。
同义字词	set apart, distinguish, discriminate
高分秘诀	▲ botanist n. 植物学家，研究植物的人 ▲ variety n. 品种，种类，变化，多样化

639. diffuse [dɪˈfjuz] [dif·fuse] ☆★★★★

v. 扩散，散播	A drop of soybean milk diffused in the water, and it became cloudy. 一滴豆浆在水中扩散，使水变得混浊不清。
adj. 散开的，弥漫的	I hate to read such kind of diffuse style. 我讨厌读这种冗赘的文体。
同义字词	spread out, scatter, dispersed, scattered
高分秘诀	▲ soybean milk 豆浆 ▲ cloudy adj. 模糊的，不透明的，不清晰的 ▲ style n. 风格，文体

640. digest [daɪˈdʒɛst] [di·gest] ☆☆★★★

| v. 消化，彻底了解 | Don't take meat at dinner, for it's not easy for our stomach to digest it.
晚餐时不要吃肉，因为肉不容易消化。 |

| n. 摘要，文摘 | The old man subscribed to "Reader's Digest" every month.
老人每月都订阅《读者文摘》。 |

同义字词　assimilate, ingest, comprehend, catch on

高分秘诀　
▲ stomach n. 胃
▲ subscribe v. 订购，预订
▲ Reader's Digest 读者文摘

641. dignity [`dɪgnətɪ] [dig·ni·ty]　☆★★★★

| n. 尊严，高贵 | A man's dignity depends upon his character not upon his wealth.
一个人高尚与否取决于他的品格，而不是财富。 |

高分秘诀　
▲ depend upon 倚赖，依靠
▲ character n. 品性，特性
▲ wealth n. 财产，财富

642. digression [daɪ`grɛʃən] [di·gres·sion]　☆☆★★★

| n. 离题，扯到枝节上 | Don't start on a digression during the speech, or you'll be cried down by the audience.
演讲中不要离题，否则你会被观众轰下台。 |

同义字词　deviation, diversion, divagation

高分秘诀　
▲ start on 开始进行
▲ cry down 把……轰下去

643. dilate [daɪ`let] [di·late]　☆☆★★★

| v. 使膨胀，使扩大 | I'm glad that I have this opportunity to dilate on my experiences in computer.
很高兴有机会向大家详述我在电脑方面的经验。 |

同义字词　expand, enlarge, widen, broaden

反义字词　contract, abbreviate, abridge

高分秘诀　
▲ opportunity n. 机会，时机
▲ dilate on sth. 详述某事
▲ computer n. 计算机，电脑

644. diligent [`dɪlədʒənt] [di·li·gent]　☆☆★★★

| adj. 勤勉的，勤奋的 | Though the boy is anything but diligent in his class, he still could get high marks.
尽管这个男孩是班上不勤奋的学生，但他总能得高分。 |

dignity ~ disadvantage

同义字词	assiduous, industrious, hard-working
高分秘诀	▲ get high marks 得高分

645. dilute [daɪˋlut] [di·lute] ☆★★★★

v. 稀释，淡化	Before painting, he diluted the paint with water. 上色前，他加水稀释颜料。
adj. 稀释的，冲淡的	I've never drunk this dilute whisky. 我从来不喝掺水的威士忌。
同义字词	weaken, attenuate, thin
高分秘诀	▲ paint n. 颜料 ▲ whisky n. 威士忌酒

646. dimension [dɪˋmɛnʃən] [di·men·sion] ☆★★★★

n. 尺寸，尺度	Could you tell me the dimensions of the room? 你能告诉我这栋屋子的面积大小吗？
高分秘诀	▲ dimensions n. 规模，面积，体积

647. diminish [dəˋmɪnɪʃ] [di·mi·nish] ☆☆★★★

v. （使）减少，（使）变小	The high medical expenses of her husband diminished their savings. 丈夫高额的医疗费用耗光了他们的积蓄。
同义字词	dwindle, reduce, decrease
反义字词	increase, raise
高分秘诀	▲ medical expenses 医疗费 ▲ saving n. 存款，储蓄金

648. diplomatic [ˌdɪpləˋmætɪk] [di·plo·ma·tic] ☆☆★★★

adj. 外交的，外交人员的	My grandfather had been in the diplomatic service. 我祖父曾在外交部门任职。
同义字词	tactful, politic, diplomatical
高分秘诀	▲ diplomatic service 外交部门，驻外单位

649. disadvantage [ˌdɪsədˋvæntɪdʒ] [dis·ad·van·tage] ☆☆★★★

n. 缺点，坏处	The lack of education was the biggest disadvantage for you to look for a job. 学历不够是你谋职时的最大不利条件。

| 同义字词 | drawback, defect, shortcoming, handicap |

高分秘诀
▲ education n. 教育
▲ look for 寻找（某人或某物）

650. disaster [dɪˈzæstə] [dis·as·ter] ☆☆★★★

n. 灾难，不幸
I think failing in the college entrance examination is a disaster to me.
没有通过大学入学考试对我来说是场灾难。

| 同义字词 | catastrophe, misfortune, calamity, tragedy |

高分秘诀 ▲ entrance examination 入学考试

651. discard [dɪsˈkɑrd] [dis·card] ☆★★★★

v. 丢弃，抛弃
Discard the siftings, there is no need to keep them.
把筛下来的杂质丢掉，没有必要再保留它们。

| 同义字词 | jettison, throw away, get rid of, cast off |

高分秘诀 ▲ siftings n. 筛屑

652. discern [dɪˈzɜn] [dis·cern] ☆☆★★★

v. 看出；察觉到
I could discern your sadness from your appearance.
我从你的样子可以察觉出你的不快。

| 同义字词 | detect, perceive |

高分秘诀
▲ sadness n. 悲哀，悲伤
▲ appearance n. 外表，外貌

653. discharge [dɪsˈtʃɑrdʒ] [dis·charge] ☆★★★★

v. 释放，排出
In the distance, there is a tall chimney discharging smoke.
远处一个大烟囱正在冒烟。

n. 排放物；释放，获准离开
Those prisoners were happy to get their discharge.
囚犯获准释放，一个个都高兴极了。

| 同义字词 | release, give off, emission, flow |

高分秘诀
▲ in the distance 在远处
▲ chimney n. 烟囱，烟筒
▲ prisoner n. 囚徒；俘虏

654. discipline [ˈdɪsəplɪn] [dis·ci·pline] ☆☆★★★

discourse ~ discourse

| n. 纪律，训练 | It's our responsibility to obey law and discipline. 遵纪守法是我们的责任。 |
| v. 训练，惩罚 | If you do well, I would not discipline anyone. 如果你们表现得好，我不会惩罚任何人。 |

同义字词: subject, field, training

高分秘诀:
▲ responsibility n. 责任；职责
▲ law n. 法，法律，法规

655. discontented [dɪskənˈtɛntɪd] [dis·con·tent·ed] ☆☆★★★

| adj. 不满的，不满足的 | I'm discontented with my present wages. 我对于目前的薪水感到不满。 |

同义字词: dissatisfied, unhappy

反义字词: content, contented

高分秘诀:
▲ wage n. 工资

656. discount [ˈdɪskaʊnt] [dis·count] ☆★★★★

| v. 不考虑，不全信 | It's a good way to promote the products by discounting all its slow-selling goods. 降价出售所有非畅销货品是一个不错的促销方法。 |
| n. 折扣 | I bought this umbrella at 70% discount. 我用七折价钱买到这把伞。 |

同义字词: deduction, reduction, disregard, doubt

高分秘诀:
▲ product n. 产品，产物
▲ slow-selling goods 冷门货

657. discourage [dɪsˈkrɜɪdʒ] [dis·cour·age] ☆☆★★★

| v. 使气馁，使沮丧 | Why are you easily discouraged by difficulties and obstacles? 为什么一遇到困难和阻碍你就容易气馁？ |

同义字词: depress, daunt, deject

高分秘诀:
▲ difficulty n. 困难，难度
▲ obstacle n. 障碍（物），妨碍

658. discourse [ˈdɪskɔrs] [dis·course] ☆☆★★

n. 讲道, 演讲	Sweet discourse makes short days and nights. 酒逢知己千杯少，话不投机半句多。
高分秘诀	▲ sweet **adj.** 悦耳的，令人高兴的

659. discreet [dɪˋskrit] [dis·creet] ☆★★★★

adj. 小心的,谨慎的	You can count on him, and he is discreet in his behavior. 你可以指望他，他是很谨慎的人。
同义字词	careful, cautious, prudent
高分秘诀	▲ count on 倚赖，依靠 ▲ behavior **n.** 行为，举止，态度

660. discrete [dɪˋskrit] [dis·crete] ☆☆★★★

adj. 分离的,截然分开的	Put those discrete events together, and you will find something new in them. 把这些不相关的事件结合在一起，你就会从中找到一些新发现。
高分秘诀	▲ event **n.** 事件，大事

661. disgust [dɪsˋgʌst] [dis·gust] ☆☆★★★

n. 厌恶, 嫌恶	The girl gave a snort of disgust, and went away quickly. 女孩厌恶地哼了一声，快速地离开了。
v. 使反感, 厌恶	I disgusted those fulsome flattery. 我讨厌过分的谄媚。
同义字词	repulsion, loathing, nauseate, repel, revolt
高分秘诀	▲ snort **n.** 喷鼻声，鼻息声（表示不耐烦、厌恶等） ▲ fulsome **adj.** 过分恭维的 ▲ flattery **n.** 奉承（话）

662. disillusion [ˌdɪsɪˋluʒən] [dis·il·lu·sion] ☆★★★★

v. 使醒悟, 理想或幻想破灭	I disillusion my daughter, for I told her that Santa Claus doesn't exist in the real world. 我戳破了女儿的幻想，因为我告诉她在真实世界中没有圣诞老人。
高分秘诀	▲ Santa Claus 圣诞老人 ▲ real world 真实世界

663. disintegrate [dɪsˋɪntəgret] [dis·in·te·grate] ☆☆★★★

discourse ~ dismember

v. (使)瓦解，(使)破裂

The taxi run into a big truck and disintegrated on impact.
出租车撞上了一辆大货车，撞得粉碎。

高分秘诀
- ▲ taxi **n.** 出租车
- ▲ truck **n.** 货车，卡车
- ▲ impact **n.** 冲击（力），碰撞

664. disinterested [dɪsˋɪntərɪstɪd] [dis·in·ter·est·ed] ☆☆★★

adj. 无个人利害关系的，公平的

We all hope that the judge could give us a disinterested verdict.
我们都希望法官能做出公正的判决。

高分秘诀
- ▲ judge **n.** 法官，裁判员，评判员
- ▲ verdict **n.** 裁决，裁定

665. dismal [ˋdɪzm!] [dis·mal] ☆☆★★

adj. 阴沉的，凄凉的

The old lady keeps on talking in a dismal strain.
这位老妇人以悲伤的语调继续说着。

同义字词　gloomy, somber, melancholy

高分秘诀
- ▲ keep on 继续前进，继续工作
- ▲ strain **n.** 写作或说话的模式或风格；语调

666. dismay [dɪsˋme] [dis·may] ☆☆★★

v. 使惊愕，使气馁

Your recklessness dismayed me much.
你的鲁莽真叫我失望。

n. 惊愕，气馁

I could see your face registered dismay at that time.
那时我看到你脸上流露出惊慌的神色。

同义字词　consternation, shock, horrify

高分秘诀
- ▲ recklessness **n.** 鲁莽，轻率，不顾一切
- ▲ register **v.** 流露

667. dismember [dɪsˋmɛmbɚ] [dis·mem·ber] ☆☆★★

v. 肢解，分割

The movie of the cannibals dismembered the boys left me with my hair standing on end.
那部食人魔肢解男孩的电影令我毛骨悚然。

同义字词　dissect, split up, divide, take apart, discerp

高分秘诀
- ▲ cannibal **n.** 食人者
- ▲ stand on end 竖立，直立

668. dismiss [dɪsˈmɪs] [dis·miss] ☆★★★★

v. 解雇，撤职 — My elder brother was dismissed from the army.
我哥哥被军队开除了。

- 同义字词: send away, fire, discharge, disband
- 反义字词: employ, engage, hire
- 高分秘诀:
  ▲ elder adj. 年长的，年龄较大的
  ▲ dismiss from 解雇，开除

669. disorganize [dɪsˈɔrgəˌnaɪz] [dis·or·ga·nize] ☆☆★★★

v. 扰乱，使混乱 — It's not easy to disorganize the enemy's defence.
破坏敌人的防守不容易。

- 高分秘诀: ▲ defence n. 防御，保卫，保护

670. dispatch [dɪˈspætʃ] [dis·patch] ☆☆★★★

v. (紧急)派遣，分发 — The king dispatched an ambassador to go abroad.
国王派遣大使到国外。

n. 派遣，重要消息 — Under the help of high-tech machine, we can solve the problems with dispatch.
在高科技机器的协助下，我们迅速解决了这些问题。

- 同义字词: send off, dispatch, expedition, dispatching
- 高分秘诀:
  ▲ ambassador n. 大使，使节
  ▲ go abroad 出国
  ▲ with dispatch 迅速地，尽快地

671. dispense [dɪˈspɛns] [dis·pense] ☆☆☆★★

v. 分发，分发 — The government dispensed emergency food to the earthquake victims.
政府把紧急救难食物发给了地震灾区的受害者。

- 同义字词: distribute, give out, deal out, allot
- 高分秘诀:
  ▲ emergency food 救急食品
  ▲ victim n. 牺牲者，受害者，受灾者

672. disperse [dɪˈspɝs] [dis·perse] ☆☆☆★★

dispute ~ dispute

v. 分散,散开	For the safety of the citizens of the city, we shall be forced to disperse the mob shortly.
	为了保护多数市民的安全，我们将采取强制手段驱散滋事分子。

同义字词　scatter, spread, distribute

高分秘诀
▲ citizen n. 市民
▲ mob n. 暴民
▲ shortly adj. 立即
▲ in an attempt to 力图，试图

673. displace [dɪsˋples] [dis·place]   ☆★★★★

v. 移置,转移	TV has displaced movies as our most popular form of entertainment nowadays.
	现今电视取代了电影的地位，成为最大众化的娱乐模式。

同义字词　move, replace, substitute, take the place

高分秘诀
▲ popular adj. 流行的，受大众欢迎的，广泛的
▲ entertainment n. 娱乐

674. display [dɪˋsple] [dis·play]   ☆☆★★★

v. 陈列,显示	The artist displayed his handicrafts on the wayside.
	这位艺术家在路边展示他的手工艺品。
n. 陈列,展览	I think most of children enjoy a fireworks display.
	我认为大多数小朋友喜爱看烟火。

同义字词　exhibit, present, show, demonstration

高分秘诀
▲ handicraft n. 手工艺，手工艺品
▲ wayside n. 路边
▲ firework n. 烟火，放烟火

675. disposal [dɪˋspozl] [dis·pos·al]   ☆★★★★

n. 清除,处理	Don't placed everything at my disposal.
	不要把一切事情都交给我处理。

同义字词　arrangement, settlement

高分秘诀　▲ at one's disposal　供任意使用，可自行支配

676. dispute [dɪˋspjut] [dis·pute]   ☆★★★★

n. 争论，纠纷	My honesty is beyond dispute. 我的诚实是毫无争议的。	
v. 争论，争执	On the meeting, we were disputing about the rights and wrongs of the case. 我们在会议上激烈争论这个事件的是非对错。	
高分秘诀	▲ beyond dispute 毫无疑问 ▲ the rights and wrongs 是非曲直	

677. disregard [ˌdɪsrɪˈɡɑrd] [dis·re·gard]   ☆☆★★★

n. 不理会，漠视	I don't like her, because she shows ruthless disregard for other people's feelings. 我不喜欢她，因为她对别人的感情漠不关心。
v. 不理会，漠视	Sometimes you could get better if you disregard the particulars. 有时别太在乎细节反而会让你做得更好一点。
同义字词	ignore, discount, take no notice of
高分秘诀	▲ ruthless **adj.** 无情的，冷酷的 ▲ particular **n.** 详情，细目

678. disrupt [dɪsˈrʌpt] [dis·rupt]   ☆☆★★★

v. 使混乱，扰乱	If the conflicts go bigger, they would disrupt the government. 如果这些冲突愈趋严重的话，有可能使政府垮台。
同义字词	upset, disorder, interrupt
高分秘诀	▲ conflict **n.** 冲突，抵触

679. disseminate [dɪˈsɛməˌnet] [dis·se·mi·nate]   ☆★★★★

v. 散布，传播	We can use the press to disseminate left-wing views. 我们可以透过报刊传播"左"翼观点。
同义字词	distribute, spread, diffuse
衍生字词	disseminator, dissemination
高分秘诀	▲ press **n.** 报刊，报界，新闻界 ▲ left-wing **adj.** "左"派的

dispute ~ distend

680. dissenter [dɪˈsɛntə] [dis·sent·er] ☆☆★★★

n. 不同意者，反对者

Be careful, the prime minister would persecute the dissenters.
小心，首相会迫害持异议的人。

同义字词: objector, protester, dissident
反义字词: consenter, sympathizer, assentor
高分秘诀:
▲ prime minister 首相
▲ persecute **v.** 迫害

681. dissimilar [dɪˈsɪmələ] [dis·si·mi·lar] ☆☆★★★

adj. 不同的，相异的

I suddenly found that your latest book is quite dissimilar from your previous one.
我突然发现你最近写的书跟以前写的大不相同。

高分秘诀:
▲ latest **adj.** 最近的，最新的
▲ previous **adj.** 先前的，以前的

682. dissipate [ˈdɪsəˌpet] [dis·si·pate] ☆★★★★

v. 消失，消散

The hyperthermia may be fatal, and measures should be taken to dissipate heat quickly.
体温过高可能致命，所以必须采取散热措施。

同义字词: disappear, vanish, scatter, disperse
高分秘诀:
▲ hyperthermia **n.** 体温过高
▲ fatal **adj.** 致命的，灾难性的
▲ heat **n.** 高温，炎热

683. dissolve [dɪˈzɑlv] [dis·solve] ☆☆★★★

v. 使溶解，解散

Those old building dissolved away, and the modern ones took their place.
古老的建筑消失了，现代建筑取代了它们的地位。

高分秘诀:
▲ dissolve away 消失，消散
▲ take one's place 代替某人

684. distend [dɪˈstɛnd] [dis·tend] ☆☆★★★

v. 膨胀，肿胀

Don't you notice her abdomen distend?
你没有注意到她的腹部涨大吗？

同义字词: dilate, bulge, swell
高分秘诀: ▲ abdomen **n.** 腹部

685. distasteful [dɪsˈtestfəl] [dis·taste·ful] ☆☆★★★

adj. (令人)不愉快的, 讨厌的

Most people find that dirty jokes are distasteful.
大多数人都认为黄色笑话低级庸俗。

同义字词 abhorrent, displeasing, disagreeable

高分秘诀 ▲ dirty joke 黄色笑话

686. distill [dɪsˈtɪl] [di·still] ☆☆★★★

v. 蒸馏, 提取

They use the traditional way to distill whiskey.
他们采用传统制法蒸馏威士忌。

同义字词 extract, distil, make pure

高分秘诀 ▲ traditional **adj.** 传统的, 惯例的
▲ whiskey **n.** 威士忌酒

687. distinct [dɪˈstɪŋkt] [dis·tinct] ☆★★★★

adj. 明确的, 确实的

There is a distinct possibility that she'll never return your money.
她不还你钱的可能性非常大。

高分秘诀 ▲ possibility **n.** 可能性; 可能的事
▲ return **v.** 还, 归还

688. distinguish [dɪˈstɪŋgwɪʃ] [dis·tin·guish] ☆☆★★★

v. 区别, 辨认

I know that the colorblind can't distinguish between colors.
我知道色盲不能辨别颜色。

同义字词 characterize, differentiate, recognize, discern

高分秘诀 ▲ colorblind **adj.** 色盲的

689. distort [dɪsˈtɔrt] [dis·tort] ☆☆★★★

v. 弄歪(形状等), 歪曲

As we all know that some newspapers distort news to attract people's attention.
我们知道有些报纸为了吸引大家的注意而歪曲事实。

同义字词 deform, twist, contort

高分秘诀 ▲ newspaper **n.** 报纸
▲ attract attention 引起注意

distasteful ~ divergent

690. distract [dɪˈstrækt] [dis·tract] ☆☆★★★

v. 使分心，分散注意力

Don't try to distract my attention. I'm not fall for it.
别想转移我的注意力，我才不会上当。

高分秘诀
▲ distract attention 分散注意力
▲ fall for 上当，听信

691. distress [dɪˈstrɛs] [dis·tress] ☆★★★★

n. 悲痛，不幸

You can't use the public fund, which would use for relieving distress among the flood victims.
你不能挪用公款，它们是用来救济困苦的洪水灾民的。

v. 使痛苦，使忧伤

My grandmother's death distressed me greatly.
外婆的去世使我很痛苦。

同义字词 discomfort, affliction, sorrow, suffering
反义字词 comfort, relief, solace
高分秘诀
▲ public fund 公款
▲ greatly **adv.** 大大地，非常

692. distribute [dɪˈstrɪbjut] [dis·tri·bute] ☆☆★★★

v. 分发，散布

The teacher distributed the food and candy among the students.
老师分发食物和糖果给学生。

同义字词 hand out, disseminate, allocate
反义字词 collect, assemble, gather

693. disturb [dɪsˈtɝb] [dis·turb] ☆★★★★

v. 打扰，扰乱

Those youngsters were arrested for disturbing the peace.
那些年轻人因扰乱社会秩序而被抓起来了。

同义字词 upset, bother, annoy
高分秘诀
▲ youngster **n.** 少年，青年，年轻人
▲ disturb the peace 扰乱治安

694. divergent [daɪˈvɝdʒənt] [di·ver·gent] ☆☆★★★

adj. 有分歧的，有差异的

I don't know which one is right, for the facts stated by two boys were widely divergent.
两个男孩所说的事实大相径庭，我不知道哪个说得对。

高分秘诀	▲ fact n. 事实，真相
	▲ state v. 陈述，叙述
	▲ widely adv. 在很大程度上，大量地

695. diverse [daɪˋvɝs] [di·verse] ☆☆★★★

adj. 不同的；变化多的	The works on display are diverse in category. 参展作品的种类十分多样化。
同义字词	various, distinct, diverse
高分秘诀	▲ on display 展出，展览 ▲ category n. 种类，类别

696. diversion [daɪˋvɝʒən] [di·ver·sion] ☆★★★★

n. 消遣，娱乐	I can tell that what he said just now was a diversion to make us forget the main point. 我能看出来刚才他所说的话是在声东击西，想借此让我们忘掉重点。
高分秘诀	▲ main point 要点，主要问题

697. divide [dɪˋvaɪd] [di·vide] ☆☆★★★

v. 划分，分开	The dying man wanted the bequest was divided among the poor, instead of leaving it to his children. 这个垂死的老人要求把遗产分给贫民，而不是留给自己的子孙。
同义字词	separate, part, split, partition
高分秘诀	▲ dying adj. 快要死的，垂死的 ▲ bequest n. 遗赠，遗产

698. divorce [dɪˋvɔrs] [di·vorce] ☆☆★★★

v. 离婚，使分离	I think there is no need to hide the fact, so I avowed openly that I was divorced. 我认为没有必要隐瞒事实，所以我坦白承认自己已经离婚。
同义字词	separate, disconnect, disjoin, dissociate
高分秘诀	▲ avow v. 公开声明，承认

699. dizzy [ˋdɪzɪ] [diz·zy] ☆☆★★★

adj. 眩晕的，头昏眼花的	I didn't feel well today, and I was kind of dizzy and nauseated. 我今天不舒服，有点昏眩作呕。
同义字词	light-headed, giddy, confused, vertiginous

diverse ~ dominant

| 高分秘诀 | ▲ nauseated adj. 作呕的，厌恶的 |

700. document [ˈdɑkjəmənt] [doc·u·ment] ☆★★★★

v. 证明；记录	If you want to document the case, you have to offer abundant evidence. 如果想证明这个案子，你必须提供充分的证据。
n. 公文，档案	The salesman persuaded me to sign the document by guile. 这个推销员用欺骗手段说服我在档案上签字。
高分秘诀	▲ evidence n. 证词，证据 ▲ salesman n. 推销员，售货员 ▲ guile n. 奸猾，狡诈，欺骗

701. dogged [ˈdɔgɪd] [dog·ged] ☆☆★★★

adj. 顽强的，顽固的	The disabled boy lacks talent, but he won the game by sheer dogged persistence. 这位残疾男孩缺少天分，却凭坚韧的毅力赢得了胜利。
同义字词	determined, persevering, tenacious, obstinate, pertinacious
高分秘诀	▲ disabled adj. 残废的，有缺陷的 ▲ sheer adj. 完全的，十足的 ▲ persistence n. 坚持不懈，执意

702. domestic [dəˈmɛstɪk] [do·mes·tic] ☆★★★★

| adj. 家庭的，家用的 | Don't let the domestic details imprison you.
不要让繁杂的家务困住你自己。 |
| 高分秘诀 | ▲ detail n. 细节，小事
▲ imprison v. 监禁 |

703. dominant [ˈdɑmənənt] [do·mi·nant] ☆☆★★★

adj. 主要的，占优势的	The man in black dinner-jacket is the dominant partner of the business. 那个穿黑礼服的男人是公司举足轻重的合作伙伴。
同义字词	major, important, outweighing
高分秘诀	▲ dinner-jacket 无尾礼服 ▲ partner n. 伙伴，合伙人，股东

704. donate [ˈdonet] [do·nate] ☆☆★★★

v. 捐赠

So many people lined up to donate blood for the boy who was on the danger list.
许多人排队等着捐血给这位病危的男孩。

同义字词 grant, contribute, bestow

高分秘诀
▲ line up 排队等候
▲ on the danger list 病势危急

705. dormant [ˈdɔrmənt] [dor·mant] ☆☆★★★

adj. 休眠的，静止的

As soon as I meet her, my dormant love for her is rekindled.
我一看到她，对她的旧情立刻重新复燃。

同义字词 hibernated, inactive, torpid

高分秘诀 ▲ rekindle **v.** 使再燃

706. doubt [daʊt] [doubt] ☆★★★★

n. 怀疑，疑虑

The old man was beyond all doubt the best artist of his day.
这位老人无疑是那个年代最优秀的艺术家。

v. 怀疑，疑虑

I don't doubt that you will succeed.
我肯定你会成功。

同义字词 question, skepticism, wonder, suspect

高分秘诀 ▲ beyond all doubt 毫无疑问地

707. draft [dræft] [draft] ☆☆★★★

n. 草图，草稿

His first draft was rejected by the press.
他的首稿被出版社退回。

v. 起草，征召……入伍

How about we ask Bob to draft the indictment?
我们请鲍伯起草诉状如何？

同义字词 rough outline, draw up, sketch, enlist

高分秘诀
▲ reject **v.** 拒绝，谢绝，驳回
▲ press **n.** 出版社，新闻社
▲ indictment **n.** 刑事起诉书，公诉书

708. drain [dren] [drain] ☆☆★★★

v. （使）流干，耗尽

We can take measures to drain away the water in time.
我们可以采取措施及时排掉水。

donate ~ drift

n. 排水沟,排水管	Oh, shit! The drain was stopped up with fallen leaves. 糟糕! 水沟被落叶堵塞了。

高分秘诀
▲ take measures 设法, 着手
▲ drain away （使）流走／流去
▲ in time 及时
▲ stop up 封住
▲ fallen leaves 落叶

709. drama [ˋdrɑmə] [dra·ma] ☆☆★★★

n. 戏剧,剧本	We all knew nothing about the Greek drama. 我们对希腊戏剧一无所知。

高分秘诀 ▲ Greek n. 希腊人, 希腊语

710. drastic [ˋdræstɪk] [dras·tic] ☆☆★★★

adj. 激烈的, 猛烈的	The drastic shortage of food drove the local people away. 当地人因为食物的严重匮乏而选择离开。

同义字词 radical, violent, severe, extreme
高分秘诀 ▲ shortage n. 不足, 缺少
▲ drive away 把……驱开, 赶走

711. dread [drɛd] [dread] ☆☆★★★

n. 畏惧, 恐怖	I have a dread of cobra. 我很怕眼镜蛇。
v. 害怕, 恐惧	I dread the interview with my future parents-in-law. 我害怕与未来的岳父母见面。

同义字词 fear, terror, horror
高分秘诀 ▲ cobra n. 眼镜蛇
▲ interview n. 面谈, 会见
▲ parents-in-law n. 岳父、岳母

712. drift [drɪft] [drift] ☆★★★★

v. 漂流, 漂泊	I watched the boat drift downstream, took my lover away. 我看着向下游漂流的船, 带走了我的爱人。
n. 漂移, 漂流	There is a drift of citizens to the countries nowadays. 近来不少市民趋向回归农村。

高分秘诀	▲ downstream adv. 在下游，顺流地
	▲ citizen n. 市民，平民
	▲ country n. 郊外，乡村

713. drill [drɪl] [drill] ☆☆★★★

n. 训练，反复练习	You'd better watch the fire drill and learn how to escape from the fire.
	你最好观看消防演习，学习如何从火场逃生。
v. 钻孔	In this area, the villagers have to drill well for water.
	这个地区的村民们需要打井取水。
同义字词	bore, pierce, practise, train
高分秘诀	▲ fire drill 消防演习
	▲ villager n. 村民

714. drowsy [ˋdraʊzɪ] [drow·sy] ☆★★★★

adj. 昏昏欲睡的	Don't take the cold medicine, for those tablets will make you drowsy.
	不要吃感冒药，它会使你昏昏欲睡。
同义字词	sleepy, soporific, oscitant, dozy
高分秘诀	▲ cold medicine 感冒药
	▲ tablet n. 药片

715. ductile [ˋdʌktl] [duc·tile] ☆☆★★★

adj. 易延展的，柔软的	Most of the educationalists believe that children's mind are ductile.
	大多数教育学家认为儿童的心智易于塑造。
同义字词	malleable, tensile, tractile, pliable, pliant
高分秘诀	▲ educationalist n. 教育学家

716. dull [dʌl] [dull] ☆★★★★

adj. 钝的，感觉或理解迟钝的	All work and no play makes Jack a dull boy.
	只工作不玩耍，聪明孩子也变傻。
同义字词	blunt, unsharpened, stupid, obtuse
高分秘诀	▲ no play 不休息

drill ~ duplicate

717. dumb [dʌm] [dumb] ☆☆★★★

adj. 哑的，愚蠢的

You can share your secret with me, and you know I'm as dumb as an oyster.
你可以把秘密告诉我，我会守口如瓶。

同义字词　mute, stupid, foolish, dense
反义字词　clever, bright, intelligent, wise
高分秘诀　▲ as dumb as an oyster 很少讲话，沉默不语

718. dump [dʌmp] [dump] ☆★★★★

v. 倾倒，丢弃

Maybe we can dump our surplus inventory on foreign countries.
或许我们可以向外国倾销剩余库存品。

n. 垃圾场

Turn left at the end of the road, then you'll see a refuse dump out there.
在这条路的尽头向左转，你就会看到一个垃圾场。

同义字词　discard, empty, throw away, garbage dump
高分秘诀　▲ surplus **adj.** 过剩的，多余的
　　　　　▲ inventory **n.** 存货 **v.** 盘点
　　　　　▲ refuse dump 垃圾场

719. duplicate [`djuplɪkɪt] [du·pli·cate] ☆☆★★★

v. 复写，复制

We got the duplicated notices of the meeting from the committee.
我们接到委员会发的会议通知副本。

adj. 完全一样的，复制的

I think she really loves you, see she gave you a duplicate key of her house.
我认为她真的爱你，看看她给了你一套她房子的钥匙。

n. 副本，复制品

You'd better keep a duplicate of the contract.
你最好储存一份合约的副本。

同义字词　reproduce, copy, identical
高分秘诀　▲ committee **n.** 委员会
　　　　　▲ contract **n.** 契约，合约

720. durable [ˈdjurəbl] [du·ra·ble] ☆☆★★★

adj. 持久的，耐用的

Those fatigue clothes were made of very durable material.
这些工作服是用非常耐用的料子做的。

同义字词　lasting, long-lasting, enduring, permanent

高分秘诀　▲ fatigue clothes 工作服，工装
　　　　　▲ material **n.** 材料，原料

721. dwarf [dwɔrf] [dwarf] ☆☆☆★★

n. 侏儒

The doctors said that some children who remain as dwarfs just because they lack a particular hormone.
医生说有些孩子长不高是因为他们身上缺少一种特殊的荷尔蒙。

v. （使）显得矮小，使相形见绌

The skyscraper dwarfs all the other buildings in the city.
这座摩天大楼使城市里其他的建筑物都显得矮小。

同义字词　midget, runt, shrimp, gnome

高分秘诀　▲ particular **adj.** 特定的，某一的
　　　　　▲ hormone **n.** 荷尔蒙，激素
　　　　　▲ skyscraper **n.** 摩天大楼

722. dwell [dwɛl] [dwell] ☆☆★★★

v. 居住，生活于

It's not good for you to dwell on past failures.
你老是想着过去的失败，这可不好。

同义字词　inhabit, live, reside

高分秘诀　▲ dwell on 老是想着
　　　　　▲ failure **n.** 失败，不成功

723. dynamic [daɪˈnæmɪk] [dy·nam·ic] ☆★★★★

adj. 动力的，动态的

I wonder why she always has a dynamic mind.
我在想为什么她总是头脑灵活。

同义字词　vigorous, animate

反义字词　static, undynamic

高分秘诀　▲ wonder **v.** 想知道，问自己

Ee 托福 TOEFL iBT

托福(TOEFL)的测验对象为母语为非英语的人
申请入学美加地区大学或研究所时,托福成绩单是必备文件之一。

- n. 名词
- v. 动词
- adj. 形容词
- adv. 副词
- prep. 介词
- art. 冠词
- pron. 代词
- aux. 助词
- conj. 连词

Ee 托福 TOEFL iBT

托福(TOEFL)的测验对象为母语为非英语的人
申请入学美加地区大学或研究所时,托福成绩单是必备文件之一。

724. eager [`igə] [ea·ger] ☆★★★★

adj. 渴望的,热心的	I know everybody is eager for success, but only few could persevere to the end. 我知道每个人都渴望成功,但只有少数人能坚持到最后。
同义字词	avid, enthusiastic, zealous, desirous, keen
反义字词	uneager, aloof, indifferent
高分秘诀	▲ be eager for 渴望 ▲ to the end 到最后,始终

725. eccentric [ɪk`sɛntrɪk] [ec·cen·tric] ★★★★★

adj. 古怪的(人),异常的(人)	Don't be an eccentric guy, or people will laugh at you. 不要当古怪的人,否则人们会嘲笑你。
n. 古怪的人,异常的人	The girl is kind of an eccentric. 这个女孩是个有点古怪的人。
同义字词	strange, odd, queer, unusual, abnormal
反义字词	common, normal, general, ordinary
高分秘诀	▲ laugh at 嘲笑,取笑

726. eclipse [ɪ`klɪps] [e·clipse] ★★★★★

n. 日食,月食	According to the newspaper, there would be an annular eclipse tomorrow. 根据报纸,明天有日环食。
v. 盖过,遮蔽	The moon gradually eclipses the sun. 月亮渐渐地遮住太阳。
同义字词	outshine, overshadow
衍生字词	▲ solar eclipse 日食 ▲ lunar eclipse 月食
高分秘诀	▲ annular eclipse (日)环食 ▲ gradually adv. 逐步地,渐渐地

eager ~ education

727. ecological [ˌɛkə`lɑdʒɪkəl] [e·co·lo·gi·cal] ☆★★★★

adj. 生态的; 生态学的

We have to take measures to deal with the dangerous ecological effects of industry.
我们必须采取措施处理工业对生态的危害。

| 同义字词 | bionomic, bionomical, ecologic |
| 高分秘诀 | ▲ dangerous **adj.** 有危险的，危险的
▲ ecological effect 生态学效应 |

728. economical [ˌikə`nɑmɪkəl] [e·co·no·mi·cal] ★★★★★

adj. 经济的, 节俭的

My grandmother was economical with cooking oil when cooking.
外婆烹饪时总是用很少的油。

同义字词	thrifty, saving
反义字词	extravagant, luxurious, uneconomical
高分秘诀	▲ cooking oil 食用油

729. edible [`ɛdəbl] [e·di·ble] ☆★★★★

adj. 可食用的

We all know that some mushrooms are edible.
我们都知道有些蘑菇是可食用的。

同义字词	eatable, comestible
反义字词	inedible, uneatable
高分秘诀	▲ mushroom **n.** 蘑菇

730. edifice [`ɛdəfɪs] [e·di·fice] ☆★★★★

n. 宏伟的建筑物

Have you ever seen the Victorian edifice in your life?
你见过维多利亚式的建筑物吗？

| 衍生字词 | ▲ skyscraper **n.** 摩天大楼
▲ volcanic edifice 火山机体 |
| 高分秘诀 | ▲ Victorian **adj.** 维多利亚时代的; **n.** 维多利亚时代的人 |

731. education [ˌɛdʒʊ`keʃən] [ed·u·ca·tion] ★★★★★

n. 教育, 培养

I think the government should take measures to improve the education, which should be geared to the children's needs and abilities.
我认为政府应该改善教育，以适应儿童的需要和能力。

| 同义字词 | upbringing, instruction, teaching, training, breeding |

| 高分秘诀 | ▲ gear to 调整（某物）使其适合……
▲ ability n. 能力，力量 |

732. efface [ɪˋfes] [ef·face] ☆☆★★★

v. 擦掉,抹去	It's impossible to efface the impression from my mind. 我不可能把这个印象从心中抹去。
同义字词	erase, obliterate, rub out
高分秘诀	▲ impossible adj. 不可能的，办不到的 ▲ impression n. 印象；看法，感觉

733. effective [ɪˋfɛktɪv] [e·ffec·tive] ★★★★★

adj. 有效的, 生效的	Fortunately, those methods have proved quite effective. 幸运的是那些方法证明是有效的。
同义字词	efficient, productive, efficacious, effectual
高分秘诀	▲ fortunately adv. 幸运地，幸亏 ▲ quite adv. 完全地，整体地，十分地

734. efficient [ɪˋfɪʃənt] [ef·fi·cient]

| adj. 生效的, 有效率的 | We have to take measures to make the heating system more efficient.
我们必须采取措施提升暖气设备的效率。 |
| 高分秘诀 | ▲ heating system 暖气系统，加热装置 |

735. eject [ɪˋdʒɛkt] [e·ject] ★★★★★

v. 喷出, 喷射	Stay away from the volcano, you know it would eject lava and ashes sometimes. 离那座火山远点，它有时会喷出熔岩和灰。
同义字词	emit, discharge, expel, force out, drive out
高分秘诀	▲ stay away from 离……远点，躲避…… ▲ volcano n. 火山 ▲ lava n. （火山喷发的）熔岩 ▲ ash n. 灰，灰烬

736. elaborate [ɪˋlæbərɪt] [e·la·bo·rate] ★★★★★

| adj. 精细的, 精心的 | The elaborate painting was too much for me.
画这样一幅精致的水彩画是我能力所不及的。 |

efface ~ element

v. 详细阐述	Don't worry, the points what I mentioned would be elaborated in the book. 不用担心，我刚才提到的几点会在书中详细阐述。
同义字词	detailed, complicated, detail, expound
反义字词	abbreviate, abridge, contract
高分秘诀	▲ painting n. 水彩画，油画 ▲ be too much for 非某人能力所及

737. elastic [ɪˈlæstɪk] [e·las·tic] ☆★★★★

adj. 有弹力的，有弹性的	As we all know that sponges are elastic. 我们都知道海绵有弹性。
n. 松紧带，橡皮圈	The elastic in my pants has gone. 我裤子的松紧带坏了。
同义字词	flexible, pliable, pliant, elastic ban, rubber band
反义字词	inelastic, stiff, rigid
高分秘诀	▲ sponge n. 海绵 ▲ pants n. 裤子，短裤

738. election [ɪˈlɛkʃən] [e·lec·tion] ★★★★★

n. 选举，当选	As we all know that presidential elections are held every four years in America. 我们都知道美国总统选举每四年举行一次。
高分秘诀	▲ presidential adj. 总统的，总统选举的

739. elegant [ˈɛləgənt] [e·le·gant] ★★★★★

adj. 优美的，文雅的	I'm falling in love with her, and you know she has a strikingly elegant and graceful bearing. 我想我爱上她了，她风采高雅又迷人。
同义字词	refined, exquisite, graceful
高分秘诀	▲ fall in love 爱上，来电 ▲ strikingly adv. 醒目地，引人注目地 ▲ graceful adj. 优美的，文雅的，得体的 ▲ bearing n. 举止，风度

740. element [ˈɛləmənt] [e·le·ment] ★★★★★

n. 成分，要素	To us, honesty, industry and kindness are elements of a good person. 对我们来说，诚实、勤奋和善良是一个好人的要素。

|同义字词| component, constituent, factor

|高分秘诀| ▲ honesty **n.** 诚实，正直，坦诚
▲ industry **n.** 勤奋，勤劳
▲ kindness **n.** 亲切，仁慈，好意

741. elevate [ˈɛləˌvet] [e·le·vate] ★★★★★

v. 举起，抬高　　I think it's your inspiring speech that elevated the audience.
我认为是你那振奋人心的谈话鼓舞了听众。

|同义字词| raise, heave, lift

|高分秘诀| ▲ inspiring **adj.** 鼓舞人的，使人感兴趣的
▲ speech **n.** 说话，演讲

742. elicit [ɪˈlɪsɪt] [e·lic·it] ☆★★★★

v. 得出，探出　　I tried my best to elicit the truth from him, but failed.
我试图从他那里得到真相，但是没有成功。

|同义字词| provoke, draw out, secure

|高分秘诀| ▲ try one's best 尽最大努力
▲ fail **v.** 失败

743. eligible [ˈɛlɪdʒəbl] [el·i·gi·ble] ☆★★★★

adj. 合格的，有资格的　　In most countries, people who are of eighteen and above are eligible to vote.
在大多数国家，年满十八岁或以上的人都有投票表决权。

|同义字词| entitled, qualified, suitable

|高分秘诀| ▲ vote **n.** / **v.** 投票，表决

744. eliminate [ɪˈlɪməˌnet] [e·li·mi·nate] ★★★★★

v. 消除，排除　　I was eliminated from the competition in the second round.
我在第二轮比赛中被淘汰了。

|同义字词| eradicate, abolish, rule out, remove

|反义字词| add, involve

|高分秘诀| ▲ competition **n.** 比赛，竞争
▲ second round 第二轮

elevate ~ elusive

745. elite [eˋlit] [e·lite] ☆★★★★

n. 精英, 中坚分子   I don't have chance to argue with those elites.
我没有机会和那些精英们争辩。

- 同义字词: elitegroup
- 高分秘诀: ▲ argue with 与……争辩，争论

746. elliptical [ɪˋlɪptɪkl] [el·lip·tical] ☆☆☆★★

adj. 椭圆的, 省略的   The teacher told us the path which the Earth rounds the sun is elliptical.
老师告诉我们地球绕太阳的轨道是椭圆形的。

- 同义字词: elliptic, egg-shaped, oval, oval-shaped
- 高分秘诀:
  ▲ path **n.** 轨迹，路径
  ▲ round **v.** 绕行

747. elongate [ɪˋlɔŋ͵get] [e·lon·gate] ☆☆☆★★

v. 延长, 伸长   I can't recognize which one is you from the photo, see all the faces are to elongated.
我认不出照片中哪个是你，因为这些脸都被拉长了。

- 同义字词: lengthen, extend, prolong, stretch
- 反义字词: contract, shrink
- 高分秘诀:
  ▲ recognize **v.** 认出，识别出
  ▲ photo **n.** 照片，相片

748. eloquent [ˋɛləkwənt] [e·lo·quent] ☆★★★★

adj. 善于表达的, 雄辩的   My parents are quite satisfied with my boyfriend, for he is eloquent and humorous as well.
父母对我男朋友很满意，因为他口才好又幽默。

- 同义字词: expressive, persuasive, well-spoken
- 高分秘诀:
  ▲ be satisfied with... 对……感到满意
  ▲ humorous **adj.** 富幽默感的
  ▲ as well 也，还有

749. elusive [ɪˋlusɪv] [e·lu·sive] ★★★★★

adj. 难以找到的, 难捉摸的   It's quite common that boys like to pursue elusive girls.
男孩们喜欢追求那些让人难以捉摸的女孩。

同义字词	baffling, subtle, evasive
反义字词	pellucid, simple
高分秘诀	▲ common adj. 普遍的，常见的 ▲ pursue v. 追求

750. emancipate [ɪˈmænsəˌpet] [e·man·ci·pate] ☆★★★★

v. 解放, 释放

It's Abraham Lincoln who emancipated the Negros from slavery.
林肯把黑人从奴隶制度下解放出来。

| 同义字词 | liberate, free, release, manumit |
| 高分秘诀 | ▲ Abraham Lincoln 亚伯拉罕·林肯
▲ Negro n. 黑种人，黑人；adj. 黑人的
▲ slavery n. 奴隶制度，奴隶身份 |

751. embarrass [ɪmˈbærəs] [em·bar·rass] ★★★★★

v. 使尴尬, 使窘迫

My father's drunken behavior embarrassed me badly.
父亲醉后的举止真让我难堪。

| 同义字词 | humiliate, shame, abash |
| 高分秘诀 | ▲ drunken adj. 酒醉的
▲ behavior n. 行为，举止，态度
▲ badly adv. 非常，在很大程度上 |

752. embellish [ɪmˈbɛlɪʃ] [em·bel·lish] ☆★★★★

v. 装饰, 美化

The dress which embellished with lace and ribbons are very beautiful.
那件有花边和缎带的连衣裙真的很漂亮。

| 同义字词 | adorn, beautify, ornament, decorate |
| 高分秘诀 | ▲ lace n. 蕾丝，花边
▲ ribbon n. 带，缎带，丝带 |

753. emblem [ˈɛmbləm] [em·blem] ☆★★★★

n. 象征, 标志

To us the olive branch is the emblem of peace.
对我们来说，橄榄枝是和平的象征。

| 高分秘诀 | ▲ olive branch 橄榄枝 |

emancipate ~ embryo

754. embody [ɪmˋbɑdɪ] [em·bod·y] ☆★★★★

v. 表现，象征   The Statue of Liberty embodies the spirit of freedom.
自由女神像体现热爱自由的精神。

同义字词   express, incarnate, include, incorporate

高分秘诀
▲ Statue of Liberty 自由女神像
▲ freedom **n.** 自由，自主，自由权

755. emboss [ɪmˋbɔs] [em·boss] ☆☆★★★

v. 装饰，浮雕（图案）   The silver bracelet is embossed with a design of dragon.
这个银手镯上刻有龙的浮雕图案。

同义字词   stamp, boss

高分秘诀
▲ silver **n.** 银；银器
▲ bracelet **n.** 手镯
▲ dragon **n.** 龙

756. embrace [ɪmˋbres] [em·brace] ☆★★★★

v. 拥抱，包含   It seemed that he was reluctant to embrace my suggestion of a return to the status quo ante.
他似乎不情愿接受我提出的恢复以前状况的建议。

同义字词   include, take up, hug, enfold, accept, take

反义字词   reject, refuse

高分秘诀
▲ reluctant **adj.** 不情愿的，勉强的
▲ suggestion **n.** 建议，意见
▲ status quo ante （拉丁）原状，以前状况

757. embroider [ɪmˋbrɔɪdɚ] [em·broi·der] ☆☆★★★

v. 刺绣，装饰   Could you spare some time to embroider a pillow cover for me?
你能否能抽点时间帮我绣一个枕头套？

同义字词   decorate, adorn, embellish

高分秘诀   ▲ pillow cover 枕头套

758. embryo [ˋɛmbrɪo] [em·bry·o] ☆★★★★

n. 胚胎，事物的萌芽期   We know nothing about the project at present, for it's still at the embryo stage.
目前我们对这个计划无从所知，因为它仍在酝酿阶段。

同义字词   conceptus, fertilized egg

高分秘诀	▲ project n. 项目，计划，方案
	▲ at present 目前，现下

759. emerge [ɪˋmɝdʒ] [e·merge] ★★★★★

v. 出现，浮现	Since the sun emerged from behind a cloud, we felt much warmer.
	太阳从云层后面钻出来，我们感到暖和多了。
同义字词	come forth, spring up, appear
高分秘诀	▲ emerge from 露出，浮现

760. emigrant [ˋɛməgrənt] [em·i·grant] ☆★★★★

n. (从本国移往他国的)移民	The American police repatriated those illegal emigrants back to their country.
	美国警方将这批非法移民遣返回国。
同义字词	migrate, emigre, outgoer
高分秘诀	▲ repatriate v. 把（某人）遣送回国，遣返
	▲ illegal adj. 不合法的，违法的

761. eminent [ˋɛmənənt] [e·mi·nent] ☆★★★★

adj. 著名的，显著的	As is known to us, Churchill was one of the world's most eminent statesmen.
	正如我们所知，丘吉尔是世界上最卓越的政治家之一。
同义字词	distinguished, notable, prominent, famous, outstanding
反义字词	nameless, unknown
高分秘诀	▲ Churchill 丘吉尔（英国首相、政治家、作家）
	▲ statesman n. 政治家

762. emit [ɪˋmɪt] [e·mit] ☆★★★★

v. 发出，放射	Some animals, such as dogs, their bodies couldn't emit perspiration.
	有些动物，比如狗，他们的身体不会出汗。
同义字词	give off, send out
高分秘诀	▲ such as 像，例如
	▲ perspiration n. 汗水，流汗

emerge ~ empty

763. emotion [ɪˋmoʃən] [e·mo·tion] ★★★★★

n. 情感, 感情

Usually this kind of utterance could reveal your emotions.
通常这种语调能暴露出你的感情。

同义字词: feeling, mood, sentiment

高分秘诀:
▲ utterance **n.** 说话模式, 语调
▲ reveal **v.** 显示, 泄露

764. emphasize [ˋɛmfəˌsaɪz] [em·pha·size] ★★★★★

v. 强调, 加强语气

Here I have to emphasize the necessity for preserving our natural resources again.
在此, 我必须再次强调保护自然资源的必要性。

同义字词: stress, underscore, highlight, underline

高分秘诀:
▲ necessity **n.** 必要性, 迫切需要
▲ preserve **v.** 保护, 维持
▲ natural resources 天然资源

765. employ [ɪmˋplɔɪ] [em·ploy] ★★★★★

v. 用, 使用

There is an old saying goes well, if you suspect a man, don't employ him; if you employ a man don't suspect him.
有句谚语说得好："疑人莫用, 用人不疑。"

同义字词: use, apply, hire, engage

反义字词: fire, dismiss, force out

高分秘诀:
▲ go well 说得好, 说得对
▲ suspect **v.** 怀疑, 不信任

766. empty [ˋɛmptɪ] [emp·ty] ★★★★★

adj. 空的, 空洞的

An empty sack cannot stand upright.
空袋不能直立。(无钱寸步难行。)

v. 腾空, 倒空

The man emptied the bottle of red wine.
这位男人把那瓶红酒喝完了。

同义字词: vacant, clean out, vacate

反义字词: fill up, make full

223

高分秘诀	▲ sack n. 麻袋，包
	▲ upright adj. 直立的，垂直的
	▲ red wine 红葡萄酒

767. enact [ɪnˋækt] [en·act] ☆★★★★

v. 通过（法案），演出

You know that Susan enacted the role of heroine in the play.
你知道的，苏珊担任了这出戏的女主角。

| 同义字词 | legislate, perform, act out |
| 高分秘诀 | ▲ heroine n. 女主角，女英雄 |

768. encase [ɪnˋkes] [en·case] ☆★★★★

v. 装入，包住

He looks like a million dollars, for his body was encased in shining armour.
他全身披着闪亮的铠甲，看上去棒极了。

同义字词	embed, enclose, incase
高分秘诀	▲ look like a million dollars 样子很神气，气宇轩昂
	▲ shining adj. 发光的，发亮的
	▲ armour n. 盔甲，铁甲

769. enclose [ɪnˋkloz] [en·close] ☆☆★★★

v. 装入，附入

I enclose her photograph with this letter, and hope you can get it.
我把她的照片放在这封信里，希望你能收到。

| 同义字词 | surround, envelop, encircle, inclose |
| 高分秘诀 | ▲ photograph n. 照片，相片 |

770. encompass [ɪnˋkʌmpəs] [en·com·pass] ☆☆★★★

v. 包括，包含

We have no chance to escape from the city, for the enemy encompassed it.
我们没有机会逃出，因为敌人已经包围了这座城市。

| 同义字词 | include, embrace, surround, circle |
| 高分秘诀 | ▲ escape from 逃避，逃出 |

771. encounter [ɪnˋkaʊntə] [en·coun·ter] ★★★★★

v. 遇到，遭遇

During my English learning, I encountered so many difficulties, but I never quit.
在我的英语学习过程中，虽然我遇到很多困难，但我从来没有放弃。

enact ~ endeavor

同义字词	face, confront, meet, come across
高分秘诀	▲ quit v. 停止，放弃

772. encourage [ɪnˈkɜrɪdʒ] [en·cour·age] ★★★★★

v. 鼓励，激励

It's better to form a system of inducement to encourage workers.
建立员工奖励制度，以此激励员工。

同义字词	activate, stimulate
高分秘诀	▲ system n. 系统，体系 ▲ inducement n. 刺激，鼓励

773. encroach [ɪnˈkrotʃ] [en·croach] ☆★★★★

v. 侵犯，侵占

I think it would be better if the new law doesn't encroach on the rights of the citizens.
我认为如果新法律不侵犯公民的权益就会更好。

同义字词	intrude, invade, infringe, trespass
高分秘诀	▲ encroach on 侵犯，蚕食 ▲ right n. 权利 ▲ citizen n. 公民，国民，市民，平民

774. endanger [ɪnˈdendʒɚ] [en·dan·ger]   ★★★★★

v. 危及，危害

What you've done would endanger your freedom and even your life.
你的所作所为将断送自己的自由，甚至生命。

同义字词	threaten, jeopardize, imperil
高分秘诀	▲ freedom n. 自由，自主

775. endeavor [ɪnˈdɛvɚ] [en·dea·vor] ★★★★★

v. 尝试，努力

Don't worry, I'll endeavor to ascertain my mother's mind.
别担心，我会努力弄清楚妈妈的想法。

n. 努力，尽力

Please make every endeavor to arrive punctually, for the boss hates people being late.
请尽量准时到达，因为老板最讨厌别人迟到。

同义字词	seek, try, attempt, strive, effort
高分秘诀	▲ ascertain v. 弄清，确定，查明 ▲ punctually adv. 如期地，准时地

776. endow [ɪnˈdaʊ] [en·dow] ☆★★★★

v. 捐赠，赋予

It's the American merchant who endows this university.
这所大学是这位美国商人捐资建造的。

同义字词　grant, award, donate, bequeath, contribute

高分秘诀　▲ American **adj.** 美国的，美国人的；**n.** 美国人
　　　　　▲ merchant **n.** 商人

777. endure [ɪnˈdjʊr] [en·dure] ★★★★★

v. 承受，忍受

Usually people can't endure seeing animals cruelly treated.
通常大家不能容忍动物受虐。

同义字词　tolerate, bear, stand, suffer, last

高分秘诀　▲ senior citizen 老年人
　　　　　▲ cruelly **adv.** 残酷地，残暴地

778. energetic [ˌɛnəˈdʒɛtɪk] [en·er·ge·tic] ★★★★★

adj. 精力充沛的，积极的

It would be very interesting to be an energetic campaigner.
做一名积极的活动家一定很有趣。

同义字词　active, up-and-coming, brisk, vigorous, gumptious

反义字词　lethargic, unenergetic

高分秘诀　▲ interesting **adj.** 令人感兴趣的，有趣的
　　　　　▲ campaigner **n.** 从军者，竞选者，出征者

779. engage [ɪnˈgedʒ] [en·gage] ★★★★★

v. 从事于，占用

Finally I found this ship is engaged in pelagic fishery.
最后我发现这艘船用于远洋渔业。

同义字词　absorb, employ, hire, occupy

高分秘诀　▲ pelagic fishery 远洋捕鱼（业）

780. engrave [ɪnˈgrev] [en·grave] ☆★★★★

v. 雕刻，铭记

The bowlder was engraved with his name and the date of his birth.
玉石上刻着他的名字和生日。

同义字词　enchase, carve, grave, inscribe

高分秘诀　▲ bowlder **n.** 玉石

781. enhance [ɪnˈhæns] [en·hance] ☆★★★★

v. 提升，增加

If you want to drive at over 300 miles per hour, you have to enhance engine power.
如果你想每小时开到三百英里，你就得加大马力。

同义字词: improve, heighten, raise, strengthen, increase

高分秘诀:
▲ miles per hour 每小时英里数
▲ engine power 发动机功率

782. enlighten [ɪnˈlaɪtn̩] [en·light·en] ☆★★★★

v. 启发，开导

He thought his mission is to enlighten the ignorant.
他认为自己的任务就是启发那些无知者。

同义字词: edify, irradiate, inspire, arouse, infuse

高分秘诀:
▲ mission **n.** 使命，任务，天职
▲ ignorant **adj.** 无知的，愚昧的

783. enormous [ɪˈnɔrməs] [e·nor·mous] ☆★★★★

adj. 巨大的，极大的

He just put all his heart on it, and totally overlooked the enormous risks involved.
他一心专注在这件事上，完全忽略其中牵涉的极大危险。

同义字词: tremendous, huge, massive, vast, giant, colossal

反义字词: tiny, diminutive

高分秘诀:
▲ totally **adv.** 完全，整个地，全部地
▲ overlook **v.** 忽视

784. enrage [ɪnˈredʒ] [en·rage] ☆★★★★

v. 激怒，使暴怒

That man's arrogance enraged me.
那个男人的傲慢让我十分恼怒。

同义字词: infuriate, anger, inflame, madden, provoke

高分秘诀:
▲ arrogance **n.** 傲慢，自大，自负

785. enrich [ɪnˈrɪtʃ] [en·rich] ☆★★★★

v. 使富有，使富裕

As we all know fertilizers can enrich the soil, but we seldom realize that they can do harm to the soil as well.
大家都知道肥料可以使土壤肥沃，但很少人意识到肥料也会给土壤带来危害。

同义字词	make rich, richen, improve, enhance
高分秘诀	▲ fertilizer **n.** 肥料，化肥 ▲ as well 也，还有

786. ensemble [ɑnˋsɑmbl] [en·sem·ble] ☆☆★★★

n. 全体，整体	Those retired workers formed an amateur ensemble. 这些退休工人成立了一个小型的业余合唱团。
同义字词	aggregate, tout ensemble, troupe, choir
高分秘诀	▲ retired worker 退休工人 ▲ amateur **adj.** 业余的，非正职的，外行的

787. entangle [ɪnˋtæŋgl] [en·tan·gle] ☆★★★★

v. 使纠缠，套住入	Unfortunately the politician got entangled in the scandal. 不幸的是这位政治家被卷入到这件丑闻中。
同义字词	involve, snare, trap, entwine, twist
反义字词	unsnarl, straighten out, disentangle
高分秘诀	▲ politician **n.** 政治家，政客 ▲ get entangled in 陷入（困境）

788. enterprising [ˋɛntɚˏpraɪzɪŋ] [en·ter·pris·ing] ☆★★★★

adj. 有进取心的，有事业心的	It's very enterprising of you to start up your own business. 你开创自己的事业真是很有魄力。
同义字词	venturesome, ambitious, industrious
反义字词	nonenterprising, unenterprising
高分秘诀	▲ start up （使）开始运转，开始

789. entertain [ˏɛntɚˋten] [en·ter·tain] ☆★★★★

v. 娱乐，款待	I like his company, for I was always entertained by his humorous stories. 我喜欢他的陪伴，因为他的幽默故事总是使我很开心。
同义字词	amuse, delight, host, treat
高分秘诀	▲ humorous **adj.** 富幽默感的，滑稽的，诙谐的

ensemble ~ envelop

790. enthusiasm [ɪnˋθjuzɪˌæzəm] [en·thu·si·asm] ☆★★★★

n. 热情，热心，巨大的兴趣

From his expression, I can tell he felt no enthusiasm for the idea.
从他的表情能看出来，他对这个主意不感兴趣。

[同义字词] intense interest, gusto, ebullience

[高分秘诀] ▲ expression **n.** 表情，表现
▲ feel no enthusiasm for 对某事不热心／没有兴趣

791. entitle [ɪnˋtaɪtl] [en·ti·tle] ☆☆★★★

v. 取名叫，叫作

Sorry, the ticket you bought doesn't entitle you to travel first class.
对不起，这张票无法让你坐头等舱。

[同义字词] name, designate, authorize, empower, title

[高分秘诀] ▲ first class 头等舱

792. entrench [ɪnˋtrɛntʃ] [en·trench] ☆★★★★

v. 用壕沟围绕或保护，牢固地确立

Ageism is entrenched in American society.
年龄歧视在美国社会根深蒂固。

[同义字词] intrench, defend

[高分秘诀] ▲ ageism **n.** 对老年人的歧视
▲ be entrenched in 盘踞在

793. envelop [ˋɛnvəˌləp] [en·ve·lop] ☆★★★★

v. 把……包住，裹住

Gloom enveloped the boss, no one dare to ask the reason.
沮丧的气氛笼罩着老板，没有人敢上前问原因。

n. 信封

When he saw the envelop, he crumpled it and tossed it into the wastebasket.
他一看到信封就把它捏成一团，随手扔进废纸篓里。

[同义字词] enclose, encase, enwrap, enfold, wrap, envelope, mailer

[高分秘诀] ▲ gloom **n.** 忧郁，沮丧，失望
▲ crumple **v.** 压皱，弄皱
▲ wastebasket **n.** 废纸篓

794. envious ['ɛnvɪəs] [en·vi·ous] ★★★★★

adj. 嫉妒的

Don't be envious of others' success, just go for it by yourself.
不要嫉妒别人的成功，要自己努力去争取成功。

同义字词: covetous, jealous

高分秘诀:
▲ success **n.** 成功，成就
▲ go for it 大胆一试，努力争取

795. envision [ɪn'vɪʒən] [en·vi·sion] ☆★★★★

v. 想象，预想

Sometimes we can envision that our life as in some sense "dull."
有时我们可以想象自己的生活在某种意义上是"平淡的"。

同义字词: picture, visualize, envisage, fancy

高分秘诀:
▲ in some sense 在某种意义上
▲ dull **adj.** 平淡的

796. ephemeral [ɪ'fɛmərəl] [e·phe·me·ral] ☆★★★★

adj. 短暂的，转瞬即逝的

Normally the stream flow can be fallen into three types: ephemeral, intermittent, and perennial.
通常河流可以分为三类：季节性河流、间歇性河流和常流河。

同义字词: short-lived, transitory, transient

反义字词: perpetual, permanent, eternal, perennial

高分秘诀:
▲ stream flow 流量，射流
▲ intermittent **adj.** 间歇的，断断续续的
▲ perennial **adj.** 经常出现的，长期的，持久的

797. epidemic [ˌɛpɪ'dɛmɪk] [e·pi·de·mic] ★★★★★

n. 传染病，流行病

Nowadays doctors can be able to get rid of the smallpox epidemic.
现在医生能制止天花传染。

adj. 流行的，传染性的

As we all know that buying goods on the installment plan has already become epidemic in these years.
我们知道最近十分流行用分期付款的方法购物。

同义字词: plague, contagious, infectious, catching

envious ~ equitable

高分秘诀
▲ smallpox n. 天花
▲ installment plan 分期付款模式

798. epoch [`ɛpək] [e·poch] ☆☆★★★

n. 时代，新时代
The invention of the bulb marked a new epoch in history.
电灯的发明标志着历史上一个新时代的开始。

同义字词　period of time, era, age

高分秘诀
▲ invention n. 发明，创造
▲ bulb n. 电灯泡

799. equal [`ikwəl] [e·qual] ★★★★★

adj. 相等的，同样的
Not every one has an equal talent or equal ability.
每个人的天资和能力并不一样。

v. 等于，比得上
I have to admit that no one equals you in English. 我必须承认，论英语没有人能和你比。

同义字词　same, identical, match, parallel, rival

高分秘诀
▲ talent n. 天资，才能
▲ ability n. 能力，才智

800. equip [ɪ`kwɪp] [e·quip] ★★★★★

v. 装备，配备
All rooms are equipped with air conditioners and computers.
每个房间都配有空调和电脑。

同义字词　furnish, provide, fit

高分秘诀　▲ equip with 用……装备起来，使具备

801. equitable [`ɛkwɪtəbl] [e·qui·ta·ble] ☆★★★★

adj. 公平的，公正的
Maybe usher in a more secure, stable, peaceful and equitable world order is everybody's dream.
也许创立一个更为安全、稳定、和平与平等的国际秩序是每个人的梦想。

同义字词　just, fair, even

反义字词　unfair, unjust, inequitable

高分秘诀
▲ secure adj. 安全的，放心的，可靠的
▲ peaceful adj. 和平的，没有战争的

802. equivalent [ɪˋkwɪvələnt] [e·qui·va·lent] ☆★★★★

n. 等同品	Do you believe that an egg is the equivalent of a pound of meat? 你相信一个鸡蛋的营养相当于一磅肉的说法吗？
adj. 相等的，等同的	Say something, you know sometimes silence is equivalent to an allowance. 说话呀，你知道缄默有时等于允许。
同义字词	interchangeable, comparable, tantamount
高分秘诀	▲ pound **n.** 磅，英磅 ▲ silence **n.** 沉默，无声 ▲ allowance **n.** 宽容，允许

803. eradicate [ɪˋrædɪˌket] [e·ra·di·cate] ☆☆★★★

v. 根除，杜绝	The general manager would have to put himself at the head of this reform movement, brutally eradicate the rot. 总经理必须领导这场改革，大刀阔斧革除弊端。
同义字词	completely destroy, eliminate, extirpate, exterminate, get rid of
高分秘诀	▲ at the head of 在……的最前面 ▲ reform **n.** 改革，改良 ▲ brutally **adv.** 残忍地，野蛮地 ▲ rot **n.** 腐烂，腐朽

804. erect [ɪˋrɛkt] [e·rect] ☆★★★★

v. 使树立，建立	A monument would be erected in the proximity of the town hall next year. 明年市政厅旁会建立一个纪念碑。
adj. 竖立的，直立的	I was attracted to those soldiers' erect posture. 我被这些站得笔直的士兵吸引住了。
同义字词	construct, stand, set up, upright, vertical
反义字词	demolish, destroy, ruin, pull down
高分秘诀	▲ monument **n.** 纪念碑 ▲ in the proximity of 在……附近 ▲ town hall 市政厅 ▲ attract to 吸引 ▲ soldier **n.** 士兵，军人 ▲ posture **n.** 姿势，姿态

equivalent ~ escape

805. erode [ɪˈrod] [e·rode] ☆★★★★

v. 腐蚀，侵蚀

The cliff face was smooth, for it was eroded by sea over years.
峭壁的表面光滑，因为它长年累月被海水冲刷着。

同义字词　wear away, corrode, wash away, eat away

高分秘诀　▲ cliff **n.** 悬崖，峭壁
▲ smooth **adj.** 光滑的，平坦的

806. erratic [ɪˈrætɪk] [er·ra·tic] ☆★★★★

adj. 不规则的，无常的

An erratic mind jump from one idea to another, you can't rely on such person.
心神不定的人反复无常，你不能依赖这种人。

同义字词　fickle, changeable, uncertain

高分秘诀　▲ rely on 倚赖，信赖

807. erupt [ɪˈrʌpt] [e·rupt] ★★★★★

v. 喷出，爆发

Don't worry, an extinct volcano can no longer erupt.
别担心，死火山不会再爆发。

同义字词　explode, burst out, break out

高分秘诀　▲ extinct volcano 死火山
▲ no longer 不再，已不

808. escalate [ˈɛskəˌlet] [es·ca·late] ☆★★★★

v. 逐步升高，逐步增强

It's difficult for us to detect the plague, besides it can quick escalate in severity.
瘟疫很难检测，而且会快速升级加重其严重性。

同义字词　rise, increase, intensify, step up

高分秘诀　▲ detect **v.** 发现，发觉，查明
▲ plague **n.** 瘟疫
▲ severity **n.** 严重，剧烈

809. escape [əˈskep] [es·cape] ☆★★★★

v. 逃脱，逃走

If the net is not strong enough, then the whale would have chance to escape.
如果网不够结实，鲸鱼就有机会逃脱。

同义字词　flee, get away, elude, avoid, evade

| 高分秘诀 | ▲ whale n. 鲸，鲸鱼 |

810. escort [ˈɛskɔrt] [es·cort] ★★★★★

v. 护送，护卫	How about you escort this young lady to the dancing party tomorrow? 你明天陪这位小姐去参加舞会好吗？
n. 护送（者），护卫队	From newspaper, I knew that the gold bullion was transported under police escort. 从报纸上得知，金块在警方的护送下已经运走。
同义字词	chaperon, accompany, bodyguard
衍生字词	▲ destroyer escort 护航驱逐舰 ▲ escort boat 救生船 ▲ escort fighter 护航战斗机 ▲ escort service 伴游服务
高分秘诀	▲ young lady 小姐，女士 ▲ gold bullion 金块

811. essential [ɪˈsɛnʃəl] [es·sen·tial] ★★★★★

adj. 绝对必要的，本质的	I think there is no essential difference between the two drafts. 我认为这两份草稿没有本质上的不同。
同义字词	necessary, critical, vital, indispensable, fundamental
反义字词	inessential, nonessential
高分秘诀	▲ difference n. 差别，差异 ▲ draft n. 草稿，草案，草图

812. estate [ɪsˈtet] [es·tate] ★★★★★

n. 地产，财产	I wonder why he waived his claim to the estate. 我不知道他为什么放弃对财产的请求权。
同义字词	property, land, demesne, inheritance, heritage
衍生字词	▲ real estate 房地产 ▲ legal estate 合法不动产 ▲ estate agent 房地产经纪人
高分秘诀	▲ waive claim 放弃要求

813. estimate [ˈɛstəˌmet] [es·ti·mate] ★★★★★

| v. 估计，评估 | It's impossible for us to estimate someone's abilities at the first sight.
我们不可能在第一次见面的时候就评定某人的才能。 |

escort ~ evaluate

| 同义字词 | assess, appraise, evaluate, gauge, figure |
| 高分秘诀 | ▲ at the first sight 一看到……就，第一次见面 |

814. eternal [ɪˋtɝn!] [e·ter·nal] ★★★★★

adj. 永恒的，永远的	The eternal is made of passing moments, and passing moments become eternal. 永恒是稍纵即逝的瞬间构成的，而每一个稍纵即逝的瞬间都会化成永恒。
同义字词	everlasting, endless, interminable, eonian
反义字词	momentary, temporary, transient
衍生字词	▲ Eternal Alexander 亚历山大大帝（罗马皇帝） ▲ eternal city 永恒之城（罗马城的别称）
高分秘诀	▲ passing adj. 经过的，短暂的 ▲ moment n. 瞬间，片刻，时刻

815. ethic [ˋɛθɪk] [eth·ic] ★★★★★

n. 道德标准，行为准则	I really appreciate that you are a staunch supporter of the work ethic. 对于你坚决支持勤奋工作的道德原则，我真的很欣赏。
同义字词	moral principle, rule of conducts
高分秘诀	▲ staunch adj. 可信赖的，可靠的，忠诚的

816. ethnic [ˋɛθnɪk] [eth·nic] ★★★★★

adj. 种族的，部落的	There are 56 ethnic groups in China. 中国有五十六个民族。
同义字词	racial, ethnical
衍生字词	▲ ethnic composition 种族构成
高分秘诀	▲ ethnic group 民族，种族群

817. evaluate [ɪˋvæljʊ͵et] [e·va·lu·ate] ★★★★★

v. 评价，估价	I asked an expert to evaluate the old pottery. 我请一位行家评估这个古老的陶器。
同义字词	judge, appraise, assess, valuate, value
高分秘诀	▲ expert n. 专家，能手 ▲ pottery n. 陶器，陶器器皿

818. evaporate [ɪˈvæpəˌret] [e·va·po·rate] ☆★★★★

v. (使)蒸发，消失

He told me that the dead body's fluids would evaporate gradually, and then the skin would blister all over.
他告诉我尸体的体液会逐渐蒸发，然后围皮肤会起水泡。

同义字词　vaporize, disappear, vanish, fade away

衍生字词　▲ evaporated milk 炼乳，脱水牛奶
▲ evaporating dish 蒸发皿

高分秘诀　▲ fluid **n.** 液体，流体
▲ blister **v.** （使）起水泡

819. eventual [ɪˈvɛntʃʊəl] [e·ven·tu·al] ★★★★★

adj. 最终的，结果的

Before we make a decision, we have to consider the eventual results.
在我们做决定前，必须考虑到最终的结果。

同义字词　ultimate, final

高分秘诀　▲ make a decision 决定下来，作出决定
▲ result **n.** 结果，效果，后果

820. evidence [ˈɛvədəns] [e·vi·dence] ★★★★★

n. 证据，证词

We don't have enough evidence to prove him guilty.
我们没有足够的证据证明他有罪。

同义字词　proof, testimony

高分秘诀　▲ prove **v.** 证明
▲ guilty **adj.** 内疚的，有罪的

821. eviscerate [ɪˈvɪsəˌret] [e·vis·cer·ate] ☆☆★★★

v. 取出内脏，除去菁华

The press eviscerated the book to make it inoffensive to the prime minister.
报社删去该书的精华以取悦首相。

同义字词　disembowel, resect

高分秘诀　▲ press **n.** 出版社，新闻社
▲ inoffensive **adj.** 无害的，不伤人的，没恶意的
▲ prime minister 总理，首相

evaporate ~ exaggerate

822. evoke [ɪ`vok] [e·voke] ☆☆★★★

v. 引起，激起

I think it's your comment that evoked the listeners' protest.
我认为是你的评论激起了听众的抗议。

| 同义字词 | bring out, arouse, prompt, kick up |

| 高分秘诀 | ▲ comment **n.** 评论，意见 |
| | ▲ protest **n.** 抗议，反对 |

823. evolve [ɪ`vɑlv] [e·volve] ★★★★★

v. 进化，发展

It's said that the modern automobile evolved from the horse and buggy.
据说现代汽车是由单马马车演化而来的。

同义字词	develop, grow, advance, progress
反义字词	degenerate, deteriorate
高分秘诀	▲ automobile **n.** 汽车
	▲ evolve from 从……逐渐发展成
	▲ buggy **n.** 轻便马车，小机动车

824. exact [ɪg`zækt] [ex·act]   ★★★★★

adj. 精确的，准确的

It's hard to tell her exact age from her appearance.
单从她的外表看，很难说出她的确切年龄。

v. 要求，索取

The gangster exacted ransoms for their hostages.
歹徒绑架人质以索取赎金。

同义字词	precise, accurate, claim, demand
高分秘诀	▲ appearance **n.** 外表，外貌
	▲ gangster **n.** 匪徒，歹徒
	▲ ransom **n.** 赎金
	▲ hostage **n.** 人质

825. exaggerate [ɪg`zædʒəˌret] [e·xag·ge·rate] ★★★★★

v. 夸大，夸张

Being a doctor, you have to tell the truth, never exaggerate, never conceal.
作为一名医生，你必须实事求是，既不能夸大其词，也不能遮遮掩掩。

同义字词	overstate, magnify, overdo, enlarge, stretch
反义字词	minimize, understate
高分秘诀	▲ conceal **v.** 隐蔽，隐瞒，遮住

826. exalted [ɪgˈzɔltɪd] [ex·alt·ed]   ☆☆★★★

adj. 崇高的，高贵的	After years of efforts, he was exalted to the eminent station. 经过多年的努力，他终于被提携到显赫的地位。	
	同义字词	superior, noble, lofty
	反义字词	inferior, ignoble
	高分秘诀	▲ eminent adj. 知名的，受人尊崇的 ▲ station n. 地位，身份

827. excavate [ˈɛkskəˌvet] [ex·ca·vate]   ☆☆★★★

v. 挖掘，挖出	The archaeologists happened to excavate a buried city last year. 去年考古学家偶然发掘出一个被埋在地下的城市。	
	同义字词	unearth, dig out, dig up
	反义字词	bury, inter
	高分秘诀	▲ archaeologist n. 考古学家 ▲ buried adj. 埋入地下的，嵌入地下的

828. exceed [ɪkˈsid] [ex·ceed]   ★★★★★

v. 超越，胜过	Because of exceeding the speed limit, my father was taken to the police station. 因为超速驾驶，爸爸被带到警察局。	
	同义字词	beat, surpass, excel, outdo, cap
	高分秘诀	▲ speed limit 速度限制 ▲ police station 警察局

829. excel [ɪkˈsɛl] [ex·cel]

v. 胜过，擅长	The boy excels at badminton. 男孩很会打羽毛球。	
	同义字词	be superior, stand out, surpass, exceed
	高分秘诀	▲ excel at（在某一活动方面）表现杰出，擅长于 ▲ badminton n. 羽毛球运动

830. exception [ɪkˈsɛpʃən] [ex·cep·tion]   ☆★★★★

n. 例外，除外	To learn a new language, you have to know that there is no grammatical rule that has no exception. 学一种新语言，你必须知道没有一条语法规则是没有例外的。	

exalted ~ excite

衍生字词	▲ exceptional adj. 异常的，杰出的
	▲ exceptionally adv. 特殊地，异常地
	▲ excepting... 除……之外
高分秘诀	▲ grammatical rule 语法规则

831. excess [ɪk`sɛs] [ex·cess] ☆★★★★

adj. 过度的，额外的	If you want to get rid of your excess weight, you have to work out every day. 如果你不想减肥，必须每天健身。
n. 过量，超过	The profit of last month was in excess of ten thousand yuan. 上个月的利润超过一万元。
同义字词	extra, superfluous, additional, surplus, nimiety, overabundance
衍生字词	▲ excess baggage 超重行李 ▲ excess cash 过剩现金
高分秘诀	▲ get rid of 除掉，去掉 ▲ excess weight 超重 ▲ work out 锻炼 ▲ profit n. 利润，收益，盈利 ▲ in excess of 多于，超出

832. exchange [ɪks`tʃendʒ] [ex·change] ★★★★★

v. 兑换，交换	It's not worth to exchange honor for wealth. 牺牲荣誉以换取财富是不值得的。
n. 兑换，交换	I think an exchange of opinions is helpful for us. 我觉得相互交换意见对我们来说是有益的。
同义字词	interchange, trade in, swap, change
衍生字词	▲ exchange contract 外汇成单，外汇合约
高分秘诀	▲ honor n. 荣誉，光荣 ▲ wealth n. 财产，财富 ▲ opinion n. 意见，看法，主张 ▲ helpful adj. 给予帮助的，有益的

833. excite [ɪk`saɪt] [ex·cite] ☆★★★★

v. 刺激，使兴奋	What he said about the ghost excited my interest. 他所说的有关鬼魂的事引起了我的兴趣。
同义字词	arouse, incite, provoke, stimulate

| 反义字词 | calm down, calm 平静 |
| 高分秘诀 | ▲ ghost **n.** 鬼，幽灵 |

834. exclaim [ɪks`klem] [ex·claim] ☆★★★★

v. 呼喊，惊叫	"It's unfair!" He exclaimed angrily. "这不公平！"他气愤地喊道。
同义字词	call, shout, clamor, cry out
高分秘诀	▲ unfair **adj.** 不公正的，不公平的 ▲ angrily **adv.** 愤怒地，生气地

835. exclude [ɪk`sklud] [ex·clude] ☆★★★★

v. 把……排除在外，排斥	I can't believe it that I was excluded from the party. 我简直不敢相信我被拒绝在聚会之外。
同义字词	leave out of, keep out of, reject, exclude from
高分秘诀	▲ exclude from 把……排斥（排除）于……之外

836. excursion [ɪk`skɝʒən] [ex·cur·sion] ☆☆★★★

n. 远足，旅行，游览	They all anticipate much pleasure from their school excursion. 他们都期盼学校的远足很好玩。
同义字词	trip, journey, jaunt, outing, tour
衍生字词	▲ excurse **v.** 远足，短程旅行，游览 ▲ excursion boat 游览船 ▲ excursion fare 旅游票价 ▲ excursion ticket 优待票，游览客票
高分秘诀	▲ anticipate **v.** 期望 ▲ pleasure **n.** 愉快，快乐，满足 ▲ school excursion 学校远足

837. excuse [ɪk`skjuz] [ex·cuse] ★★★★★

v. 原谅	She is too uncompromising to excuse our mistakes. 她坚决不肯原谅我们的错误。
n. 借口，理由	I doubt he manufactured an excuse for being late. 我怀疑他为迟到编造借口。
同义字词	forgive, pardon, alibi, pretext

exclaim ~ exempt

高分秘诀 ▲ uncompromising adj. 不妥协的，坚定的
▲ manufacture v. 制造；捏造

838. execute [`ɛksɪˌkjut] [ex·e·cute]   ★★★★★

v. 执行；将……处死
The soldier had no choice but to execute the colonel's orders.
士兵除了执行上校的命令外，别无选择。

同义字词 carry on, administer, perform
衍生字词 ▲ executive adj. 行政的
高分秘诀 ▲ colonel n. 上校

839. exemplary [ɪɡˋzɛmpləri] [ex·em·pla·ry]   ☆☆★★★

adj. 模范的，典范的
They all thought that my love life could be described as exemplary.
他们认为我的爱情生活堪称典范。

同义字词 modeled, ideal, paradigmatic
高分秘诀 ▲ love life 爱情生活
▲ describe as 描述为

840. exemplify [ɪɡˋzɛmpləˌfaɪ] [ex·em·pli·fy]   ☆☆★★★

v. 例证，作为……的例子
You'd better to offer some materials to exemplify this theory.
你最好提供一些题材举例说明这种理论。

同义字词 illustrate, instance, demonstrate
高分秘诀 ▲ material n. 素材，资料

841. exempt [ɪɡˋzɛmpt] [ex·empt]   ☆☆★★★

v. 使免除，豁免
My bad eyesight exempted me from military service.
我因视力不好而免服兵役。

adj. 被免除……的，被豁免的
According to the law, school property is exempt from all taxes.
依据法律，学校财产免除一切赋税。

同义字词 excuse, free, let off, nontaxable
反义字词 taxable, nonexempt
高分秘诀 ▲ eyesight n. 视力
▲ military service 兵役
▲ tax n. 税，税额

842. exert [ɪgˋzɝt] [ex·ert] ☆★★★★

v. 运用，行使

I exerted all my influence to make my parents accept my point.
我用尽一切影响力使父母接受我的观点。

同义字词　cause, apply, exercise, wield, put forth

高分秘诀　▲ exert influence on 对……施加影响

843. exhale [ɛksˋhel] [ex·hale] ☆★★★★

v. 呼出，呼气

Sitting on the sofa, the man was blissfully exhaling his first puff.
坐在沙发上，男人乐悠悠地吐出第一口烟。

同义字词　breathe out, emanate, expire

反义字词　inhale, breath in, inspire

高分秘诀
▲ sofa **n.** 沙发
▲ blissfully **adv.** 福祉地，充满喜悦地
▲ puff **n.** 一缕（烟、蒸汽等）

844. exhaust [ɪgˋzɔst] [ex·haust] ☆★★★★

n. 排气，排气装置

I think something must have gone wrong with truck's exhaust system.
我认为卡车的排气系统出了故障。

v. 用尽，耗尽

After a whole day's work, I'm completely exhausted.
一天工作下来，我精疲力竭。

同义字词　use up, consume, play out, spend, knock out, wear out, tire

反义字词　replenish, supply

高分秘诀
▲ truck **n.** 货车，卡车
▲ exhaust system 排气系统

845. exhibit [ɪgˋzɪbɪt] [ex·hi·bit] ★★★★★

v. 展现，展览

I'm quite surprised that she exhibited an unexpected graciousness on the party.
我非常吃惊，在晚会上她的表现出人意料地有礼貌。

n. 展览品，陈列品

The exhibits in the Great Exhibition covered and contained everything.
世界博览会上的展览可以说包罗万象。

exert ~ expand

	同义字词	display, show
	高分秘诀	▲ unexpected adj. 没有料想到的，意外的 ▲ graciousness n. 礼貌，和蔼 ▲ the Great Exhibition 世界博览会

846. exhilarate [ɪɡˋzɪləˌret] [ex·hi·la·rate] ☆★★★★

v. 使高兴, 使兴奋	Sometimes bold designs could exhilarate the audiences' imagination. 有时候大胆的设计可以激发观众的想象力。
同义字词	stimulate, inebriate, thrill, gladden, enliven, cheer, brighten
高分秘诀	▲ design n. 设计，布局 ▲ imagination n. 想象力，空想，想象

847. exorbitant [ɪɡˋzɔrbətənt] [ex·or·bi·tant] ☆★★★★

adj. (价格、索价) 过高的, 过度的	The mother was disturbed to find that the toy's price was exorbitant for the size of her purse. 那位母亲因买不起价格过高的玩具，心里感到不安。
同义字词	expensive, excessive
反义字词	cheap, inexpensive, threepenny
高分秘诀	▲ disturbed adj. 扰乱的 ▲ toy n. 玩具，玩物

848. exotic [ɛɡˋzɑtɪk] [ex·ot·ic] ★★★★★

adj. 异国的, 外来的	From the pictures we saw a lot of exotic birds from the jungle of Africa. 从照片上我们看到来自非洲热带雨林的各种珍禽。
同义字词	foreign, alien
反义字词	indigenous, endemic, native
衍生字词	▲ exotic dancer 脱衣舞娘 ▲ exotic material 特殊材料
高分秘诀	▲ jungle n. (热带) 丛林，密林 ▲ Africa n. 非洲

849. expand [ɪkˋspænd] [ex·pand] ★★★★★

v. 扩大, 膨胀	Look, the petals of the flowers which expanded in the sunshine are very beautiful. 看，花瓣在阳光下绽开，真是美丽极了。

同义字词	dilate, spread out, extend, enlarge
反义字词	contract, shrink
高分秘诀	▲ petal n. 花瓣 ▲ sunshine n. 阳光，日光

850. expedite [ˈɛkspɪˌdaɪt] [ex·pe·dite] ☆★★★★

v. 加快，派出

The businessman demanded to expedite shipment as much as possible.
那位商人要求尽可能加速装运。

| 衍生字词 | ▲ expedition n. 远征，探险，考察，迅速
▲ expeditor n. 畅通保证员，催料员
▲ expeditionary force 远征军 |
| 高分秘诀 | ▲ businessman n. 商人，实业家
▲ expedite shipment 加速发货 |

851. expel [ɪkˈspɛl] [ex·pel] ☆★★★★

v. 驱逐，开除

I doubt whether the antidote is strong enough to expel the poison.
我怀疑这种解毒药药力够不够驱散毒素。

| 同义字词 | oust, kick out, drum out |
| 高分秘诀 | ▲ antidote n. 解药，解毒剂
▲ poison n. 毒药，毒物 |

852. expenditure [ɪkˈspɛndɪtʃɚ] [ex·pen·di·ture] ☆☆★★★

n. 支出，花费

I have no choice but to adjust my expenditures to my income.
我除了量入而出外，别无选择。

同义字词	consumption, expending, outgo, outlay
反义字词	income, revenue
衍生字词	▲ expendable adj. 可消耗的，可牺牲的 ▲ expense n. 消耗，花费，费用
高分秘诀	▲ adjust to 调整，调节 ▲ income n. 收入，所得

expedite ~ explode

853. expertise [ˌɛkspɚˈtiz] [ex·per·tise] ★★★★★

n. 专门知识, 专门技能

I think if you could learn the expertise well and improving practise ability, then you would find a content job after graduation.

我认为只要你学好专业知识并且提升实践能力，毕业后就能找到令人满意的工作。

| 同义字词 | skill, expert knowledge, special knowledge |

| 衍生字词 | ▲ combat expertise 战斗专家 |

| 高分秘诀 | ▲ practise ability 实践能力
▲ content **adj.** 满意的，满足的
▲ graduation **n.** 毕业 |

854. expire [ɪkˈspaɪr] [ex·pire] ★★★★★

v. 期满, 到期, 呼气

I guess their licences have expired.
我猜想他们的执照已过期。

| 同义字词 | end, become due |

| 反义字词 | breath in, inhale, sniff |

| 高分秘诀 | ▲ licence **n.** 许可证，执照 |

855. explicit [ɪkˈsplɪsɪt] [ex·pli·cit] ☆★★★★

adj. 明确的, 清楚的

You can ask the doctor to tell you the explicit instructions on when and how to take the medicine.

你可以请医师告诉你该何时以及如何服药。

| 同义字词 | clear, distinct, unequivocal |

| 反义字词 | implicit, inexplicit, vague |

| 高分秘诀 | ▲ instruction **n.** 讲授，使用说明，操作指南 |

856. explode [ɪkˈsplod] [ex·plode] ★★★★★

v. 爆炸, 爆发

The boy exploded with rage when he heard the bad news.
听到这个坏消息，男孩勃然大怒。

| 同义字词 | blow up, detonate, burst |

| 高分秘诀 | ▲ explode with 突然发作
▲ rage **n.** 狂怒，盛怒 |

857. exploit [ˈɛksplɔɪt] [ex·ploit] ★★★★★

v. 利用，开发
They spend much time and money on exploiting oil reserves.
他们不惜花时间和金钱开发石油储藏。

n. 业绩，功绩
I really admire you, you always performing many daring exploits.
我真的很佩服你，你总有许多大胆的举动。

同义字词　utilize, make use of, advance, tap

高分秘诀　▲ oil reserves 石油储量
　　　　　▲ perform **v.** 执行，履行
　　　　　▲ daring **adj.** 勇敢的，无畏的

858. explore [ɪkˈsplor] [ex·plore] ★★★★★

v. 探险，勘探
Those scientists explored the Arctic regions last year.
去年，那些科学家们探测了北极地带。

同义字词　investigate, probe, search, research

高分秘诀　▲ Arctic **adj.** 北极的，北极区的
　　　　　▲ region **n.** 地区，地带，区域，范围

859. exposition [ˌɛkspəˈzɪʃən] [ex·po·si·tion] ☆★★★★

n. 博览会，讲解
They are planning to hold an international exposition next year.
他们计划明年召开一次国际博览会。

同义字词　exhibition, fair, expo, explanation, presentation

高分秘诀　▲ international **adj.** 国际的，国家间进行的

860. expose [ɪkˈspoz] [ex·pose] ★★★★★

v. 曝光，暴露
Fortunately, their scheme was exposed before it happens.
幸运的是，他们的阴谋在事发前曝光。

同义字词　disclose, reveal, uncover, unmask

反义字词　cover, hide, conceal

高分秘诀　▲ fortunately **adv.** 幸运地，幸亏
　　　　　▲ scheme **n.** 阴谋，诡计

exploit ~ exterminate

861. express [ɪkˋsprɛs] [ex·press] ★★★★★

v. 表达，表示
First I have to express my gratitude for your kindness.
首先对于你的好意我必须要表示感谢。

n. 快车，快递
You can take the No.8 special express to Paris.
你可以乘坐开往巴黎的第8号特快车。

同义字词　describe, show, present, dispatch, express mail, expressage

衍生字词　▲ express train 特快列车

高分秘诀　▲ gratitude **n.** 感激，感谢
　　　　　▲ special express 特快列车

862. extend [ɪkˋstɛnd] [ex·tend] ★★★★★

v. 延长，扩大
Normally the tourist season extends from May till October.
通常旅游季节从五月延续到十月。

同义字词　stretch, prolong, increase, expand, enlarge

反义字词　contract, shrink

高分秘诀　▲ normally **adv.** 通常，正常地
　　　　　▲ tourist season 旅游季节
　　　　　▲ May **n.** 五月
　　　　　▲ October **n.** 十月

863. exterior [ɪkˋstɪrɪɚ] [ex·te·ri·or] ★★★★★

n. 外部，外表
My father is a good man with rough exterior.
我父亲是一个外表粗野的好人。

adj. 外面的，外部的
The exterior surface of the hollow ball is black.
这个空心球的外表是黑色的。

同义字词　outside, appearance

反义字词　interior, internal, inter

高分秘诀　▲ rough **adj.** 粗野的，粗鲁的
　　　　　▲ exterior surface　外表面
　　　　　▲ hollow **adj.** 空的，凹的

864. exterminate [ɪkˋstɝməˏnet] [ex·ter·mi·nate] ☆★★★★

v. 根除，灭绝
You can buy some spray to exterminate the termites.
你可以买些喷剂消灭这些白蚁。

同义字词	eliminate, annihilate, eradicate, extirpate, kill off
高分秘诀	▲ spray n. 喷剂 ▲ termite n. 白蚁

865. external [ɪk`stɝnəl] [ex·ter·nal] ☆★★★★

adj. 外部的，表面的	Read the instruction, it says that this ointment is for external use only. 看看说明书，上面说此药膏仅供外用。
同义字词	exterior, outer, outside, extraneous
高分秘诀	▲ instruction n. 使用说明书 ▲ ointment n. 软膏，油膏

866. extinct [ɪk`stɪŋkt] [ex·tinct] ★★★★★

adj. 灭绝的，熄灭的	I'm afraid the Northeast Tigers are in danger of becoming extinct. 我担心东北虎有绝种的危机。
同义字词	nonexistent, vanished, dead, past
反义字词	active, extant
衍生字词	▲ extinct volcano 死火山 ▲ extinct species 灭绝物种
高分秘诀	▲ Northeast Tiger 东北虎 ▲ in danger of 在危险中，有……的危险

867. extinguish [ɪk`stɪŋgwɪʃ] [ex·tin·guish] ☆★★★★

v. 使熄灭，扑灭	A few of minutes later, the firemen arrived at the spot and extinguished the blaze quickly. 几分钟后，消防人员赶到现场迅速把火势扑灭了。
同义字词	put out, crush out, snuff out, blow out
反义字词	kindle, light, ignite
高分秘诀	▲ a few of 少许，少数 ▲ fireman n. 消防队员 ▲ arrive at 到达，来到 ▲ blaze n. 火焰，烈火

868. extol [ɪk`stol] [ex·tol] ☆☆☆★★

v. 赞扬，赞美	I hate to listen to Mike talking about his girlfriend, this guy extolled his girlfriend to the skies. 我讨厌听麦克谈他女友，这家伙把他的女友捧上了天。

external ~ exuberant

| 同义字词 | praise, exalt, laud, glorify |
| 高分秘诀 | ▲ to the sky 无保留地，过分地 |

869. extract [ɪkˋstrækt] [ex·tract] ☆★★★★

| v. 拔出，榨取 | I guess this substance is extracted from seaweed.
我猜想这种物质是从海藻中提取出来的。 |
| n. 摘录，引用，浓缩物 | How about you read several extracts from the poem for me?
你为我朗读这首诗的其中几段好吗？ |

| 同义字词 | distil, draw out, squeeze, essence, substance |
| 高分秘诀 | ▲ substance n. 物质
▲ seaweed n. 海草，海藻
▲ poem n. 诗，韵文 |

870. extraordinary [ɪkˋstrɔrdənɛrɪ] [ex·tra·or·di·nary] ☆★★★★

| adj. 特别的，非凡的 | The girl is really an extraordinary genius.
这个女孩真是非比寻常的天才。 |

同义字词	exceptional, remarkable, outstanding, extraordinaire
反义字词	general, ordinary
高分秘诀	▲ genius n. 天才人物

871. extremity [ɪkˋstrɛmətɪ] [ex·trem·i·ty] ☆☆★★★

| n. 极端，绝境 | The old man was driven crazy by the extremity of pain.
极度的痛苦使老人发狂。 |

同义字词	end, utmost point, limit
衍生字词	▲ extremism n. 极端性，极端主义 ▲ extremist n. 极端主义者，偏激的人
高分秘诀	▲ crazy adj. 疯狂的，发疯的 ▲ pain n. 痛苦，身体某部分的疼痛（不适）

872. exuberant [ɪgˋzjubərənt] [ex·u·ber·ant] ☆☆★★★

| adj. 兴高采烈的，（植物）繁茂的 | After returning, she gave us an exuberant account of the exhibition.
回来之后，她向我们生动地介绍了那场展览的情形。 |

| 同义字词 | high-spirited, lively, ebullient |

| 高分秘诀 | ▲ return v. 返回，回来
▲ account n. 记述，描述，报道
▲ exhibition n. 展览，展览会 |

873. eyewitness [ˈaɪˈwɪtnɪs] [eye·wit·ness] ☆★★★★

n. 目击者	It's the eyewitness's testimony that proves that the guy was guilty. 目击者的证词证明那个人有罪。
同义字词	witness, spectator
衍生字词	▲ eyewitness memory 视觉记忆 ▲ eyewitnesser n. 目击报道，见证者的报告
高分秘诀	▲ testimony n. 证词，证明，证据 ▲ guilty adj. 内疚的，有罪的

Ff 托福 TOEFL iBT

托福(TOEFL)的测验对象为母语为非英语的人
申请入学美加地区大学或研究所时,托福成绩单是必备文件之一。

- n. 名词
- v. 动词
- adj. 形容词
- adv. 副词
- prep. 介词
- art. 冠词
- pron. 代词
- aux. 助词
- conj. 连词

Ff 托福 TOEFL iBT

托福(TOEFL)的测验对象为母语为非英语的人
申请入学美加地区大学或研究所时,托福成绩单是必备文件之一。

874. fable [ˋfebl] [fa·ble]
☆☆★★★

n. 寓言,神话
The teacher had some reason in telling this fable to the children.
老师讲这个寓言故事给小朋友听是有用意的。

同义字词　fairy tale, myth, allegory, lay, untruth, mendacity

875. fabric [ˋfæbrɪk] [fab·ric]
☆☆★★★

n. 织物,布,架构
I think this water-repellent fabric is better than that one.
我认为这块防水布比那块好。

同义字词　cloth, stuff, material, textile, structure, framework

高分秘诀　▲ water-repellent **adj.** 防水的,拒水的

876. face [fes] [face]
★★★★★

v. 面对
Maybe next year the telephone users will be facing higher bills.
也许明年电话用户将面临电话费涨价的问题。

n. 脸,面孔,外表
I can hardly recognize her, her face is thin and very tanned.
我差点没有认出她来,她现在脸颊消瘦,晒得黑黑的。

同义字词　confront, encounter

衍生字词　▲ face mask 面罩,面具

高分秘诀　▲ telephone use 电话用户
▲ bill **n.** 账单,清单,票据
▲ hardly **adv.** 几乎没有,几乎不
▲ tan **v.** (使)晒成棕褐色

877. facilitate [fəˋsɪlə͵tet] [fa·ci·li·tate]
☆★★★★

v. 使容易,有助于,促进
This new system facilitates the navigation of the seas.
这套新系统促进了海上航行。

fable ~ factual

| 同义字词 | promote, expedite, |
| 反义字词 | alleviate, ease |

高分秘诀
▲ system n. 系统，体系
▲ navigation n. 航行（学），航海（术）

878. facsimile [fæk`sɪməlɪ] [fac·sim·i·le] ☆★★★★

n. 传真, 传真机

Born of the facsimile transceivers has brought many conveniences into the office.
无线电传真机的发明为办公室带来了许多便利。

同义字词　reproduction, duplicate, fax, facsimile machine

衍生字词
▲ facsimile equipment 传真设备
▲ facsimile posting 传真过程

高分秘诀
▲ facsimile transceiver 传真收发两用机
▲ convenience n. 方便，便利

879. faction [`fækʃən] [fac·tion] ☆☆★★★

n. 派别, 宗派

We have to take action to heal the deep divide between the two factions.
我们必须采取措施解除这两个派系之间的隔阂。

同义字词　group, sect, cabal

高分秘诀
▲ take action 采取行动，行动起来
▲ heal v. 调停，消除
▲ divide n. 隔阂，分歧

880. factor [`fæktə] [fac·tor] ★★★★★

n. 元素, 要素

Before taking a decision, you have to analyze the various factors.
在下决定之前，你必须分析各种要素。

同义字词　element, ingredient

高分秘诀
▲ decision n. 决定，决心
▲ various adj. 各种不同的，各种各样的

881. factual [`fæktʃuəl] [fac·tu·al] ☆★★★★

adj. 事实的, 实际的

I hope you could give a factual account of what really happened.
我希望你能实际说明，到底发生了什么事。

同义字词　real, actual

衍生字词　▲ factualist n. 事实主义者

高分秘诀　▲ account n. 记述，描述，报道

882. faculty [ˋfæk|tɪ] [fac·ul·ty] ☆☆★★★

n. 教职工的总称，才能
I astonished that the boy has a great faculty for mathematics.
我很吃惊那个男孩有很强的数学能力。

同义字词　staff, teachers, ability, aptitude

衍生字词
▲ faculty adviser 指导教师
▲ faculty member 教职工
▲ faculty club 教授俱乐部

高分秘诀
▲ astonish v. 使惊讶，使大为吃惊
▲ mathematics n. 数学

883. fade [fed] [fade] ★★★★★

v. 褪色，枯萎
I guess the flowers faded for want of water.
我猜想这些花是因缺水而凋谢的。

同义字词　disappear, die out, evanesce

高分秘诀　▲ for want of 因缺乏

884. faint [fent] [faint] ★★★★★

adj. 微弱的，模糊的
He is going to pass out, for his breathing became faint.
他快要昏倒了，因为他的呼吸变得很微弱。

v. 晕倒，昏倒
When he heard that his daughter got hit by a car, he fainted on the spot.
听到女儿被车撞到时，他一下子晕了过去。

同义字词　dim, hazy, feeble, weak, keel over

反义字词　strong, powerful, clear

高分秘诀
▲ breathing n. 呼吸
▲ daughter n. 女儿
▲ on the spot 立即，当场

885. fair [fɛr] [fair] ★★★★★

adj. 公平的，公正的
I can say I won the game fair and square.
我敢说我赢得这次比赛是公平的。

同义字词　impartial, just, fairish

高分秘诀　▲ fair and square 公正地

886. faithful [`feθfəl] [faith·ful] ★★★★★

adj. 忠实的	As I always said a faithful friend helps in times of trouble. 正如我常说的，一个忠实的朋友在困难时会帮助你。	
同义字词	loyal, devoted	
反义字词	faithless, unfaithful	
衍生字词	▲ faith-cure n. 信仰疗法	
高分秘诀	▲ in time of 在……的时候	

887. fake [fek] [fake] ★★★★★

n. 赝品, 假货	It's quite common to discover several fakes in the art collection. 在艺术收藏品中发现几件赝品是很正常的。
adj. 假的, 伪造的	I was hoodwinked into buying fake diamond. 我被骗买到了假钻石。
同义字词	imitation, counterfeit, disguise, postiche, sham
反义字词	mccoy, the genuine
高分秘诀	▲ several adj. 几个, 数个, 一些
	▲ collection n. 收集, 收藏, 收藏品, 收集的东西
	▲ hoodwink v. 欺诈, 哄骗
	▲ diamond n. 金刚钻, 钻石

888. falcon [`fɔlkən] [fal·con] ☆☆★★★

n. 猎鹰	Though the caracara looks little like a true falcon, it is a member of the falcon family. 虽然这只卡拉卡拉鹰看起来一点都不像真正的猎鹰，但它确实属于猎鹰属。
同义字词	hawk, skystinger, eagle
衍生字词	▲ falconer n. 养猎鹰者, 放鹰狩猎人
	▲ falconry n. 鹰猎, 猎鹰训练术
高分秘诀	▲ caracara n. 卡拉卡拉鹰

889. famine [`fæmɪn] [fam·ine] ☆★★★★

n. 饥荒, 饥饿	I'm glad that those villagers lasted out the famine. 真高兴那些村民们度过饥荒。

同义字词	shortage of food, starvation
反义字词	plenty, abundance
高分秘诀	▲ villager n. 村民 ▲ last out 在困难中坚持下去

890. fanatic [fə`nætɪk] [fa·nat·ic] ☆★★★★

n. 狂热者，入迷者	Most of the boys in my classroom are basketball fanatics. 我们班上大部分的男孩子都是篮球迷。
adj. 狂热的，盲信的	My father always told me there is nothing blinder than fanatic passion. 我父亲总是对我说，再没有比盲从更盲目的。
同义字词	fanatical, crazy, frenetic, excessively enthusiastic
反义字词	uninterested, disinterested
高分秘诀	▲ classroom n. 教室，课堂 ▲ basketball n. 篮球（运动） ▲ blind adj. 盲目的

891. fancy [`fænsɪ] [fan·cy] ★★★★★

adj. 新奇的，精美的	The girl was born with a sliver spoon in her mouth, and she always has so many fancy clothes. 这个含着银汤匙出生的女孩总是有很多精美的服饰。
v. 想象，设想	I couldn't fancy what you did during the whole day. 我真想象不出你一整天都在做什么。
同义字词	elegant, ornate, visualize
高分秘诀	▲ be born with a silver spoon in one's mouth 生于富贵之家，含着银汤匙出生 ▲ during prep. 在……期间，在……之时

892. fantastic [fæn`tæstɪk] [fan·tas·tic] ☆★★★★

adj. 极大的，异乎寻常的	The girl had some fantastic idea that her parents are evil and want to poison her. 这个女孩有个怪异至极的想法，认为她父母很邪恶并且想要毒害她。
同义字词	excellent, outstanding, unusual, incredible
衍生字词	▲ fantasy n. 幻想，白日梦 ▲ fantasia n. 幻想曲，即兴作品

fanatic ~ fasten

高分秘诀
▲ ghost n. 鬼，幽灵
▲ poison v. 毒死，毒杀

893. farce [fɑrs] [farce] ☆☆★★★

n. 笑剧，闹剧

The famous movie star played a shameful role in this farce.
这个著名的电影明星在这场闹剧中扮演了可耻的角色。

同义字词　comedy, farcetta
反义字词　tragedy 悲剧
高分秘诀
▲ famous adj. 著名的，出名的
▲ movie star 电影明星
▲ shameful adj. 可耻的，丢脸的

894. fascinate [ˋfæsn͵et] [fas·ci·nate] ☆★★★★

v. 使着迷，使神魂颠倒

Every time I took my daughter out, she was fascinated by the toy in the shop window.
每次我带女儿出去，她总是被商店橱窗里的玩具所吸引。

同义字词　enchant, attract, enthrall, captivate, enamor
高分秘诀
▲ toy n. 玩具
▲ shop window 橱窗

895. fashion [ˋfæʃən] [fash·ion]

n. 流行，风尚

Purple is quite in fashion this year.
今年很流行紫色。

同义字词　vogue, style, mode
高分秘诀
▲ purple n. 紫色
▲ in fashion 流行的

896. fasten [ˋfæsn̩] [fas·ten] ☆★★★★

v. 使固定，系

Before you ride the horse, please fasten the saddle on its back.
骑马之前，先把马鞍系在马背上。

同义字词　attach, affix, tie
反义字词　loose, unfasten
高分秘诀
▲ ride v. 乘，骑，驾
▲ saddle n. 马鞍，鞍状物

897. fatal [`fetl] [fa·tal] ☆★★★★

adj. 致命的，灾难性的

I'm sorry to know that your father suffered from a fatal disease.
得知你父亲罹患不治之症，我深感遗憾。

同义字词: deadly, mortal, disastrous, fateful

衍生字词:
▲ fatalist n. 宿命论者，听天由命者
▲ fatalistic adj. 宿命论的，听天由命的

高分秘诀:
▲ suffer from 患（某种病），受（某种病痛）折磨
▲ fatal disease 不治之症

898. fateful [`fetfəl] [fate·ful] ☆★★★★

adj. 重大的，灾难性的

I can't help reliving those fateful days over and over in my mind.
我脑子忍不住回想起灾难的那段日子。

同义字词: decisive, critical, crucial

高分秘诀:
▲ relive v. （在想象中）重新过……的生活，再经历
▲ over and over 反复，再三
▲ in one's mind 在某人的脑海里

899. fatigue [fə`tig] [fa·tigue] ★★★★★

n. 疲乏，劳累

I hate to work overtime, for it always leaves me great fatigue.
我讨厌加班，因为那总是让我精疲力竭。

同义字词: weariness, exhaustion, tiredness

反义字词: refreshness, freshness

衍生字词: ▲ fatigue curve 疲劳曲线

高分秘诀: ▲ work overtime 加班

900. fault [fɔlt] [fault] ★★★★★

n. （地质学）断层，过错

A proverb goes well, every man has his faults.
有句谚语说得好："人非圣贤，孰能无过。"

同义字词: crack, defect, flaw, shortcoming

反义字词: merit, virtue

高分秘诀: ▲ proverb n. 谚语，格言

901. flora [ˋflorə] [flo·ra] ☆☆☆★★

n. 植物群

I know nothing about the Neotropical flora and fauna.
对于新热带植物群和动物群我一无所知。

同义字词　botany, plant, vegetation

高分秘诀　▲ neotropical **adj.** 新热带区的

902. favorable [ˋfevərəbl] [fa·vor·a·ble] ☆☆★★★

adj. 有利的，有助的

It's lucky for you to regain a former favorable position.
你重返原本的职位真幸运。

同义字词　propitious, beneficial, well-disposed

反义字词　unfavorable, adverse

高分秘诀　▲ regain **v.** 失而复得，赢回
▲ former **adj.** 以前的

903. feasible [ˋfizəbl] [fea·si·ble] ☆☆★★★

adj. 切实可行的，可能且合理的

You have to ask the boss whether it is feasible to proceed in this manner.
你必须先问老板这样做是否可行。

同义字词　practicable, viable, workable, executable, possible

反义字词　unfeasible, infeasible, impracticable, impossible

高分秘诀　▲ whether **conj.** 是否
▲ proceed **v.** 前进，行进，继续下去
▲ in this manner 如此，照这样

904. feat [fit] [feat] ☆☆★★★

n. 功绩，壮举

Richard Winter's heroic feats made him a legend in his own time.
理察·温特斯的英雄事迹使他成为那个时代的传奇人物。

同义字词　achievement, accomplishment, exploit

高分秘诀　▲ heroic **adj.** 英勇的，英雄的
▲ legend **n.** 传说，传奇故事，传奇人物
▲ in one's time 在自己一生中，一度

905. feeble [ˈfibl] [fee·ble] ☆★★★★

| adj. 虚弱的，衰弱的 | The old man insisted that he was not guilty and even bleated out a feeble excuse.
老人坚持自己无罪，并以微弱的声音说出一个无法令人信服的借口。 |

同义字词	weak, faint, frail
反义字词	intense, strong, tough
衍生字词	▲ feeble-minded 智障的，低能的
高分秘诀	▲ insist v. 坚持认为 ▲ bleat v. 轻声诉说 ▲ excuse n. 理由，辩解

906. feed [fid] [feed] ★★★★★

| v. 喂养，饲养 | Send one of the zoo keepers to feed the tiger.
派一位动物饲养员喂这只老虎。 |
| n. 饲养，饲料 | Sometimes oat and wheat are used as animal feed.
有时候燕麦和小麦都被用来当作牲口饲料。 |

| 同义字词 | forage, food, raise |
| 高分秘诀 | ▲ keeper n. 饲养员，保管人
▲ tiger n. 老虎
▲ wheat n. 小麦 |

907. feminine [ˈfɛmənɪn] [fem·i·nine] ☆★★★★

| adj. 女子气的，适于女子的 | As we all know that there are few feminine members in this committee.
正如我们所知，这个委员会里女性成员很少。 |

同义字词	female
反义字词	masculine, virile
衍生字词	▲ feminism n. 女权运动 ▲ feminist n. 女权主义者 ▲ femicide n. 杀害女人
高分秘诀	▲ member n. 成员，会员 ▲ committee n. 委员会

feeble ~ ferry

908. fend [fɛnd] [fend] ☆☆★★★

v. 独立生活，挡开，避开

Since his father passed away, he has to fend for himself.
他父亲去世了，他不得不自己谋生。

[同义字词] resist, stand

[高分秘诀] ▲ pass away 去世
▲ fend for oneself 自己谋生

909. ferment [`fɝmɛnt] [fer·ment] ☆☆★★★

v. 使发酵，（使）动乱

His rude remarks fermented trouble among the public.
他粗鲁的言语在公众中引起了骚动。

n. 激动, 动乱

During the Great Depression, the whole country was in a state of ferment.
在大萧条期间，整个国家全部处于动乱状态。

[同义字词] agitate, ruffle, stir

[衍生字词] ▲ fermentation **n.** 发酵，激动，纷扰

[高分秘诀] ▲ rude remark 粗鲁的言语
▲ public **n.** 公众，大众，民众
▲ Great Depression 大萧条

910. ferry [`fɛrɪ] [fer·ry] ★★★★★

n. 渡口, 渡船

The girl is standing on the bank, waiting for the ferry to return.
女孩站在岸上，等候渡船返回。

v. 渡运, 运送

There is only one boats ferry people back and forth on that river.
那条河上，只有一艘小船往返为人摆渡。

[同义字词] shuttle, barge, carry, haul, transport

[衍生字词] ▲ ferry boat 渡船，渡轮
▲ ferry bridge 浮桥

[高分秘诀] ▲ bank **n.** （河的）岸，堤
▲ back and forth 来回地

911. fertile [ˋfɝtl] [fer·tile] ★★★★★

adj. 多产的,富饶的

The boy is very clever, he is fertile of imagination.
这个男孩很聪明,想象力也很丰富。

同义字词	rich, fruitful, creative
反义字词	infertile, barren, steril
衍生字词	▲ fertilized egg 受精卵 ▲ fertilizer **n.** 肥料 ▲ ertility **n.** 肥沃,多产,丰富 ▲ fertilizable **adj.** 可受精的
高分秘诀	▲ clever **adj.** 聪明的 ▲ imagination **n.** 想象,空想,想象力

912. fervor [ˏfɝvɚ] [fer·vor] ☆☆★★★

n. 热情,热烈

Speaking of the religious fervor, no one can compare to you.
说起宗教热情,没人比得过你。

同义字词	enthusiasm, passion, fervency
高分秘诀	▲ speak of 谈到,讲到 ▲ religious **adj.** 宗教的,笃信宗教的,虔诚的 ▲ compare to 与……相比

913. festive [ˋfɛstɪv] [fes·tive] ☆★★★★

adj. 欢宴的,节日的

The atmosphere of the party is quite festive and friendly.
宴会的气氛真是欢乐而美好。

同义字词	merry, gay, happy, joyous, jovial
反义字词	gloomy, melancholy
高分秘诀	▲ atmosphere **n.** 气氛,环境 ▲ friendly **adj.** 友好的,和睦的

914. feud [fjud] [feud] ☆☆★★★

n. 世仇,长期不和

The feuds between the two families were deeply seated.
两家之间长期不合。

v. 长期争斗,结仇

I don't think you can make it, for the two families have been feuding for generations.
我想你无法调停,数代以来,这两个家族彼此仇视。

fertile ~ fiction

同义字词	enmity, vendetta, animosity 世仇
衍生字词	▲ family feud 家庭争夺 ▲ internal feud 同室操戈 ▲ blood feud 族仇
高分秘诀	▲ deeply adv. 强烈地，深刻地 ▲ for generations 一连好几代，几代相传

915. feudal [ˋfjudl] [ˈfeu·dal] ☆☆★★★

adj. 封建制度的	According to the history, feudal China was gradually reduced after 1840 to a semicolonial and semifeudal country. 依据历史，一八四○年后，封建的中国逐渐变成半殖民地半封建的国家。
衍生字词	▲ feudal hierarchy 封建等级制度 ▲ feudal society 封建社会 ▲ feudal system 封建制度
高分秘诀	▲ gradually adv. 逐步地，渐渐地 ▲ semicolonial adj. 半殖民地的 ▲ semifeudal adj. 半封建的

916. feverish [ˋfivərɪʃ] [ˈfe·ver·ish] ☆☆★★★

adj. 发烧的，狂热的	Last night you were feverish and rambled in your talk. 昨晚你因发烧而胡说八道。
同义字词	excited, agitated, feverous
高分秘诀	▲ ramble v. 漫谈，说话东拉西扯

917. fiction [ˋfɪkʃən] [ˈfic·tion] ★★★★★

n. 小说，（虚构）故事	The crime he described last night was a complete fiction. 他昨晚讲的那个犯罪事件纯粹是虚构的。
同义字词	story, legend, novel
衍生字词	▲ science fiction 科幻小说 ▲ fictionalize v. 把（历史事件等）编成小说，使小说化
高分秘诀	▲ crime n. 罪，罪行，犯罪 ▲ complete adj. 完全的，完整的

918. fierce [fɪrs] [fierce] ★★★★★

adj. 凶猛的，凶狠的	In the old days, people always said that tyranny is fiercer than a tiger. 过去，人们常说"苛政猛于虎。"

- 同义字词：ferocious, savage, wild
- 反义字词：gentle, meek, quiet
- 高分秘诀：▲ tyranny n. 专横，暴政，苛政

919. file [faɪl] [file] ★★★★★

n. 档案，队列	The file was stapled to some letters. 这个档案和一些信件钉在一起。
v. 归档	Your mission is to file those letters carefully. 你的任务就是把那些信件仔细分类。

- 同义字词：arrange, categorize, classify, sort, document
- 高分秘诀：
  - ▲ staple v. 用订书机钉住
  - ▲ mission n. 任务，使命
  - ▲ carefully adv. 仔细地，小心谨慎地

920. filter [ˈfɪltɚ] [fil·ter] ☆★★★★

v. 过滤	Before you use it, you have to filter out the dirt. 在使用前，你必须滤除尘垢。
n. 过滤器	Would you like to buy a coffee filter for me when you go shopping? 你去逛街的时候帮我买一个咖啡过滤器好吗？

- 同义字词：strain, purify, sift, refine
- 高分秘诀：
  - ▲ filter out 滤除，过滤
  - ▲ dirt n. 污垢，灰尘
  - ▲ coffee n. 咖啡
  - ▲ go shopping 去逛街，去购物

921. finance [faɪˈnæns] [fi·nance] ★★★★★

n. 财政，拨款	She said her major is international finance. 她说她的专业是国际金融。
v. 资助	The schoolmaster is financing for the housing project. 校长正在为住宅计划筹措资金。

fierce ~ fitting

| 同义字词 | funding, pay for, fund, sponsor, support |
| 高分秘诀 | ▲ major n. 专业，主修科目
▲ international finance 国际金融
▲ schoolmaster n. 男校长
▲ housing project 住房建造计划 |

922. finesse [fə'nɛs] [fi·nesse] ☆☆★★★

n. 精密技巧，手腕	Though she is a little girl she managed that situation with great finesse. 虽然只是个小女孩，但对于那个情况，她处理得很高明。
同义字词	delicacy, adroitness, tact, discreetness, diplomacy
高分秘诀	▲ manage v. 办理，设法应付 ▲ situation n. 情势，情况

923. firm [fɝm] [firm] ★★★★★

adj. 结实的，牢固的	I don't think this cupboard is firm enough to stand on. 我觉得这个碗橱不够坚固，不能久用。
同义字词	hard, solid, determined
反义字词	flimsy, fragile
高分秘诀	▲ cupboard n. 碗橱

924. fishy ['fɪʃɪ] [fish·y]   ☆★★★★

adj. 鱼的，腥臭的，可疑的	I'm convinced that there is something fishy about the whole matter. 我觉得这件事有点可疑。
同义字词	shady, suspect, suspicious
高分秘诀	▲ convince v. 使相信，使明白 ▲ matter n. 事情，问题

925. fitting ['fɪtɪŋ] [fit·ting] ☆★★★★

| adj. 适合的，恰当的 | It's a fitting evening for a walk.
这是个适合散步的夜晚。 |
| n. 设备，家具 | If you want to finish it on time, you have to have all the necessary fittings.
如果想及时完成，你就必须拥有齐全的设备。 |

同义字词	apt, proper, equipment, facility
反义字词	unfitting, improper
高分秘诀	▲ on time 按时，准时 ▲ necessary adj. 必要的，必需的

926. fixed [fɪkst] [fixed] ☆★★★★

adj. 固定的，确定的	The guy is enough stubborn, and he has a fixed pattern of behavior. 这家伙很固执，信守自己的一套不变的行为模式。
同义字词	stationary, settled, established
反义字词	floating, unfixed
衍生字词	▲ fixed star 恒星 ▲ fixture n. 固定设备 ▲ fixity n. 固定性，固定物，不变性
高分秘诀	▲ stubborn adj. 顽固的，固执的 ▲ pattern n. 模式，形式 ▲ behavior n. 行为，举止

927. flabby [ˋflæbɪ] [flab·by] ☆☆★★★

adj. （肌肉等）不结实的，松弛的	Stay in shape, or you will be flabby. 保持体形，否则你的肌肉会松弛。
同义字词	flaccid, soft, slack, lax
反义字词	firm, compact
高分秘诀	▲ stay in shape 保持体型

928. flair [flɛr] [flair] ☆☆★★★

n. 天资，才能	By the time he was seven, the boy started to show a flair for the game. 在男孩七岁的时候，他开始展现出在这个运动上的天赋。
同义字词	talent, knack, genius
衍生字词	▲ flair point 识别点，明显的物点
高分秘诀	▲ by the time 到……的时候 ▲ show v. 表现出，显露出

929. flake [flek] [flake] ☆☆★★★

n. 薄片	Suddenly it began to snow big, flat flakes. 突然间开始下起大雪。

fixed ~ flash

同义字词	slice, chip
衍生字词	▲ snowflake n. 雪花 ▲ flaky adj. 薄片的，成片的
高分秘诀	▲ suddenly adv. 意外地，忽然，冷不防 ▲ flat adj. 平的，扁平的

930. flamboyant [flæm`bɔɪənt] [flam·boy·ant] ☆☆★★★

adj. 辉耀的，华丽的	Don't believe this flamboyant charlatan. 不要相信这个夸夸其谈假冒内行的人。
同义字词	showy, ostentatious, florid, flashy
反义字词	faint, grave
衍生字词	▲ flamboyantism n. 过分华丽的格调 ▲ flamboyant Gothic 哥特式的火焰装饰
高分秘诀	▲ charlatan n. 冒充内行者，骗子

931. flare [flɛr] [flare] ☆★★★★

n. 闪光，闪耀	Suddenly I saw a brilliant flare popped off right over my head. 突然一颗耀眼的照明弹在我头顶上炸开了。
v. 闪光，闪耀	The door opened and the breeze flared the candle. 门开了，微风进来，烛光闪动。
同义字词	flash, glare, shine, glow, blaze
衍生字词	▲ flare-path n. 夜间照明跑道
高分秘诀	▲ brilliant adj. 闪光的，明亮的 ▲ pop off 爆炸 ▲ breeze n. 微风，轻风 ▲ candle n. 蜡烛

932. flash [flæʃ] [flash] ☆★★★★

n. 闪光，闪现	Suddenly a flash of lightning crossed the sky. 突然一道闪电划过天空。
v. 闪光，反射	I saw a lighthouse was flashing in the distance. 我看见灯塔在远处发出闪烁的光。
同义字词	flare, spark, glare, sparkle, gleam
衍生字词	▲ flashlight n. 手电筒，闪光灯 ▲ flashbulb n. 闪光灯泡

高分秘诀	▲ lightning n. 闪电
	▲ lighthouse n. 灯塔
	▲ in the distance 在远处，在很远的那边

933. flavor [`flevə] [fla·vor] ★★★★★

n. 味，风味	You may choose your favorite flavor among these chocolates. 你可以从这些巧克力中选择你最喜欢的口味。
v. 加香味于	We always flavor the fish with sugar and vinegar. 我们总是用糖和醋为鱼调味。
同义字词	season, taste, savor, spice
高分秘诀	▲ favorite adj. 中意的
	▲ among prep. 在……中
	▲ chocolate n. 巧克力
	▲ sugar n. 糖
	▲ vinegar n. 醋

934. fleeting [`flitɪŋ] [fleet·ing] ☆☆★★★

adj. 短暂的，飞逝的	I couldn't recall his appearance, for last time I only got a fleeting glimpse of him. 我想不起他长什么样子，因为上次我只是瞥了他一眼。
同义字词	transient, brief, temporary, momentary, transitory
反义字词	permanent 永久的
衍生字词	▲ fleet n. 舰队，船队，军队，机群
高分秘诀	▲ recall v. 回忆起，回想
	▲ glimpse n. 一瞥，一看
	▲ last time 上次

935. flexible [`flɛksəbl] [flex·i·ble] ☆★★★★

adj. 易弯曲的，柔软的	I'm glad that the policy of our company is more flexible than before. 真高兴我们公司的政策比过去灵活多了。
同义字词	pliant, elastic, docile, flexile
反义字词	inflexible, sturdy
高分秘诀	▲ policy n. 政策，方针
	▲ company n. 公司

flavor ~ flounder

936. flicker [ˋflɪkə] [flick·er] ☆★★★★

| v. (通常指灯光) 闪烁, 摇曳 | The electricity has just failed, the boy was still reading by the flickering light of the candle.
停电了，男孩借着闪烁的烛光读书。 |

- 同义字词: twinkle, glint, blink
- 高分秘诀: ▲ electricity n. 电，电流

937. float [flot] [float] ★★★★★

| v. 漂浮, 使漂浮 | In the distance there is an iceberg floating in the sea.
远处一座冰山在海上漂浮。 |

- 同义字词: drift along, drift
- 反义字词: go down, go under, sink
- 衍生字词: ▲ floating adj. 不固定的，流动的，浮动的
- 高分秘诀: ▲ iceberg n. 冰山，流冰

938. flock [flɑk] [flock] ★★★★★

| n. (畜、禽)群, 大量 | I saw a flock of wild geese fly in a V-shaped formation.
我看见一群雁排成人字形一起飞。 |
| v. 蜂拥, 群集 | Birds of a feather flock together.
物以类聚，人以群分。 |

- 同义字词: group, herd, crowd, cluster
- 衍生字词: ▲ flocky adj. 毛茸茸的，毛丛状的
- 高分秘诀:
  ▲ a flock of 一群
  ▲ wild goose 大雁
  ▲ V-shaped formation 人字队
  ▲ feather n. 羽毛

939. flounder [ˋflaʊndə] [floun·der] ☆☆☆★★

| n. 比目鱼 | Have you ever read the Flounder, a novel of new historicism?
你读过《比目鱼》这部新历史主义小说吗？ |
| v. 挣扎，艰难地移动 | The children floundered through deep snow to get home.
孩子们费力地踏着厚重的积雪回家。 |

同义字词	struggle, stumble, have trouble
高分秘诀	▲ novel n. 小说 ▲ historicism n. 历史相对论 ▲ flounder through 挣扎通过，跟跄通过

940. flourish [ˋflɜrɪʃ] [flour·ish] ☆☆★★★

v. 繁荣，茂盛，挥动	This type of plant flourishes in the subtropics. 这种植物在亚热带地区生长茂盛。
同义字词	thrive, prosper
反义字词	decay, decline
高分秘诀	▲ plant n. 植物 ▲ subtropics n. 亚热带地方

941. fluctuate [ˋflʌktʃʊˌet] [fluc·tu·ate] ☆☆★★★

v. 波动，起伏	I don't know what I should do, just fluctuating between hopes and fears. 我不知道该怎么办，只是在希望与失望之间徘徊。
同义字词	alternate, vary, vacillate, waver
衍生字词	▲ fluctuating demand 波动需求 ▲ fluctuating current 波动电流
高分秘诀	▲ Fluctuate between hopes and fears. 忽喜忽忧，在希望与失望之间徘徊。

942. fluent [ˋfluənt] [flu·ent] ☆★★★★

adj. 流利的，流畅的	I think speak fluent English is a distant thing for me. 我认为说一口流利的英语对我来说是遥不可及的事。
同义字词	articulate, eloquent, facile
衍生字词	▲ fluent aphasia 流畅失语症
高分秘诀	▲ distant adj. 远隔的，遥远的

943. fluorescent [fluəˋrɛsn̩t] [flu·o·res·cent] ☆☆☆★★

adj. 荧光的	How about you buy a fluorescent lamp for me when you go shopping? 你去购物的时候帮我买一个荧光灯如何？

flourish ~ foe

同义字词	luminous, bright
衍生字词	▲ fluorescent antibody 荧光抗体
高分秘诀	▲ fluorescent lamp 荧光灯（管），日光灯（管）

944. fluster ['flʌstɚ] [flus·ter]
☆☆☆★★

v. 使忙乱，使慌乱	The old man always get flustered by the honking of horns. 听到汽车喇叭的声音，老人总感到慌乱。
n. 慌乱，不安	I was put in a fluster by knowing that my immediate superior would come this afternoon. 得知我的上司下午要来，我很紧张。
同义字词	perturbation, confusion, confuse, excite
反义字词	calm, compose, quiet
高分秘诀	▲ honk n. 汽车的喇叭声 v. 按喇叭 ▲ horn n. 喇叭，报警器 ▲ immediate superior 直接上司（级）

945. flux [flʌks] [flux]
☆☆☆★★

n. 不断的变动，通量，流动	Gradually I know that all things are in a state of flux. 渐渐地我知道万物都在不断变动。
同义字词	conversion, change, drift, current
衍生字词	▲ flux density 通量密度，辐射流密度 ▲ flux line 通量线，力线 ▲ flux material 焊剂，熔剂
高分秘诀	▲ gradually adv. 逐步地，渐渐地 ▲ be in a state of flux 不断变动

946. foe [fo] [foe]
☆★★★★

n. 敌人，敌军，反对者	A courageous foe is better than a cowardly friend. 勇敢的敌人胜过懦弱的朋友。
同义字词	enemy, adversary, opponent
高分秘诀	▲ courageous adj. 勇敢的，无畏的 ▲ cowardly adj. 胆小的，怯懦的

947. fog [fɑg] [fog] ☆☆★★★

n. 雾

A dim shape loomed up in the dense fog.
浓雾中出现一个模糊的身影。

- 同义字词: haze, mist
- 衍生字词: ▲ foghorn **n.** 雾号（浓雾信号）
- 高分秘诀:
  ▲ dim **adj.** 隐约的，模糊不清的
  ▲ loom up 突然出现
  ▲ dense fog 浓雾

948. fold [fold] [folded] ☆★★★★

v. 折叠

The girl fold up the newspaper in a hurry and put it in her bag.
女孩快速折起报纸，放进自己的袋子里。

n. 折痕，折

You can tear the paper along the fold.
你可以沿着褶痕把纸撕下来。

- 同义字词: pucker, bend back
- 反义字词: unfold, open, spread
- 高分秘诀:
  ▲ fold up 折叠起来
  ▲ newspaper **n.** 报纸
  ▲ in a hurry 匆忙地，迅速地
  ▲ tear **v.** 撕，扯
  ▲ along **prep.** （表示方向）沿着，循着，顺着

949. folly [`fɑlɪ] [fol·ly] ☆☆★★★

n. 愚笨，愚蠢

Be careful! You know sometimes the folly has cost you dearly.
小心！有时候愚蠢会让你损失惨重。

- 同义字词: foolishness, absurdity, stupidity, silliness
- 反义字词: wisdom, wiseness, sagacity
- 高分秘诀:
  ▲ sometimes **adv.** 有时
  ▲ dearly **adv.** 非常，（损失、损坏等）极大地

950. foment [fo`mɛnt] [fo·ment] ☆★★★★

v. 煽动，助长

I know your intention; you just want to foment dissension.
我知道你的企图；你就是想挑拨离间。

fog ~ foray

同义字词	stir up, instigate, agitate
衍生字词	▲ fomenter n. 挑唆者，煽动者 ▲ foment war 煽动战争
高分秘诀	▲ intention n. 意图，打算 ▲ foment dissension 挑拨离间

951. foolish [ˈfulɪʃ] [fool·ish] ☆★★★★

adj. 愚蠢的, 笨的	I can tell you just pretend to be foolish intentionally. 我可以看出来你有意装傻。
同义字词	silly, ridiculous, stupid
反义字词	wise, sagacious
高分秘诀	▲ pretend v. 假装，伪装 ▲ intentionally adv. 有意地，故意地

952. forage [ˈfɔrɪdʒ] [for·age] ☆☆★★★

v. 搜寻（食物）	The commander asked me to go foraging for wood to make a fire. 指挥官叫我搜寻木柴点火。
同义字词	hunt for, search, look, fodder
衍生字词	▲ forager n. 强征（粮食）者，抢劫者 ▲ forage acre 饲料面积单位，饲料亩 ▲ forage cap 军便帽
高分秘诀	▲ commander n. 指挥官 ▲ forage for 搜寻，搜查 ▲ make a fire 生火

953. foray [ˈfɔre] [for·ay] ☆☆★★★

n. 突袭, 偷袭	We would go on foray into enemy territory tonight. 今晚我们准备袭击敌区。
v. 突袭, 偷袭	It's the first time for the laptop company to foray into the computer market. 这家手提电脑公司首次打入电脑市场。
同义字词	assault, maraud, raid, plunder, pillage
高分秘诀	▲ territory n. 领土，地盘，领域，范围 ▲ tonight n. 今晚 adv. （在）今晚 ▲ laptop n. 便携式电脑，手提电脑 ▲ computer market 电脑市场

954. forbid [fə`bɪd] [for·bid] ☆★★★★

v. 禁止

Recently a new law passed which forbids smoking in public.
最近颁布一项新法律，禁止在公共场合吸烟。

同义字词: prohibit, prevent, ban, taboo
反义字词: allow, permit
高分秘诀:
▲ recently **adv.** 最近，近来
▲ in public 公开地，当众

955. forebear [`for‚bɛr] [fore·bear] ☆☆★★★

n. 祖先

More and more data proved that ape is our forebear.
愈来愈多的资料证明人猿就是我们的祖先。

同义字词: forefather, ancestor
反义字词: offspring, descendant
衍生字词: ▲ immediate forebear 直系祖先
高分秘诀:
▲ data **n.** 资料，材料
▲ ape **n.** 猿

956. forecast [`for‚kæst] [fore·cast] ☆★★★★

n. 预言，预报

Have you listened to today's weather forecast?
你收听今天的天气预报了吗？

v. 预言，预报

No one can forecast the future.
没有人能预言未来。

同义字词: prediction, outlook, prognosis, predict, foresee
衍生字词:
▲ forecaster **n.** 预报员
▲ forecast period 预测期，预报期
高分秘诀:
▲ weather forecast 天气预报
▲ future **n.** 未来，将来

957. foresee [for`si] [fore·see] ★★★★★

v. 预见，预知

I think most of difficulties can not be foreseen.
我认为大多数困难都无法预见。

同义字词: anticipate, predict, envision, foreknow
衍生字词:
▲ foreseer **n.** 有先见之明的人
▲ foresight **n.** 预见，先见之明，深谋远虑

forbid ~ formidable

高分秘诀 ▲ difficulty n. 困难，难事，麻烦

958. forestall [fɔr`stɔl] [fore·stall] ☆★★★★

v. 预防，预先阻止

There is a saying that to forestall is better than to amend.
有句谚语说，与其补救于已然，不如防范于未然。

同义字词 prevent, thwart, foreclose, preclude

衍生字词 ▲ forestallment n. 预防，预先阻止

高分秘诀 ▲ saying n. 谚语，格言，名言
▲ amend v. 修改，修正

959. forge [fɔrdʒ] [forge] ☆★★★★

v. 铸造，仿造

When I entered, the blacksmith was forging the horseshoes out of iron.
当我进去的时候，那个铁匠正在铸造马蹄铁。

同义字词 counterfeit, falsify, fake

高分秘诀 ▲ blacksmith n. 铁匠，锻工
▲ horseshoe n. 马蹄铁
▲ iron n. 铁

960. formation [fɔr`meʃən] [for·ma·tion] ☆★★★★

n. 形成，构成

It's a long process for the formation of one's character.
人的性格的形成是一个长期的过程。

同义字词 synthesis, configuration, pattern

高分秘诀 ▲ process n. 过程，进程
▲ character n. 品性，特性，特色

961. formidable [`fɔrmɪdəbl] [for·mi·da·ble] ☆★★★★

adj. 可怕的，难对付的

Sometimes I think it's a good thing to grapple with an unexpectedly formidable opponent.
有时候，我想能与一名出乎意料难对付的对手竞争是件好事。

同义字词 dreadful, frightening, redoubtable

高分秘诀 ▲ grapple with 与……搏斗，尽力解决
▲ unexpectedly adv. 未料到地，意外地
▲ opponent n. 对手，敌手

962. formulate [ˈfɔrmjəˌlet] [for·mu·late] ☆★★★★

v. 构想出，规划

I don't think I can formulate my ideas in a few words.
我觉得几句话无法阐明我的思想。

| 同义字词 | explicate, describe, express, define |
| 高分秘诀 | ▲ idea **n.** 想法，主意，思想 |

963. fortify [ˈfɔrtəˌfaɪ] [for·ti·fy] ☆★★★★

v. 加强，巩固

A cup of hot milk tea would fortify you against cold.
一杯热奶茶可以帮助你御寒。

同义字词	reinforce, strengthen
反义字词	demilitarise, disarm, weaken
高分秘诀	▲ milk tea 奶茶
	▲ fortify again 使……更强大以抵制

964. fortuitous [fɔrˈtjuətəs] [for·tu·i·tous] ☆☆★★★

adj. 偶然的，意外的

In my opinion, the occurrence of such things is by no means fortuitous.
在我看来，出现这种问题绝不是偶然的。

同义字词	serendipitous, accidental, haphazard, causeless
反义字词	intentional
高分秘诀	▲ in my opinion 依我看来
	▲ occurrence **n.** 发生，出现
	▲ by no means 绝不，一点也不

965. fortune [ˈfɔrtʃən] [for·tune] ★★★★★

n. 财富，财产

Recently my fortune was at its nadir.
最近我的运气坏到了极点。

同义字词	treasure, riches, wealth, chance, prosperity
衍生字词	▲ fortune cookie 幸运饼干
	▲ Fortuna **n.** 福耳图那（罗马神话中的命运女神）
高分秘诀	▲ nadir **n.** 最低点；最压抑、最消沉等的时刻

966. fossil [ˈfɑsl] [fos·sil] ☆★★★★

n. 化石，老顽固

After much study, the archaeologist finally dated the fossil.
经过认真的研究，那位考古学家终于确定了该化石的年代。

formulate ~ fragile

同义字词	fogey, fogy, dodo
高分秘诀	▲ archaeologist **n.** 考古学家
	▲ date **v.** 鉴定……的年代

967. foster ['fɔstə] [fos·ter] ★★★★★

v. 鼓励, 养育	She is sterile, so she decided to foster a little girl. 她无法生育, 所以决定领养一个小女孩。
同义字词	encourage, promote, raise, feed, nourish
衍生字词	▲ foster father 养父
	▲ foster daughter 养女
高分秘诀	▲ sterile **adj.** 不生育的, 不能生殖的

968. foul [faul] [foul] ☆★★★★

adj. 污秽的, 肮脏的	The girl is very pretty, but I really was shocked by her foul language. 这个女孩很漂亮, 可是她的粗话让我感到震惊。
同义字词	disgusting, filthy, dirty, nasty
高分秘诀	▲ pretty **adj.** 漂亮的, 可爱的
	▲ foul language 粗话, 骂人的话

969. fracture ['fræktʃə] [frac·ture] ☆★★★★

n. 骨折; 破裂	The water is leaking, for there is a fracture in the water pipe. 漏水了, 因为水管有裂缝。
同义字词	break, crack
高分秘诀	▲ leak **v.** 漏
	▲ water pipe 水管

970. fragile ['frædʒəl] [fra·gile] ★★★★★

adj. 易碎的, 脆弱的	I saw a warning on the container, which says: Fragile — handle with care. 我看到容器上贴有警告语: "易碎——小心轻放。"
同义字词	delicate, brittle, breakable, weak, frail, slight
反义字词	solid , strong, sturdy, tough
衍生字词	▲ fragile cargo 易碎货物
高分秘诀	▲ warning **n.** 警告语, 告诫
	▲ container **n.** 容器, 货柜
	▲ handle with care 小心轻放

971. fragrant [`fregrənt] ['fra·grant] ☆★★★★

adj. 香的，芬芳的	I read a beautiful sentence, which says love is a fragrant flower, and friendship is a sweet fruit. 我读到一句优美的句子："爱情是一朵芬芳的鲜花，友情是一颗甜美的果实。"

- 同义字词: aromatic, odorous
- 反义字词: stinky, malodorous, ill-smelling
- 高分秘诀:
  - ▲ sentence **n.** 句子
  - ▲ friendship **n.** 友情，友谊
  - ▲ fruit **n.** 果实

972. fray [`fre] [fray] ☆☆★★★

v. 磨损，磨破	The cuffs were broken, as the constant rubbing had frayed them. 袖子破损是因为不断的磨损。
n. 吵架，冲突	Don't join the fray between them. 不要加入他们的争吵。

- 同义字词: wear out, rub, frazzle
- 高分秘诀:
  - ▲ cuff **n.** 袖口
  - ▲ constant **adj.** 不断的，连续发生的
  - ▲ rubbing **n.** 摩擦

973. freight [fret] [freight] ☆★★★★

n. 货物，货运	They don't have time to load freight. 他们没有时间装货。
v. 装货，运送	It's better to freight merchandise than to mail it. 货运商品比邮寄更好。

- 同义字词: cargo, load, goods
- 衍生字词:
  - ▲ freighter **n.** 货车
  - ▲ freight bill 运货单，运费单
  - ▲ freight container 货物货柜
- 高分秘诀:
  - ▲ merchandise **n.** 商品，货物
  - ▲ mail **v.** 邮寄

974. frenetic [frɪ`nɛtɪk] [fre·net·ic] ☆☆★★★

adj. 狂乱的，发狂的	I really don't know what led to the frenetic activity. 我真的不知道是什么导致了这次狂热的行动。

fragrant ~ frugal

同义字词	crazy, wild, frantic, frenzied, phrenetic
高分秘诀	▲ lead to 导致，引起 ▲ activity n. 活动性，活力

975. friction [ˋfrɪkʃən] [fric·tion] ☆★★★★

n. 摩擦，冲突	I need to buy new shoes, the constant friction wore out the heels of them. 我需要买一双新鞋，我的鞋跟被不断的摩擦磨损。
同义字词	abrasion, scraping, conflict, clash
高分秘诀	▲ wear out 用坏，穿破 ▲ heel n. 后跟

976. frigid [ˋfrɪgɪd] [frig·id] ☆★★★★

adj. 寒冷的，冷漠的	It seemed that she disgust me, for she returned my smile with a frigid glance. 她好像厌恶我，对我的微笑她竟报以冷冷的一瞥。
同义字词	chilly, cold, icy, glacial, gelid
高分秘诀	▲ disgust v. 厌恶 ▲ glance n. 一瞥，瞥视

977. frivolity [frɪˋvɑlətɪ] [fri·vol·i·ty] ☆☆☆★★

n. 轻浮	I don't want to accompany him, because I can't tolerate his frivolity. 我不想陪伴他，因为我受不了他的轻浮。
同义字词	flippancy, levity
反义字词	seriousness, earnestness
高分秘诀	▲ accompany v. 陪伴，陪同 ▲ tolerate v. 忍受，容忍

978. frugal [ˋfrugl] [fru·gal] ☆☆★★★

adj. 节约的，节俭的	I want to get married with a girl who is a frugal housekeeper. 我想和一位勤俭持家的女孩结婚。
同义字词	sparing, economical, thrifty
反义字词	wasteful, luxurious, extravagant, uneconomical
高分秘诀	▲ get married with 和（某人）结婚 ▲ housekeeper n. 主妇，女管家

979. frustrate [ˋfrʌsˌtret] [frus·trate] ☆★★★★

v. 挫败, 破坏

He committed suicide just because he was frustrated by repeated failure.

他因一再失败而灰心丧气,最终自杀了。

同义字词	discourage, depress, foil
高分秘诀	▲ commit suicide 自杀
	▲ repeated **adj.** 反复的, 再三的, 重复的
	▲ failure **n.** 失败, 不成功的

980. furious [ˋfjuərɪəs] [fu·ri·ous] ★★★★★

adj. 狂怒的, 暴怒的

Your sister-in-law will be furious if the news reaches her ears.

如果这个消息传到你嫂嫂的耳朵里,她一定会大发雷霆。

同义字词	angry, rageful, fighting mad
反义字词	gentle, meek, mild, quiet
高分秘诀	▲ sister-in-law **n.** 老公或老婆的姐妹

981. furnish [ˋfɝnɪʃ] [fur·nish] ★★★★★

v. 布置, 装备

We scouted around for some unique furniture to furnish our new apartment.

我们到处寻找独特的家具装饰新居。

同义字词	provide, supply, equip, outfit
高分秘诀	▲ scout around for 到处寻找
	▲ unique **adj.** 独一无二的, 特有的, 少见的
	▲ furniture **n.** 家具

982. fuse [fjuz] [fuse] ☆☆★★★

v. 熔合

I think it's the common interests drove the two companies fused together.

我认为共同利益促使这两公司结合。

n. 保险丝, 导火线

You'd better keep a spare fuse handy by the fuse box.

你最好在保险丝盒旁边放一根备用保险丝。

同义字词	combine, blend, melt, solder, weld
高分秘诀	▲ common interests 共同利益
	▲ fuse together 熔合
	▲ spare fuse 备用熔断器
	▲ fuse box 保险丝盒

Gg 托福 TOEFL iBT

托福(TOEFL)的测验对象为母语为非英语的人
申请入学美加地区大学或研究所时，托福成绩单是必备文件之一。

- n. 名词
- v. 动词
- adj. 形容词
- adv. 副词
- prep. 介词
- art. 冠词
- pron. 代词
- aux. 助词
- conj. 连词

Gg 托福 TOEFL iBT

托福(TOEFL)的测验对象为母语为非英语的人
申请入学美加地区大学或研究所时，托福成绩单是必备文件之一。

983. gallant [`gælənt] [gal·lant] ☆★★★★

adj. （对女子）殷勤的, 英勇的	My sister got married with a gallant knight. 我姐姐和一位勇敢的骑士结婚了。
同义字词	courtly, chivalrous, brave, courageous
反义字词	cowardly, timid
高分秘诀	▲ knight n. 骑士，武士

984. galvanize [`gælvəˌnaɪz] [gal·va·nize] ☆☆★★★

v. 通电流于, 刺激	Those days I always wonder how I can galvanize my workers into taking the responsibility for their word. 这几天我一直在想怎样才能激励员工对他们的工作负起责任。
同义字词	stimulate, invigorate
高分秘诀	▲ wonder v. 想知道，问自己
	▲ take responsibility for... 对……负有责任，负起对……的责任

985. gauge [gedʒ] [gauge] ☆☆★★★

v. 测量, 计量	Before taking measures, we have to put out some feelers to gauge people's reactions. 在采取措施之前，我们必须试探一下，看大家对这些措施的回应。
n. 量规, 量表	Can you tell me what the scale, dial, gauge read? 你能告诉我比例尺、标度盘和量规显示的计数是多少吗？
同义字词	measure, judge, assess, size up, estimate, appraise
高分秘诀	▲ feeler n. 对他人观点或回应的试探
	▲ reaction n. 回应，回应
	▲ scale n. 比例尺
	▲ dial n. 标度盘

986. gear [gɪr] [gear] ☆☆★★★

n. 齿轮，传动装置 — I found the gear of this machine is unique.
我发现这个机器上的齿轮很独特。

v. 使适合，使一致 — Don't worry, I geared myself up for the job.
不用担心，我已经为这项工作做好了准备。

- 同义字词：gear wheel, toothed wheel
- 衍生字词：▲ gear drive 齿轮传动
- 高分秘诀：▲ gear up 使做好行动准备

987. generalize [ˈdʒɛnərəˌlaɪz] [ge·ne·ra·lize] ☆★★★★

v. 归纳，概括 — It would take much time to generalize from a large collection of data.
从一大堆资料中概括地归纳出结论，这将会花费不少时间。

- 同义字词：reach conclusion, infer, deduce
- 高分秘诀：
  ▲ generalize from 从（一定实例）中归纳出……
  ▲ a collection of 很多
  ▲ data **n.** 资料，材料

988. generate [ˈdʒɛnəˌret] [ge·ne·rate] ☆★★★★

v. 造成，导致 — Everybody knows that the dynamo is used to generate electricity.
大家都知道发电机用来发电。

- 同义字词：make happen, produce, render
- 高分秘诀：
  ▲ dynamo **n.** 发电机
  ▲ generate electricity 发电

989. generous [ˈdʒɛnərəs] [ge·ne·rous] ★★★★★

adj. 慷慨的，大量的 — I don't know why the boy sniffed at my generous offer.
我不知道为什么这个男孩对我的慷慨嗤之以鼻。

- 同义字词：magnanimous, bighearted, liberal
- 反义字词：mean, stingy, ungenerous
- 高分秘诀：▲ sniff at... 对……嗤之以鼻……

990. genetic [dʒəˈnɛtɪk] [ge·net·ic] ☆★★★★

adj. 遗传的，起源的 — A heart diseas is a genetic disease.
心脏病是一种遗传性疾病。

同义字词	hereditary, inherited, genic, genetical
衍生字词	genetics n. 遗传学 heredity
	genesis n. 起源，产生
高分秘诀	▲ heart disease 心脏病
	▲ genetic disease 遗传疾病

991. genial [ˈdʒinjəl] [ge·ni·al] ☆☆★★★

adj. 和蔼的，亲切的	It's terrific that the boy I liked has a genial personality.
	我喜欢的那个男孩为人和蔼可亲，真是棒极了。
同义字词	friendly, cordial, amiable, good-natured, kindly
高分秘诀	▲ terrific adj. 极好的，太棒了
	▲ personality n. 人格，个性

992. gibe [dʒaɪb] [gibe] ☆☆★★★

v. 嘲弄，讥笑	It's impolite to gibe at other's mistakes.
	嘲笑别人的错误是不礼貌的。
同义字词	deride, mock, jeer, scoff, taunt
高分秘诀	▲ impolite adj. 不礼貌的，失礼的

993. gigantic [dʒaɪˈgæntɪk] [gi·gan·tic] ☆★★★★

adj. 巨大的，庞大的	How I wish I could go to the Tombs to see the gigantic stone sculptures with my own eyes!
	我多么希望我能去陵墓亲眼看看那些巨大的石雕！
同义字词	mammoth, huge, enormous, immense, tremendous
反义字词	diminutive, little, small
高分秘诀	▲ sculpture n. 雕刻，雕塑，雕刻品
	▲ with one's own eyes 亲眼

994. glacial [ˈgleʃəl] [gla·ci·al] ☆★★★★

adj. 冰的，冰冷的	Her glacial smile gave me the gooseflesh.
	她冷冰冰的笑容让我起鸡皮疙瘩。
同义字词	frigid, frosty, gelid, icy
衍生字词	▲ glacier n. 冰川

genial ~ glean

| 高分秘诀 | ▲ gooseflesh n. 鸡皮疙瘩 |

995. glamorous [ˋglæmərəs] [glam·or·ous] ☆★★★★

| adj. 迷人的，富有魅力的 | I really admired your glamorous lifestyle.
我真的很羡慕你绚丽多彩的生活。 |

| 同义字词 | attractive, charming, alluring, appealing |
| 高分秘诀 | ▲ lifestyle n. 生活模式 |

996. glare [glɛr] [glare] ☆★★★★

| v. 闪耀，怒目而视 | Though the couple didn't argue, they glared at each other.
虽然这对夫妻没有争吵，但他们怒目相对。 |

| 同义字词 | light, brightness, flare, glow, flash |
| 高分秘诀 | ▲ glare at 用愤怒的目光注视 |

997. glaze [glɛz] [glaze] ☆★★★★

| v. 装玻璃，上釉 | Sorry I can't help you, because I don't know how to glaze a window.
对不起我无法帮你，因为我不知道怎么装窗户玻璃。 |
| n. 釉料 | Why you scratched the glaze of the chair?
你为什么刮掉椅子上的釉? |

同义字词	coat, cover, gloss, luster, polish
衍生字词	▲ glaze coat 上釉面层 ▲ glazed brick 釉面砖，瓷砖
高分秘诀	▲ window n. 窗户，玻璃窗 ▲ scratch v. 刮伤

998. glean [glin] [glean] ☆☆★★

| v. 点滴搜集，拾 | The boy has spent the whole day gleaning through the bookstore.
男孩花了一整天，找遍书店收集资料。 |

| 同义字词 | gather, collect |
| 高分秘诀 | ▲ bookstore n. 书店 |

999. glide [glaɪd] [glide] ☆★★★★

v. 滑动,滑行

Please cherish your time, for youth would glide past without your awareness.
请珍惜你的时间,青春在不知不觉中就会逝去。

同义字词 slide, slip

高分秘诀 ▲ cherish v. 珍爱,珍视
▲ awareness n. 察觉,觉悟

1000. glimpse [glɪmps] [glimpse] ☆★★★★

n. 一瞥,一看

The old man caught a glimpse of me when he passed by.
老人从我身边走过时,看了我一眼。

v. 瞥见

As he smiled at me, he glimpsed at my new glad rags.
他对我笑笑,看了一眼我新买的晚礼服。

同义字词 glance, see briefly, catch sight of

反义字词 gaze, stare

高分秘诀 ▲ catch a glimpse of 瞥见,瞥一眼
▲ pass by 经过,过去
▲ smile at 对……微笑
▲ glad rags 晚礼服

1001. glorify [ˈglorə,faɪ] [glo·ri·fy] ☆★★★★

v. 美化,赞扬

The media glorified the guy's heroic deed.
媒体称颂那位男人的英雄事迹。

同义字词 exalt, laud, praise, beautify, prettify

反义字词 defame, uglify, blame, reprove, reproach

高分秘诀 ▲ media n. 媒体
▲ heroic adj. 英雄的,英勇的

1002. glossy [ˈglɔsɪ] [gloss·y] ☆☆★★★

adj. 平滑的,有光泽的

I bought a book with glossy paper backs the other day.
前几天我买了一本有光泽的平装书。

同义字词 shiny, polished, glistening, silken, satiny

高分秘诀 ▲ glossy paper 蜡光纸
▲ the other day 前几天

glide ~ graft

1003. gnaw [nɔ] [gnaw] ☆★★★★

v. 咬, 啃

The rabbit in the cage gnawed listlessly at a carrot.
笼子里的兔子无精打采地啃着一根胡萝卜。

同义字词 nibble, bite, gnash, chew

衍生字词 ▲ gnawer **n.** 日齿动物

高分秘诀 ▲ rabbit **n.** 兔子
▲ gnaw at 啃, 咬, 侵蚀
▲ listlessly **adv.** 无精打采地, 冷淡地
▲ carrot **n.** 胡萝卜

1004. gorgeous [ˋgɔrdʒəs] [gor·geous] ☆★★★★

adj. 华丽的, 灿烂的

On the evening of the Mid-Autumn Festival, we sat under the tree and enjoyed the gorgeous moon.
中秋节晚上，我们坐在树下欣赏皎洁的月光。

同义字词 beautiful, magnificent, stunning, splendid

高分秘诀 ▲ Mid-Autumn Festival 中秋节

1005. gourmet [ˋgurme] [gour·met] ★★★★★

n. 美食家

Some people flavor the dishes with gourmet powder.
有些人在菜里加味精调味。

同义字词 epicure, foodie, gastronome

衍生字词 ▲ gourmand **n.** 美食家
▲ gourmet coffee 精制的咖啡
▲ gourmet festival 美食节

高分秘诀 ▲ dish **n.** 菜肴, 一道菜
▲ gourmet powder 味精

1006. graft [græft] [graft] ☆☆★★★

v. 移植, 行贿

The surgeon grafted the donated kidney into the patient.
这位外科医生将捐赠的肾移植到病人身上。

同义字词 implant, transplant, engraft, ingraft

高分秘诀 ▲ surgeon **n.** 外科医生
▲ donated **adj.** 捐赠的
▲ kidney **n.** 肾
▲ patient **n.** 病人

1007. grandeur [ˈɡrændʒə] [gran·deur] ☆★★★★

n. 宏伟, 壮观

I'm sorry I couldn't accept the worker who has delusions of grandeur.
对不起，我无法接受这种自以为了不起的员工。

同义字词: magnificence, grandness, brilliance

高分秘诀: ▲ delusion of grandeur 夸大妄想

1008. gravitational [ˈɡrævəˈteʃənl] [grav·i·ta·tion·al] ☆★★★★

adj. 地心引力的, 重力的

The phenomenon was caused by the gravitational force.
这种现象是由地心引力引起的。

衍生字词:
▲ gravitation **n.** 引力, 重力
▲ gravitational field 重力场
▲ gravitational force 地心引力

高分秘诀: ▲ phenomenon **n.** 现象

1009. grind [ɡraɪnd] [grind] ☆★★★★

v. 磨碎, 碾碎

I'm afraid it won't grind down any finer than that.
恐怕不能磨得比那个更细。

同义字词: crush, pulverize, squash, grate

高分秘诀: ▲ grind down 用磨等磨碎

1010. grope [ɡrop] [grope] ☆★★★★

v. 摸索, 探索

It would take me much time to grope for a solution to this problem.
寻求解决问题的方法历时很长。

同义字词: fumble, probe, feel around

高分秘诀:
▲ grope for 探索
▲ solution **n.** 解决, 解答, 解决方法

1011. grumble [ˈɡrʌmbl] [grum·ble] ☆★★★★

n. 抱怨, 发牢骚

I don't know why you've got everything you want, but still have a lot of grumbles.
我不知道为什么你得到了想要的东西，但仍然抱怨个不停。

v. 抱怨, 发牢骚

There is no need to grumble about having to work overtime.
没有必要抱怨加班。

grandeur ~ gymnastic

同义字词	complain, mutter, grouch, murmur, rumble
衍生字词	▲ grumbler n. 爱抱怨的人，发牢骚的人
高分秘诀	▲ grumble about 抱怨 ▲ work overtime 加班

1012. guarantee [ˌgærənˈti] [guar·an·tee] ★★★★★

v. 保证, 担保 — No one can guarantee the punctual arrival of trains in the snowy day.
下雪时没有人能保证火车准时到达。

同义字词	assure, ensure, undertake, vouch, warrant
衍生字词	▲ guarantor n. 保证人 ▲ guarantee clause 保证条款 ▲ guarantee deposit 保证金，押金
高分秘诀	▲ punctual adj. 严守时刻的，准时的，整点的 ▲ snowy adj. 下雪的，积雪的

1013. gulp [gʌlp] [gulp] ☆★★★★

v. 吞, 吞咽 — Maybe she is so thirty, she just gulped down the hot water.
可能她太渴了，所以就大口大口地喝热水。

n. 吞, 吞咽 — It's late for work; I just took a gulp of milk and rushed out of home.
上班快迟到了，我喝了一大口牛奶就冲出家门。

| 同义字词 | swallow, devour, quaff, swig |
| 高分秘诀 | ▲ gulp down 狼吞虎咽地吃
▲ hot water 热水 |

1014. gush [gʌʃ] [gush] ☆☆★★★

v. 喷涌, 涌流 — Springwater gushed from the well.
天然泉水从井中喷出。

| 同义字词 | flow, flood, flush, pour, spout |
| 高分秘诀 | ▲ springwater n. 天然泉水
▲ well n. 井 |

1015. gymnastic [dʒɪmˈnæstɪk] [gym·nas·tic] ☆☆★★★

adj. 体操的, 体育的 — Congratulations! You've passed the qualification for the Olympic gymnastic competition.
恭喜你获得奥运体操比赛的资格。

同义字词	athletic 体育的
高分秘诀	▲ congratulation n. 祝贺，恭喜
	▲ qualification n. 资格，条件
	▲ Olympic adj. 奥运的
	▲ competition n. 比赛

1016. gyrate [ˈdʒaɪret] [gy·rate]   ☆☆★★

v. 旋转, 回旋	Those dancers gyrated on the dance floor. 舞者在舞池不停地旋转。
同义字词	revolve, move around, spin
高分秘诀	▲ dance floor 舞池

Hh 托福 TOEFL iBT

托福(TOEFL)的测验对象为母语为非英语的人

申请入学美加地区大学或研究所时，托福成绩单是必备文件之一。

- n. 名词
- v. 动词
- adj. 形容词
- adv. 副词
- prep. 介词
- art. 冠词
- pron. 代词
- aux. 助词
- conj. 连词

Hh 托福 TOEFL iBT

托福(TOEFL)的测验对象为母语为非英语的人
申请入学美加地区大学或研究所时，托福成绩单是必备文件之一。

1017. habitat [ˈhæbəˌtæt] [ha·bi·tat]   ☆★★★★

n. 产地，栖息地　Nowadays most people prefer to see animals in their natural habitat, rather than in zoos.
如今愈来愈多的人喜欢看生活在自然栖息地的动物而非动物园里的动物。

同义字词　natural environment, home ground

高分秘诀
▲ prefer to 较喜欢，宁愿
▲ rather than （要）……而不……

1018. hail [hel] [hail] ☆★★★★

n. 冰雹，欢呼　Hail is a meteoric phenomenon, it would harm the crops and hurt people.
冰雹是一种大气现象，它会造成农作物的损害，而且会砸伤人。

v. 致敬，向……欢呼　So many audience lined the street to hail this famous movie star.
很多观众排列在街道的两旁向这位有名的电影明星欢呼。

同义字词　acclaim, salute, greet, welcome

高分秘诀
▲ meteoric **adj.** 大气的，流星的
▲ crop **n.** 作物，庄稼
▲ famous **adj.** 著名的，出名的

1019. halt [hɔlt] [halt] ★★★★★

n. （使）停止　I waved to a taxi, and it rolled to a halt.
我朝出租车招手，车慢慢地停下来。

v. （使）停止　We only have a few minutes to halt, then we have to march again.
我们只能停几分钟，然后得继续前进。

同义字词　stop, pause, quit

反义字词　start, get going, march

高分秘诀
▲ wave to 朝……挥手
▲ taxi **n.** 出租车

habitat ~ harmonize

1020. hamper [`hæmpə] [ham·per] ☆☆★★★

v. 妨碍，使困难

The bad weather hampered my original plan.
坏天气妨碍我原来的计划。

同义字词	impede, hinder, block, obstruct
反义字词	assist, expedite
衍生字词	▲ hamper traffic 阻碍交通 ▲ hamper production 妨碍生产
高分秘诀	▲ bad weather 恶劣天气 ▲ original **adj.** 起初的，原来的

1021. handicap [`hændɪˌkæp] [han·di·cap] ☆★★★★

n. 障碍，不利条件

Losing such kind of player like you was a handicap to the team.
失去像你这样的运动员对我们不利。

v. 严重妨碍，削弱

You have to study hard; your father was handicapped by illiteracy.
你必须好好学习；你父亲就因不识字而吃亏。

| 衍生字词 | ▲ handicapism **n.** 身（心）残疾者差别（主义）
▲ handicapper **n.** 主管障碍赛跑的裁判人员
▲ handicapped room 残疾人客房 |
| 高分秘诀 | ▲ study hard 好好学习
▲ illiteracy **n.** 文盲，无知，缺乏教育 |

1022. haphazard [ˌhæp`hæzəd] [hap·haz·ard] ☆☆★★★

adj. 偶然的，随便的

I should have known that my haphazard remarks would hurt her.
我真没有想到我随口说出的那些话会伤害到她。

| 同义字词 | indiscriminate, random, aimless, casual, chance |
| 高分秘诀 | remark **n.** 话语，评论 |

1023. harmonize [`hɑrməˌnaɪz] [har·mo·nize]

v. （使）协调，（使）和谐

It would be better if we could harmonize these two different opinions.
如果我们能把这两种不同意见调和折中一下就太好了。

| 同义字词 | correspond, attune, harmonise, reconcile |
| 高分秘诀 | ▲ different **adj.** 不同的
▲ opinion **n.** 意见，看法，主张 |

1024. harness [ˈhɑrnɪs] [har·ness]

v. 给(马等)装上挽具,利用
They wonder how to harness the sun's energy to heat homes.
他们在想怎样才能利用太阳能为住宅供暖气。

n. (全套)马具
Of course bridle is one part of a horse's harness.
笼头当然属于马具的一部分。

同义字词 utilize, make use of, saddle

衍生字词 ▲ harness bull / harness cop (美俚)穿制服的警察

高分秘诀 ▲ sun's energy 太阳能
▲ bridle **n.** 马笼头,马缰

1025. harsh [hɑrʃ] [harsh]

adj. 粗糙的,严酷的
Speaking of the harsh discipline and harsh management, I think the harsher the better.
说起严格的纪律以及严格的管理,我认为越严格越好。

同义字词 rough, coarse, acrimonious

衍生字词 ▲ harsh reality 残酷的现实

高分秘诀 ▲ speak of 谈到,讲到
▲ discipline **n.** 纪律
▲ management **n.** 管理,经营

1026. hatch [hætʃ] [hatch]

v. 孵化
I bought an incubator to hatch chicken.
我买一个孵蛋器孵小鸡。

同义字词 breed, emerge from the egg, incubate

高分秘诀 ▲ incubator **n.** 孵化器

1027. haul [hɔl] [haul]

v. 拖,拉
It took the fisherman much time and toil to haul the net aboard.
渔夫费了很大的劲儿才把渔网拖上渔船。

同义字词 drag, draw, pull, tow, tug

高分秘诀 ▲ fisherman **n.** 渔夫,渔民
▲ aboard **prep.** /**adv.** 在船(飞机、车)上

harness ~ heal

1028. haunt [hɔnt] [haunt] ★★★★★

v. 经常出没于，萦绕心头
I tried my best to forget it, but the memories of the past always haunted me.
我试图去忘记，但过去的记忆总是萦绕心头。

n. 常去的地方
The little bookstore is one of my haunts.
这个小书店是我经常出入的地方。

同义字词	hang around, frequent, obsess
衍生字词	▲ haunted **adj.** 闹鬼的，鬼魂出没的，受到折磨的
	▲ Haunted Boat《海上慌踪》（电影名）
	▲ The Haunted Mansion《鬼屋》（电影名）
	▲ haunted house 鬼屋

1029. hazard [ˈhæzəd] [haz·ard] ★★★★★

n. 危险，危害物
Explosions are the biggest occupational hazard for the coal-miners.
爆炸是煤矿工人职业中最大的危险。

v. 尝试着去做，冒风险
Don't hazard your life by going rock climbing.
不要去冒生命危险攀岩。

同义字词	danger, risk, gamble, venture
反义字词	safety, security
高分秘诀	▲ occupational hazard 职业病
	▲ coal-miner **n.** 矿工，煤矿工人
	▲ go rock climbing 去攀岩

1030. heal [hil] [heal] ★★★★★

v. 康复，治愈
I don't know how to heal the rift between me and my husband.
我不知道如何缓和我和老公之间的不和。

同义字词	cure, remedy, mend
反义字词	injure, wound, hurt
衍生字词	▲ heal the breach 调停，使和解
	▲ heal the pain 结束痛苦
高分秘诀	▲ rift **n.** 裂缝，分裂，不和

1031. heed [hid] [heed] ☆★★★★

n. 注意，留意
My father is a good leader who always pays heed to the voice of the masses.
爸爸是个好领导者，他经常倾听群众的心声。

v. 注意，留意
I don't think I can persuade her, and you know she didn't heed my advice.
我想我说服不了她，她根本就不听我的劝告。

同义字词　attention, consideration, notice, attend, observe, regard

反义字词　heedlessness, inattentiveness

高分秘诀
▲ pay heed to... 注意……，留心……
▲ mass **n.** 群众
▲ persuade **v.** 说服，劝告

1032. herald [ˈhɛrəld] [her·ald] ☆★★★★

v. 宣布……的消息，预示……的来临
The new manager rise to power heralded the end of the my freedom.
新经理的上任代表着我的自由结束。

n. 使者，预报者
The Englishmen believe that the cuckoo is the herald of spring.
英国人认为杜鹃是报春的使者。

同义字词　announce, proclaim, foretell, predict, harbinger

高分秘诀
▲ rise to power 掌权
▲ freedom **n.** 自由
▲ Englishmen **n.** 英国人
▲ cuckoo **n.** 杜鹃，布谷鸟

1033. herd [hɝd] [herd] ☆★★★★

n. 兽群，人群
My boyfriend is such kind of person who has no opinions of his own just follow the herd.
我男友是那种无主见、人云亦云的人。

v. 把……赶在一起放牧，群集
After school, I often helped my sister herd cattle.
放学后，我经常帮姐姐放牛。

同义字词　flock, crowd, gather

衍生字词　▲ shepherd **n.** 牧羊人

高分秘诀
▲ follow the herd 随大流
▲ cattle **n.**（总称）牛，牲口

heed ~ heterogeneous

1034. heredity [hə`rɛdətɪ] [he·red·i·ty] ☆★★★★

n. 遗传

I think that the heredity and environment determine a man's character.
我认为遗传和环境可以决定一个人的性格。

同义字词: genetics, inheritance, genetic endowment

高分秘诀:
▲ environment **n.** 环境，周围状况，自然环境
▲ character **n.** 品质，性格，特色

1035. heritage [`hɛrətɪdʒ] [he·ri·tage] ★★★★★

n. 遗产，继承物

Being a human being, you should take care to preserve our heritage.
作为一个人，你应该保护我们的遗产。

同义字词: legacy, bequest, inheritance

衍生字词:
▲ heritage foundation 传统基金会，遗产基金会
▲ heritage movement 文化遗产保护运动
▲ heritage preservation 遗产维护

高分秘诀:
▲ preserve **v.** 保护，维持
▲ national **adj.** 国家的，民族的

1036. hesitate [`hɛzə,tet] [he·si·tate] ★★★★★

v. 犹豫，踌躇

Don't hesitate to call on me if I can be of service.
如果有我可以帮忙的地方，尽管来找我。

同义字词: vacillate, fluctuate, falter

高分秘诀:
▲ call on 号召，要求，请求
▲ service **n.** 服务，服役，任职

1037. heterogeneous [,hɛtərə`dʒinɪəs] [het·er·o·ge·ne·ous] ☆☆★★★

adj. 异类的，不同的

Though Americans are heterogeneous in their origins, they constantly try their best to rediscover what they have in common.
尽管美国人的祖先来自四面八方，他们总是尽最大的努力找出大家的共同点。

同义字词: miscellaneous, variant, different, heterogenous

高分秘诀:
▲ origin **n.** 出身，血统
▲ rediscover **v.** 再次（重新）发现
▲ in common 共有

1038. hibernate [ˈhaɪbəˌnet] [hi·ber·nate] ☆★★★★

v. 过冬，冬眠，蛰伏	In the cold weather the polar bears would hibernate. 寒冷的天气，北极熊会冬眠。
同义字词	be dormant, slumber, hole up
反义字词	aestivate, estivate
高分秘诀	▲ polar bear 北极熊

1039. hierarchy [ˈhaɪəˌrɑrkɪ] [hi·er·arch·y] ☆☆★★★

n. 阶层，等级制度	Though he is the general manager, he is not very important in the company hierarchy. 虽然他是总经理，但在公司的领导层中似乎无多大权力。
同义字词	class, order, power structure, pecking order
高分秘诀	▲ important **adj.** 重要的，有势力的，有地位的

1040. highlight [ˈhaɪˌlaɪt] [high·light] ★★★★★

v. 使显著，突出	The professor's remarks highlighted the need for educational reform. 教授的言语强调教育改革的必要性。
n. 最显著或重要的部分	Don't miss this piece; it is one of the highlight of the programme. 别漏掉这节；这可是节目中最精彩的一部分。
同义字词	emphasize, stress, foreground, spotlight
反义字词	downplay, play down
衍生字词	▲ highlighter **n.** 荧光笔，亮光笔
高分秘诀	▲ educational reform 教育改革 ▲ piece **n.** 片，段，部分 ▲ programme **n.** 节目，节目单

1041. hike [haɪk] [hike] ☆★★★★

v. 远足，徒步旅行	The soldiers hiked out to the marsh. 士兵们徒步行经沼泽。
n. 徒步旅行	It's necessary to take a canteen with you on a hike. 徒步旅行的时候带个水壶是很有必要的。
同义字词	travel, walk, tramp

hibernate ~ horizon

高分秘诀
- ▲ marsh n. 沼泽，湿地
- ▲ necessary adj. 必要的，必需的
- ▲ canteen n. 水壶，水罐

1042. hinder [`hɪndə] [hind·er] ☆★★★★

v. 阻碍，妨碍
Be optimistic! You know downhearted thoughts would hinder progress.
乐观点！消极的思想有碍进步。

同义字词　stunt, inhibit, tie up, hamper, impede

反义字词　assist, expedite

高分秘诀
- ▲ optimistic adj. 乐观的
- ▲ downhearted adj. 沮丧的，灰心丧气的
- ▲ progress n. 进步

1043. hint [hɪnt] [hint] ★★★★★

n. 提示，线索
I coughed, and then he quickly took the hint.
我咳了一下，他立即就明白了。

v. 暗示，示意
What he said just hinted at my love affairs.
他说的话间接提到我的风流韵事。

同义字词　allusion, clue, intimate, suggest, insinuate, imply

高分秘诀
- ▲ cough v. 咳嗽
- ▲ hint at 暗示（某事）
- ▲ love affair 风流韵事

1044. homogenize [ho`mɑdʒəˌnaɪz] [ho·mo·ge·nize] ☆★★★★

v. 使均匀，使同类
Before trying an experiment, please homogenize the main ingredients.
做实验前，要先把这些主要原料调匀。

同义字词　equalize, homogenise

高分秘诀
- ▲ experiment n. 实验，试验
- ▲ ingredient n. 配料，组成部分

1045. horizon [hə`raɪzn̩] [ho·ri·zon] ☆★★★★

n. 地平线，视野
After floating on the sea for several days, they finally saw an island on the horizon.
在海上漂流数日后，他们终于见到地平线上的一个岛。

同义字词　range, limit, purview, apparent horizon

高分秘诀	▲ float v. 漂浮
	▲ island n. 岛，岛屿

1046. hospitable [ˈhɑspɪtəbl] [hos·pi·ta·ble] ★★★★★

adj. 好客的，热情友好的	Chinese have the reputation of being very hospitable people. 中国人以好客出名。
同义字词	generous, receptive, cordial, friendly, neighborly
高分秘诀	▲ reputation n. 名气，名声，名誉

1047. hostile [ˈhɑstɪl] [hos·tile] ☆★★★★

adj. 敌对的，不友善的	The young man fixed me with a decidedly hostile look. 年轻人恶狠狠地瞪着我。
同义字词	unfriendly, antagonistic
反义字词	amiable, friendly
衍生字词	▲ hostile fire （保险业）意外失火险 ▲ hostile witness 恶意证人
高分秘诀	▲ decidedly adv. 果断地，断然地

1048. hover [ˈhʌvə] [hov·er] ☆★★★★

v. 翱翔，摇摆不定	In the distance, I saw an eagle was hovering over the valley. 远远地我看见一只老鹰在山谷中飞翔。
同义字词	levitate, float, drift, waver, vacillate, hesitate
高分秘诀	▲ eagle n. 鹰 ▲ hover over 停留于，盘旋于 ▲ valley n. 山谷，流域

1049. huddle [ˈhʌdl] [hud·dle] ☆☆★★★

v. 聚成一堆，挤成一团	Children feared so much and they huddled together like a flock of sheep. 小朋友们很害怕，他们像一群羊一样挤在一起。
n. 杂乱的一堆，拥挤	When the movie star appeared, there was a huddle of people around him. 当电影明星出现的时候，一群人围着他。
同义字词	crowd, gather, cluster, assemble

hospitable ~ humiliate

| 高分秘诀 | ▲ huddle together 挤在一起 |
| | ▲ a huddle of 杂乱的一群 |

1050. humanity [hjuˋmænətɪ] [hu·man·i·ty] ☆★★★★

n. 人性，博爱	The prison guard always treat the prisoners with humanity.
	这名狱警总是人道地对待俘虏。
同义字词	humanness, kindness, virtue, humankind, human beings
衍生字词	▲ humanitarian n. / adj. 人道主义者，人道主义的
高分秘诀	▲ prison guard 狱警
	▲ prisoner n. 囚徒，俘虏

1051. humble [ˋhʌmbl] [hum·ble] ☆★★★★

adj. 谦逊的，谦虚的	To my surprise, most famous people are surprisingly humble.
	令我吃惊的是许多知名人士都非常谦虚。
v. 使谦卑，使地位降低	I'm an ordinary kid and have to humble myself in the presence of the prime minister.
	我只是个普通小孩，在首相面前只能低声下气。
同义字词	meek, submissive, lowly
高分秘诀	▲ to my surprise 使某人惊奇的是
	▲ surprisingly adv. 惊人地，出人意料地
	▲ ordinary adj. 普通的，平常的，平庸的
	▲ in the presence of... 在……面前
	▲ prime minister 总理，首相

1052. humid [ˋhjumɪd] [hu·mid] ☆★★★★

adj. 潮湿的	The weather here in summer is torrid and humid.
	这里夏天的天气酷热且潮湿。
同义字词	damp, wet, moist, muggy
衍生字词	▲ humidor n. 保湿烟盒
高分秘诀	▲ weather n. 天气
	▲ summer n. 夏季
	▲ torrid adj. 灼热的，炎热的

1053. humiliate [hjuˋmɪlɪˌet] [hu·mi·li·ate] ☆★★★★

| v. 羞辱，使丢脸 | You can't imagine it; he humiliated his wife beyond endurance. |
| | 你根本想象不到，他把自己的妻子羞辱得无地自容。 |

同义字词	embarrass, shame, disgrace, dishonor
高分秘诀	▲ beyond endurance 忍无可忍

1054. hurl [hɝl] [hurl]　　☆☆★★★

v. 用力投掷，大声叫骂	The girl bristled with anger and hurls all her boyfriend's things out from the window. 女孩怒气冲冲，把男友的所有东西都扔出了窗外。
同义字词	throw, cast, toss, fling
衍生字词	▲ hurling n. 爱尔兰的曲棍球
高分秘诀	▲ bristle with 密集，充满

1055. hurricane [ˈhɝɪˌken] [hur·ri·cane]　　☆★★★★

n. 飓风	Stay inside, you know the hurricane screamed outside. 待在屋内别出来，外面飓风狂吹。
同义字词	cyclone, squall, tornado
衍生字词	▲ hurricane deck 最上层甲板 ▲ hurricane lamp 防风灯 ▲ outside broadcast 实况广播，实况转播 ▲ outside lane 外侧行车道，外（车）道 ▲ outside one's ken 在……的知识范围之外 ▲ outside-the-box 创造性的，打破传统的 ▲ inside lane 慢车道，（圆形跑道的）内圈 ▲ inside out 里朝外地 ▲ inside sales 内勤销售（在办公室以电话洽谈生意或接见来访的潜在消费者的一种产品销售方式） ▲ inside track （圆形跑道的）内圈，有利位置
高分秘诀	▲ stay inside 待在屋内 ▲ scream v. 发出尖叫声

1056. hustle [ˈhʌsl] [hus·tle]　　☆★★★★

v. 催促，赶紧	The cop hustled the shoplifter into the car and took him into the police station. 警察把窃贼推进车内，并把他送到警察局。
n. 忙碌，匆忙	To tell you the truth I really don't like the hustle and bustle of life in the big city. 老实说我真不喜欢大城市热闹繁忙的生活。

hurl ~ hypothesis

衍生字词	▲ toss a coin 抛硬币（决定） ▲ as trunk as a tosspot 形容某人醉得不省人事 ▲ toss-up （决胜负的）掷钱币，胜负各半的机会
高分秘诀	▲ cop n. 警察 ▲ shoplifter n. 商店窃贼 ▲ police station 警察局 ▲ to tell you the truth 老实说 ▲ hustle and bustle 熙熙攘攘，忙碌 ▲ big city 大城市

1057. hygiene [ˈhaɪdʒin] [hy·giene] ☆☆★★★

n. 卫生，卫生学	In the interests of hygiene, please quit smoking. 为了健康着想，请戒烟。
同义字词	cleanliness, sanitation, hygienics
高分秘诀	▲ in the interest of 为了……的利益

1058. hypersensitive [ˈhaɪpəˈsɛnsətɪv] [hy·per·sen·si·tive] ☆☆★★★

adj. 高灵敏度的，感觉过敏的	I'm not the least bit hypersensitive; on the contrary, I'm quite normal. 我一点都不神经过敏；相反地，我很正常。
同义字词	allergic, hypersensitized, supersensitised, supersensitized
高分秘诀	▲ not the least 一点也没有 ▲ on the contrary （与此）相反，正相反

1059. hypothesis [haɪˈpɑθəsɪs] [hy·po·the·sis] ☆★★★★

n. 假设，假说	How many conclusions could get from this hypothesis? 从这个假设中能得出几种结论？
同义字词	assumption, theory, conjecture, possibility
高分秘诀	▲ conclusion n. 结论

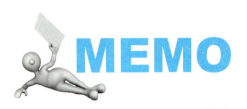

Ii 托福 TOEFL iBT

托福(TOEFL)的测验对象为母语为非英语的人
申请入学美加地区大学或研究所时,托福成绩单是必备文件之一。

- n. 名词
- v. 动词
- adj. 形容词
- adv. 副词
- prep. 介词
- art. 冠词
- pron. 代词
- aux. 助词
- conj. 连词

Ii 托福 TOEFL iBT

托福(TOEFL)的测验对象为母语为非英语的人
申请入学美加地区大学或研究所时，托福成绩单是必备文件之一。

1060. icon [ˈaɪkɑn] [i·con] ★★★★★

n. 偶像，符号	I was told that each icon can only positioned once on the picture. 他们告诉我每个图示只能在图案上被定位一次。
同义字词	idol, image, ikon, symbol
高分秘诀	▲ position v. 将（某物）放在（某一）位置上

1061. identical [aɪˈdɛntɪkl̩] [i·den·ti·cal] ☆★★★★

adj. 同一的，完全相同的	I know that no two person have identical fingerprints in the world. 我知道世界上没有两个人的指纹完全相同。
同义字词	identic, duplicate, alike, same
衍生字词	▲ identical twins 同卵双生
高分秘诀	▲ fingerprint n. 指纹

1062. identify [aɪˈdɛntəˌfaɪ] [i·den·ti·fy] ★★★★★

v. 识别，认出	Sorry, I can't identify the signature. 对不起，我辨识不出这是谁的签名。
同义字词	detect, spot, find out, discover
高分秘诀	▲ signature 签名，签字

1063. ideology [ˌaɪdɪˈɑlədʒɪ] [id·e·ol·o·gy] ☆★★★★

n. 思想(意识)，意识形态	Nowadays most of people criticize the ideology of going after fame and wealth. 如今大多数人都批评追求名利的思想。
同义字词	beliefs, ideas, philosophy
高分秘诀	▲ go after 追逐，追求 ▲ fame n. 名声，名望 ▲ wealth n. 财产，财富

icon ~ ignore

1064. idyllic [aɪˋdɪlɪk] [i·dyl·lic] ☆★★★★

adj. 田园诗的，田园风光的

It looks like an idyllic life to an outsider, but in fact it is not like that.
局外人觉得这看来好像是一种田园式的生活，但事实并非如此。

- 同义字词: pastoral, rural
- 衍生字词: ▲ idylist **n.** 田园诗人
- 高分秘诀:
  - ▲ outsider **n.** 局外人，门外汉
  - ▲ in fact 实际上，其实
  - ▲ like that 那样地，类似地

1065. ignite [ɪgˋnaɪt] [ig·nite] ☆★★★★

v. 点燃，引发

You have to know that it's the oppression ignited the hatred of the people.
你必须知道压迫会激起人民的仇恨。

- 同义字词: catch fire, burn, light, kindle
- 反义字词: extinguish, blow out, quench
- 高分秘诀:
  - ▲ oppression **n.** 压迫，压制
  - ▲ hatred **n.** 仇恨，憎恶

1066. ignorant [ˋɪgnərənt] [ˈig·no·rant] ★★★★★

adj. 无知的，不了解的

Don't hang around that ignorant and incompetent guy.
不要整天和那个不学无术的家伙混在一起。

- 同义字词: unlearned, uneducated, unenlightened, nescient, unaware, unknowing
- 反义字词: aware, knowing, educated, learned
- 高分秘诀:
  - ▲ hang around 闲逛，闲待着
  - ▲ incompetent **adj.** 无能力的，不胜任的

1067. ignore [ɪgˋnor] [ig·nore] ★★★★★

v. 忽视，不顾

I learned a sentence from the newspaper, which says: ripe person is it pass by to ignore, clever person ignore now, optimistic person ignore future.
我在报纸上看到一句话："成熟的人不问过去，聪明的人不问现在，豁达的人不问未来。"

- 同义字词: disregard, overlook, neglect, slight, snub

高分秘诀	▲ sentence n. 句子
	▲ ripe adj. 成熟的
	▲ optimistic adj. 乐观的，豁达的

1068. illuminate [ɪˈluməˌnet] [il·lu·mi·nate] ★★★★★

v. 照明，照亮	I'm sitting at the foot of the mountain, and seeing the moonlight illuminated the valley.
	我坐在山脚下，看着月光照亮山谷。
同义字词	light up, brighten, clarify, explain, illustrate
高分秘诀	▲ foot of the mountain 山脚下
	▲ moonlight n. 月光

1069. illusion [ɪˈljuʒən] [il·lu·sion] ☆★★★★

n. 幻觉，错觉	He is under the illusion that the girl still loves him.
	他误以为那女孩还爱着他。
同义字词	misconception, delusion, fancy
高分秘诀	▲ be under the illusion 有错觉，误以为

1070. illustrate [ˈɪləstret] [il·lus·trate] ☆★★★★

v. 给……加插图，阐明	This cartoonist would illustrate the book.
	这位漫画家将为这本书画插图。
同义字词	represent, demonstrate, depict, portray
高分秘诀	▲ cartoonist n. 漫画家

1071. image [ˈɪmɪdʒ] [im·age] ★★★★★

n. 图像，肖像，形象	I guess the hero of the book is the spitting image of the author.
	我猜书中的主角是作者的真实写照。
同义字词	picture, figure, likeness
高分秘诀	▲ spitting image 简直一模一样的人
	▲ author n. 作家，作者

1072. imbibe [ɪmˈbaɪb] [im·bibe] ☆☆★★★

v. 吸，吸收	On the celebration they imbibed freely of champagne.
	庆功会上他们开怀畅饮香槟。
同义字词	drink, absorb, take in, suck up

illuminate ~ immigrant

高分秘诀	▲ celebration n. 庆祝会（仪式） ▲ freely adv. 自由地，随意地 ▲ champagne n. 香槟酒

1073. imitate [ˈɪməˌtet] [im·i·tate] ☆★★★★

v. 仿效，模仿	It's quite common for children to imitate adults. 孩子们喜欢模仿成年人，这很常见。
同义字词	mimic, emulate, copy, simulate
反义字词	create, invent
高分秘诀	▲ adult n. 成人

1074. immediate [ɪˈmidɪɪt] [im·me·di·ate] ★★★★★

adj. 立即的，直接的	Before he take immediate and resolute action, something bad happened to him. 他还没有来得及采取坚决果断的行动，坏事就发生了。
同义字词	prompt, instantaneous
高分秘诀	▲ take action 采取行动，行动起来 ▲ resolute adj. 坚决的，刚毅的

1075. immense [ɪˈmɛns] [im·mense] ☆★★★★

adj. 巨大的，极大的	I felt so good when my eyes ranged over an immense extend of wilderness. 当我的目光扫过这片蛮荒时，我感觉好极了。
同义字词	enormous, colossal, huge, mammoth, vast
高分秘诀	▲ range over 扫视 ▲ wilderness n. 荒野，沙漠

1076. immigrant [ˈɪməgrənt] [im·mi·grant] ☆★★★★

n. （自外国移入）移民	Unfortunately these immigrants were subjected to barbarous treatment. 不幸的是，这些移民受到了野蛮的对待。
同义字词	alien, non-native
反义字词	emigrant
高分秘诀	▲ unfortunately adv. 不幸地 ▲ be subjected to 受…… ▲ barbarous adj. 野蛮的，残暴的 ▲ treatment n. 处理，对待

1077. immune [ɪˋmjun] [im·mune] ☆★★★★

adj. （对……）免疫的，不受影响的

Save your breath, the boy was immune to all persuasion.
别浪费口舌，那男孩对所有的劝说都无动于衷。

同义字词　exempt, resistant, free

衍生字词　▲ immune system 免疫系统

高分秘诀　▲ save one's breath 别白费口舌
　　　　　▲ persuasion **n.** 劝说，说服（力），信仰

1078. impact [ˋɪmpækt] [im·pact] ★★★★★

n. 影响，作用

The boy collapsed under the full impact of the blow.
男孩受到重击而倒下。

v. 影响，冲击

It's obvious that the book will impact on children.
显而易见，这本书会对儿童产生影响。

同义字词　bear upon, bear on, affect, wallop, burn, bump

高分秘诀　▲ collapse **v.** 倒下
　　　　　▲ blow **n.** 一击，打击
　　　　　▲ obvious **adj.** 明显的，显而易见的

1079. impair [ɪmˋpɛr] [im·pair] ☆★★★★

v. 损害，削弱

Sometimes fatigue and illness can impair people's judgment.
有时候疲劳和疾病会降低人的判断力。

同义字词　hurt, damage, harm, weaken

高分秘诀　▲ fatigue **n.** 疲劳，劳累
　　　　　▲ illness **n.** 病，疾病
　　　　　▲ judgment **n.** 判断

1080. impart [ɪmˋpɑrt] [im·part] ☆☆★★★

v. 传授，告知

I think pink is better; the pink curtain can impart a certain elegance to the room.
我认为粉红色的比较好；粉红色的窗帘能使房间更加高雅。

同义字词　add, give, contribute, convey, disclose, reveal

高分秘诀　▲ pink **adj.** 粉红色的
　　　　　▲ curtain **n.** 窗帘，门帘
　　　　　▲ elegance **n.** 高雅，典雅，雅致

immune ~ imperative

1081. impartial [ɪm`pɑrʃəl] [im·par·tial] ☆★★★★

adj. 公正的，无偏见的

The judge is an impartial and incorruptible one, and he's never taken bribes.
这位法官铁面无私，他从来不收贿。

同义字词 unbiased, fair, unprejudiced

反义字词 partial, biased, prejudiced

高分秘诀
▲ judge **n.** 法官
▲ incorruptible **adj.** 不腐败的，清廉的
▲ take bribes 受贿

1082. impede [ɪm`pid] [im·pede] ☆☆★★★

v. 妨碍，阻碍

It rained heavily last week and the muddy roads impede our journey.
上个星期雨下得很大，泥泞的道路阻碍了我们的旅程。

同义字词 hinder, interrupt, hamper, obstruct

高分秘诀
▲ heavily **adv.** 严重地，大量地
▲ muddy road 泥泞道路
▲ journey **n.** 旅行，行程

1083. impending [ɪm`pɛndɪŋ] [im·pend·ing] ☆★★★★

adj. 即将发生的，逼近的

Sometimes the agitated activity by certain animals can by a sign of an impending earthquake.
有时某些动物的烦躁不安很可能是地震来临前的预兆。

同义字词 approaching, imminent, at hand, impendent

高分秘诀
▲ agitated **adj.** 不安的，焦虑的，激动的
▲ certain **adv.** 某，某些
▲ earthquake **n.** 地震

1084. imperative [ɪm`pɛrətɪv] [im·per·a·tive] ☆★★★★

adj. 必要的，强制的

The life of the sick man is at stake, an immediate operation was imperative.
病人的生命危在旦夕，非立刻动手术不可。

n. 命令，需要

Accumulating enough money to buy a house has become an imperative for the young generation.
存下足够的钱买栋房子成了年轻一代必须做的事。

同义字词 necessary, essential, compelling, compulsory, mandatory

衍生字词	▲ imperative mood 祈使式，祈使语气
	▲ imperative sentence 祈使句，命令句
高分秘诀	▲ at stake 在紧要关头（危如累卵）
	▲ immediate operation 立即操作，立即做手术
	▲ young generation 年轻一代

1085. impersonal [ɪmˈpɜsn̩] [im·per·son·al]   ☆★★★★

adj. 客观的，无私的	Though his son was involved in this matter, he still made an impersonal comment on it. 尽管这件事与自己的儿子有关，他仍然作了客观的评论。
同义字词	detached, disinterested, objective, impartial
衍生字词	▲ impersonal entity 法人单位
高分秘诀	▲ be involved in 涉及，专心
	▲ comment on 就……发表看法（评论）

1086. impersonate [ɪmˈpɜsn̩ˌet] [im·per·son·ate]   ☆☆★★★

v. 模仿，扮演	By the time he was fifteen he started to show a flair for impersonate many well-known politicians. 十五岁的时候，他开始展现模仿知名政治人物的天分。
同义字词	mimic, imitate, personate, portray, pose
高分秘诀	▲ by the time 到……时候为止
	▲ flair n. 天资，天分，才华
	▲ well-known adj. 出名的，众所周知的，熟悉的
	▲ politician n. 政治家

1087. impetus [ˈɪmpətəs] [im·pe·tus]   ☆☆★★★

n. 推动（力），激励（物）	The government reform gave fresh impetus to commerce. 政府改革进一步推动商业的发展。
同义字词	driving force, incentive, push, momentum, impulse
高分秘诀	▲ government reform 政府改革
	▲ commerce n. 商业，贸易

1088. implement [ˈɪmpləmənt] [im·ple·ment]   ☆☆★★★

n. 工具，器具	How about you buy some agricultural implements for me when you come back? 你回来的时候能否为我买些农具？

impersonal ~ improvise

v. 实行,实施	One of my rules is that I've never undertake a project unless I can implement it. 我的原则之一是：除非我能完成这项计划，否则我不会接案。
同义字词	tool, instrument, execute, carry out, perform
高分秘诀	▲ agricultural implements 农具 ▲ come back 回来 ▲ undertake v. 担任，承揽

1089. imply [ɪmˈplaɪ] [im·ply] ★★★★★

v. 暗示,意味	I knew him quite well, his silence implied agreement. 我很了解他，他的沉默意味着同意。
同义字词	suggest, hint, intimate, insinuate
高分秘诀	▲ silence n. 沉默 ▲ agreement n. 同意

1090. import [ɪmˈport] [im·port] ★★★★★

v. (贸易)进口	The Korean didn't import any goods from Japan. 韩国人不从日本进口任何产品。
n. (贸易)进口	I found that the import of chemicals went up sharply these days. 我发现近来化学药品的进口量急速上升。
同义字词	importation, introduce
高分秘诀	▲ Korean n. 韩国人，韩国国民 ▲ Japan n. 日本 ▲ chemicals n. 化学药品，化学制剂（品）

1091. impose [ɪmˈpoz] [im·pose] ☆★★★★

v. 把……强加于,施加影响	I don't think it is right to impose your thoughts on others. 我觉得把你的想法强加于别人是不对的。
同义字词	demand, force, inflict, enforce
反义字词	free, liberate
高分秘诀	▲ impose on 把……加于

1092. improvise [ˈɪmprəvaɪz] [im·pro·vise] ☆★★★★

v. 即席创作,即兴表演	I haven't made any preparation for the speech, so I have to improvise. 这次演讲我没有做任何准备，只好即兴发挥。

同义字词	think up on the spot, extemporize, extemporise, improvize
衍生字词	▲ improvisational adj. 即兴的
高分秘诀	▲ preparation n. 准备，预备

1093. impulse [ˈɪmpʌls] [im·pulse] ☆★★★★

n. 冲动；刺激	On impulse, I bought this big plush toy for myself. 我一时冲动，为自己买下了这个大毛绒玩具。
同义字词	force, urge, compulsion
衍生字词	▲ impulse circuit 脉冲电路 ▲ impulse buying 即兴购买（一时冲动的购物行为）
高分秘诀	▲ on impulse 一时冲动 ▲ plush toy 绒毛玩具

1094. inanimate [ɪnˈænəmɪt] [in·an·i·mate] ☆☆★★★

adj. 无生命的，无精打采的	Don't inflict your anger on those inanimate things. 不要把怒气发泄在无生命的事物上。
同义字词	lifeless, nonliving, pulseless
高分秘诀	▲ inflict v. 把……强加给，使承受，遭受

1095. inaugurate [ɪnˈɔgjəˌret] [in·au·gu·rate] ☆★★★★

v. 开创，使就职	It was Watt who inaugurated the age of steam. 瓦特开创了蒸汽时代。
同义字词	begin, initiate, install, set up, instate
衍生字词	▲ inauguration n. 就职典礼，开幕式 ▲ inauguration day （美国）总统就职日
高分秘诀	▲ Watt 瓦特（苏格兰发明家、蒸汽机发明人）

1096. incense [ˈɪnsɛns] [in·cense] ☆☆★★★

n. 香	I'm allergic to the mosquito coil incense. 我对蚊香过敏。
v. 激怒，焚香	I found he became incensed at my behavior. 我发现他对我的行为感到愤怒。
同义字词	anger, enrage, exasperate, infuriate
衍生字词	▲ incense burner 香炉 ▲ incense paper 香纸

impulse ~ inclination

高分秘诀 ▲ be allergic to 对……过敏
▲ mosquito coil incense 蚊香

1097. incentive [ɪnˋsɛntɪv] [in·cen·tive] ☆☆★★★

n. 动机, 刺激

The workers have no incentive to work harder because they know that the boss is bound not to give them a pay raise.
工人们没有努力工作的动力，因为他们知道老板必定不会加薪。

同义字词 motivation, motive, inducement, stimulus
衍生字词 ▲ incentive pay 奖金，奖励津贴
高分秘诀 ▲ work hard 努力工作
▲ be bound to 一定，注定
▲ pay raise 加薪

1098. incessant [ɪnˋsɛsn̩t] [in·ces·sant] ☆☆★★★

adj. 不停的, 连续的

She is a chatterbox and always keeps incessant talking.
她是个喋喋不休的人，总是说个不停。

同义字词 unending, constant, unceasing, ceaseless, nonstop
高分秘诀 ▲ chatterbox **n.** 喋喋不休的人，话匣子

1099. incisive [ɪnˋsaɪsɪv] [in·ci·sive] ☆☆★★★

adj. 深刻的, 尖锐的

In fact I really appreciate his incisive criticism.
事实上，我真的很感激他中肯的批评。

同义字词 sharp, penetrating, penetrative
高分秘诀 ▲ in fact 实际上，其实
▲ criticism **n.** 批评，指责，评论

1100. inclination [ˌɪnkləˋneʃən] [in·cli·na·tion] ☆☆★★★

n. 嗜好, 爱好

From his expression I can tell he hasn't the inclination to parley.
从他的表情，我能看出他没有和谈的倾向。

同义字词 preference, tendency, leaning
高分秘诀 ▲ expression **n.** 表情
▲ parley **n.**/**v.** 和谈，谈判

1101. incongruity [ˌɪnkɑnˈgruətɪ] [in·con·gru·i·ty] ☆☆★★★

n. 不一致, 不和谐

I didn't felt any sense of incongruity from what you talk.
从你说的话中,我没有感到任何矛盾的地方。

同义字词 incompatibility, disharmony, incongruousness, incongruence

反义字词 congruity, congruence, congruousness

高分秘诀 ▲ sense **n.** 感觉,辨别

1102. incorporate [ɪnˈkɔrpəˌret] [in·cor·po·rate] ☆☆★★★

v. 合并, 并入

It would be better if you incorporate the new suggestion with the old.
如果你们把新旧建议合并就更好了。

同义字词 merge, unite, integrate, contain, comprise

高分秘诀 ▲ suggestion **n.** 建议,意见

1103. incur [ɪnˈkɝ] [in·cur] ☆★★★★

v. 招致, 引起, 遭受

His father died, so he had to incur liabilities.
他父亲去世了,所以他不得不扛下债务。

同义字词 cause, arouse

高分秘诀 ▲ liabilities 债务,负债

1104. indicate [ˈɪndəˌket] [in·di·cate] ★★★★★

v. 指示, 指出

See the arrow on the sign, which indicates the right way to go.
看牌子上的箭头,上面指示该走哪条路。

同义字词 show, reflect, evidence, imply, suggest, express

高分秘诀 ▲ arrow **n.** 箭头
▲ sign **n.** 标记,符号

1105. indiscriminate [ˌɪndɪˈskrɪmənɪt] [in·dis·crim·i·nate] ☆☆★★★

adj. 不加区别的, 不加选择的

Don't be indiscriminate in the choice of sexual partners, or you would catch the sexually transmitted diseases.
选择性伴侣的时候要谨慎,否则会感染性病。

同义字词 indiscriminative, unselective, indiscriminating

高分秘诀 ▲ sexual partner 性伴侣
▲ sexually transmitted diseases(STD 性病)

incongruity ~ infectious

1106. induce [ɪn`djus] [in·duce] ☆☆★★★

v. 诱使，促使

I can't agree more that too much food induces sleepiness.
对于吃得太饱会突然想睡，我很赞同。

同义字词: bring about, cause, evoke, lead on

衍生字词:
▲ induced abortion 人工流产
▲ induced charge 电荷

高分秘诀:
▲ I can't agree more. 我完全同意
▲ sleepiness **n.** 睡意，嗜睡

1107. industrious [ɪn`dʌstrɪəs] [in·dus·tri·ous] ☆★★★★

adj. 勤劳的，勤奋的

Thoreau once said that it's not enough to be industrious; you have to know what you are industrious about.
美国作家梭罗曾说过光勤劳是不够的，你必须知道自己为什么而勤劳。

同义字词: assiduous, diligent, sedulous, energetic, hardworking

反义字词: idle, indolent, lazy

高分秘诀:
▲ Thoreau 梭罗（美国作家，思想家）
▲ not enough 不够的

1108. inert [ɪn`ɝt] [in·ert] ☆☆★★★

adj. 惰性的，不活泼的

The management team in our company is inert, so I don't want to work here.
我们公司的管理层死气沉沉，所以我不想在这里工作。

同义字词: inactive, listless, sluggish

衍生字词:
▲ inert atmosphere 惰性气氛
▲ inert gas 惰性气体

高分秘诀:
▲ management team 管理层

1109. infectious [ɪn`fɛkʃəs] [in·fec·tious] ☆★★★★

adj. 传染性的，易传染的

AIDS is a fatal infectious disease.
艾滋病是一种致命的传染病。

同义字词: contagious, contaminating, infective

高分秘诀:
▲ AIDS (Acquired Immune Deficiency Syndrome) **n.** 艾滋病
▲ serious disease 重病

1110. inferior [ɪnˈfɪrɪə] [in·fe·ri·or] ★★★★★

adj. （社会地位、品质等）差的

One of my colleagues is always thought that she is inferior to others in many respects.
我有一个同事总是认为自己在许多方面不如别人。

同义字词 poor, worse, lower, secondary, subordinate

反义字词 superior, superordinate

衍生字词
▲ inferiority complex 自卑情结
▲ inferiority n. 自卑感

高分秘诀
▲ colleague n. 同事
▲ be inferior to 在……之下，次于，不如
▲ in many respects 在许多方面

1111. infest [ɪnˈfɛst] [in·fest] ★★★

v. 骚扰，大批滋生

The gnats and mosquitoes infested the field by the river.
小昆虫和蚊子群集在河边的田野。

同义字词 beset, overrun, swarm, spread

高分秘诀
▲ gnat n. 叮人小虫
▲ mosquito n. 蚊子
▲ by the river 在河边

1112. infiltrate [ɪnˈfɪltret] [in·fil·trate] ★★★

v. 使透过，渗透

No on can get the bottom of the sea, you know there is no light can infiltrate there.
没有人可以抵达海底，那里连光线都照射不进。

同义字词 spread to, permeate, penetrate, pass through

高分秘诀
▲ bottom n. 底部，水底
▲ light n. 光，光线

1113. inflate [ɪnˈflet] [in·flate] ★★★

v. 使膨胀，使充气

Susan, it's your turn to inflate the bicycle.
苏珊，轮到你帮自行车充气了。

同义字词 expand, fill with air or gas, blow up, swell

衍生字词 ▲ inflation n. 通货膨胀

高分秘诀
▲ it's one's turn 轮到某人……
▲ bicycle n. 自行车

inferior ~ influx

1114. inflict [ɪn`flɪkt] [in·flict] ☆★★★★

v. 造成；（使）遭受（痛苦、损伤等）

We should inflict severe punishment on criminals.
我们应该对罪犯施加严厉的惩罚。

| 同义字词 | impose, cause, bring about |

高分秘诀
▲ severe **adj.** 严重的，严厉的
▲ punishment **n.** 处罚，受罚
▲ criminal **n.** 罪犯，犯人

1115. influential [ˌɪnfluˋɛnʃəl] [in·flu·en·tial] ★★★★★

adj. 有影响的，有权势的

He is such an apple polisher, and always fawns on anyone in an influential position.
他是个马屁精，总是向身居要职的人谄媚。

| 同义字词 | important, powerful, significant |

高分秘诀
▲ apple polisher 拍马屁的人
▲ fawn on 奉承，拍马
▲ position **n.** 职位，地位，身份

1116. influenza [ˌɪnfluˋɛnzə] [in·flu·en·za] ★★★★★

n. 流行性感冒

I can't take part in the party, because I had an influenza epidemic.
我不能参加晚会，因为我感染了流行性感冒。

| 同义字词 | flu, grippe |

衍生字词
▲ influenza flu 流感
▲ influenza vaccine 流感疫苗

高分秘诀
▲ take part in 参加，参与……活动
▲ epidemic **n.** 流行病

1117. influx [ˋɪnflʌks] [in·flux] ☆★★★★

n. 流入，汇集

Before I know it, there was a influx of goods onto the market.
不知不觉地，大批商品涌入市场。

| 同义字词 | arrival, inward flow, inflow |
| 反义字词 | efflux, outflow, effluence |

高分秘诀
▲ before I know it 不知不觉地
▲ market **n.** 市场

1118. infuse [ɪn`fjuz] [in·fuse] ☆★★★★

v. 注入, 灌输
We must infuse new blood into the club.
我们必须为俱乐部注入新鲜的血液。

同义字词　instill, impregnate, inculcate

高分秘诀　▲ infuse new blood into 给(企业、团体)增加新成员

1119. ingenious [ɪn`dʒinjəs] [in·gen·ious] ☆★★★★

adj. 机灵的, 有独创性的
We should try our best to promote this ingenious contrivance.
我们应该大力推广这个有独创性的发明。

同义字词　clever, crafty, inventive, imaginative

反义字词　clumsy, awkward, unskillful

高分秘诀
▲ try one's best 尽最大努力
▲ promote **v.** 推销, 推动, 促进
▲ contrivance **n.** 发明, 发明才能, 发明物

1120. inhabit [ɪn`hæbɪt] [in·ha·bit] ☆★★★★

v. 居住于, 栖息于
It is so cold in the South Pole, and it is not inhabited.
南极太冷了, 没有人居住。

同义字词　live in, occupy, reside in, dwell

高分秘诀
▲ North Pole 北极
▲ South Pole 南极

1121. inherent [ɪn`hɪrənt] [in·her·ent] ☆☆★★★

adj. 固有的, 内在的
The little boy has an inherent modesty, and he always stammers in the presence of strangers.
这个小男孩天生羞怯, 在陌生人面前说话总是结巴。

同义字词　intrinsic, built in, natural

高分秘诀
▲ modesty **n.** 谦虚, 谦逊
▲ stammer **v.** 结巴地说出
▲ in the presence of 在……面前

1122. inherit [ɪn`hɛrɪt] [in·her·it] ☆★★★★

v. 继承
The young man has inherited his father's skill in making money.
这个年轻人继承了父亲赚钱的本领。

高分秘诀　▲ make money 挣钱

infuse ~ innate

1123. inhibit [ɪnˋhɪbɪt] [in·hib·it] ☆★★★★

v. 抑制，阻止

The teacher told me that this kind of compounds can inhibit the microbial growth.
老师告诉我这种化合物能抑制微生物的生长。

| 同义字词 | restrain, curb, hinder, deter |

衍生字词
▲ inhibitory adj. 禁止的，抑制的
▲ inhibiter n. 抑制剂，缓蚀剂

高分秘诀
▲ compound n. 复合物，化合物
▲ microbial adj. 微生物的

1124. initiate [ɪˋnɪʃɪ͵et] [in·i·ti·ate] ☆★★★★

v. 开始，发起

The education and library board is considering about initiating a new course of studies.
教委会正在考虑开设一门新课程。

同义字词 begin, originate, start, pioneer, lead

高分秘诀
▲ education and library board 教委会
▲ course of study 研究课程，学科

1125. inject [ɪnˋdʒɛkt] [in·ject] ☆★★★★

v. 注射，注入，灌溉

Sometime it would be better to inject a note of humor into the story.
有时候在故事中增添一点幽默会比较好。

同义字词 put in, infuse, insert, interpose, shoot

高分秘诀
▲ a note of 一点
▲ humor n. 幽默，诙谐

1126. innate [ˋɪnˋet] [in·nate] ☆☆★★★

adj. 先天的，天生的

As I told you before the correct ideas are not innate in mind, but come from social practice.
正如我以前告诉你的，正确的思想不是天生的，而是来自社会经验。

同义字词 inborn, congenital, unconditioned

反义字词 acquired

衍生字词 ▲ innate immunity 先天免疫，自然免疫

高分秘诀
▲ come from 来自某处
▲ social practice 社会实践

1127. innocent [ˈɪnəsn̩t] [in·no·cent] ☆★★★★

adj. 无辜的，清白的

I can offer ample reason to prove that I am innocent.
我能提供充分理由证明我是无辜的。

同义字词： naive, gullible, ingenuous

高分秘诀：
▲ ample **adj.** 足够的，大量的，丰富的
▲ prove **v.** 证明

1128. innovation [ˌɪnəˈveʃən] [in·no·va·tion] ☆★★★★

n. 改革，创新

If you have some bold innovation, please share it with us.
如果你有大胆的创新，跟我们分享一下。

同义字词： novelty, creation, invention

高分秘诀：
▲ bold **adj.** 大胆的，勇敢的
▲ share with 把（自己的感受）告诉（某人），分享

1129. inquiry [ɪnˈkwaɪrɪ] [in·qui·ry] ☆★★★★

n. 质问，调查

I doubted what he said, so I made a detailed inquiry about the facts.
我怀疑他说的话，于是我追问事实真相

同义字词： investigation, quest, interrogation, query, question, enquire

衍生字词： ▲ inquiry agency 调查所，征信机构

高分秘诀：
▲ doubt **v.** 怀疑，疑惑
▲ detailed **adj.** 详细的，精细的，复杂的

1130. insanity [ɪnˈsænətɪ] [in·san·i·ty] ☆★★★★

n. 精神错乱，疯狂

He must be mad; you know its insanity to drive a car without any brakes.
他一定是疯了；驾驶一部没有刹车的汽车真是愚不可及。

衍生字词： ▲ insane **adj.** （患）精神病的，精神失常的

高分秘诀： ▲ brake **n.** 制动器，刹车

1131. insert [ɪnˈsɝt] [in·sert] ☆★★★★

v. 插入

According to the instruction, the next procedure is to insert the battery.
依照说明书，下一步要安装电池。

同义字词： input, enter, enclose, tuck, put in, set in

innocent ~ instinct

高分秘诀
▲ instruction n. 使用说明书，操作指南
▲ procedure n. 步骤，程序
▲ battery n. 电池

1132. insist [ɪnˈsɪst] [in·sist] ★★★★★

v. 坚持认为，坚决主张
I think we should insist on the importance of being punctual.
我认为我们应该强调守时的重要性。

同义字词 assert, maintain, contend, urge

高分秘诀
▲ insist on 坚持，强调
▲ importance n. 重要（性）
▲ punctual adj. 严守时刻的，准时的

1133. inspect [ɪnˈspɛkt] [in·spect] ★★★★★

v. 检查，审查
The mayor would come to inspect the new power station.
新任市长要来视察那座新的发电站。

同义字词 look over, examine, scrutinize

高分秘诀
▲ mayor n. 市长
▲ power station 发电所，发电站

1134. inspire [ɪnˈspaɪr] [in·spire] ★★★★★

v. 鼓舞，启迪
It's obvious that the novel inspired the young generation.
很明显地，这本小说激励着年轻一代。

同义字词 encourage, inspirit

高分秘诀
▲ obvious adj. 明显的，显而易见的
▲ novel n. 小说

1135. instantaneous [ˌɪnstənˈtenɪəs] [in·stan·ta·ne·ous] ☆☆★★★

adj. 瞬间的，即刻的
The little girl made it. It's the instantaneous and strong impulse moved her to battle with her desperate fate.
女孩会成功是因为有一股强有力的冲动促使她挑战坎坷的命运。

高分秘诀
▲ battle with 与……战斗
▲ desperate fate 坎坷的命运

1136. instinct [ˈɪnstɪŋkt] [in·stinct] ☆★★★★

n. 本能，直觉
Most of time I act on instinct.
通常我凭直觉行动。

同义字词	instant, drive, nature, inherent aptitude
衍生字词	▲ instinct noodles 速食面，泡面
高分秘诀	▲ act on instinct 凭直觉行动

1137. insulation [ˌɪnsəˈleʃən] [in·su·la·tion] ☆★★★★

n. 绝缘，隔离	Plastic is often used for insulation. 塑胶经常被当作绝缘材料。
同义字词	isolation, separation
衍生字词	▲ insulant n. 绝缘材料 ▲ insularism n. 岛国特性；胸襟狭窄 ▲ acoustic insulation 隔音 ▲ cold insulation 隔冷，绝热保冷 ▲ wire insulation 导线绝缘

1138. insult [ˈɪnsʌlt] [in·sult] ★★★★★

v. 侮辱，凌辱	The little boy always insulted others with filthy language. 这个小男孩经常用脏话侮辱人。
同义字词	offend, affront, humiliate
反义字词	esteem, honor, respect
高分秘诀	▲ filthy adj. 肮脏的，污秽的，下流的

1139. intact [ɪnˈtækt] [in·tact] ☆★★★★

adj. 尚未被人碰到的，完整的	Though the businessman experienced much misfortunes, his faith and optimism remained intact. 尽管这个商人经历很多不幸，但他的信心和乐观丝毫未减。
同义字词	unaltered, uninjured, untouched, integrated, whole, complete, entire
反义字词	incomplete, nonholonomic
高分秘诀	▲ misfortune n. 不幸，灾难 ▲ faith n. 信心 ▲ optimism n. 乐观，乐观主义

1140. integrate [ˈɪntəˌɡret] [in·te·grate]  ☆☆★★★

| v. 使成为整体，使一体化 | When you learn some new things, just integrate theory with practice.
当你学新东西时，要把理论和实践相结合。 |
| 同义字词 | unify, synthesize, coordinate, amass |

insulation ~ intersect

| 高分秘诀 | ▲ theory n. 理论
▲ practice n. 实践，实际 |

1141. intelligent [ɪnˈtɛlədʒənt] [in·tel·li·gent] ☆★★★★

adj. 聪明的，有才智的	I wonder whether the earth has been visited by intelligent creatures from outer space. 我想知道太空的智慧生物是否已经访问过地球。
同义字词	ingenious, wise, bright, sensible
反义字词	stupid, unintelligent
高分秘诀	▲ whether conj. 是否 ▲ intelligent creature 智慧生物 ▲ outer space 太空，外太空

1142. interfere [ˌɪntɚˈfɪr] [in·ter·fere] ☆★★★★

v. 妨碍，干涉	I don't like others interfere with my business. 我不喜欢别人干涉我的事情。
同义字词	disrupt, hinder, obstruct, meddle
高分秘诀	▲ interfere with 干预，妨碍，阻止

1143. intermittent [ˌɪntɚˈmɪtnt] [in·ter·mit·tent] ☆☆★★★

adj. 间歇的，断断续续的	The boy stuck to nothing long, for he has intermittent bursts of interest. 男孩做任何事都做不久，因为他的兴趣总是一阵一阵的。
同义字词	periodic, recurrent, snatchy
反义字词	continued, continuous
高分秘诀	▲ burst n. 突发 ▲ interest n. 兴趣，爱好，嗜好

1144. interrupt [ˌɪntəˈrʌpt] [in·ter·rupt] ☆★★★★

v. 打断，使中断	No one ventured to interrupt the boss when he spoke. 没有人敢在老板说话的时候打断他。
同义字词	impede, discontinue, cut off, disturb
高分秘诀	▲ venture v. 敢于，冒险

1145. intersect [ˌɪntɚˈsɛkt] [in·ter·sect] ☆☆★★★

| v. 相交，横断 | In my city streets usually intersect at right angles.
在我们的市区，马路通常以直角交叉。 |
| 同义字词 | cross, meet |

衍生字词	▲ intersection n. 十字路口，交叉点
	▲ intersect struggle 内部派系斗争
高分秘诀	▲ street n. 大街，街道
	▲ right angle 直角

1146. interval [ˈɪntəvl] [in·ter·val] ☆☆★★★

| n. 间隔，距离 | The traffic policeman told us that the proper intervals should be maintained between vehicles. 交警告诉大家，车辆之间应该保持适当的间距。 |

同义字词	pause, break, interim, interlude, intermission, recess
高分秘诀	▲ traffic policeman 交通警察
	▲ proper adj. 适合的，适当的
	▲ vehicle n. 交通工具，车辆

1147. intervention [ˌɪntəˈvɛnʃən] [in·ter·ven·tion] ☆★★★★

| n. 干涉，介入 | Don't get in the middle of it; you know your intervention would bring their quarrel to a climax. 不要卷入此事，你的干涉会使他们的口角更加激烈。 |

同义字词	interference, intercession, intrusion
高分秘诀	▲ in the middle of 在……的中间
	▲ quarrel n. 争吵，不和，口角
	▲ climax n. 顶点，极点，高潮

1148. intimate [ˈɪntəmɪt] [in·ti·mate] ☆★★★★

| adj. 亲密的，熟知的，精通 | Though they are not native sisters, they are more intimate than that. 虽然他们不是亲姐妹，但亲密更胜亲姐妹。 |
| v. 示意，暗示 | He didn't say it explicitly, only intimated that he didn't agree. 他没有明讲，只是暗示他不同意。 |

同义字词	close, familiar, deep, profound
高分秘诀	▲ native sisters 亲姐妹
	▲ explicitly adv. 明白地，明确地

1149. intoxication [ɪnˌtɑksəˈkeʃən] [in·tox·i·ca·tion] ☆★★★★

| n. 陶醉，酒醉 | A certain man saw you were in a state of beastly intoxication last night. 昨晚有人看见你醉醺醺的。 |

| 同义字词 | inebriation, drunkenness |

interval ~ intrinsic

反义字词	sobriety, soberness
衍生字词	▲ intoxicant n. 酒类饮料，麻醉品 ▲ food intoxication 食物中毒 ▲ chronic intoxication 慢性中毒
高分秘诀	▲ in a state 处于激动（焦躁）的情绪中 ▲ beastly adv. 非常，极

1150. intrepid [ɪnˈtrɛpɪd] [in·trep·id]

adj. 无畏的，勇敢的

Though he is my adversary and failed in the game, I admired his intrepid spirit.
虽然他是我的手下败将，我却敬佩他无畏的精神。

| 同义字词 | fearless, courageous, brave, bold, dauntless, valiant |
| 高分秘诀 | ▲ adversary n. 对手，敌手
▲ fail in （使）在……方面失败了 |

1151. intricate [ˈɪntrəkɪt] [in·tri·cate]

adj. 复杂的，错综的

The author is good at writing such kind of novels with intricate plots.
这名作家擅长写情节错综复杂的小说。

| 同义字词 | complex, complicated, entangled, involved |
| 高分秘诀 | ▲ author n. 作家，作者
▲ be good at 擅长
▲ plot n. 故事情节，剧情 |

1152. intrigue [ɪnˈtrig] [in·trigue]

v. 激起……的兴趣，阴谋诡计

How dare you intrigue against me!
你竟敢阴谋陷害我。

n. 阴谋，诡计

In the old royal palace was filled with intrigue.
古时候的皇宫充满钩心斗角。

| 同义字词 | fascinate, captivate, conspiracy, plot, scheme, machination |
| 高分秘诀 | ▲ intrigue against 与……密谋反对……
▲ royal palace 皇宫 |

1153. intrinsic [ɪnˈtrɪnsɪk] [in·trin·sic]

adj. 固有的，内在的

It's hard to change a man's intrinsic worth.
改变一个人的价值观真的很难。

| 同义字词 | inherent, essential, fundamental, intrinsical |
| 高分秘诀 | ▲ intrinsic worth 价值观 |

1154. introspective [ˌɪntrəˈspɛktɪv] [in·tro·spec·tive] ☆☆★★★

adj. 自省的，反省的

I found my little nephew became increasingly introspective.
我发现我的外甥越来越内向。

| 同义字词 | self-examining, introverted, contemplative |
| 反义字词 | extrospective, extroverted |

1155. intrusion [ɪnˈtruʒən] [in·tru·sion] ☆★★★★

n. 闯入，干涉

Your intrusion into my private life is illegal.
你侵扰我的私生活是违法的。

同义字词	encroachment, invasion, trespass, infringement, violation
衍生字词	▲ intruder **n.** 入侵者，闯入者
高分秘诀	▲ private **adj.** 私人的，个人的 ▲ illegal **adj.** 不合法的，违法的

1156. inundate [ˈɪnʌnˌdet] [in·un·date] ☆☆★★★

v. 淹没，（洪水般地）涌来

We should prepare for the flood protection, for the river would inundate the valley any time.
我们应该做好防洪工作，因为这条河流随时都会泛滥。

| 同义字词 | flood, overflow, deluge, overwhelm |
| 高分秘诀 | ▲ prepare for 为……准备
▲ flood protection 防洪，防汛，防洪工作
▲ valley **n.** 山谷 |

1157. invade [ɪnˈved] [in·vade] ☆★★★★

v. 侵略，侵犯

After the press reported the old town's beautiful scene, thousands of tourists invaded it.
媒体报道这座古城的美景后，数以千计的观光客涌入这座城市。

| 同义字词 | move into, intrude, aggress, encroach, trespass |
| 高分秘诀 | ▲ the press 报刊
▲ scene **n.** 景色，景象
▲ thousands of 数千的
▲ tourist **n.** 旅行者，观光客 |

introspective ~ ironic

1158. inventory [ˈɪnvənˌtɔrɪ] [in·ven·to·ry] ☆★★★★

n. 存货清单，库存品
I have to take time to complete the inventory.
我得找时间填好这张库存单。

同义字词	check list, stock list
衍生字词	▲ inventory account 存货账户 ▲ inventory analysis 库存分析 ▲ inventory control 存货控制
高分秘诀	▲ take time 花点时间.

1159. investigate [ɪnˈvɛstəˌget] [in·ves·ti·gate] ★★★★★

v. 调查，研究
I think it's necessary to investigate the matter further.
我认为有必要进一步调查此事。

| 同义字词 | explore, research, survey, search, probe, enquire, look into |
| 高分秘诀 | ▲ necessary adj. 必要的，必需的
▲ further adv. 进一步地 |

1160. inviting [ɪnˈvaɪtɪŋ] [in·vit·ing] ☆★★★★

adj. 诱人的，引人心动的
My mouth is watering, for the food you cooked is so inviting.
你准备的美食太诱人，我的口水直流。

| 衍生字词 | ▲ inviting views 诱人景色 |
| 高分秘诀 | ▲ My mouth is watering. 我在流口水。 |

1161. ironic [aɪˈrɑnɪk] [i·ron·ic] ☆★★★★

adj. 讽刺的
His ironic expression really hurt me.
他嘲讽的表情深深地刺伤了我。

| 同义字词 | satiric, ironical, wry |
| 衍生字词 | ▲ Iron Age 铁器时代
▲ Iron Curtain 铁幕（指第二次世界大战后冷战期间，苏联及其东欧附庸国彻底封闭的状态）
▲ iron gray 铁灰色
▲ iron hand 铁腕，坚强严厉的手段 |

▲ iron horse 火车头，自行车，监狱
▲ iron lung 铁肺（一种人工呼吸器）
▲ iron out 消除
▲ iron pyrites 二硫化铁
▲ iron rations 军用干粮，野战应急口粮
▲ iron wedding 铁婚
▲ have (too) many irons in the fire 同时有几件事要办
▲ Strike while the iron is hot. 趁热打铁

高分秘诀　▲ expression n. 表情

1162. irreversible [ˌɪrɪˈvɜsəbl] [ir·re·ver·si·ble] ☆★★★★

adj. 不可改变的，不可撤销的
I can tell you that the lapse of time is irreversible.
我可以告诉你流逝的时光不可能逆转。

同义字词　irrevocable, final, unchangeable

高分秘诀　▲ lapse of time 时光的流逝

1163. irrigate [ˈɪrəˌɡet] [ir·ri·gate] ☆☆★★★

v. 灌溉
We can irrigate our crops with water from the near river.
我们可以引进邻近河流的水源灌溉作物。

高分秘诀　▲ crop n. 庄稼，作物

1164. irritate [ˈɪrəˌtet] [ir·ri·tate] ☆★★★★

v. 激怒，使过敏
I was irritated by my former boyfriend's insolence.
我被前男友的蛮横态度激怒了。

同义字词　prickle, annoy, provoke, agitate, foment

反义字词　appease, calm

高分秘诀　▲ former adj. 过去的，以前的
▲ insolence n. 傲慢，无礼

1165. isolate [ˈaɪsˌlet] [i·so·late] ★★★★★

v. 使隔离，使孤立
It's the heavy snowfall isolated our little village with the outside.
大雪把我们这小村庄和外界隔离了。

同义字词　seclude, separate, set apart, segregate

衍生字词　▲ isolate selection 隔离选择
▲ isolator n. 隔音装置，绝缘体

irreversible ~ itinerary

1166. issue [ˋɪʃjʊ] [is·sue] ★★★★★

n. 问题，(报刊的)期
The professor had published so many issues on energy preservation.
教授已经出版了很多有关能源节约问题的期刊。

v. 发行
Tell you a good news that the post office issued new stamps last month.
告诉你一个好消息，上个月邮局发行了新邮票。

| 同义字词 | subject, topic, problem, edition, publication, release, publish |

衍生字词	▲ issue to 发给……，核发……
	▲ issue from 由……产生，由……核发
	▲ at issue 争议中的，讨论中的

| 高分秘诀 | ▲ energy preservation 能源节约 |
| | ▲ post office 邮局 |

1167. itinerary [aɪˋtɪnəˏrɛrɪ] [i·tin·er·ar·y] ☆★★★★

n. 路线，行程
I think an itinerary which could leave us plenty of leeway would be better.
我觉得能提供我们很多自由活动的旅行计划就是好计划。

| 同义字词 | route, course, path |

| 高分秘诀 | ▲ plenty of 很多，大量的 |
| | ▲ leeway **n.** 灵活性 |

Jj 托福 TOEFL iBT

托福(TOEFL)的测验对象为母语为非英语的人
申请入学美加地区大学或研究所时,托福成绩单是必备文件之一。

- n. 名词
- v. 动词
- adj. 形容词
- adv. 副词
- prep. 介词
- art. 冠词
- pron. 代词
- aux. 助词
- conj. 连词

Jj 托福 TOEFL iBT

托福(TOEFL)的测验对象为母语为非英语的人
申请入学美加地区大学或研究所时,托福成绩单是必备文件之一。

1168. jar [dʒɑr] [jar] ☆☆☆★★

n. 罐,广口瓶	Before put it into the refrigerator, make sure the top is screwed back tightly onto the jar. 把它放进冰箱之前,一定要把罐子盖紧。
v. 震动,震惊	The quarrel between my parents really jars on my nerves. 父母间的争吵真让我心烦意乱。

高分秘诀
▲ refrigerator **n.** 冰箱
▲ screw **v.** 旋,扭,拧
▲ tightly **adv.** 紧紧地,坚固地,牢固地
▲ quarrel **n.** 争吵,不和,口角
▲ jar on 使人心烦,听起来令人难受

1169. jealousy [ˈdʒɛləsɪ] [jea·lou·sy] ★★★★★

n. 妒忌,羡慕	Please forgive me; you know I acted out of jealousy. 请原谅我,你知道我这样做是出于妒忌。

同义字词 envy, covetousness, green-eyed monster, jealousness
衍生字词 ▲ jealous delusion 嫉妒妄想
高分秘诀 ▲ forgive **v.** 原谅,饶恕
▲ act out 付诸行动

1170. jibe [dʒaɪb] [jibe] ☆☆★★★

v.(与……)相符,一致	I found your report does not jibe with the facts. 我发现你的报告与事实不符。

同义字词 correspond, agree, match
高分秘诀 ▲ report **n.** 报告,报道
▲ jibe with 与……一致

jar ~ jumble

1171. jolt [dʒolt] [jolt] ☆☆★★★

n. 震动，颠簸

The news that he got accepted by one famous university really gave me a jolt.

他考上了一所知名的大学，这消息真令我震惊。

v. 使颠簸，使震惊

The bus jolted me terribly when it zigzagged along the mountain road.

公交车沿着弯曲山路行驶时，颠簸得很严重。

| 同义字词 | shake, jounce, shock, startle |

| 高分秘诀 | ▲ terribly **adv.** 很，非常，极 |
| | ▲ mountain road 山路 |

1172. journal [`dʒɝnl] [jour·nal] ☆★★★★

n. 期刊，（航海）日记

My father is a doctor who often contributes to the medical journal.

我爸爸是位医生，经常为医学刊物撰稿。

| 同义字词 | magazine, periodical, log, diary |

衍生字词	▲ journalist **n.** 新闻记者
	▲ journalistic **adj.** 新闻事业的，新闻工作的
	▲ journalism **n.** 新闻业，新闻报道

| 高分秘诀 | ▲ contribute to 为……贡献 |
| | ▲ medical **adj.** 医学的，医疗的，医术的 |

1173. jubilant [`dʒublənt] [ju·bi·lant] ☆☆★★★

adj. 兴高采烈的，喜气洋洋的

All the members of the team are in a jubilant mood after they won the game.

赢得比赛后，所有的队员都非常高兴。

| 同义字词 | exultant, happy, merry, delighted, overjoyed, gleeful |

| 高分秘诀 | ▲ member **n.** 成员，会员 |

1174. jumble [`dʒʌmbl] [jum·ble] ☆☆★★★

v. 使混乱，混杂

Your clothes and mine were jumble together; I don't know which one is mine and which one is yours.

你的衣服和我的混在一起，我不知道哪件是你的，哪件是我的。

n. 混乱，杂乱的一堆

I got confused by the nonsensical jumble of words of you.

我被你那堆无意义的话给搞糊涂了。

同义字词	mix, confuse, mingle, scramble, chaos, mess, mixture
高分秘诀	▲ jumble together 搞乱，混在一起 ▲ confuse v. 使困惑，把……弄糊涂 ▲ nonsensical adj. 无意义的，荒谬的

1175. justify [ˈdʒʌstəˌfaɪ] [jus·ti·fy]　★★★★★

v. 证明……是正当的或有理的；为……辩护	If you cheat on an exam, nothing can justify it. 如果你考试作弊，没什么好狡辩的。
同义字词	vindicate, defend
反义字词	condemn
高分秘诀	▲ cheat on 作弊

1176. juvenile [ˈdʒuvənl] [ju·ve·nile]　☆★★★★

n. 青少年（的）	Sometimes we should give the juvenile a chance at a fresh start. 有时候我们应该给青少年重新开始的机会。
adj. 青少年（的）	I bought several juvenile books for my niece. 我为外甥女买了几本儿童读物。
同义字词	youth, adolescent, children's, young, youthful
衍生字词	▲ juvenile court 少年法庭 ▲ juvenile delinquent 少年犯
高分秘诀	▲ a fresh start 新的起点，新的开始 ▲ niece n. 侄女，外甥女

1177. juxtaposition [ˌdʒʌkstəpəˈzɪʃən] [jux·ta·po·si·tion]　☆☆☆★★

n. 毗邻，并置	The juxtaposition of these two remarks really startled me. 这两句话连在一起真让我震惊。
高分秘诀	▲ startle v. 使惊吓，使大吃一惊

Kk 托福 TOEFL iBT

托福(TOEFL)的测验对象为母语为非英语的人
申请入学美加地区大学或研究所时，托福成绩单是必备文件之一。

- n. 名词
- v. 动词
- adj. 形容词
- adv. 副词
- prep. 介词
- art. 冠词
- pron. 代词
- aux. 助词
- conj. 连词

Kk 托福 TOEFL iBT

托福(TOEFL)的测验对象为母语为非英语的人
申请入学美加地区大学或研究所时，托福成绩单是必备文件之一。

1178. keen [kin] [keen] ★★★★★

adj. （感觉、观察等）敏锐的，敏捷的

Being an excellent author, you have to have a remarkably keen insight into human nature.
作为一名出色的作家，你必须对人性有极为敏锐的洞察力。

- 同义字词: acute, incisive, quick, sharp-witted
- 反义字词: blunt, dull, obtuse
- 高分秘诀:
  - ▲ excellent **adj.** 优秀的，卓越的
  - ▲ remarkably **adv.** 引人注目地，明显地，非常地
  - ▲ insight **n.** 洞察力，深刻的见解
  - ▲ human nature 人性，人情

1179. kerosene [ˈkɛrəˌsin] [ker·o·sene] ☆☆☆★★

n. 煤油

There is nothing on the table, only a kerosene lamp.
桌上除了一盏煤油灯外什么也没有。

- 同义字词: coil oil, kerosine, lamp oil
- 衍生字词:
  - ▲ gas burner 煤气炉，煤气灯，煤气喷嘴
  - ▲ gas canister 汽化炉
  - ▲ gas chamber 毒气室，毒气行刑室
  - ▲ gas fire 煤气炉，取暖炉
  - ▲ gas guzzler 吃油车（美国在五六十年代制造的耗油大车）
  - ▲ gas holder 煤气容器，煤气桶
  - ▲ gas jet 煤气喷嘴口，煤气灯的火焰
  - ▲ gas log （煤气暖炉用的）圆木状燃烧嘴
  - ▲ gas main 煤气总管
  - ▲ gas mask 防毒面具
  - ▲ gas meter 煤气计表
  - ▲ gas pedal （汽车）油门，加速器，加速踏板
  - ▲ gas permeable lens 透气隐形眼镜
  - ▲ gas ring （环形喷火头的）煤气炉
  - ▲ gas station 加油站

| 高分秘诀 | kerosene lamp 煤油灯 |

1180. kidnap [ˈkɪdnæp] [kid·nap] ☆★★★★

v. 诱拐，绑架	When the woman got the news that her son was kidnapped, she hit the panic button. 当这位妇女得知自己的儿子被绑架后，她惊慌失措。
同义字词	abduct, carry off, snatch, hijack
高分秘诀	▲ hit the panic button 惊慌失措（非常恐惧、紧张）

1181. kindle [ˈkɪndl] [kin·dle] ☆☆★★★

v. 燃烧，激起（感情等）	The man's insult kindled hatred in my heart. 这个男人的侮辱，激起了我的憎恨。
同义字词	arouse, provoke, stir up, trigger
反义字词	extinguish, stifle, smother
高分秘诀	▲ insult n. 侮辱，冒犯 ▲ hatred n. 仇恨，憎恶 ▲ in one's heart 在内心深处

1182. kinetic [kɪˈnɛtɪk] [ki·ne·tic] ☆☆★★★

adj. 运动的；动力学的	The teacher told us that kinetic energy is the energy arising from motion. 老师告诉我们动能就是由于运动而产生的能量。
同义字词	energising, energizing, dynamic
高分秘诀	▲ kinetic energy 动能 ▲ arise from 产生于，起因于 ▲ motion n. 运动

Ll 托福 TOEFL iBT

托福(TOEFL)的测验对象为母语为非英语的人
申请入学美加地区大学或研究所时，托福成绩单是必备文件之一。

- n. 名词
- v. 动词
- adj. 形容词
- adv. 副词
- prep. 介词
- art. 冠词
- pron. 代词
- aux. 助词
- conj. 连词

Ll 托福 TOEFL iBT

托福(TOEFL)的测验对象为母语为非英语的人
申请入学美加地区大学或研究所时，托福成绩单是必备文件之一。

1183. laborious [lə`borɪəs] [la·bo·ri·ous] 　☆☆★★★

| adj. 费力的，艰难的 | I had spent many laborious hours on this project, but failed in the end.
这项工程让我费时费力，但最终却失败了。 |

同义字词　arduous, painstaking, toilsome, operose

高分秘诀　▲ project n. 专案，计划，方案
　　　　　▲ in the end 最后，结果

1184. labyrinth [`læbə‚rɪnθ] [lab·y·rinth]　☆☆★★★

| n. 迷宫，错综复杂的事件 | I can't find out the intricate windings of the labyrinth.
我找不到迷宫错综复杂的路线。 |

同义字词　maze, intricacy, complex, tangle

高分秘诀　▲ intricate adj. 错综复杂的
　　　　　▲ winding n. 绕，缠

1185. lag [læg] [lag] 　☆★★★★

| v. 走得极慢，落后 | Some girls were lagging behind in the race.
有些女孩子在比赛中落后了。 |

同义字词　delay, drag, dillydally, linger, loiter

衍生字词　▲ lag compensation 滞后补偿

高分秘诀　▲ lag behind 落后，落后于
　　　　　▲ in the race 在比赛中

1186. lament [lə`mɛnt] [la·ment]　☆☆★★★

| v. 为……悲痛，痛惜 | Have you ever heard an old saying "short pleasure, long lament?"
你听过一句老谚语"痛快一时，痛苦一世"吗？ |

同义字词　deplore, complain about, bemoan, grieve, mourn, sorrow

高分秘诀　▲ saying n. 谚语，格言，名言
　　　　　▲ pleasure n. 快乐，满足

laborious ~ lateral

1187. larva [ˈlɑrvə] [lar·va] ☆☆☆★★

n. 幼虫 — I guess this worm is the larva of a beetle.
我猜想这种虫子是甲虫的幼虫。

- 同义字词: cysticerci, caseworm, nepit, nit
- 反义字词: imago, adult, prosopon, imageo
- 高分秘诀:
  - ▲ worm **n.** 虫，蠕虫
  - ▲ beetle **n.** 甲虫

1188. larynx [ˈlærɪŋks] [lar·ynx] ☆☆☆☆★

n. [解]喉 — There would be no choice but to remove the larynx if the cancer can get out of hand.
如果癌症难以控制，除了割除喉头外别无他法。

- 同义字词: voice box, throat, jaws, fauces, gorge
- 高分秘诀:
  - ▲ remove **v.** 移走，割除
  - ▲ cancer **n.** 癌症
  - ▲ get out of hand 难以控制，失控

1189. lash [læʃ] [lash] ☆★★★★

v. 抽打，鞭打 — It rained heavily outside and the rain lashed against the window.
外面雨下得很大，雨滴一直敲打着窗户。

- 同义字词: whip, strike, hit
- 衍生字词: ▲ lash the waves（风）吹打海浪，徒劳无益，白费力气
- 高分秘诀:
  - ▲ heavily **adv.** 严重地，大量地
  - ▲ lash against 敲打

1190. latent [ˈletn̩t] [la·tent] ☆☆★★★

adj. 潜伏的，隐藏的 — Sometimes it's the hard task which draw out our latent talents.
有时候艰难的任务可以发掘出我们潜在的才能。

- 同义字词: potential, dormant, hidden, covered, underlying
- 高分秘诀:
  - ▲ draw out 诱发，引出
  - ▲ talent **n.** 天资，才能

1191. lateral [ˈlætərəl] [la·ter·al] ☆☆★★★

adj. 侧面的，旁边的 — Can you draw a lateral view of the building?
你能画出这座建筑物的侧面图吗？

| 同义字词 | parallel, side, sidelong |
| 高分秘诀 | ▲ lateral view 侧面图
▲ building n. 建筑物，楼房 |

1192. latitude [ˈlætəˌtjud] [la·ti·tude]   ☆★★★★

n. 纬度，范围

From the globe, we know that the two cities are at approximately the same latitude.
从地球仪上，我们得知这两个城市差不多在同一纬度上。

同义字词	parallel, freedom
反义字词	longitude
衍生字词	▲ latitude effect 纬度效应
高分秘诀	▲ globe n. 地球仪 ▲ approximately adv. 近似地，大约

1193. launch [lɔntʃ] [launch]   ★★★★★

n. 发射，升空

The launch of a rocket received much media coverage.
火箭的发射广获传媒报道。

v. 发动，(使)升空

We have to make careful preparation and to launch a counterattack on the enemy.
我们必须做好准备，以便向敌人反攻。

| 同义字词 | begin, originate, initiate, start |
| 高分秘诀 | ▲ rocket n. 火箭
▲ media n. 媒体
▲ coverage n. 新闻报道，报道量
▲ preparation n. 准备，筹备
▲ counterattack n. 反攻，反击 |

1194. laurels [ˈlɔrəl] [lau·rel]   ☆★★★★

n. 桂冠，荣誉

This lucky girl was crowned with laurel in the beauty contest.
这个幸运的女孩在选美大赛中摘取桂冠。

| 同义字词 | honor, honour, accolade, credit |
| 高分秘诀 | ▲ be crowned with laurel 获得桂冠
▲ beauty contest 选美比赛 |

latitude ~ leak

1195. lavish [`lævɪʃ] [la·vish] ☆☆★★★

adj. 过分慷慨的,浪费的

Though the man is not very rich, he is lavish and ostentatious.
虽然这个男人并不是很富裕,但他花钱不手软而且喜欢摆阔。

同义字词: magnificent, generous, abundant, ample

高分秘诀: ▲ ostentatious **adj.** 好夸耀的,炫耀的

1196. lawsuit [`lɔˌsut] [law·suit] ☆★★★★

n. 诉讼

An old lady filed a lawsuit against this famous movie star.
一位老妇人对这位电影明星提出诉讼。

同义字词: litigation, prosecution, case, suit

衍生字词: ▲ lawsuit of patent 专利诉讼

高分秘诀: ▲ file **v.** 提交(申请等),呈递

1197. layout [`leˌaut] [lay·out] ☆★★★★

n. 规划, 设计

The layout of the mansion is so fantastic.
这个豪宅的设计真是太棒了。

高分秘诀:
▲ mansion **n.** 公馆,大厦
▲ fantastic **adj.** 极好的,极出色的,了不起的

1198. league [lig] [league] ☆★★★★

n. 同盟, 联盟

I found this official is privately in league with some bandits.
我发现这位官员暗中和一些歹徒勾结。

同义字词: association, union

衍生字词:
▲ English Premier League 英格兰(足球)超级联赛
▲ League Cup 联赛杯

高分秘诀:
▲ official **n.** 行政官员
▲ privately **adv.** 私下地,不公开地
▲ in league with 和……联合着
▲ bandit **n.** 土匪,强盗

1199. leak [lik] [leak] ☆★★★★

v. 渗, 泄露

The faucet in the kitchen is leaking; I have to find someone to repair it.
厨房的水龙头漏水了,我必须找人修理。

| 反义字词 | keep secret, hold out, conceal |
| 高分秘诀 | ▲ faucet n. 水龙头
▲ kitchen n. 厨房
▲ repair v. 修理，修补 |

1200. leap [lip] [leap] ☆★★★★

n. 跳跃

According the calendar, this year is a leap year.
依照日历，今年是闰年。

v. 跳跃

Think twice and don't leap to conclusions.
好好考虑一下，不要贸然作出结论。

| 同义字词 | jump, hop, bounce, bound, spring |
| 高分秘诀 | ▲ calendar n. 日历，年度
▲ leap year 闰年
▲ think twice 三思，再三考虑
▲ leap to conclusion 贸然断定，过早下结论 |

1201. lease [lis] [lease] ☆★★★★

n. 租约

The lease on this instrument expires at the end of the next year.
这机器的租约到明年年底到期。

v. 出租，租借

How about you lease your house to me?
把你的房子租给我好吗？

| 同义字词 | rent, charter, engage, hire |
| 高分秘诀 | ▲ instrument n. 器具，仪器
▲ expire v. 期满，（期限）终止 |

1202. legacy [ˈlɛgəsɪ] [le·ga·cy] ☆★★★★

n. 遗产，遗物

His parents left him a legacy of a million dollars.
他父母留下百万家产给他。

同义字词	inheritance, bequest, heritage
衍生字词	▲ legacy tax 遗产税
高分秘诀	▲ million n. 百万

1203. legendary [ˈlɛdʒəndˌɛrɪ] [leg·end·ar·y]   ☆★★★★

adj. 传奇的

Since the old man has beaten the dragon, he became a household legendary figure.
自从老人击败恶龙，他成为家喻户晓的传奇性人物。

leap ~ lethargic

衍生字词 ▲ legend n. 传说，传奇文学
高分秘诀 ▲ dragon n. 龙
▲ household adj. 家喻户晓的

1204. legible [ˋlɛdʒəbl] [le·gi·ble] ☆☆★★★

| adj. （指印刷或字迹）清楚的，易读的 | As time goes on, the sign was no longer legible, for much of the lettering had worn away.
随着时间的流逝，这块招牌已看不清楚，因为大部分字已经被磨损了。 |

同义字词 readable, distinct, plain

高分秘诀 ▲ as time goes on 随着时间的推移
▲ no longer 不再，已不
▲ lettering n. 字体
▲ wear away 磨损，磨掉，侵蚀

1205. legislate [ˋlɛdʒɪsˏlet] [leg·is·late] ☆★★★★

| v. 立法，制定法律 | Of course it's impossible to legislate for every contingency.
为每一个偶发事件都立法当然是不可能的。 |

同义字词 make laws, enact law

衍生字词 ▲ legislature n. 立法机关
▲ legislation n. 立法，法规

高分秘诀 ▲ contingency n. 意外事故

1206. lethal [ˋliθəl] [le·thal] ☆★★★★

| adj. 致命的，有害的 | Don't touch them, those lethal weapons are so dangerous.
不要碰这些致命武器，它们很危险。 |

同义字词 fatal, mortal, deadly

高分秘诀 ▲ lethal weapon 致命武器
▲ dangerous adj. 危险的

1207. lethargic [lɪˋθɑrdʒɪk] [le·thar·gic] ☆☆★★★

| adj. 昏睡的，懒洋洋的 | As soon as I touched the hammock, I immediately felt lethargic.
我一躺到吊床上，就感到昏昏欲睡。 |

同义字词 slumberous, sluggish, torpid, languid

高分秘诀 ▲ hammock n. 吊床
▲ immediately adv. 立即，马上

1208. lettuce [ˈlɛtɪs] [let·tuce] ☆☆★★★

n. 莴苣，生菜

Come on and have a taste of the lettuce salad!
过来尝尝生菜沙拉！

同义字词　lactu ca sativa, tossed green

衍生字词　▲ leek **n.** 韭菜
　　　　　▲ spinach **n.** 菠菜
　　　　　▲ Chinese cabbage 大白菜

高分秘诀　▲ lettuce salad 生菜沙拉

1209. libel [ˈlaɪb(ə)l] [li·bel] ☆☆★★★

n. 以文字损害名誉，诽谤

He threatened me that he would sue me for libel.
他威胁要告我诽谤。

同义字词　slander, defamation

高分秘诀　▲ threaten **v.** 恐吓，威胁
　　　　　▲ sue **v.** 起诉，控告

1210. liberate [ˈlɪbəˌret] [li·be·rate] ☆★★★★

v. 释放，使自由

It's a wrong thing to liberate prisoners in jail.
释放监狱中的囚犯是错误的。

同义字词　free, discharge, release

反义字词　compel, restrain, restrict

1211. lineage [ˈlɪnɪdʒ] [lin·e·age] ☆☆★★★

n. 血统，世系

It's lucky for you to have a family of royal lineage.
你生在贵族家庭真幸运。

同义字词　ancestry, family, race, descent

高分秘诀　▲ royal **adj.** 王室的，皇家的

1212. linger [ˈlɪŋɡə] [lin·ger] ☆★★★★

v. 逗留，徘徊

I lingered away the whole winter at this beautiful resort.
我在这个美丽的度假村消磨整个冬天。

同义字词　stay, stroll, hover, tarry

反义字词　hasten, hotfoot, hie

lettuce ~ litter

| 高分秘诀 | ▲ linger away 虚度（时间）
▲ resort n. 度假胜地 |

1213. linguistic [lɪŋˋgwɪstɪk] [lin·guis·tic] ☆★★★★

adj. 语言上的，语言学上的	Can you explain what the linguistic convention is? 你能解释什么是约定俗成（的用语）吗？
同义字词	lingual, linguistical
反义字词	nonlinguistic
衍生字词	▲ linguistics n. 语言学 ▲ linguist n. 语言学家
高分秘诀	▲ explain v. 讲解，解释 ▲ linguistic convention 语言学约定

1214. literate [ˋlɪtərɪt] [li·te·rate] ★★★★★

adj. 有文化的，有阅读和写作能力的	Though these villagers come from remote mountain areas, they are all literate. 虽然这些村民来自偏远山区，但他们都会读会写。
n. 识字的人，有学问的人	The old lady couldn't read so she had to ask a literate to read the letter for her. 这位老太太不识字，因此她请一位读过书的人为她读信。
同义字词	educated, schooled, cultured, learned
高分秘诀	▲ villager n. 村民 ▲ remote adj. 遥远的，偏僻的 ▲ mountain area 山区

1215. litter [ˋlɪtɚ] [lit·ter] ☆★★★★

v. 乱丢，乱丢垃圾	The teacher warned us that don't litter up the floor with scraps of paper. 老师警告我们别往地上乱丢纸屑。
n. 垃圾	I saw there were piles of litter in the yard. 我看见院子里堆着成堆的垃圾。
同义字词	garbage, refuse, rubbish, trash
高分秘诀	▲ warn v. 警告，提醒，告诫 ▲ litter up 把（某处）搞得乱糟糟 ▲ scrap n. 碎片，碎屑 ▲ pile n. 一堆，一叠 ▲ yard n. 院子

1216. livelihood [ˈlaɪvlɪˌhʊd] [live·li·hood] ☆★★★★

n. 生计，谋生

This man is so old but he still picked up a livelihood by hawking fruit.
这个男人年纪很大，但仍以沿街叫卖水果为生。

同义字词 subsistence, sustenance, bread and butter, living, support

衍生字词 livelihood education 生计教育

高分秘诀
▲ pick up 学到，获得
▲ hawk **v.** 沿街叫卖
▲ fruit **n.** 水果

1217. loathsome [ˈloðsəm] [loath·some] ☆☆★★★

adj. 令人讨厌的

As I see it, murder is a vile and loathsome crime.
在我看来，谋杀是邪恶且令人发指的罪行。

同义字词 repulsive, disgusting, abhorrent, disgustful

高分秘诀
▲ as I see it 在我看来
▲ vile **adj.** 极坏的，可耻的
▲ crime **n.** 罪，罪行

1218. lobby [ˈlɑbɪ] [lob·by] ☆★★★★

n. 大厅，休息厅

Would you mind to shepherd us to the lobby?
你能把我们带到大厅去吗？

v. 游说议员

This young man tried his best to lobby the parliament members, but failed.
这个年轻人使尽浑身解数向国会议员游说，但还是失败了。

同义字词 hall, room, foyer, influence, persuade

高分秘诀
▲ shepherd **v.** 带领，引导
▲ parliament member 议员

1219. locate [loˈket] [lo·cate] ★★★★★

v. 找出，指出

My apartment was located in our city's commercial centre.
我的公寓位于商业中心。

同义字词 find, monitor, situate, settle, place

高分秘诀
▲ apartment **n.** 公寓，住宅
▲ commercial centre 商业中心

livelihood ~ loop

1220. locomote [ˌlokəˈmot] [lo·co·mote] ☆☆★★★

v. 移动, 行动	The group of children is locomoting down the alley. 这群孩子顺着巷子前进着。
同义字词	go, move, travel
反义字词	stay in place
高分秘诀	▲ alley n. 小巷, 小径

1221. lodge [lɑdʒ] [lodge] ☆☆★★★

n. (山林)小屋, 艺术室(工厂、学校的)	The dog died in a small lodge. 这只狗死在一间小屋内。
v. 寄存, 临时住宿, 射入, 刺进	The doctor couldn't take out the bullet, because it lodged in the spine. 医生取不出子弹, 因为它嵌在脊椎骨里。
同义字词	stay, accommodate, deposit
高分秘诀	▲ take out 取出 ▲ bullet n. 子弹 ▲ spine n. 脊柱, 脊椎

1222. logical [ˈlɑdʒɪkl̩] [lo·gi·cal] ★★★★★

adj. 合乎逻辑的, 合理的	It is logical to assume that she will accept the job offer. 照理说, 她应该会接受那个工作机会。
同义字词	coherent, reasonable, rational, sensible, sound
反义字词	absurd, unlogical

1223. loop [lup] [loop] ☆★★★★

v. 把……圈成环, 缠绕	The little girl looped the curtain up to let the sunlight in. 小女孩卷起窗帘, 让阳光直射进来。
n. 圈, 环	The news that he got accepted by a famous university knocked me for a loop. 他考上名校的消息的确让我大吃一惊。
同义字词	circle, ring, curl, coil
高分秘诀	▲ knock for a loop 使震惊, 使激动

1224. lore [lor] [lore] ☆☆★★★

n. 口头传说，学问

The tribal lore and custom have been passed down orally from generation to generation.
部落的知识和风俗经由口耳相传一代代地保留下来。

同义字词 | legend, wisdom, knowledge
高分秘诀 | ▲ tribal **adj.** 部落的
▲ custom **n.** 习惯，风俗，惯例
▲ pass down 使流传
▲ from generation to generation 世代相传

1225. lucrative [ˈlukrətɪv] [lu·cra·tive] ☆☆★★★

adj. 赚钱的，有利可图的

You are lucky enough to land a lucrative billet with a joint adventure.
你真幸运在一家合资企业找到了一个报酬很高的职位。

同义字词 | profitable, remunerative, moneymaking
反义字词 | nonprofitable, gainless
高分秘诀 | ▲ billet **n.** 工作职位
▲ joint adventure 合资企业

1226. lull [lʌl] [lull] ☆☆★★★

v. 使平静，使安静

It took me much time to lull my little daughter to sleep.
我花很久才把我的小女儿哄睡着。

同义字词 | appease, calm, quiet, quieten
反义字词 | agitate, commove, rouse
衍生字词 | ▲ lullaby **n.** 摇篮曲，催眠曲
高分秘诀 | ▲ lull to sleep 轻哼或轻摇使之入睡
▲ daughter **n.** 女儿

1227. lumber [ˈlʌmbə] [lum·ber] ☆☆★★★

n. 木材，木料

I saw piles of lumber were stacked along the wall.
我看见大量的木堆在墙边。

同义字词 | board, timber, wood
衍生字词 | ▲ lumbering **n.** 采伐林木
▲ lumber room 杂物堆放室
高分秘诀 | ▲ stack **v.** 堆积

lore ~ luxurious

1228. luminous ['lumənəs] [lu·mi·nous] ☆★★★★

adj. 发光的, 明亮的

Have you ever seen the luminous bacteria in your life?
你一生中是否看过会发光的细菌?

同义字词 glowing, fluorescent, bright, radiant, shining

衍生字词
▲ luminous body 发光体
▲ luminous density 发光密度

高分秘诀
▲ luminous bacteria 发光细菌
▲ in one's life 在某人的一生中

1229. lure [lʊr] [lure] ☆★★★★

v. 引诱, 诱惑

It's the enticement of the big city lure me away from my hometown.
大城市的种种诱惑吸引我离开家乡。

n. 饵, 诱惑

I can say only few people could resist the lure of money.
我敢说只有少数人能抵抗金钱的诱惑。

同义字词 attract, entice, draw on, tempt

高分秘诀
▲ enticement **n.** 引诱（物），怂恿
▲ hometown **n.** 家乡，故乡
▲ resist **v.** 抵抗

1230. lustrous ['lʌstrəs] [lus·trous] ☆☆★★★

adj. 光亮的, 有光泽的

I saw his lustrous eyes flashing defiance.
我看到他发亮的眼睛闪着挑战的光芒。

同义字词 shiny, glowing, burnished, glistening, glossy

高分秘诀
▲ flash **v.** 发出闪光，闪耀
▲ defiance **n.** 挑衅的态度，蔑视

1231. luxurious [lʌg'ʒʊrɪəs] [lux·u·ri·ous] ☆★★★★

adj. 奢侈的, 豪华的

You've lived in the luxurious surroundings and never gone through this kind of things.
你生活在奢侈的环境中，从来没有经历过这些事。

同义字词 sumptuous, lavish, deluxe, luxuriant

高分秘诀
▲ surroundings **n.** 环境
▲ go through 遭受，经历

1232. lyric [`lɪrɪk] [ly·ric] ☆ ★ ★ ★ ★

n. 抒情诗，歌词   Can you tell me who wrote the lyrics for the song?
你能告诉我谁为这首歌谱写的歌词吗？

adj. 抒情的   The poet sang a lyric love poem to his lover.
这位诗人唱了一首爱情抒情诗给他的爱人。

高分秘诀
▲ poet **n.** 诗人
▲ poem **n.** 诗，韵文
▲ lover **n.** 情人，爱人

Mm 托福 TOEFL iBT

托福(TOEFL)的测验对象为母语为非英语的人
申请入学美加地区大学或研究所时,托福成绩单是必备文件之一。

- n. 名词
- v. 动词
- adj. 形容词
- adv. 副词
- prep. 介词
- art. 冠词
- pron. 代词
- aux. 助词
- conj. 连词

Mm 托福 TOEFL iBT

托福(TOEFL)的测验对象为母语为非英语的人
申请入学美加地区大学或研究所时，托福成绩单是必备文件之一。

1233. magic [ˈmædʒɪk] [ma·gic]   ☆★★★★

n. 魔法，魔力	It's the magician who thrilled the audience with his feats of magic. 这位魔术师的魔术表演使观众情绪激动。
adj. 魔法的，有魔力的	When I was a little girl, I admired the wizard's magic wand. 小时候，我非常羡慕巫师的魔杖。

- 同义字词: wizardry, sorcery, magical, sorcerous, witching, wizard
- 高分秘诀:
  - ▲ thrill v. 使兴奋，使激动
  - ▲ feat n. 技艺
  - ▲ wizard n. 男巫，术士
  - ▲ magic wand 魔杖

1234. magnetic [mæɡˈnɛtɪk] [mag·ne·tic] ☆★★★★

adj. 磁的，有吸引力的	I was ravished with her magnetic personality. 她迷人的风采令我着迷不已。

- 同义字词: captivating, attractive, drawing, charismatic
- 反义字词: nonmagnetic, repulsive
- 高分秘诀:
  - ▲ sweep away ravish v. 使心醉，使着迷
  - ▲ personality n. 人格，个性

1235. magnificent [mæɡˈnɪfəsənt] [mag·ni·fi·cent] ☆★★★★

adj. 华丽的，高尚的	You know the view from the hilltop is so magnificent. 从山顶看到的景色非常壮观。

- 同义字词: gorgeous, lavish, brilliant, glorious, splendid
- 高分秘诀:
  - ▲ view n. 景色，风景
  - ▲ hilltop n. 山顶

magic ~ malleable

1236. magnify [ˈmæɡnəˌfaɪ] [mag·ni·fy] ☆★★★★

v. 放大, 扩大

She is always complaining and inclined to magnify difficulties.
她总是抱怨并夸大困难。

同义字词: intensify, increase, enlarge, amplify

反义字词: minimise, scale down

高分秘诀:
▲ complaining adj. 诉苦的, 抱怨的
▲ be inclined to 倾向于
▲ difficulty n. 困难, 难事

1237. majestic [məˈdʒɛstɪk] [ma·jes·tic] ☆☆★★★

adj. 壮观的, 庄严的

I found most of the openings and closing were all accomplished with majestic rituality in China.
我发现在中国, 几乎所有的开幕和闭幕都是以隆重的仪式完成。

同义字词: stately, royal, majestical

衍生字词:
▲ majesty n. 威严, 最高权威
▲ majestically adv. 雄伟地, 庄严地, 威严地

高分秘诀: ▲ rituality n. 仪式

1238. malfunction [mælˈfʌŋkʃən] [mal·func·tion] ☆★★★★

n. 故障, 失灵

We can do nothing to this kind of destructive malfunction.
对于这种破坏性故障我们一点儿办法也没有。

同义字词: failure, breakdown, misfunction

高分秘诀:
▲ destructive adj. 破坏性的, 毁灭性的
▲ destructive malfunction 破坏性故障

1239. malleable [ˈmælɪəbl] [mal·le·a·ble] ☆☆★★★

adj. 可锻造的, 有延展性的

My teacher taught us that the lead and tin are malleable metals.
老师告诉我们铅和锡都是有延展性的金属。

同义字词: changeable, adaptable, elastic, flexible

衍生字词: ▲ malleability n. 可塑性, 延展性

高分秘诀:
▲ lead n. 铅
▲ tin n. 锡
▲ malleable metal 可锻金属

1240. mandate [ˈmændet] [man·date] ☆☆★★★

n. 命令，要求

It's the union membership who asked us to carry out the mandate.
工会会员要求我们执行这项命令。

[同义字词] command, decree

[高分秘诀]
▲ union **n.** 工会
▲ membership **n.** 全体会员
▲ carry out 执行，贯彻

1241. maneuver [məˈnuvɚ] [ma·neu·ver] ☆★★★★

v. （敏捷地）操纵，调动

It's difficult but my father maneuvered our car into the garage.
虽然有些困难，但爸爸还是设法把汽车开进了车库。

n. 策略，谋略

Don't worry; Mr. Smith has already foreseen their oblique political maneuvers.
不用担心，史密斯先生已经识破了他们阴险的政治计谋。

[同义字词] move, control, drive, guide, tactic, strategy

[衍生字词] ▲ maneuvering area 起飞着陆和滑行地带

[高分秘诀]
▲ garage **n.** 车库
▲ foresee **v.** 预知，预见
▲ oblique **adj.** 间接的，不光明正大的
▲ political **adj.** 政治的，政治上的

1242. mania [ˈmenɪə] [ma·ni·a] ☆☆★★★

n. 狂热

My grandfather has a mania for bunnies.
我外公特别喜欢兔子。

[同义字词] craze, madness, passion

[高分秘诀] ▲ bunny **n.** 兔子

1243. manifestation [ˌmænəfɛsˈteʃən] [ma·ni·fes·ta·tion]   ☆☆★★★

n. 表现，显示

Usually cough is one manifestation of a cold.
咳嗽通常是着凉的一种表现。

[同义字词] revelation, indication, demonstration

[高分秘诀]
▲ usually **adv.** 通常，惯常地
▲ cough **n.** 咳嗽

1244. manipulate [mə`nɪpjəˌlet] [ma·ni·pu·late] ☆★★★★

v. 操作，操纵

Being an airplane pilot, you have to know how to manipulate various controls.
作为一个飞行员，你必须知道如何操纵不同的控制仪器。

[同义字词] maneuver, control, operate, manage, conduct

[高分秘诀] ▲ airplane **n.** 飞机
▲ various **adj.** 各种不同的，各式各样的

1245. margin [`mɑrdʒɪn] [mar·gin] ☆☆★★★

n. 边缘，余地

I have a good habit of inscribing in the margin of a page.
我有在书页边作注释的好习惯。

[同义字词] edge, border, rim, room, leeway

[衍生字词] ▲ margined marginal **adj.** 边缘的，临界的
▲ margin deposit 保证金，押金

[高分秘诀] ▲ habit **n.** 习惯，习性
▲ inscribe **v.** 写

1246. marine [mə`rin] [ma·rine] ☆★★★★

adj. 航海的，海军陆战队的

Do you know how many clauses in the marine policies?
你知道海运险包括哪些条款吗？

n. 海军陆战队员

My grandfather was a marine when he was young.
我外公年轻的时候曾是一名海军陆战队员。

[同义字词] sea-dwelling, maritime, nautical, devil dog, leatherneck

[衍生字词] ▲ marine animal 海洋动物
▲ marine climate 海洋气候

[高分秘诀] ▲ clause **n.** 条款
▲ marine policy 海洋政策

1247. marvel [`mɑrvl] [mar·vel] ☆☆★★★

n. 奇迹，令人惊奇的事物

It's a marvel that the little girl was unhurt when she fell from the fourth floor.
这个小女孩从四楼掉下来竟然毫发无伤，真是一个奇迹。

v. 惊奇，对……感到惊奇

I marveled that how he can make it without any help.
对于他独自一人完成此事，我感到惊诧不已。

同义字词	wonder, miracle
高分秘诀	▲ unhurt adj. 没有受害的，没有受伤的 ▲ make it 成功，做成或完成某事

1248. mason [ˈmesn̩] [ma·son] ☆☆☆☆★

n. 石匠，泥水工人	Please asked a mason to flush the joint with mortar. 请一位泥工把接缝处用灰浆嵌平。
同义字词	bricklayer, stonemason, masonry
高分秘诀	▲ flush joint 平头接合，齐平接缝 ▲ mortar n. 灰浆，砂浆

1249. massacre [ˈmæsəkɚ] [mas·sa·cre] ☆★★★★

v. 大屠杀	It's the German fascists who massacred so many Jews during the World War II. 第二次世界大战期间，德国法西斯分子屠杀了很多犹太人。
n. 大屠杀	Nanking Massacre was taken as a worldwide humiliation. 南京大屠杀是全世界的耻辱。
同义字词	pogrom, slaughter, carnage, mass murder, mow down
衍生字词	▲ Nanking Massacre 南京大屠杀
高分秘诀	▲ fascist n. 法西斯主义的支持者 ▲ Jews n. 犹太人 ▲ World War II 第二次世界大战

1250. meager [ˈmigɚ] [mea·ger] ☆☆★★★

adj. 缺乏的，不足的	The meager monetary allowance from the government can't support the old couples. 政府的少量津贴根本无法让这对老夫妻生活。
同义字词	scanty, poor, skimpy
反义字词	ample, plentiful, rich
高分秘诀	▲ monetary adj. 货币的，金融的 ▲ allowance n. 津贴，补助 ▲ couple n. 一对，夫妻，情侣

1251. mechanical [məˈkænɪkl] [me·cha·ni·cal] ☆☆★★★

adj. 机械的，机械性的	We asked this machine works to produce the mechanical device for us. 我们请这家机械厂生产这种机械装置。

mason ~ memorial

同义字词	automatic, monotonous
反义字词	nonmechanical
高分秘诀	▲ machine works 机械厂 ▲ device n. 装置，设备，器具

1252. mediate [ˋmidɪ͵et] [me·di·ate] ☆★★★★

v. 斡旋，调停	It's difficult to mediate between two warring countries. 在两个交战国之间进行斡旋不是件容易的事。
同义字词	arbitrate, negotiate, intercede, intervene
高分秘诀	▲ mediate between 在……之间调解（调停） ▲ warring adj. 交战的，敌对的

1253. medieval [͵mɪdɪˋivəl] [me·di·e·val] ☆★★★★

adj. 中世纪的	The study shows that this temple is a classic example of medieval architecture. 经过研究，我们得知这间寺庙是中世纪建筑的典型风格。
衍生字词	▲ Medieval Greek 中古希腊语 ▲ medievalism n. 中世纪精神，中世纪性质 ▲ medievalist n. 中世纪研究家，中古史学家
高分秘诀	▲ temple n. 庙，寺，殿 ▲ classic adj. 典范的；典型的，标准的 ▲ architecture n. 建筑风格，建筑式样

1254. melodious [məˋlodɪəs] [me·lo·di·ous] ☆☆★★★

adj. 旋律优美的，悦耳的	When I opened the window, the melodious song of a bird coming in. 我一打开窗户，就听到鸟儿悦耳的歌声。
同义字词	harmonious, euphonic, tuneful, musical
反义字词	tuneless, unmelodic, unmelodious, unmusical
高分秘诀	▲ come in 进入

1255. memorial [məˋmorɪəl] [me·mo·ri·al] ☆★★★★

n. 纪念物，纪念碑	The government decided to set up a memorial to the martyrs. 政府决定为烈士建一座纪念碑。
adj. 纪念的，记忆的	Do you know who read this memorial speech? 你知道是谁念出这篇悼词的吗？

| 同义字词 | monument, commemoration, remembrance |
| 高分秘诀 | ▲ set up 建立，竖立
▲ martyr n. 烈士
▲ memorial speech 悼词 |

1256. menace [ˈmɛnɪs] [men·ace] ☆★★★★

n. 危险，威胁	I can tell there is a tone of menace entered into your voice. 我觉察到你的声音带着威胁的口吻。
v. 威吓，胁迫	The gangster menaced me with a rifle. 这名歹徒用来福枪威胁我。
同义字词	danger, threat, threaten, intimidate
高分秘诀	▲ tone n. 腔调，语气 ▲ enter into 包括；参与 ▲ rifle n. 步枪；来复枪

1257. mention [ˈmɛnʃən] [men·tion] ★★★★★

v. 提及，说起	It's insensitive of you to mention that kind of things to your father. 你跟父亲提起那种事实在很迟钝。
同义字词	refer to, indicate, bring up
高分秘诀	▲ insensitive adj. 感觉迟钝的，麻木不仁的

1258. merchandise [ˈmɝtʃənˌdaɪz] [mer·chan·dise] ☆★★★★

n. 商品	We bought these distressed merchandise at reduced prices. 我们以低价买进这些廉价商品。
同义字词	objects for sale, goods, product
高分秘诀	▲ distress merchandise 廉价出售的商品 ▲ reduced price 折扣价格，降低的价格

1259. merge [mɝdʒ] [merge] ☆★★★★

v. (使)合并，(使)融合	Maybe merge our company with our major rival is a good choice. 或许将我们公司与主要对手合并会是不错的选择。
同义字词	combine, unite, coalesce
反义字词	break apart, disunify
高分秘诀	▲ major adj. 主要的；rival n. 竞争对手

1260. mesmerize [ˈmɛsməˌraɪz] [mes·me·rize]

v. 施催眠术，迷住

Nowadays more and more youngsters got mesmerized by computer games.
如今越来越多的青少年沉迷于电脑游戏。

同义字词: hypnotize, hypnotise, fascinate, captivate, bewitch, magnetise

高分秘诀:
▲ youngster **n.** 青年，少年
▲ computer game 电脑游戏

1261. metabolism [mɛˈtæblˌɪzəm] [me·ta·bo·lism]

n. 新陈代谢

I think the dosage would be better if it could work on the infected cells, at the same time it doesn't upset the normal metabolism.
我认为药量若能对付感染细胞，同时又不会干扰正常的新陈代谢比较好。

同义字词: metabolic process, metastasis, metamorphosis

高分秘诀:
▲ dosage **n.** 药量
▲ infected **adj.** 被感染的
▲ at the same time 同时
▲ upset **v.** 打乱，扰乱

1262. metaphor [ˈmɛtəfɚ] [me·ta·phor]

n. 隐喻，暗喻

If you want to use metaphor, you have to find an appropriate one.
如果要用隐喻，你必须找个贴切的。

高分秘诀:
▲ appropriate **adj.** 适当的，恰当的

1263. meteorology [ˌmitɪəˈrɑlədʒɪ] [me·te·or·ol·o·gy]

n. 气象学，气象状态

The scientist pay much attention to the air pollution meteorology.
这位科学家很关注空气污染气象学。

同义字词: weather forecasting

衍生字词:
▲ meteorologic / meteorological **adj.** 气象的，气象学的
▲ meteorologist **n.** 气象学者

高分秘诀:
▲ pay attention to 注意，关注
▲ air pollution meteorology 空气污染气象学

1264. methodology [ˌmɛθəˈdɑlədʒɪ] [meth·od·ol·o·gy]

n. 方法论，方法学

I got confused by this methodology of genetic studies.
这个遗传学研究的方法让我很困惑。

同义字词	methodological analysis
高分秘诀	▲ confuse v. 使困惑，把……弄糊涂 ▲ genetic adj. 遗传（学）的，基因的

1265. methodical [məˋθɑdɪkəl] [meth·o·di·cal] ☆★★★★

adj. 有条理的，井然有序的	You can count on me, and I'm methodical. 你可以相信我，我做事有条不紊。
同义字词	systematical, orderly, methodic
高分秘诀	▲ count on 相信，指望

1266. meticulous [məˋtɪkjələs] [me·tic·u·lous] ☆☆★★★

adj. 一丝不苟的，过细的	Be meticulous please! You know the sloppy work would enrage the boss. 请小心谨慎！要知道草率的工作会激怒老板。
同义字词	punctilious , scrupulous, cautious
反义字词	careless, incautious
高分秘诀	▲ sloppy adj. 草率的，粗心的 ▲ enrage v. 使暴怒

1267. metropolitan [ˌmɛtrəˋpɑlətn̩] [me·tro·po·li·tan] ☆★★★★

adj. 主要都市的，大城市的	I don't like to live in a metropolitan city, especially its crowded streets. 我不喜欢住在繁华的大都市，尤其不喜欢拥挤的街道。
同义字词	civic, municipal, urban
高分秘诀	▲ crowded adj. 水泄不通的，拥挤的

1268. migrate [ˋmaɪˌgret] [mi·grate] ☆★★★★

v. 移动，迁徙	I found these years so many people migrate to urban area. 我发现近年愈来愈多的人向市区迁移。
同义字词	move from one place to another. transmigrate
衍生字词	▲ migration n. 定期迁移，迁居 ▲ migratory adj. 迁移的，流浪的 ▲ migrant n. 候鸟，移民 ▲ emigrant n. 移居外国者，移民 ▲ immigrant n. （从外国移入的）移民，侨民
高分秘诀	▲ urban area 城市地区

methodical ~ minimal

1269. milieu [mi`ljə] [mi·lieu] ☆☆★★★

n. 环境，出身背景

Yoghourt provided a good milieu for the persistence of bacteria.
优酪乳为细菌提供一个良好的栖息所。

同义字词: environment, surroundings

高分秘诀:
▲ yoghourt **n.** 优酪乳
▲ bacterium **n.** 细菌（复数bacteria）

1270. militant [`mɪlətənt] [mil·i·tant] ☆★★★★

adj. 好战的，激进的

I was infected by those militant protesters.
我的情绪被这些激动的抗议者感染。

同义字词: fighting, belligerent, warlike, combative

高分秘诀:
▲ infect **v.** 影响，（受）传染
▲ protester **n.** 抗议者，反对者，拒绝者

1271. mimetic [mɪ`mɛtɪk] [mi·met·ic] ☆☆★★★

adj. 模仿的，(生物)拟态的

Her eyes focus on this mimetic diagram.
她的眼睛专注在这张模拟图上。

同义字词: imitative, mimic, simulative

高分秘诀:
▲ focus on 使聚焦于，对……予以注意
▲ mimetic diagram 模拟图

1272. mimic [`mɪmɪk] [mi·mic] ☆☆★★★

n. 模仿者，小丑

We have to admit that parrot is an amazing mimic.
我们不得不承认鹦鹉很会学舌。

v. 模仿，模拟

The boy mimicked his father's voice and gestures perfectly.
男孩把爸爸的声音和姿势模仿得惟妙惟肖。

同义字词: mime, imitate, copy, copycat, parrot

高分秘诀:
▲ parrot **n.** 鹦鹉
▲ amazing **adj.** 令人惊异的
▲ gesture **n.** 姿势，姿态

1273. minimal [`mɪnəməl] [mi·ni·mal] ☆★★★★

adj. 最小的，最少的

When I visited England, I stayed with one of my friends, so my expenses were minimal.
我去英格兰的时候住在一位朋友家，所以花费很低。

同义字词	the fewest, minimum
反义字词	maximal, maximum
高分秘诀	▲ England n. 英格兰，英国 ▲ expense n. 消耗，花费，费用

1274. mitigate [`mɪtə‚get] [mi·ti·gate] ☆★★★★

v. 使减轻,使缓和	I really appreciate your kind words, it mitigated my suffering. 我真的很感激，因为你亲切的话语让我的痛苦减轻了。
同义字词	alleviate, relieve, palliate
反义字词	aggravate, deteriorate
高分秘诀	▲ suffering n. 身体或心灵的痛苦，折磨

1275. mobile [`mobɪl] [mo·bile] ☆★★★★

adj. 可移动的,易变的	How I wish I could buy a mobile home! 真希望我能买一个拖车屋！
同义字词	moveable, fluid, changeable
高分秘诀	▲ mobile homes 拖车住宅，可移式住宅

1276. mock [mɑk] [mock] ☆★★★★

v. (模仿性的)嘲笑	We should not mock at others' appearance. 我们不应该嘲笑他人的外貌。
同义字词	ridicule, jeer, bemock, scoff
高分秘诀	▲ mock at 取笑，嘲弄 ▲ appearance n. 外貌，外表

1277. modify [`mɑdə‚faɪ] [mo·di·fy] ★★★★★

v. 修改,变更	If you intend to persuade her, you'd better modify your tone. 如果你打算说服她，你最好改一下语气。
同义字词	alter, change, adjust
高分秘诀	▲ persuade v. 说服，劝告 ▲ tone n. 语气，音调

1278. molecule [`mɑlə‚kjul] [mo·le·cule] ☆☆★★★

n. 分子	We all know that a molecule of water consists of two atoms of hydrogen and one atom of oxygen. 我们都知道水分子含两个氢原子和一个氧原子。

mitigate ~ monotonous

衍生字词	▲ atom n. 原子
	▲ particle n. 粒子
	▲ proton n. 质子
	▲ neutron n. 中子
高分秘诀	▲ hydrogen n. 氢
	▲ oxygen n. 氧

1279. molten [`moltən] [mol·ten]

adj. 熔融的，熔化的

Suddenly the volcano poured out molten rock.
突然间，火山喷出熔岩。

同义字词	melted, fused, liquefied
高分秘诀	▲ volcano n. 火山
	▲ pour out 涌出，倒出，使流出
	▲ molten rock 熔融岩石

1280. monarch [`mɑnək] [mon·arch]

n. 君主，帝王

Those rioters are planning to launch a revolution to overthrew the monarch.
这些暴民正准备发动革命推翻君主。

同义字词	king, ruler, emperor
高分秘诀	▲ rioter n. 暴徒，暴民
	▲ launch a revolution 发动革命
	▲ overthrow v. 打倒，推翻，使终止

1281. monopolize [mə`nɑpl‚aɪz] [mo·no·po·lize]

v. 独占，垄断

The girl is a motor mouth, and she always monopolized the conversation.
这个女孩很爱说话，总是一个人说个没完，别人根本无法插嘴。

同义字词	dominate, occupy, monopolise
衍生字词	▲ monopolism n. 独占主义
	▲ monopoly n. 独占，垄断
高分秘诀	▲ motor mouth 滔滔不绝，没完没了地说话
	▲ conversation n. 交谈，谈话

1282. monotonous [mə`nɑtənəs] [mo·no·to·nous]

adj. 单调乏味的，无变化的

My professor's monotonous voice put me to sleep.
教授单调的声音让我想睡觉。

同义字词	boring, dull, humdrum, tedious
反义字词	various
高分秘诀	▲ put to sleep 使某人入眠

1283. morphology [mɔr`fɑlədʒɪ] [mor·pho·lo·gy]

n. 形态学，形态论

The cellular morphology is only a branch of morphology.
细胞形态学只是形态学中的一个分支。

| 高分秘诀 | ▲ cellular morphology 细胞形态学 |
| | ▲ branch **n.** 分科，分支 |

1284. motif [mo`tif] [mo·tif] ☆☆★★★

n. (作品)主题，主旨

When you read books, you have to grasp the motif of the literature.
阅读时要抓住文学作品的主旨。

| 同义字词 | theme, design, subject |
| 高分秘诀 | ▲ literature **n.** 文学，文学作品 |

1285. motivate [`motə‚vet] [mo·ti·vate] ☆★★★★

v. 激发，刺激

The main reason I hire you just to let you motivate my employees.
我雇用你的主要原因就是让你激发我的职员。

同义字词	prompt, stimulate, impel, propel
高分秘诀	▲ main reason 主要原因
	▲ employee **n.** 雇工，雇员

1286. multiply [`mʌltəplaɪ] [`mul·tiply] ☆★★★★

v. 繁殖，增加，乘

We have to multiply our efforts to realize my dream.
我必须加倍努力实现我的梦想。

同义字词	proliferate, procreate, increase, advance, grow, rise
衍生字词	▲ multiple **adj.** 多样的，多重的
	▲ multiple choice 多项选择
高分秘诀	▲ effort **n.** 努力，尽力
	▲ realize dream 实现梦想

morphology ~ mythical

1287. mundane [ˈmʌnden] [mun·dane] ☆☆☆★★

adj. 世俗的，平凡的
I've never meddled in the mundane affairs.
我从来不管世俗琐事。

- 同义字词: worldly, earthly, secular, ordinary, everyday, quotidian
- 衍生字词:
  - ▲ mundane world 红尘
  - ▲ mundanely **adv.** 世俗地，平常地
- 高分秘诀:
  - ▲ meddle in 干预，管闲事
  - ▲ mundane affairs 俗事

1288. myriad [ˈmɪrɪəd] [my·ri·ad] ☆☆★★★

n. 许多，无数
Suddenly a myriad of ideas run into my mind, but no one is proper.
一时间无数想法涌入我的脑海，但没有一个合适的。

adj. 无数的
I wish I could own myriad money.
我希望拥有数不尽的金钱。

- 同义字词: countless, numberless, innumerous, innumerable
- 衍生字词:
  - ▲ myriads **n.** 无数，众生
- 高分秘诀:
  - ▲ a myriad of 无数
  - ▲ run into 突然进入
  - ▲ proper **adj.** 适合的，适当的

1289. mysterious [mɪsˈtɪrɪəs] [mys·te·ri·ous] ☆★★★★

adj. 神秘的，难以理解的
Speaking of the mysterious Egyptian pyramids, no one knows how they build them.
谈到神秘的埃及金字塔，没有人知道古埃及人是如何建造它们的。

- 同义字词: cryptical, mystic, mystical
- 衍生字词:
  - ▲ mystery **n.** 神秘（性），秘密（性），神秘的事
  - ▲ mysticism **n.** 神秘主义
- 高分秘诀:
  - ▲ Egyptian **adj.** 埃及的，埃及人的；**n.** 埃及人；古埃及语
  - ▲ pyramid **n.** 金字塔

1290. mythical [ˈmɪθɪkəl] [my·th·ical] ☆★★★★

adj. 神话的，虚构的
In the fairy tales, there are always some mythical creatures out there.
神话故事中有许多虚构的生物。

同义字词	mythic, legendary, fictitious
衍生字词	▲ myth n. 神话，神话故事 ▲ mythology adj. （总称）神话 ▲ mythologist n. 神话学者
高分秘诀	▲ fairy tale 神话故事 ▲ creature n. 生物，动物

Nn 托福 TOEFL iBT

托福(TOEFL)的测验对象为母语为非英语的人
申请入学美加地区大学或研究所时,托福成绩单是必备文件之一。

- n. 名词
- v. 动词
- adj. 形容词
- adv. 副词
- prep. 介词
- art. 冠词
- pron. 代词
- aux. 助词
- conj. 连词

Nn 托福 TOEFL iBT

托福(TOEFL)的测验对象为母语为非英语的人
申请入学美加地区大学或研究所时,托福成绩单是必备文件之一。

1291. narcotic [nɑrˋkɑtɪk] [nar·co·tic] ☆☆☆★★

adj. 麻醉的,催眠的	I'm glad that I'm free from narcotics addiction. 真高兴我摆脱了毒瘾。
n. 麻醉剂	The man was sent to prison on a narcotics charge. 那名男子被指控贩卖毒品,因而被关进了监狱。
同义字词	narcotising, soporiferous, soporific
衍生字词	▲ narcotherapy n. 麻醉疗法 ▲ narcotically adv. 麻醉地,催眠地 ▲ narcotic analgesic 麻醉性镇痛药
高分秘诀	▲ free from 从……释放出来,使摆脱 ▲ narcotics addiction 麻醉药成瘾(毒瘾) ▲ send to prison 送进监狱

1292. navigate [ˋnævəˏget] [na·vi·gate] ☆★★★★

v. 航行,航海,航空	Do you know who was the first to navigate the Atlantic alone? 你知道谁是第一位单独横渡大西洋的人吗?
同义字词	steer, voyage, sail, pilot
衍生字词	▲ navigation area 导航区 ▲ navigate channel 航道 ▲ navigating instrument 导航仪
高分秘诀	▲ Atlantic n. 大西洋

1293. negative [ˋnɛɡətɪv] [neg·a·tive] ★★★★★

adj. 否定的,消极的	I think most of the criticisms were not negative; they were really good for us. 我认为大多数批评并不是负面的,反而对我们有益。
同义字词	adverse, disparaging, pessimistic
反义字词	affirmative, positive
高分秘诀	▲ criticism n. 批评,批判

1294. neglect [nɪgˋlɛkt] [neg·lect] ★★★★★

n. 疏忽，忽略
I don't think you can change him, and you know he has shown a persistent neglect of duty.
我认为你无法改变他，他一贯玩忽职守。

v. 疏忽，遗漏
It serves him right that he was dismissed for neglecting his duty.
他因玩忽职守而被解雇，活该！

同义字词	disregard, ignore, leave out
反义字词	attend to, take to heart
高分秘诀	▲ persistent **adj.** 持续的，不断的 ▲ it serves him right 他活该 ▲ dismiss **v.** 解雇，撤职，开除

1295. negotiate [nɪˋgoʃɪ͵et] [ne·go·ti·ate] ☆★★★★

v. 谈判，协商
The President never negotiates with terrorists.
总统绝对不会与恐怖分子谈判。

| 同义字词 | intervene, mediate, confer |
| 高分秘诀 | ▲ negotiate with 与……进行交涉（以达成协定）
▲ terrorist **n.** 恐怖主义者，恐怖分子 |

1296. neutralize [ˋnjutrəl͵aɪz] [neu·tra·lize] ☆☆★★★

v. 抵消，中和
I got a raise, but the rising prices neutralized increased wage.
虽然我的薪水增加了，但是与物质的涨价相互抵消了。

同义字词	offset, counterbalance, counteract, neutralise
衍生字词	▲ neutral **adj.** 中性的，中立的，中性的
高分秘诀	▲ raise **n.** 增加 ▲ rising **adj.** 上升的，增长的 ▲ increased **adj.** 增加的，增强的

1297. nocturnal [nɑkˋtɝnl] [noc·tur·nal] ☆☆★★★

adj. 夜的，夜间活动的
Bats and owls belong to nocturnal animals.
蝙蝠和猫头鹰属于夜行动物。

| 衍生字词 | ▲ nocturnally **adv.** 夜间地，夜间活动地
▲ nocturnal cooling 夜间冷却
▲ nocturia **n.** 夜尿症，遗尿症
▲ nocturnal emission 梦遗 |

|高分秘诀| ▲ bat n. 蝙蝠
▲ owl n. 猫头鹰

1298. nomadic [noˈmædɪk] [no·mad·ic] ☆☆★★★

| adj. 游牧的，流浪的 | It's said that the nomadic Arabs did not farm.
据说游牧的阿拉伯人并不耕种。|

|同义字词| wandering, itinerant, roving

|高分秘诀| ▲ Arab n. 阿拉伯人 adj. 阿拉伯的，阿拉伯人的
▲ farm v. 耕作，经营农场

1299. nominate [ˈnɑməˌnet] [no·mi·nate] ☆★★★★

| v. 提名，任命 | Susan had been nominated as candidate for the general manager.
苏珊已被提名为总经理候选人。|

|同义字词| designate, appoint, constitute

|衍生字词| ▲ nominee n. 被提名的人，被任命者
▲ nominator n. 提名者，任命者

|高分秘诀| ▲ candidate n. 候选人

1300. nonsense [ˈnɑnsɛns] [non·sense] ☆★★★★

| n. 胡说，废话 | A man in his right senses would not be fooled with nonsense like that.
凡是有理智的人都不会被那种胡说八道愚弄。|

|同义字词| rubbish, bunk, poppycock, hokum

|高分秘诀| ▲ in one's right senses 神志清醒
▲ fool v. 愚弄，耍弄

1301. nostalgia [nɑsˈtældʒɪə] [nos·tal·gi·a] ☆☆☆★★

| n. 思家病，怀旧 | The scene of mother and daughter met and embraced emotionally inspired him with nostalgia.
母女相会相互拥抱的情景激起他的思乡之情。|

|同义字词| homesickness, reminiscence

|衍生字词| ▲ nostalgic adj. 对往事怀恋的，怀旧的
▲ nostalgist n. 怀乡者，怀旧者

|高分秘诀| ▲ embrace v. 拥抱
▲ emotionally adv. 感情上，情绪上

nomadic ~ novice

1302. notation [noˋteʃən] [no·ta·tion] ☆☆★★★

n. 符号, 记号

A few days later a more convenient notation will be given.
几天后就会提供较为方便的标示方法。

- 同义字词: sign, mark, note
- 衍生字词: ▲ notational system 符号系统
- 高分秘诀: ▲ convenient **adj.** 方便的, 便利的

1303. notorious [noˋtorɪəs] [no·to·ri·ous] ☆★★★★

adj. 恶名昭彰的, 声名狼藉的

The city is notorious for its casinos.
这个村庄因其众多的赌场而远近皆知。

- 同义字词: disreputable, infamous, ill-famed
- 反义字词: renowned, well-known, famous
- 衍生字词: ▲ notoriously **adv.** 声名狼藉地
- 高分秘诀: ▲ casino **n.** 赌场, 娱乐场

1304. nourish [ˋnɝɪʃ] [nour·ish] ☆★★★★

v. 养育, 滋养

It's the sunlight and water nourish the plants.
阳光和水分滋养植物生长。

- 同义字词: feed, nurture, nurse
- 衍生字词: ▲ eye nourisher 眼霜
- 高分秘诀:
  ▲ sunlight **n.** 阳光
  ▲ plant **n.** 植物

1305. novice [ˋnɑvɪs] [no·vice] ☆☆★★★

n. 生手, 新手

The period of being a novice is not finished yet.
新手的时期尚未结束。

- 同义字词: beginner, new hand, fresher, neophyte, tyro
- 反义字词: adept, veteran, old hand, go-getter
- 衍生字词: ▲ novice nun （佛教）比丘尼
- 高分秘诀: ▲ period **n.** （一段）时间；时期, 时代

1306. noxious [`nɑkʃəs] [nox·ious] ☆★★★★

adj. 有害的，有毒的

A lot of factories discharged noxious chemical wastes, which seriously poisoned the air.
很多工厂排放有毒化学废弃物，严重污染空气。

同义字词 harmful, injurious, nocuous

反义字词 harmless, innocuous

衍生字词
▲ noxious bacteria 有害细菌
▲ noxious gas 有害气体

高分秘诀
▲ discharge **v.** 放出，流出
▲ chemical waste 化学废弃物

1307. null [nʌl] [null] ☆☆★★★

adj. 无效的，空的

You should recognize which state or quality is null.
你应该认得出哪个状况或品质没有价值。

同义字词 invalid, void, nullified

反义字词 valid, effective

衍生字词 ▲ nullity **n.** 无效，无法律约束力

高分秘诀
▲ recognize **v.** 认出，识别出
▲ quality **n.** 品质，特征，特性

1308. numerous [`njumərəs] [nu·mer·ous] ☆★★★★

adj. 众多的，很多的

When the athlete appeared, he was surrounded by his numerous fans.
当这位运动员出现时，他的众多粉丝们向前将他包围。

同义字词 many, various, abundant, considerable

反义字词 little, few

高分秘诀
▲ athlete **n.** 运动员，体育家
▲ fan **n.** 狂热爱好者，迷

1309. nutritious [njuˋtrɪʃəs] [nu·tri·tious] ☆★★★★

adj. 有营养成分的，滋养的

Nowadays placenta is thought to be very nutritious.
现今胎盘被认为很有营养。

同义字词 nutritional, healthy, nourishing, nutrient, alimental

衍生字词
▲ nutritionist **n.** 营养学家
▲ nutriment **n.** 营养品

高分秘诀 ▲ placenta **n.** 胎盘

Oo 托福 TOEFL iBT

托福(TOEFL)的测验对象为母语为非英语的人
申请入学美加地区大学或研究所时，托福成绩单是必备文件之一。

n. 名词
v. 动词
adj. 形容词
adv. 副词
prep. 介词
art. 冠词
pron. 代词
aux. 助词
conj. 连词

Oo 托福 TOEFL iBT

托福(TOEFL)的测验对象为母语为非英语的人
申请入学美加地区大学或研究所时,托福成绩单是必备文件之一。

1310. obligate [ˈɑbləˌget] [ob·li·gate]
☆★★★★

v. 使(在法律或道义上)负有责任或义务

I don't think we are obligated to attend the opening ceremony.
我认为我们没有必要参加开幕式。

衍生字词 ▲ obligated adj. 有义务的,有责任的
高分秘诀 ▲ be obligated to 对……负有责任
▲ opening ceremony 开幕式

1311. oblige [əˈblaɪdʒ] [o·blige]
☆★★★★

v. 迫使, 使负义务

I'm obliged not to give up my claim.
我不得不放弃我的要求。

同义字词 force, compel, coerce

衍生字词 ▲ obliger n. 施惠于人者
▲ obliged adj. 必须的,有责任的
▲ obligee n. 债权人,权利人

高分秘诀 ▲ be obliged to 不得不
▲ give up 放弃,认输

1312. obliterate [əˈblɪtəˌret] [ob·li·te·rate]
☆☆★★★

v. 擦掉, 彻底破坏或毁灭

We can't get enough proof, as the heavy rain obliterated all footprints.
我们找不到足够的证据,因为大雨把所有的脚印都冲掉了。

同义字词 delete, erase, efface, wipe out, destroy, demolish
高分秘诀 ▲ heavy rain 大雨
▲ footprint n. 足迹,脚印

1313. obscure [əbˈskjur] [ob·scure]
☆★★★★

v. 隐藏, 使……模糊

I can't drive, as the smog obscured my view.
我无法开车,因为大雾模糊了我的视野。

obligate ~ obstacle

adj. 朦胧的,模糊的	I don't think his composition was good, see the meaning in it was obscure. 我认为他的作文写得不好，文字意义晦涩。
同义字词	conceal, veil, unclear, vague, indefinite
反义字词	clear
衍生字词	▲ obscured adj. 遮蔽的，湮没的 ▲ obscuration n. 昏暗，暗淡，朦胧 ▲ obscure glass 毛玻璃，不透玻璃
高分秘诀	▲ smog n. 烟雾 ▲ composition n. 作文，作品

1314. obsession [əb`sɛʃən] [ob·ses·sion] ★★★★★

n. 入迷,固执的念头	I don't know why she has an unhealthy obsession with death. 我不知道她为什么有一种不健康的念头，总是想着死亡。
同义字词	fascination, mania, fixation, compulsion

1315. obsolete [`ɑbsəˌlit] [ob·so·lete] ☆★★★★

adj. 废弃的,过时的	I think the root and branch reform is necessary, for our method is obsolete. 我认为彻底改革势在必行，因为我们的方法都太老套。
同义字词	out-of-date, outmoded, old-fashioned, antiquated
反义字词	up to date, fashionable
衍生字词	▲ obsolete information 失效信息
高分秘诀	▲ root and branch 彻底的 ▲ necessary adj. 必要的，必需的

1316. obstacle [`ɑbstəkl] [ob·sta·cle] ★★★★★

n. 障碍	I'm confident that these obstacles can be superable. 我有信心可以超越这些障碍。
同义字词	obstruction, impediment, hindrance, barrier
反义字词	help
衍生字词	▲ obstacle course 超载障碍训练场 ▲ obstacle race 障碍赛跑 ▲ obstacle avoidance 排除故障

1317. obstruct [əbˋstrʌkt] [ob·struct]

v. 阻塞（道路、通道等）

It is a crime for any government officials to obstruct justice.
任何政府官员阻挠司法都是犯罪。

同义字词　stop, impede, block, hinder

高分秘诀
▲ government official 政府官员
▲ justice **n.** 司法，审判

1318. occur [əˋkɝ] [oc·cur] ★★★★★

v. 发生，出现

No one had a prior knowledge when the accident occurred.
没有人事先知道意外何时发生。

同义字词　happen, take place, transpire, come about

高分秘诀
▲ prior **adj.** 预先的，在前的
▲ plane crash 飞机坠毁事件
▲ take-off 飞机起飞

1319. offensive [əˋfɛnsɪv] [of·fen·sive] ☆★★★★

adj. 讨厌的，无礼的

The company advertised their goods, never knew that the advertisement was highly offensive to the customers.
这家公司登广告宣传产品，没想到广告令顾客大为反感。

同义字词　disgusting, loathsome, disagreeable, aggressive

反义字词　inoffensive

衍生字词
▲ offensive grenade 进攻性手榴弹
▲ offensive minefield 攻势性雷区

1320. olfactory [ɑlˋfæktərɪ] [ol·fac·to·ry]   ☆☆★★★

adj. 嗅觉的

The olfactory nerves of dogs are very sensitive.
狗的嗅觉神经非常灵敏。

同义字词　olfactive

衍生字词　▲ olfaction **n.** 嗅觉

高分秘诀
▲ olfactory nerve 嗅觉神经
▲ sensitive **adj.** 灵敏的，敏感的

1321. omit [oˋmɪt] [o·mit] ☆☆★★★

v. 省略，省去

It's okay to omit the minor details.
可以省掉无关紧要的细枝末节。

同义字词	dispense with, bypass, neglect, leave out
反义字词	attend to
衍生字词	▲ omission n. 省略，遗漏 ▲ ommittance n. 遗漏
高分秘诀	▲ minor details 次要细节

1322. ooze [uz][ooze] ☆☆★★★

n. 软泥	This kind of heavy-metal ooze are rare. 这种重金属软泥很稀有。
v. 渗出，泄漏	I was shot with a bullet, and now blood is still oozing from the wound. 我被子弹射中了，伤口现在还在渗血。
同义字词	mud, mire, seep, flow, leak, filter
衍生字词	▲ ooze calf 植鞣小牛绒面革
高分秘诀	▲ wound n. 创伤，伤口 ▲ heavy-metal ooze 重金属软泥

1323. opaque [o`pek][o·paque] ☆☆★★★

adj. 不透明的，晦涩难懂的	Can you buy a bottle of opaque finish for me? 你能帮我买一瓶不透光的涂料吗?
同义字词	nontransparent；obscure, unintelligible, unclear
反义字词	clear
衍生字词	▲ opaqueness n. 不透明性 ▲ opaque glass 不透明玻璃
高分秘诀	▲ opaque finish 不透明涂饰剂

1324. optical [`ɑptɪkl][op·ti·cal] ☆★★★★

adj. 视觉的，光学的	I think that's only an optical illusion, for there is no ghosts in the world. 我觉得那是一种幻觉，因为这个世界上根本没有鬼。
同义字词	optic, visual
衍生字词	▲ optometrist n. 验光师 ▲ optics n. 光学 ▲ optician n. 眼镜商；配制眼镜技师 ▲ optical image 光学图像

1325. optimal [ˈɑptəməl] [op·ti·mal] ☆★★★★

adj. 最佳的，最理想的

I think 25 degrees Celsius is the optimal temperature for the growth of plants.
我认为摄氏二十五度是植物生长的最佳温度。

同义字词： most advantageous, optimum, ideal

衍生字词：
▲ optimal control 最优控制
▲ optimal design 优化设计，最佳设计

高分秘诀：
▲ degree Celsius 摄氏温度，摄氏度
▲ degree Fahrenheit 华氏温度
▲ temperature **n.** 温度，气温

1326. optimistic [ˌɑptəˈmɪstɪk] [op·ti·mis·tic] ☆★★★★

adj. 乐观的，乐观主义的

The boy's behavior embodied the spirit of optimistic materialism.
男孩的行为体现乐观的实利主义精神。

同义字词： hopeful, positive, affirmative

反义字词： pessimistic

衍生字词： ▲ optimistic striver 乐观奔命者

高分秘诀： ▲ materialism **n.** 物质主义，实利主义

1327. optional [ˈɑpʃənl] [op·tion·al] ☆★★★★

adj. 可自由选择的

Don't worry, the insurance cover is optional.
不要担心，保险范围可以随意选择。

同义字词： not compulsory, alternative, selectiona

衍生字词： ▲ optional course 选修课

高分秘诀： ▲ insurance cover 保险范围

1328. orient [ˈorɪənt] [o·ri·ent] ☆★★★★

v. 使适应，确定方向

If you are lost in the forest, you can orient yourself by finding a familiar landscape.
如果你在森林迷路，你可以先找一个熟悉的景色，进而确定自己所处的方位。

衍生字词： ▲ orientation **n.** 定向，介绍性指导

高分秘诀： ▲ familiar **adj.** 熟悉的，通晓的

optimal ~ outlast

1329. ornament [`ɔrnəmənt] [or·na·ment] ☆★★★★

n. 装饰，装饰物

The thief stole some ornaments and money from that mansion.
这个小偷从那所豪宅偷走了一些饰物和钱财。

- 同义字词：decoration, adornment, embellishment, garnish
- 衍生字词：▲ ornamentation **n.** 装饰，装饰品
- 高分秘诀：mansion **n.** 宅第，公馆，大厦

1330. oust [aʊst] [oust] ☆★★★★

v. 驱逐，赶走

The chairman ousted a rival from the committee.
主席将对手从委员会中赶了出去。

- 同义字词：drive out, eject, expel
- 高分秘诀：▲ rival **n.** 竞争者，对手

1331. outbreak [`aʊt,brek] [out·break] ★★★★★

n. 爆发，暴动

No one could have resisted a similar outbreak of enthusiasm.
没人能抵抗这样的热情。

- 同义字词：disturbance, eruption, explosion
- 衍生字词：▲ polar outbreak 寒潮
  ▲ periodic outbreak 周期性大发作

1332. outgoing [`aʊt,goɪŋ] [out·going] ★★★★★

adj. 外出的，外向的

The outgoing and incoming correspondence is kept in that file.
收件和寄件的信函存在那个文件里。

- 同义字词：sociable, extroverted
- 反义字词：incoming
- 衍生字词：▲ outgoing call 去话呼叫
  ▲ outgoing feeder 输出线路
- 高分秘诀：▲ correspondence **n.** 信件，符合，一致

1333. outlast [`aʊt`læst] [out·last] ★★★★★

v. 比……长久

Ancient earth and sky, marvel that love's passion should outlast all time.
古老的天地之间总是孕育许多天长地久的恋情。

| 衍生字词 | ▲ to outlast those dark clouds. 乌云会侵入你的生活。|

1334. outrage [ˈaʊtˌredʒ] [out·rage] ☆★★★★

n. 暴行, 愤怒	The government has been dilatory in condemning the outrage. 政府迟迟才谴责这次暴行。
v. 凌辱, 触犯	Such conduct outrages our rules of morality. 这种行为违背我们的道德准则。
同义字词	atrocity, barbarity, anger, enrage, offend
高分秘诀	▲ dilatory **adj.** 缓慢的, 拖延的 ▲ morality **n.** 道德, 品行

1335. outright [ˈaʊtˈraɪt] [out·right] ☆★★★★

adv. 率直地, 立刻地	I told him outright what I thought of his treason. 我把我对他的背叛的看法直率地告诉了他。
同义字词	altogether, entirely, completely
衍生字词	▲ outright forward 直接报价法 ▲ outright purchase 买断

1336. overdue [ˈovəˈdju] [over·due] ☆★★★★

adj. 过期的, 未兑的	Suspicion was only aroused when they became overdue. 他们逾期账款很久还未到达，这才引起怀疑。
同义字词	late, delayed, delinquent
衍生字词	▲ overdue account 逾期账款 ▲ overdue fine 滞纳金 ▲ overdue bill 到期未付票据

1337. overhaul [ˌovəˈhɔl] [over·haul] ☆★★★★

v. 分解检查, 精细检查	The fast cruiser soon overhauled the old cargo boat. 快速巡逻艇很快就赶上了那艘旧货船。
同义字词	restore, repair, fix, mend
高分秘诀	▲ cruiser **n.** 巡洋舰 ▲ cargo **n.** 货物

outrage ~ overwhelm

1338. overlap [ˋovɚˋlæp] [over·lap] ☆☆★★★

v. 部分重叠，与……交搭

There is no pericope of overlap between the two courses.
这两门课程之间不存在重叠的问题。

衍生字词 ▲ overlap fault 超复断层
高分秘诀 ▲ pericope **n.** 章节，选段

1339. oversee [ˋovɚˋsi] [o·ver·see] ☆★★★★

v. 向下看，监督

The manager is overseeing the process in the factory.
经理正在监督工厂的工作流程。

同义字词 supervise, manage, administer
衍生字词 ▲ overseer **n.** 监督人，工头

1340. overt [oˋvɝt] [o·vert] ☆☆★★★

adj. 明显的，公然的

They showed overt hostility to us.
他们向我们表示公开的敌意。

衍生字词 ▲ overt culture **n.** 外表文化
高分秘诀 ▲ hostility **n.** 敌对，敌意

1341. overwhelm [ˌovɚˋwɛlm] [o·ver·whelm] ☆★★★★

v. 战胜，压倒

Butcheries on a gigantic scale overwhelmed all detached sentiment.
大规模的屠杀压倒一切分歧意见。

衍生字词 ▲ overwhelmingly **adv.** 压倒性地，不可抵抗地
高分秘诀 ▲ gigantic **adj.** 巨大的，庞大的

Pp 托福 TOEFL iBT

托福(TOEFL)的测验对象为母语为非英语的人
申请入学美加地区大学或研究所时,托福成绩单是必备文件之一。

- n. 名词
- v. 动词
- adj. 形容词
- adv. 副词
- prep. 介词
- art. 冠词
- pron. 代词
- aux. 助词
- conj. 连词

Pp 托福 TOEFL iBT

托福(TOEFL)的测验对象为母语为非英语的人
申请入学美加地区大学或研究所时,托福成绩单是必备文件之一。

1342. pack [pæk] [pack] ☆★★★★

v. 装, 塞满	Susan is packing right now because she is leaving for London. 苏珊正在整理行李,因为她即将前往伦敦。
n. 一群, 包裹	Most tourists carried a pack on their backs. 大部分观光客都背着背包。

同义字词: cram, fill, load, stuff

衍生字词:
▲ packed adj. 压紧的,压实的
▲ backpack v. 背包

高分秘诀: ▲ coach bus 长途客车

1343. painstaking [penzˌtekɪŋ] [pains·tak·ing] ☆★★★★

adj. 辛苦的,辛勤的,极小心的

Though she made painstaking efforts to learn English, her English was not fluent.
虽然苦学英语,但她的英语依然不流利。

同义字词: arduous, diligent, careful, meticulous, scrupulous

衍生字词:
▲ painstaker v. 勤恳的人,刻苦的人
▲ painstakingly adv. 刻苦地,煞费苦心地

1344. palatable [ˈpælətəbl] [pal·at·a·ble] ☆★★★★

adj. 美味的,合意的

My mouth is watering as soon as I see the palatable food.
一看到可口的饭菜,我就口水直流。

同义字词: tasty, delicious, toothsome, luscious, savory

高分秘诀: ▲ as soon as 一……就……

1345. panic [ˈpænɪk] [pa·nic] ☆★★★★

n. 恐慌, 惊慌

I got into a panic when I thought the approaching examination.
一想到即将到来的考试,我就惊慌。

pack ~ paramount

v. (使)恐慌

Keep secret, or this idea would panic the investors.
保守秘密，否则这个想法会使投资者惶恐不安。

同义字词 alarm, fear, scare, terror

衍生字词
▲ panicky **adj.** 恐慌的，易恐慌的
▲ panic attack 惊恐发作（一种病症）
▲ panic barrier 紧急栏障

1346. parallel [ˋpærəˌlɛl] [par·al·lel] ☆★★★★

v. 与……平行，匹敌

Don't paralleled your life with others, and you know comparisons are odious.
不要把你的生活和别人比，人比人会气死人。

n. 类似，相似

It seems that the parallels can come together in the distance.
平行线似乎在远处交合。

adj. 平行的，相似的

The girl can keep her balance on the parallel bars.
这个女孩可以在双杠上保持平衡。

同义字词 compare, match, similarity, analogy, even, equal

衍生字词
▲ parallel circuit 并联电路
▲ parallel interface（计）平行界面

1347. paralysis [pəˋræləsɪs] [pa·ral·y·sis] ☆★★★★

n. 瘫痪

It's so pity that the car accident left the girl with paralysis of the limbs.
真遗憾，意外使那个女孩的四肢瘫痪了。

衍生字词
▲ paralysed **adj.** 瘫痪的，麻痹的
▲ paralysis agitans 帕金森病，震颤性麻痹

1348. paramount [ˋpærəˌmaʊnt] [par·a·mount] ☆★★★★

adj. 最高的，至上的

To the government the paramount thing is to reduce the unemployment.
对政府来说，最重要就是降低失业率。

同义字词 predominant, superior, primary, principal, uppermost

衍生字词
▲ paramount clause 最高条款
▲ paramount interest 首要权益
▲ paramountship **n.** 最高权威

1349. paraphrase [ˈpærəˌfrez] [par·a·phrase]

v. 将……释义，改写
Can you paraphrase the passage into two paragraphs?
你能把这节文章意译成两段吗？

n. 释义，意译
I think the monologue paraphrase is better than the former one.
我认为独白式讲述比前面的那个要好。

同义字词　restate, reword, explanation, interpretation, paraphrasis

衍生字词　▲ paraphrasable **adj.** 可意译的
　　　　　▲ paraphrasing **n.** 释义，意译，改写

1350. parasite [ˈpærəˌsaɪt] [par·a·site]

n. 寄生虫，食客
The sluggard was a parasite on his family.
这个懒惰鬼是他家的寄生虫。

衍生字词　▲ parasite plant 寄生植物

1351. passionate [ˈpæʃənɪt] [pas·sion·ate]

adj. 充满热情的，热烈的
Maybe it's my passionate speech which had an effect on their emotions.
也许是我热情的演讲打动了他们。

同义字词　ardent, zealous, enthusiastic

衍生字词　▲ passion **n.** 激情，热情
　　　　　▲ passionately **adv.** 热情地，激昂地

1352. pastel [pæsˈtɛl] [pas·tel]

adj. 柔和的，彩色蜡笔的
You should change the color of your curtain, and you know pastel colour is restful to the eyes.
你应该换换窗帘的颜色，柔和的颜色对眼睛较好。

同义字词　bland, soft

衍生字词　▲ pastel chalk 彩色粉笔
　　　　　▲ pastel drawing 蜡笔画；彩粉画

1353. patent [ˈpætn̩t] [pat·ent]

n. 专利
The patent runs out in five years time.
这项专利的期限有五年。

v. 取得……的专利权，申请专利
It's your right to patent your invention.
为你的发明申请专利是你的权利。

paraphrase ~ peck

| 同义字词 | license, apply for patent, patent pending |
| 衍生字词 | ▲ patentable adj. 可以取得专利的 |

1354. patriarch [ˈpetrɪˌɑrk] [pa·tri·arch] ☆☆☆★★

n. 家长，族长

The old man is the patriarch of the herd.
这位老人是这里的大家长。

| 同义字词 | master, chief, paterfamilias |
| 衍生字词 | ▲ patriarchism n. 家长制度，族长制度 |

1355. patriot [ˈpetrɪət] [pa·tri·ot] ☆☆★★★

n. 爱国者

If there were so many noble-minded patriots, then our nation would not be destroyed.
如果我们有许多爱国主义者，民族就不会灭亡。

| 衍生字词 | ▲ patriotic adj. 爱国的
▲ patriotism n. 爱国主义，爱国精神 |

1356. patrol [pəˈtrol] [pa·trol] ☆★★★★

v. 巡逻，巡视

There are so many soldiers patrolling the streets with army rifles on their backs.
街上许多士兵在背着枪巡逻。

| 衍生字词 | ▲ patroller n. 巡警
▲ patrolman n. 公路巡查员 |
| 高分秘诀 | ▲ army rifle 步枪 |

1357. patron [ˈpetrən] [pa·tron] ☆★★★★

n. 赞助人，资助人

Most of the shop would give their regular patrons some discount.
大部分商店会给他们的老主顾一些折扣。

| 同义字词 | benefactor, helper, customer, client |
| 衍生字词 | ▲ patron saint 守护神
▲ patronage n. 赞助；惠顾 |

1358. peck [pɛk] [peck] ☆★★★★

v. 啄，啄起

Don't touch the pullus, or the mamma bird would peck you.
不要摸幼鸟，否则鸟妈妈会啄你。

| 同义字词 | pick, pick at |

衍生字词	▲ peck order 啄序，啄的等级
	▲ peck and boose 酒肉，饮食

1359. peculiar [pɪˋkjuljə] [pe·cul·iar]   ☆★★★★

adj. 特有的，奇怪的	Though he looks ugly, he is really a peculiar talent. 虽然他其貌不扬，但确是个天才。
同义字词	special, characteristic, unusual, odd, bizarre, weird
衍生字词	▲ peculiarity n. 特性，怪癖 ▲ peculiarly adv. 异常地，古怪地
高分秘诀	▲ peculiar talent 鬼才

1360. pedagogy [ˋpɛdəˏgodʒɪ] [ped·a·go·gy]   ☆☆★★★

n. 教育学，教学法	I'm taking applied pedagogy as an elective this year. 今年我准备选修应用教育学。
同义字词	education, teaching method, pedagogics, didactics
衍生字词	▲ pedagog / pedagogue n. （卖弄学问的）教师 ▲ pedagogic adj. 教育学的

1361. peer [pɪr] [peer]   ☆★★★★

v. 凝视，仔细看	My girlfriend peered at me closely, as if she didn't know me. 我女朋友仔细地盯着我，好像她不认得我一样。
n. 同辈，同侪	My father is so kind that it would be hard to find his peer. 我爸爸为人很好，简直找不出第二个像他的人。
同义字词	gaze, stare, fellow, companion
衍生字词	▲ peer machine 个别系统，对等机 ▲ peeress n. 贵族夫人，有爵位的妇女

1362. penal [ˋpinl] [pe·nal]   ☆☆★★★

adj. 刑罚的，刑法上的	Don't do that kind of thing, you know robbery is a penal offense. 不要去做那种事，抢劫是刑事犯罪。
衍生字词	▲ penalty clause 合同中违约罚款的规定 ▲ penalty area （足球）罚球区
高分秘诀	▲ penal offense 刑事犯罪

peculiar ~ perch

1363. penchant [ˈpɛntʃənt] [pen·chant]

n. 爱好, 嗜好

It's impossible for her falling in love with you, and you are poor and she has a penchant for luxury and opulence.
她不可能爱上你，你那么穷，而她又崇尚奢华的生活。

同义字词　liking, inclination, predilection, preference

1364. pendant [ˈpɛndənt] [pend·ant] ☆★★★★

n. 垂饰, 下垂物

How about set an emerald in a pendant?
在垂饰上镶绿宝石你觉得如何?

同义字词　hanging

衍生字词
▲ pendant cloud（气象学）漏斗云
▲ pendant control 控制板
▲ pendant lamp 吊灯

高分秘诀　▲ emerald **n.** 绿宝石

1365. penetrate [ˈpɛnəˌtret] [pe·ne·trate] ☆★★★★

v. 穿透, 渗透

The wolf's sharp claws penetrated my skin. It hurts.
狼的尖爪刺入我的皮肤，真是痛。

同义字词　pierce, go through, permeate

1366. pensive [ˈpɛnsɪv] [pen·sive] ☆★★★★

adj. 沉思的, 忧郁的

There are always some paintings which can inspire a pensive mood.
有些画总能引人沉思。

同义字词　meditative, contemplative, brooding, broody

1367. perceive [pəˈsiv] [per·ceive] ☆★★★★

v. 感知, 察觉

I perceived there are some changes in my husband's behavior.
我察觉老公的行为有些变化。

同义字词　sense, detect

1368. perch [pɝtʃ] [perch]

n. 栖枝, 栖木

Most of the birds took their perches on the tree branch.
大多数鸟类栖息在树枝。

v. (使)栖息	There are two birds perched on the antenna. 有两只鸟停在天线上。
同义字词	pole, rod, settle, sit, alight, roost

1369. percolate [ˈpɝkəˌlet] [per·co·late]   ☆★★★★

v. 过滤,渗透	The rumour percolated through the whole village. 那谣言在村子里慢慢流传。
同义字词	filter, leach, permeate
高分秘诀	▲ percolate through 渗透过

1370. perennial [pəˈrɛnɪəl] [per·en·ni·al]   ☆★★★★

adj. 四季不断的, 终年的	The shortage of capital is a perennial phenomenon to my family. 资金短缺对我们家来说是长久的现象。
同义字词	continuous, perpetual, year-round
衍生字词	▲ perennially adv. 永久地,终年地 ▲ perennial plant 多年生植物

1371. perform [pɚˈfɔrm] [per·form]   ★★★★★

v. 履行,执行	I can count on Tom, for he always performs his duty faithfully. 我可以依赖汤姆,因为他总是履行自己的职责。
同义字词	handle, execute, carry out
衍生字词	▲ performance n. 履行,执行,表演,演奏 ▲ performable adj. 可执行的,可完成的
高分秘诀	▲ perform one's duty 履行职责 ▲ faithfully adv. 忠实地

1372. peripheral [pəˈrɪfərəl] [pe·riph·er·al]   ☆★★★★

adj. 周边的,周边的	Can you tell me what the peripheral war is? 你能告诉我什么是边缘战争吗?
高分秘诀	▲ peripheral war (军)边缘战争

1373. perishable [ˈpɛrɪʃəbl] [per·ish·a·ble]   ☆★★★★

adj. (尤指食物)易腐的,易坏的	Food are not perishable if they are kept in refrigerator. 食物保存在冰箱不易坏。

percolate ~ perpetuate

衍生字词	▲ perish v. 丧生，消亡，腐烂
	▲ perishability n. 易腐烂性，易朽性
	▲ perishable food 易腐食品
高分秘诀	▲ refrigerator n. 冰箱

1374. permanent ['pɝmənənt] [per·ma·nent]　☆★★★★

adj. 长久的，永久的

I've been on the run for so many years and decided to buy a permanent abode in Beijing.
我奔波多年，想在北京买一处永久性的居所。

衍生字词	▲ permanence n. 永久，持久
高分秘诀	▲ on the run 忙碌，奔波
	▲ abode n. 住所，公寓

1375. permeate ['pɝmɪ,et] [per·me·ate]　☆★★★★

v. 弥漫，渗透

A mood of excitement permeated the whole class.
兴奋之情感染全班。

同义字词	pass through, penetrate, saturate, soak
衍生字词	▲ permeable adj. 有浸透性的，能透过的
	▲ permeation n. 渗入，透过
高分秘诀	▲ excitement n. 兴奋，激动

1376. perpendicular [,pɝpən'dɪkjəlɚ] [per·pen·dic·u·lar]　☆★★★★

adj. 垂直的，直立的

The wall is out of the perpendicular, and I have to ask for some builders to repair it.
这堵墙有些倾斜，我需要找些建筑工人修理。

同义字词	vertical, upright
反义字词	inclined, oblique
衍生字词	perpendicularly adv. 垂直地，直立地
高分秘诀	▲ be out of 没有
	▲ ask for 请求，要求

1377. perpetuate [pə'pɛtʃu,et] [per·pet·u·ate]　☆★★★★

v. 使……延续，使永存

We set up a monument to perpetuate the memory of the martyrs.
我们立了一座纪念碑纪念烈士。

同义字词	eternalize

衍生字词	▲ perpetual adj. 永久的，没完没了的
	▲ perpetuated adj. 永存的
	▲ perpetuator n. 永久保存的人
	▲ perpetual bond 永久债券
	▲ perpetual calendar 万年历
高分秘诀	▲ monument n. 纪念碑
	▲ martyr n. 烈士

1378. perplex [pə`plɛks] [per·plex] ☆★★★★

v. 使迷惑，使混乱	I don't think little Tom could answer the question, even the most knowledgeable man would get perplexed to such question.
	我想小汤姆回答不出这个问题，即使知识最渊博的人也会被这样的问题考倒。
同义字词	baffle, confuse, bewilder, puzzle
反义字词	simplify
衍生字词	▲ perplexing adj. 使人困惑的，令人费解的
	▲ perplexed adj. 困惑的，不知所措的
	▲ perplexity n. 困惑，混乱
高分秘诀	▲ knowledgeable adj. 博学的，知识渊博的

1379. persevere [ˌpɝsə`vɪr] [per·se·vere] ☆★★★★

v. 坚持不懈，不屈不挠	Every time I face the difficulty, I would grit my teeth and persevere.
	每当遇到困难，我就咬紧牙关坚持下去。
同义字词	endure, persist, keep on, hang on, hold on
衍生字词	▲ perseverance n. 坚定不移
	▲ perseveringly adv. 坚定地
高分秘诀	▲ difficulty n. 困难，麻烦
	▲ grit one's teeth 咬紧牙关

1380. persist [pə`sɪst] [per·sist] ★★★★★

v. 坚持，持续	If you persist in violating the traffic rules, one day you would get hurt in the car accident.
	如果你继续违反交通规则，总有一天会意外受伤。
同义字词	continue, insist, persevere, endure, last
反义字词	desist, stop

衍生字词　▲ persistence n. 坚持不懈，持续
　　　　　▲ persistent adj. 坚持不懈的

高分秘诀　▲ violate the traffic rule 违反交通规则

1381. perspective [pəˋspɛktɪv] [per·spec·tive] ★★★★★

n. （判断事物的）角度，方法
First I have to remind you to see things in perspective.
首先，我要提醒你必须正确观察事物。

同义字词　viewpoint, view, position

衍生字词　▲ perspectival adj. 透视性的
　　　　　▲ perspectival issues 观点议题
　　　　　▲ perspective correction 透视校正
　　　　　▲ perspective glass 望远镜

高分秘诀　▲ in perspective 正确地；符合透视法地

1382. perspire [pəˋspaɪr] [per·spire] ☆★★★★

v. 出汗
I began to perspire as I pedaled the bicycle.
我一骑自行车就出汗。

同义字词　sweat, exude perspiration

衍生字词　▲ perspiration n. 汗水，出汗
　　　　　▲ perspired adj. 被出汗的
　　　　　▲ perspirable adj. 可随汗液排出的，汗液通过的
　　　　　▲ hidropoiesis n. 流汗

1383. persuade [pəˋswed] [per·suade] ☆★★★★

v. 说服，劝说
I really don't know how I can persuade you of my sincerity.
我真的不知道如何能够说服你相信我的诚意。

衍生字词　▲ persuasive adj. 有说服力的，善说服的

高分秘诀　▲ sincerity n. 真实，诚挚，诚实

1384. pertinent [ˋpɝtnənt] [per·ti·nent] ☆★★★★

adj. 相关的，切题的
If you trust me, please tell me the pertinent details.
如果相信我，请告诉我相关的细节。

同义字词　relevant, apposite, appropriate

反义字词　impertinent

衍生字词	▲ pertinence / pertinency n. 相关性，有关性
	▲ pertinently adv. 有关地
高分秘诀	▲ detail n. 细节，详情

1385. pestilence [ˈpɛstləns] [pes·ti·lence] ☆★★★★

n. 瘟疫

We have to take measures to control the pestilence, or it would overhang the whole country.
我们必须采取措施控制瘟疫，否则它会威胁整个国家。

同义字词	epidemic, plague, murrain
衍生字词	▲ pestilential adj. 引起瘟疫的
	▲ pestilent adj. 致命的，致死的，有害的
高分秘诀	▲ overhang v. 威胁

1386. petition [pəˈtɪʃən] [pe·ti·tion] ☆★★★★

n. 请愿书

There are a lot of people file a petition against the law.
很多人申请取消这项法律。

v. 请愿

There are several organizations petitioned the government for cancelling the rules.
很多组织向政府请愿，请求取消法规。

同义字词	plea, request, appeal, request
衍生字词	▲ bankruptcy petition 破产呈请书
	▲ appellate petition 上诉申请，上诉状
高分秘诀	▲ file a petition 提出诉状
	▲ organization n. 团体，机构，组织

1387. philology [fɪˈlɑlədʒɪ] [phi·lol·o·gy] ☆☆★★★

n. 语言学，文献学

The woman devoted her life to the study of the comparative philology.
这位妇女把毕生精力投入到研究比较语言学上。

同义字词	linguistics, literature
衍生字词	▲ philological / philologic adj. 语言学的，文献学的
高分秘诀	▲ devote one's life to 献身于……
	▲ comparative philology 比较语言学

1388. philosophy [fəˈlɑsəfɪ] [phi·los·o·phy] ☆★★★★

n. 哲学，原理

He told me that ethics is only a branch of philosophy.
他告诉我伦理学只是哲学的一个分科。

pestilence ~ pinch

同义字词	philosophical system
衍生字词	▲ philosopher n. 哲学家，哲人
	▲ philosophical / philosophic adj. 哲学上的
	▲ philosophize / philosophise v. 像哲学家般思考或辩论

1389. physiology [ˌfɪzɪˋɑlədʒɪ] [phys·i·ol·o·gy] ☆★★★★

n. 生理学	The intelligent woman was awarded the Nobel Prize for physiology and medicine.
	这位聪明的女士获得诺贝尔生理学和医学奖。
衍生字词	▲ physiologist n. 生理学家，生理学研究者
	▲ physiological character 生理状态
	▲ physiological clock 生物钟，生理钟
高分秘诀	▲ award v. 授予，奖给
	▲ Nobel Prize 诺贝尔奖

1390. picturesque [ˌpɪktʃəˋrɛsk] [pic·tur·esque] ☆★★★★

adj. 如画的，美丽的	Have you ever been to that picturesque borderland village?
	你去过那个风景如画的边界村落吗？
同义字词	scenic, beautiful
衍生字词	▲ picturesque views 景色如画
	▲ picturesque scenery 山清水秀，景色如画
	▲ picturesquely adv. 如画地，别致地，生动地
高分秘诀	▲ borderland v. 边疆，边境

1391. pierce [pɪrs] [pierce] ☆★★★★

v. 刺入，穿透	Nowadays more and more girls pierced through ears for earrings.
	如今越来越多的女孩子穿耳洞戴耳环。
同义字词	penetrate, perforate, puncture, stab, thrust
衍生字词	▲ pierce die 冲孔模
	▲ pierce ears 穿耳孔
高分秘诀	▲ pierce through 穿破，穿过
	▲ earring n. 耳环

1392. pinch [pɪntʃ] [pinch]   ☆★★★★

v. 捏，掐，夹，拧	I like to pinch my little brother's pink cheek.
	我喜欢拧我弟弟的粉红脸颊。
同义字词	clutch, squeeze, nip

| 衍生字词 | ▲ pinch bar 爪棍，尖头长杆
▲ pinch and save 节衣缩食地攒钱，省吃俭用
▲ pinch cock 弹簧夹子 |
| 高分秘诀 | ▲ pink adj. 粉红色的，淡红色的
▲ cheek n. 脸颊，脸蛋 |

1393. pinpoint [ˈpɪnˌpɔɪnt] [pin·point] ☆★★★★

| v. 准确地确定 | After a few minutes' searching, the radar quickly pinpointed the attacking planes.
经过几分钟的搜索，雷达很快确定了来袭敌机的精确方位。 |
| 衍生字词 | ▲ pinpoint oiler 注油器
▲ pinpoint gate （工程）针孔型浇注孔
▲ pinpoint target （军械）针点状目标 |
| 高分秘诀 | ▲ search v. 搜索，找寻
▲ radar n. 雷达（装置）
▲ attacking plane 来袭飞机 |

1394. pique [pik] [pique] ☆☆★★★

| v. 激起，引起（好奇等） | The dark house piqued my curiosity.
这座坟墓激起了我的好奇心。 |
| 同义字词 | arouse, provoke, irritate, offend |
| 衍生字词 | ▲ piqued adj. 激怒的，不满的 |
| 高分秘诀 | ▲ dark house 冥穴，坟墓
▲ curiosity n. 好奇心 |

1395. pivot [ˈpɪvət] [piv·ot] ☆☆★★★

| n. 枢轴，中心点 | It took me hours to find the pivot of the whole argument.
我花了几个小时才找到论据的关键。 |
| 同义字词 | axis, focus, center |
| 衍生字词 | ▲ pivotal adj. 枢轴的，关键的
▲ pivotal figure 关键人物 |
| 高分秘诀 | ▲ argument n. 论据，论点 |

1396. plagiarism [ˈpledʒəˌrɪzəm] [pla·gi·a·rism] ☆★★★★

| n. 剽窃，抄袭 | The principal said that plagiarism is akin to theft.
校长说抄袭与偷窃无异。 |

pinpoint ~ pledge

衍生字词
- ▲ plagiarise v. 剽窃，抄袭
- ▲ plagiarization n. 剽窃，抄袭
- ▲ plagiarist n. 剽窃者，抄袭者
- ▲ plagiaristic adj. 抄袭的

1397. plague [pleg] [plague] ☆★★★★

n. 瘟疫，灾祸
The plague raged for months before it could be controlled.
瘟疫盛行好几个月才被控制住。

v. 折磨，使苦恼
It's so pity that the severe back injury plagued the soldier all his life.
严重的背伤终身折磨着这个士兵，真令人感到遗憾。

衍生字词
- ▲ plague city 瘟疫城市
- ▲ plague serum 抗疫病血清
- ▲ plague spot 疹子

1398. plainspoken [`plen`spokən] [plain·spoken] ☆☆★★★

adj. 直言不讳的
To tell the truth, I like this plainspoken country doctor.
老实说，我喜欢这个说话很直接的乡村医生。

同义字词　forthright, frank, free-spoken

高分秘诀
- ▲ to tell the truth 说实话
- ▲ country doctor 乡村医生

1399. platitude [`plætə͵tjud] [plat·i·tude] ☆★★★★

n. 陈词滥调
What you said is no more than a platitude to me.
对我来说，你说的这些话都是老生常谈。

同义字词　trite saying, cliché, bromide, commonplace

衍生字词
- ▲ platitudinize/ platitudinise v. 说平凡的话，说陈腔滥调
- ▲ platitudinous adj. 陈词滥调的，陈腐的

高分秘诀　▲ no more than 只是

1400. pledge [plɛdʒ] [pledge] ☆★★★★

n. 保证，誓言
Though the little boy scared to death, he still bravely kept his pledge to.
虽然这个小男孩吓得半死，但仍勇敢地遵守誓言。

v. 发誓，保证
She pledged never to let the secret out, but she lied.
她发誓绝不说出这个秘密，但最终还是泄露出去了。

同义字词	promise, oath, guarantee
衍生字词	▲ pledge of blood 血的誓约 ▲ Pledge of Allegiance 效忠誓言
高分秘诀	▲ scare to death 吓得要死 ▲ let out 泄密，透露

1401. pliable [ˋplaɪəb!] [pli·a·ble] ☆★★★★

adj. 易弯的，柔软的	The willow twigs are lightweight, soft and pliable. 这些柳条重量轻，柔软易弯曲。
同义字词	malleable, lithe, ductile, elastic
衍生字词	▲ pliability n. 易曲折，顺从，柔软
高分秘诀	▲ willow twig 柳条 ▲ lightweight adj. 轻量的

1402. pliant [ˋplaɪənt] [pli·ant] ☆☆★★★

adj. 易弯的，柔韧的	We have to pay much attention to children's education; they have pliant natures. 我们必须关心儿童的教育，因为他们有着可塑的本性。
衍生字词	▲ pliancy n. 柔软，柔顺 ▲ pliantly adv. 易弯地，柔韧地
高分秘诀	▲ pay attention to 注意 ▲ children's education 儿童教育

1403. plight [plaɪt] [plight] ☆★★★★

n. （恶劣的）情势，困境	I'm in sympathy with the refugees' plight. 我同情难民的困苦。
同义字词	misfortune, predicament, quandary
衍生字词	▲ plighted lovers 山盟海誓的一对恋人
高分秘诀	▲ in sympathy with 同情 ▲ refugee n. 避难者，难民

1404. plump [plʌmp] [plump] ☆☆★★★

adj. 胖嘟嘟的，丰满的	I saw a short plump man walking along the pavement towards me. 我看见一个矮胖的男人沿着人行道向我走来。

pliable ~ polish

同义字词	chubby, fat, zaftig, plumpy
反义字词	lean
衍生字词	▲ plumpen v. 使长胖；使变得胖鼓鼓的 ▲ plumper n. 含在嘴里的东西；猛跌
高分秘诀	▲ pavement n. 人行道

1405. plunge [plʌndʒ] [plunge] ☆★★★★

v. 跳进，投入，陷入	I saw a diver plunging into the deep water suddenly. 我看见一个潜水员猛然跳进深水中。

同义字词	dive, submerge, plummet
衍生字词	▲ plunge pool 瀑布下的水潭 ▲ plunge chip 冲头 ▲ plunger n. 活塞，潜水者
高分秘诀	▲ diver n. 潜水员 ▲ plunge into 投入，跳入

1406. polarize [ˈpoləˌraɪz] [po·lar·ize] ☆☆★★★

v. 使极化，使两极分化	It turned out the public opinion has polarized on the issue. 结果公众的意见在问题上呈现两极化。

同义字词	polarize
衍生字词	▲ polar adj. 两极的，极地的 ▲ polaris n. 北极星
高分秘诀	▲ turn out 结果是，原来是 ▲ public opinion 舆论，民意

1407. polish [ˈpɑlɪʃ] [pol·ish] ☆★★★★

v. 擦亮	Don't polish your glasses with a handkerchief. 不要用手帕擦拭眼镜。
n. 光泽，上光剂	It's said that the car polish is an effective shield against rust. 据说汽车上光蜡的防锈功能很棒。

同义字词	shine, burnish, furbish
衍生字词	▲ polished adj. 擦亮的；精致的，完美的，优雅的 ▲ polished bolt 抛光螺栓 ▲ polisher n. 磨光机

1408. pollinate [ˈpɑləˌnet] [pol·li·nate] ☆☆★★★

v. 对……授粉

Wild bees are our human's friends, and they help us to pollinate human crops.

野蜂是人类的朋友，他们有助于农作物授粉。

同义字词 fertilize, pollenate, cross-pollinate

衍生字词
▲ pollination n. 授粉
▲ pollen n. 花粉
▲ pollinator n. 传粉媒介，传粉昆虫

1409. pollute [pəˈlut] [pol·lute] ★★★★★

v. 污染, 玷污

Some factories' chimneys poured a large volume of smoke to pollute the air; I think the government should forbid them to do that.

一些工厂的烟囱排放烟雾污染空气，我认为政府应该阻止他们。

同义字词 contaminate, foul, defile, profane

衍生字词
▲ pollution n. 污染，玷污
▲ pollutant n. 污染物质

1410. polygon [ˈpɑlɪˌgɑn] [pol·y·gon] ☆☆★★★

n. 多边形, 多角形

Draw a polygon whose angles are equal on the paper.

在纸上画一个等角多边形。

衍生字词
▲ polygonal adj. 多角形的，多边形的
▲ polygon geometry 多边形几何体
▲ polygon ground（地质学）多边形土

高分秘诀
▲ angle n. 角，角度
▲ equal adj. 相等的，同样的

1411. porous [ˈpɔrəs] [po·rous] ☆☆★★★

adj. 可渗透的, 多孔的

Can you buy a new clay pot for me? This one is porous.

你能帮我买个新的陶罐吗？这个会渗水。

同义字词 permeable, poriferous, holey

反义字词 nonporous

衍生字词
▲ porousity n. 渗透性
▲ porousness n. 多孔性
▲ porous brick 多孔钻
▲ porous layer 多孔岩层

pollinate ~ possess

高分秘诀 ▲ clay pot 泥罐

1412. portable [ˋpɔrtəbl] [port·a·ble] ☆★★★★

adj. 便于携带的，手提式的

I'm planning to save up money to buy a portable computer.
我计划存钱买一部手提电脑。

同义字词 mobile, conveyable, transferable

衍生字词
▲ portability n. 可携带，轻便
▲ portable appliance 手提（式）仪表，可移动的用具

高分秘诀
▲ save up 储存起来
▲ portable computer 手提电脑

1413. portend [pɔrˋtɛnd] [por·tend] ☆★★★★

v. 预兆，预示

There is no doubt that the threatening skies portend a storm.
毫无疑问，恶劣的天气通常预告一场暴风雨即将到来。

同义字词 herald, foreshadow, forecast, betoken

衍生字词
▲ portent n. 预兆，征兆
▲ portentous adj. 预兆的，凶兆的

高分秘诀
▲ no doubt 毫无疑问
▲ threatening adj. 胁迫的，险恶的
▲ storm n. 暴风雨（雪）

1414. portray [pɔrˋtre] [por·tray] ☆★★★★

v. 描述，绘制

The picture portrays a beautiful sunrise.
这幅画描绘了日出的美景。

同义字词 depict, describe, draw

衍生字词
▲ portrayal n. 饰演，描画
▲ portrait n. 肖像，画像，描写
▲ portraitist n. 肖像画家
▲ portraiture n. 肖像画法

1415. possess [pəˋzɛs] [pos·sess] ★★★★★

v. 拥有，占有

It's horrible if you were possessed by devils.
要是被魔鬼附身就太骇人了。

同义字词 have, own, occupy, hold

衍生字词
▲ possession n. 拥有，占有，财产
▲ possesser n. 拥有者
▲ possessed adj. 疯狂的，着魔的

| 高分秘诀 | ▲ horrible adj. 可怕的，令人恐惧的 |

1416. postdate [ˋpostˋdet] [post·date] ☆☆★★★

| v. 填迟……的日期 | I asked the policeman who is in charge of household registration to postdate my day of birth.
我请求这位调查户籍的警察把我的生日日期填晚一些。 |

反义字词	antedate
衍生字词	▲ postdated cheque 未到期支票
高分秘诀	▲ be in charge of 管理 ▲ household registration 户籍登记

1417. posthumous [ˋpɑstjuməs] [post·hu·mous] ☆☆★★★

| adj. 死后的，身后的 | There is no use to confer posthumous honours on him.
等他去世后再授予荣耀，根本于事无补。 |

| 衍生字词 | ▲ posthumously adv. 于死后，于身后
▲ posthumous child 遗腹子 |
| 高分秘诀 | ▲ confer posthumous honours on 追赠，溢封 |

1418. postpone [postˋpon] [post·pone] ☆★★★★

| v. 推迟，使延期 | After a long meditation, I decided to postpone deliver a lecture.
经过一番考虑，我决定延期演讲。 |

| 同义字词 | put off, delay, defer, procrastinate, hold over |
| 衍生字词 | ▲ postponer n. 延迟者，使延缓者
▲ postponable adj. 可以延缓的 |

1419. postulate [ˋpɑstʃə͵let] [pos·tu·late] ☆★★★★

| v. 要求，假定 | Let's postulate the existence of matter.
让我们假设物质的存在。 |

同义字词	assume, presume
衍生字词	▲ postulant n. 请求者，志愿者 ▲ postulation n. 假定，要求 ▲ postulational method 拟设法
高分秘诀	▲ existence n. 存在 ▲ matter n. 物质，物体

1420. potent ['potn̩t] [po·tent]

adj. 强有力的，有效的

If he drinks the potent toxin, he must die.
如果他喝下强力毒药，他一定会死。

同义字词: powerful, forceful, mighty, effective

衍生字词:
▲ potential **adj.** 可能的，潜在的
▲ potentiality **n.** 潜能，潜力

高分秘诀: ▲ toxin **n.** 毒素

1421. preach [pritʃ] [preach]

v. 布道，宣扬

I think we should preach the virtues of socialism.
我认为我们应该宣传社会主义的长处。

衍生字词:
▲ preacher **n.** 说教者，鼓吹者
▲ preaching **n.** 讲道，讲道法
▲ preach to deaf ears 对牛弹琴，对聋子讲道

高分秘诀:
▲ virtue **n.** 优点，长处
▲ socialism **n.** 社会主义

1422. precarious [prɪˋkɛrɪəs] [pre·car·i·ous]

adj. 不稳定的，危险的

When he lost his job, the whole family lived a precarious existence.
失业后，全家人过着不稳定的生活。

同义字词: doubtable, unstable, shaky, dangerous, hazardous

衍生字词: ▲ precariously **adv.** 不安全地，不牢靠地

高分秘诀: ▲ existence **n.** 生存，生活（方式）

1423. precaution [prɪˋkɔʃən] [pre·cau·tion]

n. 预防措施，警惕

Please take a raincoat as a precaution.
带着雨衣吧，有备无患。

同义字词: prevention, forethought

衍生字词:
▲ precautionary **adj.** 预先警戒的，预防的
▲ precautionary measure 预防措施

1424. precede [prɪˋsid] [pre·cede]

v. 在……之前，早于

Mr. Smith preceded me as a first lieutenant.
史密斯比我早担任陆军中尉。

同义字词	come before, antecede
反义字词	follow, come after, succeed
衍生字词	▲ precedent n. 先例 ▲ unprecedented adj. 空前的 ▲ preceding adj. 在前的
高分秘诀	▲ first lieutenant n. 陆军中尉

1425. precious [ˈprɛʃəs] [pre·cious] ★★★★★

adj. 宝贵的，珍贵的	The New Concept English is my most precious possession. 这本新概念英语是我最珍贵的财产。
同义字词	valued, valuable, costly, priceless
反义字词	valueless
衍生字词	▲ precious metal 贵金属 ▲ precious moon 惜月（乐曲）
高分秘诀	▲ New Concept English 新概念英语 ▲ possession n. 财产，财物

1426. precipitate [prɪˈsɪpəˌtet] [pre·cip·i·tate] ★★★★★

v. 促成，加速	It's your rude behavior precipitated my decision. 你粗鲁的行为促使我作出决定。
n. 沉淀物，降雨	The professor took the chemical precipitates to the laboratory. 教授把这些化学沉淀物带回实验室。
同义字词	urge, accelerate, come down, fall
衍生字词	▲ precipitation n. 仓促，降雨量 ▲ precipitous adj. 陡峭的 ▲ precipitable adj. 可沉淀的 ▲ precipitator n. 催促的人，沉淀剂
高分秘诀	▲ chemical precipitates n. 化学沉淀物

1427. precision [prɪˈsɪʒən] [pre·ci·sion] ☆★★★★

n. 精确，精密度	I don't think you are fit for the job, you know it entails precision. 我认为你不适合这个工作，因为需要精确性。
同义字词	exactness, accuracy, preciseness

precious ~ predict

衍生字词 ▲ precise adj. 精确的，准确的，精密的
高分秘诀 ▲ be fit for 适合于，胜任
▲ entail v. 使……成为必要，需要

1428. precursor [prɪˋkɝsɚ] [pre·cur·sor] ☆★★★★

n. 先驱，先行者 | Here I have to point out that the precursor of the car was not horse-drawn carriage.
在此我不得不指出汽车的前身并不是马车。

同义字词 forerunner, harbinger, herald

衍生字词 ▲ precursory adj. 前兆的
▲ precursor chemicals 易制毒化学品

高分秘诀 ▲ point out 指出
▲ horse-drawn adj. 用马拖的
▲ carriage n. 车辆，车厢，四轮马车

1429. predatory [ˋprɛdəˌtorɪ] [pred·a·to·ry] ☆★★★★

adj. 掠夺的，食肉的 | She is such a person with a rapacious and predatory nature.
她是那种贪婪又具有掠夺性格的人。

同义字词 carnivorous, predaceous, predatorial, marauding

衍生字词 ▲ predator n. 掠夺者，食肉动物
▲ predatory bird 猛禽，捕食鸟
▲ predatory dumping 恶意倾销

高分秘诀 ▲ rapacious adj. 贪婪的，贪财的
▲ nature n. 天性，性格，性质

1430. predict [prɪˋdɪkt] [pre·dict] ☆★★★★

v. 预言，预告 | The astronomers predict that there would be an eclipse next month.
天文学家预测下个月会有日食。

同义字词 forecast, foretell, portend, prophesy

衍生字词 ▲ prediction n. 预言，预报
▲ predictive adj. 预言性的，成为先兆的
▲ predictable adj. 可预见的

高分秘诀 ▲ astronomer n. 天文学者，天文学家
▲ eclipse n. （日、月）食

1431. predominate [prɪˋdɑməˌnet] [pre·dom·i·nate] ☆☆★★★

v. 统治，成为主流

When she got promoted to the manager, she began to predominate over us.
当她升职为经理后，就开始支配我们。

同义字词　control, rule, prevail, dominate

衍生字词
▲ predominance **n.** 优势，主导或支配的地位
▲ predominant **adj.** 支配的，主要的
▲ predomination **n.** 支配，优势

1432. preeminent [priˋɛmɪnənt] [pre·e·min·ent] ☆★★★★

adj. 卓越的，出类拔萃的

I think it's a good thing to have a preeminent competitor.
我认为一个出类拔萃的对手对我们来说是一件好事。

同义字词　distinguished, notable, renowned, eminent

衍生字词
▲ preeminence **n.** 卓越，杰出
▲ preeminently **adv.** 卓越地，出类拔萃地

高分秘诀　▲ competitor **n.** 竞争者，对手

1433. prefabricate [priˋfæbrəˌket] [pre·fab·ri·cate] ☆★★★★

v. 预制

I've already prefabricated sections of houses, and I have to ask the workers to assemble them.
我已经构思好房屋的各个部分，剩下来就要找工人把它们组装起来。

同义字词　preassemble

衍生字词
▲ prefabricated **adj.** 预制的
▲ prefabrication **n.** 预制

高分秘诀
▲ section **n.** 部分
▲ assemble **v.** 装配，组合

1434. preliminary [prɪˋlɪməˌnɛrɪ] [pre·lim·i·nar·y] ☆★★★★

adj. 预备的，初步的

If you want to learn English very well, you have to lay a preliminary groundwork.
如果你想学好英语，你必须打好基础。

同义字词　initial, introductory, preparatory, prior

衍生字词
▲ preliminary agreement 初步协议
▲ preliminary candidate 初步候选人
▲ preliminary design 初步设计

predominate ~ preponderance

1435. premature [ˌprimə`tjur] [pre·ma·ture] ☆★★★★

adj. 早熟的，不成熟的
The doctor said that this kind of disease could produce premature aging of the brain.
医生说这类疾病会使大脑早衰。

同义字词 too soon, too early, previous, untimely

衍生字词
▲ prematuration **n.** 不够成熟
▲ premature babies 早产婴儿

1436. premium [`primɪəm] [pre·mi·um] ☆★★★★

n. 保险金，奖金
I think it's a better way to buy the premium bonds.
我认为购买政府增额债券是个不错的方法。

adj. 高级的，高价的
You get what you pay for; you know these machines have premium properties.
一分价钱一分货，你知道这些机器都有优良的性能。

同义字词 bounty, prize, insurance premium

衍生字词
▲ premium price 溢价
▲ premium gasoline 高级汽油

高分秘诀
▲ premium bonds 政府增额债券（英国）

1437. preoccupation [priˌɑkjə`peʃən] [pre·oc·cu·pa·tion] ☆☆★★★

n. 主要考虑因素，全神贯注
I think such an excessive preoccupation with money can't be normal.
我认为如此过分关注金钱是不正常的。

同义字词 concern, involvement, absorption, engrossment

衍生字词
▲ preoccupied **adj.** 全神贯注的；被先占的
▲ preoccupant **adj.** 抢先占据的，抢先占有的

高分秘诀
▲ excessive **adj.** 过度的，过分的，极度的
▲ normal **adj.** 正常的，平常的

1438. preponderance [prɪ`pɑndərəns] [pre·pon·der·ance] ☆☆★★★

n. （数量或力量上的）优势
We shouldn't meet the enemy head on, as there is no sufficient preponderance over them in the front line.
我们不应该和敌人针锋相对，因为与他们相比，我们在前线并没有显著的优势。

衍生字词
▲ preponderant **adj.** 占有优势的
▲ preponderate **v.** （在重量、数量、力量等方面）占优势

高分秘诀	▲ head on 迎面地
	▲ sufficient adj. 足够的,充足的
	▲ front line 前线,第一线

1439. prerequisite [ˌpriˈrɛkwəzɪt] [pre·req·ui·site] ☆☆★★★

n. 先决条件	Honesty and meticulous is the prerequisite condition to apply for the work. 诚实和心细是申请这份工作的先决条件。
同义字词	requirement, necessity
衍生字词	▲ prerequisition land 预征土地
高分秘诀	▲ apply for 申请

1440. prescribe [prɪˈskraɪb] [pre·scribe] ☆★★★★

v. 指示,开药方	You have to keep in mind that the law prescribes heavy penalties for this offence. 你必须牢记,法律规定这种不法行为从严惩处。
衍生字词	▲ prescription n. 药方,处方 ▲ prescriber n. 处方者,开药者,建议者 ▲ prescribed book 指定教科书
高分秘诀	▲ keep in mind 记住 ▲ offence n. 违法行为,罪行

1441. preserve [prɪˈzɝv] [pre·serve] ☆★★★★

v. 保存,保持	Don't take it for granted that your parents should support you all your life, you know you should preserve your independence. 不要认为父母养你一辈子是天经地义的事,你应该保持自己的独立性。
同义字词	uphold, retain, maintain, save
衍生字词	▲ preservable adj. 可保存的,可保管的,能储藏的 ▲ preservative n. 防腐剂
高分秘诀	▲ take it for granted 视为当然 ▲ all one's life 一生 ▲ independence n. 独立,自主,自立

1442. prestige [prɛsˈtiʒ] [pres·tige] ☆★★★★

| n. 威望,声望 | I advised you not risk your prestige at stake.
我建议你不要拿自己的名声冒险。 |

prerequisite ~ prey

同义字词	fame, reputation, prominence
衍生字词	▲ prestigious adj. 有名望的，有威信的
	▲ prestigeful adj. 有名望的，有声望的
	▲ prestige pricing 声望定价

1443. presumable [prɪˋzuməbl] [pre·sum·a·ble] ☆★★★★

adj. 可推测的

The Japanese authority is trying their best to dig out the presumable causes of the disaster.
日本当局正在尽力找出引起灾难的可能原因。

同义字词	surmisable, supposable
衍生字词	▲ presumably adv. 推测起来，大概
高分秘诀	▲ authority n. 官方，当局
	▲ try one's best 尽力
	▲ dig out 寻找，发掘
	▲ disaster n. 灾难，灾祸

1444. pretension [prɪˋtɛnʃən] [pre·ten·sion] ☆★★★★

n. 要求，自命

Though he is a famous engineer, he has no pretensions to being an expert on the subject.
虽然他是位著名的工程师，但从来并不以这方面的专家自居。

同义字词	claim, assertion, pretence, pretense, pretentiousness
衍生字词	▲ pretensioned adj. 主张的
	▲ pretensioning n. 主张
高分秘诀	▲ engineer n. 工程师，机械师
	▲ subject n. 题目，科目，主题

1445. prevail [prɪˋvel] [pre·vail] ☆★★★★

v. 盛行，居主导地位

Suddenly the tide turned the unfortunate prevailed.
突然之间形势改变了，弱者占了优势。

同义字词	dominate, predominate, triumph
衍生字词	▲ prevalent adj. 普遍的，流行的
	▲ prevaiiing adj. 流行的，盛行的
高分秘诀	▲ unfortunate adj. 不幸的，倒霉的 n. 不幸的人

1446. prey [pre] [prey] ★★★★★

n. 牺牲品，猎物

The big eagle carried its prey in its claws.
这只大鹰用爪子抓着捕获物。

| v. 捕食，掠食 | It's quite normal that the strong animals prey upon weaker ones in nature.
自然界中，弱肉强食是一种自然现象。 |

| 同义字词 | victim, food, quarry, target, hunt, victimize, raven |
| 衍生字词 | ▲ preyer n. 猛兽，猛禽
▲ preying adj. 捕食性的，掠夺的 |

1447. primal [`praɪml] [pri·mal]   ☆★★★★

| adj. 原始的，最初的 | Though money was a primal necessity to human, it is not everything.
虽然金钱是人们的主要需求，但它并不是万能的。 |

| 同义字词 | primeval, initial, aboriginal, fundamental, key |
| 衍生字词 | ▲ primal fear 一级恐惧
▲ primary adj. 主要的，首要的
▲ primate adj. 首要的，第一的 n. 灵长目动物 |
| 高分秘诀 | ▲ necessity n. 必要（性），必需品 |

1448. primordial [praɪ`mɔrdɪəl] [pri·mor·di·al]   ☆☆★★★

| adj. 原始的，最初的 | This biologist is studying the primordial matter.
这位生物学家研究原生物质。 |

| 同义字词 | primeval, primitive, fundamental |
| 衍生字词 | ▲ primordial broth （生物学）原生汤
▲ primordial follicle 原始卵泡
▲ primordial meristem （生物学）原生生组织 |
| 高分秘诀 | ▲ biologist n. 生物学家
▲ primordial matter 原生物质 |

1449. privilege [`prɪvlɪdʒ] [priv·i·lege]   ☆★★★★

| v. 给予……特权，特免 | It's the pass which privilege you to attend the meeting.
有了这张通行证，你就可以出席这场会议。 |
| n. 特权 | She got married with a millionaire and lived a life of luxury and privilege.
她嫁给一个百万富翁，过着养尊处优的生活。 |

| 同义字词 | exclusive right, prequisite, prerogative, favor |

primal ~ proclaim

衍生字词
▲ privileged adj. 享有特权的
▲ privilege violation 特权行为
▲ privilege cab 特许在车站接客的马车

1450. probe [prob] [probe] ☆★★★★

v. 调查, 查究

The auditor was sent to probe into several financial scandals.
这位审计员被派往调查几起财务丑闻。

同义字词　detect, find out, dig into, investigate, explore

衍生字词
▲ probe card 探针板
▲ prober n. 探查者
▲ probing adj. 探索的，寻根究底的

高分秘诀
▲ auditor n. 审计员，稽核员
▲ probe into 细查，深究
▲ financial adj. 财政的，金融的
▲ scandal n. 丑闻

1451. proceed [prəˋsid] [pro·ceed] ☆★★★★

v. 前进, 行进

The old man paused for some minutes then proceeded with his speech.
老人暂停几分钟，然后继续他的演讲。

同义字词　continue, advance, go ahead, progress

衍生字词
▲ proceeds n. 收益
▲ proceeding n. 行动，进行

高分秘诀
▲ pause v. 停顿，暂停
▲ proceed with 继续做……

1452. proclaim [prəˋklem] [pro·claim] ☆★★★★

v. 声明, 宣告

It's your accent proclaimed that you are northlander.
你的口音显示你是北方人。

同义字词　declare, announce, promulgate

衍生字词
▲ proclaiming tone 宣称性语调
▲ proclaimer n. 宣称者

高分秘诀
▲ accent n. 口音，腔调
▲ northlander n. 北方人，北方居民

1453. proclivity [prə`klɪvətɪ] [pro·cliv·i·ty] ☆☆★★★

n. 倾向, 癖性

Oh, please! The proclivity to faultfinding is disgusting.
噢, 拜托! 吹毛求疵的个性真是让人讨厌。

同义字词　tendency, disposition, inclination, propensity, leaning

高分秘诀
▲ faultfinding **n.** 挑剔
▲ disgusting **adj.** 令人作呕的, 令人厌恶的

1454. prod [prɑd] [prod] ☆☆★★★

v. 戳, 刺

Don't fall into the bad habit of prodding yourself into action with a crisis.
不要养成事到临头才被迫采取行动的坏习惯。

同义字词　poke, thrust, stimulate

衍生字词
▲ prod cast 锥模, 冲击模
▲ prod mark 戳痕, 椎痕

高分秘诀
▲ fall into bad habit 染上恶习
▲ crisis **n.** 危机, 危急关头

1455. prodigious [prə`dɪdʒəs] [pro·di·gious] ☆★★★★

adj. 巨大的, 挥霍的

Though she is a little girl only in ten years old, she overwhelmed the audience with her prodigious memory.
虽然这个小女孩只有十岁, 但观众却被她惊人的记忆力折服。

同义字词　huge, amazing, stupendous, colossal

衍生字词
▲ prodigality **n.** 挥霍, 浪费
▲ prodigalize **v.** 浪费, 挥霍

高分秘诀
▲ overwhelm **v.** 压倒, 制服, 打败
▲ audience **n.** 观众, 听众

1456. prodigy [`prɑdədʒɪ] [prod·i·gy] ☆☆★★★

n. 非凡之人, 天才

My son is an infant prodigy, you know when he was three years old, he could read novels.
我儿子是个天才神童, 他三岁的时候就能读小说。

同义字词　marvel, genius, talent

高分秘诀　▲ infant prodigy 天才神童

proclivity ~ prominent

1457. proficient [prə`fɪʃənt] [pro·fi·cient] ☆★★★★

adj. 熟练的，精通的

Though I'm not a tailor, I can say I'm quite proficient at tailoring.
虽然我不是个裁缝，但我敢说我对裁缝很在行。

- 同义字词: skilled, expert, masterful
- 反义字词: unskilled
- 衍生字词:
  - ▲ proficiency **n.** 熟练，精通
  - ▲ proficience **n.** 前进，进步
  - ▲ proficiency test 水准测试，熟练测验
- 高分秘诀:
  - ▲ tailor **n.** 裁缝
  - ▲ tailoring **n.** 裁缝业，成衣业

1458. prohibit [prə`hɪbɪt] [pro·hi·bit] ☆★★★★

v. 禁止

I'm afraid that my prior engagement will prohibit me from joining your birthday party.
我有约在先，恐怕不能参加你的生日晚会。

- 同义字词: ban, taboo, forbid
- 衍生字词:
  - ▲ prohibitive **adj.** 禁止的，抑制的
  - ▲ prohibitively **adv.** 令人望而却步地
  - ▲ prohibited article 禁运物品，违章夹带物品
- 高分秘诀:
  - ▲ engagement **n.** 约会，约定
  - ▲ birthday party 生日聚会

1459. proliferate [prə`lɪfəˌret] [pro·li·fe·rate] ☆★★★★

v. 激增，繁殖

Nowadays sports stores proliferate in this region.
如今这个地区的体育用品商店在增加。

- 同义字词: multiply, propagate, reproduce
- 衍生字词:
  - ▲ proliferation **n.** 繁殖，大量增殖
  - ▲ prolific **adj.** 多产的，多结果的
  - ▲ proliferative **adj.** 增生性的，增殖的
- 高分秘诀:
  - ▲ sports stores 体育用品商店
  - ▲ region **n.** 地区，地带，区域

1460. prominent [`prɑmənənt] [prom·i·nent] ☆★★★★

adj. 杰出的，突出的

I envy him very much, because his work allowed him to access to some very prominent people.
我很羡慕他，因为他的工作可以接近一些名人。

同义字词	distinguished, famous, conspicuous, outstanding
衍生字词	▲ prominence n. 显著，突出 ▲ prominent character 主要特性 ▲ prominent teacher 优秀教师
高分秘诀	▲ access to 接近

1461. promote [prə`mot] [pro·mote] ☆★★★★

v. 晋级，使升级	I think it's the government's duty to promote commerce with neighbouring countries. 我认为促进与邻国的贸易是政府的职责。
同义字词	advertise, further, encourage
衍生字词	▲ promoter n. 促进者 ▲ promotion n. 提升，晋升 ▲ promo n. 商品推销，商品广告
高分秘诀	▲ commerce n. 商业，贸易 ▲ neighbouring adj. 邻近的

1462. prompt [prɑmpt] [prompt] ☆★★★★

v. 鼓动，促进	My boyfriend's evasive reply prompted my suspicions. 男友含糊其辞的回答引起了我的猜疑。
adj. 迅速的，按时地	It's Jack's prompt action that saved the drowning boy. 杰克的及时行动救了那个溺水的男孩。
同义字词	motivate, incite, encourage
衍生字词	▲ prompter n. 敦促者 ▲ promptitude n. 敏捷，迅速
高分秘诀	▲ evasive adj. 逃避的，推托的 ▲ suspicion n. 怀疑，猜疑，疑心

1463. prone [pron] [prone] ☆★★★★

adj. 易于……的，倾向于……的	The boy was spoiled, and he's prone to anger. 这孩子被宠坏了，动不动就发脾气。
衍生字词	▲ pronounced adj. 显著的，明显的 ▲ prone position 卧姿 ▲ prone pressure method 俯压式人工呼吸法

promote ~ propensity

高分秘诀
▲ spoiled adj. 被宠坏的
▲ prone to 倾向于……

1464. proofread [`prufˌrid] [proof·read] ☆☆★★★

v. 校正，校对

I asked my teacher to proofread my report.
我请老师帮我校正报告。

同义字词: proof, collate, check error

衍生字词:
▲ proofreader n. 校对者，校对员
▲ proofreading n. 校正，校对

高分秘诀: ▲ report n. 报告，报道

1465. propagate [`prapəˌget] [prop·a·gate] ☆☆★★★

v. 繁殖，散布

Butterflies propagate themselves by means of eggs.
蝴蝶产卵繁殖后代。

同义字词: raise, reproduce, spread, disperse, diffuse, disseminate

衍生字词:
▲ propagation n. 繁殖，增值，传播
▲ propagated adj. 被繁殖的
▲ propagator n. 传播者，宣传者

高分秘诀:
▲ butterfly n. 蝴蝶
▲ by means of 用，依靠
▲ egg n. 卵，蛋

1466. propel [prə`pɛl] [pro·pel] ☆☆★★★

v. 推进，促进

It's his ambition which propelled him into craziness.
他的野心使他疯狂。

同义字词: drive forward, push, motivate, impel

衍生字词:
▲ propeller n. 螺旋桨，推进器
▲ propeller blade 螺旋桨叶片

高分秘诀:
▲ ambition n. 雄心，野心
▲ craziness n. 发狂，疯狂

1467. propensity [prə`pɛnsətɪ] [pro·pen·si·ty] ☆☆★★★

n. 倾向，癖好

He knew his own propensity to evil, but he was reluctant to change it.
虽然他意识到自己生性作恶，却不愿悔改。

同义字词: inclination, tendency, disposition, aptness

衍生字词: ▲ propensity to invest 投资倾向

| 高分秘诀 | ▲ evil n. 邪恶，罪恶 |
| | ▲ reluctant adj. 不情愿的，勉强的 |

1468. proponent [prə`ponənt] [pro·po·nent] ☆★★★★

n. 支持者，拥护者 — Mr. Smith is a fervent and even militant proponent of tax increase.
史密斯先生是增加税收的拥护者。

同义字词	advocate, supporter, exponent
反义字词	rival, adversary, opponent
衍生字词	▲ project proponent 案子提议者
	▲ proponent supporters 支持者
高分秘诀	▲ fervent adj. 热诚的，热烈的
	▲ militant adj. 激进的，好战的

1469. proportion [prə`porʃən] [pro·por·tion] ☆★★★★

n. 比例，比率 — The boy looks funny; you know his head is out of proportion to the size of his body.
这个男孩看起来很滑稽；他的头和身体大小不成比例。

同义字词	amounts, percentage, ratio
反义字词	disproportion
衍生字词	▲ disproportionate adj. 不成比例的
	▲ proportionment n. 比例，匀称，调和
	▲ proportionable adj. 成比例的，相称的
高分秘诀	▲ out of proportion to 和……不成比例，和……不相称

1470. propose [prə`poz] [pro·pose] ★★★★★

v. 提议，建议 — I wish to propose a toast to the newlyweds.
我提议为这对新婚夫妇干杯。

同义字词	advance, suggest, advise
衍生字词	▲ proposer n. 申请人，提案人
	▲ proposal n. 提案，建议
高分秘诀	▲ propose a toast 敬一杯，提议为……干杯
	▲ newlywed n. 新婚的人

1471. proprietor [prə`praɪətə] [pro·pri·e·tor] ☆★★★★

n. 所有者，业主 — If you are not satisfied with our service, you can write a complaint to the proprietor of the hotel.
如果你对我们的服务不满意，你可以写信向饭店老板投诉。

proportion ~ prospect

同义字词	owner
衍生字词	▲ proprietorship n. 所有权 ▲ proprietary articles 专利品 ▲ proprietor account 业主账户
高分秘诀	▲ be satisfied with 对……感到满意 ▲ complaint n. 投诉，控告

1472. propulsion [prə`pʌlʃən] [pro·pul·sion] ☆★★★★

n. 推进，推进力

Can you explain the principle of jet propulsion?
你能为我解释喷气推进的原理吗？

同义字词	push, actuation, driving force
衍生字词	▲ propulsive adj. 推进的，有推进力的 ▲ propulsion device 推进器 ▲ propulsion engine 推进发动机
高分秘诀	▲ principle n. 原则，原理 ▲ jet propulsion 喷气推进

1473. prosecute [`prɑsɪˌkjut] [pro·se·cute] ☆★★★★

v. 对……起诉，告发

It's quite common for us to see the sign "unauthorized reproduction will be prosecuted" on the trademark.
我们经常在商标上看到"仿冒必究"这样的标记。

同义字词	sue, indict
反义字词	defend, represent
衍生字词	▲ prosecutable adj. 可提起公诉的 ▲ prosecution n. 起诉，检举 ▲ prosecuting attorney 检察官
高分秘诀	▲ unauthorized adj. 未经授权的，未经许可的

1474. prospect [`prɑspɛkt] [pros·pect] ☆★★★★

n. 前景，期望

I was disappointed in her, as there was no prospect of an improvement in her condition.
我对她很失望，因为她没有任何改进的希望。

v. 勘探，采矿

We formed a team to prospect for oil.
我们成立了一个小组勘探石油。

同义字词	possibility, hope, outlook
衍生字词	▲ prospecting n. 探矿 ▲ prospector n. 勘探者，采矿者 ▲ prospective adj. 预期的，未来的，可能的

| 高分秘诀 | ▲ be disappointed in 对……失望 |

1475. prosper [ˈprɑspɚ] [pros·per]   ☆★★★★

| v. 繁荣，成功 | My business is prospering with each passing day.
我的生意正蒸蒸日上。 |

| 衍生字词 | ▲ prosperity n. 繁荣，兴旺
▲ prosperous adj. 成功的，繁荣的 |
| 高分秘诀 | ▲ with each passing day 日益地，一天天地 |

1476. protagonist [proˈtæɡənɪst] [pro·tag·o·nist]   ☆★★★★

| n.（戏剧、小说的）主角 | I found most of the protagonists in his novels are lazy, selfish and hypocritical.
我发现他小说中的主角大部分都是懒惰、自私又虚伪的人物。 |

同义字词	champion, supporter, booster, character
衍生字词	▲ protagonism n. 主体主义
高分秘诀	▲ selfish adj. 自私的，利己的 ▲ hypocritical adj. 虚伪的，伪善的

1477. protest [prəˈtɛst] [pro·test]   ☆★★★★

| n. 抗议 | After he finished speaking, his proposals was met by a storm of protest.
他刚说完建议，就遭到激烈反对。 |
| v. 抗议 | I think you are brave enough to protest to the boss that the salary was too low.
我认为你真勇敢，敢向老板抗议工资太低。 |

同义字词	outcry, objection, dissent
衍生字词	▲ protester n. 抗议者，反对者 ▲ protestingly adv. 抗议地，不服地
高分秘诀	▲ a storm of 一阵（狂似暴风雨之物），某些物品密集地降落

1478. prototype [ˈprotəˌtaɪp] [pro·to·type]   ☆☆★★★

| n. 原型 | There are so many biological prototypes which were on display at the exhibition.
许多生物原型在这次展览中出现了。 |

| 同义字词 | model, archetype, epitome, paradigm |

protagonist ~ provoke

衍生字词	▲ prototypal adj. 原型的
	▲ prototypal inheritance pattern 原型继承模式
	▲ prototype machine 样机，原型机
高分秘诀	▲ biological prototype 生物原型
	▲ exhibition n. 展览，展览会

1479. protrudent [prə'trudənt] [pro·tru·dent] ☆☆★★★

adj. 突出的,伸出的	I saw an eagle owl was seating on a protrudent rock.
	我看见一只大猫头鹰栖息在一块突出的岩石上。
同义字词	protruding, protrusive
衍生字词	▲ protrude v. （使某物）伸出，(使某物)突出
	▲ protrudentable adj. 可伸出的
高分秘诀	▲ eagle owl 大猫头鹰

1480. provincialism [prə'vɪnʃəlˌɪzəm] [provin·cial·ism] ☆☆★★★

n. 地方主义，地方偏狭观念	He tried his best to escape from the provincialism of the small town, but failed in the end.
	他试图摆脱小城镇的地方主义桎梏，但是最后失败了。
同义字词	regionalism, localism, sectionalism
衍生字词	▲ provincial adj. 省的，偏狭的，地方的
	▲ province n. 省份，大行政区
高分秘诀	▲ escape from 逃避，摆脱

1481. provoke [prə'vok] [pro·voke] ☆★★★★

v. 激怒,惹起	It's my brother's rudeness provoked my father to strike him.
	哥哥的粗鲁激怒父亲揍了他一顿。
同义字词	irritate, annoy, anger, aggravate
衍生字词	▲ provocative adj. 挑拨的，煽动的
	▲ provocation n. 激怒，挑拨，刺激
	▲ provoking adj. 令人生气的，使人恼火的
高分秘诀	▲ rudeness n. 粗鲁，无礼貌
	▲ strike v. 打，击

1482. prudent [ˈprudn̩t] [pru·dent]

| adj. 审慎的，深谋远虑的 | Susan is a prudent housekeeper; she can always fits her standard of living to her budget.
苏珊是一位谨慎的主妇，她总能使生活水准符合收支预算。 |

同义字词：wary, cautious, discreet, careful

衍生字词：
▲ prudence n. 审慎，慎重
▲ care for 喜欢，照料，计较
▲ in care of 由……转交
▲ take care of 照顾，处理
▲ care giver 照料者，看护人
▲ care label （衣服上的）使用须知标签
▲ care naught for 对……不感兴趣
▲ care package （为远离家庭的人寄送的）食品和礼物包裹
▲ care worker 护理人员
▲ care-laden 劳苦的

高分秘诀：
▲ housekeeper n. 主妇，女管家
▲ fit to （使）与……相配（相称），相对应
▲ budget n. 预算，预算额，经费

1483. psychology [saɪˈkɑlədʒɪ] [psy·chol·o·gy]

| n. 心理学，心理 | I'm taking psychology as an elective course next year.
我明年将选修心理学。 |

衍生字词：
▲ psychologic adj. 心理学的，精神上的
▲ psychologist n. 心理学家，心理学研究者
▲ psychological adj. 心理的，精神的，心理学的
▲ psychological warfare 心理战

高分秘诀：
▲ elective course 选修课
▲ in course of 在……过程中
▲ in due course 在适当的时候
▲ in the course of 在……期间，在……过程中
▲ in the course of time 最终
▲ in the ordinary course of nature/events/things 在通常情况下
▲ of course 当然
▲ run/take one's course 顺其发展，听其自然
▲ course book 课本，教科书
▲ course of action 行动方针，做法
▲ course work 作业

psychology ~ purify

1484. puncture [ˈpʌŋktʃə] [punc·ture] ☆★★★★

v. 刺穿，戳破

It's your practical joke punctured the girl's pride, since then she couldn't take any joke.
你们的恶作剧伤害了女孩的自尊心，以后她再也经不起任何玩笑了。

同义字词	prick, impale, pierce, stab
衍生字词	▲ puncturable **adj.** 可穿孔的，可穿刺的 ▲ puncture needle 穿刺针，采血针 ▲ puncture outfit 穿刺器，穿刺装备 ▲ puncture tester 穿击试验仪，耐（电）压试验器
高分秘诀	▲ practical joke 恶作剧

1485. pungent [ˈpʌndʒənt] [pun·gent] ☆☆★★★

adj. （气味、味道）刺激的

I was stabbed to the heart by the teacher's pungent remark.
我被老师尖锐的批评刺伤了。

同义字词	penetrating, sharp, acrid, harsh, spicy
衍生字词	▲ pungency **n.** 辛辣，刺激性，尖刻 ▲ pungent odor 刺激气味
高分秘诀	▲ stab to the heart 刺伤了心 ▲ pungent criticism 尖锐的批评

1486. purify [ˈpjurəˌfaɪ] [pu·ri·fy] ☆★★★★

v. 提炼，精炼

Distilling can be used to purify water.
通过蒸馏可以净化水。

同义字词	refine, make pure
衍生字词	▲ purification **n.** 纯化，净化 ▲ purifier **n.** 清洁者，清洁器，精炼者 ▲ purificatory **adj.** 精炼的，精制的，净化的
高分秘诀	▲ distilling **n.** 蒸馏（作用）

新托福核心单词速记

Qq 托福 TOEFL iBT

托福(TOEFL)的测验对象为母语为非英语的人
申请入学美加地区大学或研究所时,托福成绩单是必备文件之一。

- n. 名词
- v. 动词
- adj. 形容词
- adv. 副词
- prep. 介词
- art. 冠词
- pron. 代词
- aux. 助词
- conj. 连词

Qq 托福 TOEFL iBT

托福(TOEFL)的测验对象为母语为非英语的人
申请入学美加地区大学或研究所时，托福成绩单是必备文件之一。

1487. quaint [kwent] [quaint]   ☆☆☆★★

| adj. 奇怪的, 离奇有趣的 | I've never seen such quaint dialect words.
我从来没有见过这么古怪的方言单词。 |

- 同义字词：strange, unusual, curious
- 衍生字词：▲ quaintly adv. 离奇有趣地
- 高分秘诀：▲ dialect n. 方言，土语

1488. qualified [ˈkwɑləˌfaɪd] [qua·li·fied] ★★★★★

| adj. 合格的 | Since our team has qualified for the semi-final, then we would have chance to win.
既然我们这一队已有资格进入半决赛，我们就有机会拿第一。 |

- 同义字词：competent, certified, eligible
- 衍生字词：
  - ▲ qualifiable adj. 可修饰的，可限制的
  - ▲ qualification n. 资格，条件
  - ▲ qualify v. （使）具有资格，（使）合格
  - ▲ quality assurance （商品及服务的）质量保证
  - ▲ quality control 品质控制，品质管理
  - ▲ quality newspaper 品位报纸（指版面、内容都很严肃认真的大报）
  - ▲ quality time 珍贵时光，上班族能跟家人相聚的时间
  - ▲ good quality 品质好
  - ▲ poor quality 品质差
  - ▲ qualified for 有……的资格
  - ▲ qualify for 使具有资格，使合格
  - ▲ qualify as 取得资格，具备合格条件
- 高分秘诀：▲ semi-final n. 半决赛

1489. quench [kwɛntʃ] [quench] ☆☆☆★★

| v. 淬火, 熄灭 | I think there is nothing like plain boiled water to quench one's thirst.
我认为白开水是解渴最好的饮料。 |

quaint ~ quota

同义字词	extinguish, put out, slake
衍生字词	▲ quencher n. 淬火，骤冷 ▲ quenchless adj. 不可熄灭的
高分秘诀	▲ plain boiled water 白开水 ▲ thirst n. （口）渴，渴感

1490. quest [kwɛst] [quest] ☆☆★★★

n. 寻找, 探索　The detective was on a quest for further evidence.
侦探正在到处寻找更多证据。

| 衍生字词 | ▲ quester n. 探求者，追求者
▲ questing knight 探险骑士
▲ questing adj. 寻求的，探求的，追求的 |

1491. quiescent [kwaɪˋɛsn̩t] [qui·es·cent] ☆☆☆★★

adj. 静止的, 寂静的　It's unlikely that people who have a hot temper could remain quiescent for long.
脾气急躁的人不太可能长期保持沉默。

同义字词	motionless, inactive, static
衍生字词	▲ quiescence n. 静止，沉默 ▲ quiescently adv. 静止地，寂静地
高分秘诀	▲ hot temper 急躁的脾气

1492. quota [ˋkwotə] [quo·ta] ☆★★★★

n. 配额, 定量　I wish I could fulfill this month's quota ahead of time.
我希望我能提前完成这个月的配额。

同义字词	share, ration, proportion
衍生字词	▲ quotation n. 引用语 ▲ quota control 配额管制 ▲ quota period 配额期限 ▲ quantitative adj. 定量的；数量的
高分秘诀	▲ ahead of time 提前

Rr 托福 TOEFL iBT

托福(TOEFL)的测验对象为母语为非英语的人

申请入学美加地区大学或研究所时,托福成绩单是必备文件之一。

- n. 名词
- v. 动词
- adj. 形容词
- adv. 副词
- prep. 介词
- art. 冠词
- pron. 代词
- aux. 助词
- conj. 连词

Rr 托福 TOEFL iBT

托福(TOEFL)的测验对象为母语为非英语的人
申请入学美加地区大学或研究所时，托福成绩单是必备文件之一。

1493. radiate [ˈredɪet] [ra·di·ate]   ☆★★★★

v. 放射，辐射　　It is a truth that the sun radiates light and heat.
太阳散发光和热是真理。

- 同义字词　spread out, effuse, beam, glow
- 衍生字词　▲ radiation **n.** 辐射，发光，放热
  　　　　　▲ radiant **adj.** 发光的，容光焕发的
  　　　　　▲ nonradiation **n.** 不辐射
- 高分秘诀　▲ light and heat 光和热

1494. radical [ˈrædɪkl] [rad·i·cal] ☆★★★★

adj. 根本的，激进的　　The lawyer often had some radical political views.
这个律师经常有激进的政治观点。

- 同义字词　drastic, extreme, greatest, utmost
- 反义字词　conservative, superficial
- 衍生字词　▲ radically **adv.** 根本上
  　　　　　▲ radicalism **n.** 激进主义，激进的思想和原则
  　　　　　▲ radical change 彻底的改变
  　　　　　▲ radical errors 基本错误

1495. rage [redʒ] [rage] ☆☆★★★

n. 风尚，大怒　　The eccentric boy has a rage for pop music.
这个古怪的男孩对流行音乐有狂热爱好。

v. 大发脾气，动怒　　The girl raged when her jewels were stolen while under police protection.
在警察保护下，这个女孩的珠宝还是被偷了，她气死了。

- 同义字词　fashion, vogue, furor, mania
- 衍生字词　▲ be (all) the rage 流行，风靡一时
  　　　　　▲ fly into a rage 勃然大怒
  　　　　　▲ have a rage for 对……具有狂热爱好
  　　　　　▲ in a rage 一怒之下

radiate ~ rally

| 高分秘诀 | ▲ eccentric adj. 古怪的
▲ pop music 流行歌曲 |

1496. ragged [`rægɪd] [rag·ged] ☆☆★★★

adj. 褴褛的，破烂的	A ragged old man begged his bread along the avenue. 一个衣衫褴褛的老人沿街乞讨。
同义字词	torn, worn, frazzled, seedy, shabby
衍生字词	▲ raggedy adj. 有点破烂的，不大完整的 ▲ be run ragged 因过度使用而破旧
高分秘诀	▲ beg one's bread 讨口饭吃，乞食

1497. raid [red] [raid] ☆☆★★★

v. 袭击，劫夺	The troop of enemy raided the docks where our troop stayed. 敌军突然袭击我军所在的码头。
n. 攻击，突袭	The bombing raid practically leveled the tiny town. 空袭几乎把整座小城镇夷为平地。
同义字词	invasion, attack, assault, offense, onslaught
衍生字词	▲ raid the market v. 扰乱市场 ▲ stage a raid 发动袭击 ▲ air raid n. 空袭

1498. rally [`rælɪ] [ral·ly] ☆☆★★★

v. 召集，集合	The troops rallied to defend their motherland. 部队再次被召集保卫祖国。
n. 集会，大会	All the teaching and administrative staff held a celebration rally. 全体教职员工举行一次庆祝大会。
同义字词	unite, combine, assemble, collect, congregate
反义字词	segregate, apart, dissociate
衍生字词	▲ rallyist n. 参加汽车竞赛者 ▲ rallying cry 战斗口号
高分秘诀	▲ defend v. 保卫 ▲ motherland n. 祖国 ▲ a celebration rally 庆祝大会

1499. rampant [ˈræmpənt] [ramp·ant] ☆☆★★★

adj. 蔓生的，猖獗的

Sickness was rampant in the rural areas of this nameless country.
这个不知名国家的农村地区疾病正肆虐。

| 同义字词 | uncontrolled, unruly |

| 高分秘诀 | ▲ rampantly **adv.** 蔓生地，猖獗地
▲ a rampant arch 跛拱 |

1500. ranch [ræntʃ] [ranch] ☆☆★★★

n. 农场，牧场

It is said that these are group of huts for housing ranch workers.
据说这些是供牧场工人居住的棚屋。

| 同义字词 | farm, homestead, plantation, range |

| 衍生字词 | ▲ ranching **adj.** 放牧的
▲ rancher **n.** 大农场经营者 |

1501. ratify [ˈrætəˌfaɪ] [rat·i·fy] ☆★★★★

v. 批准，通过

These important files have been ratified by the end of this year.
这些重要文件将在今年年底批准生效。

| 同义字词 | endorse, approve, uphold, validate |

| 反义字词 | disapprove, disagree |

| 衍生字词 | ▲ ratification **n.** 批准
▲ to ratify the treaty 批准条约
▲ ratify an amendment to a constitution 批准宪法修正案 |

| 高分秘诀 | ▲ important files 重要文件
▲ by the end of this year 今年年底前 |

1502. ration [ˈræʃən] [ra·tion] ☆★★★★

n. 定量，配给量

The famous country cut the tobacco ration last year.
这个国家去年削减了烟草配给量。

v. 定量配给

The government of that nameless country had to ration petrol during the war.
那个不知名国家的政府不得不在战争期间限量汽油的供应量。

| 同义字词 | allotment, allowance, portion, allot |

rampant ~ realization

衍生字词
▲ rationing n. (食物等的)配给
▲ rational adj. 理性的，合理的
▲ an iron /emergency ration (备急用的)军用干粮

1503. rattle [ˈrætl] [rat·tle] ☆☆★★★

n. 拨浪鼓, 格格声 — This wonderful thing is a drum-shaped rattle for children.
这个有趣的东西是小朋友玩的拨浪鼓。

v. 喋喋不休地说话 — The boring man rattled on about his job, not noticing how bored the listener was.
这个无聊的人只顾喋喋不休地说自己工作上的事，没注意到倾听者有多么厌烦。

衍生字词
▲ rattlesnake n. 响尾蛇
▲ rattleroot n. 任何可治蛇咬的植物
▲ rattle on 喋喋不休地说，轻快地说
▲ rattle up 激起

1504. raucous [ˈrɔkəs] [rau·cous] ☆☆★★★

adj. 沙哑的, 喧嚣的 — I recognized the personnel manager by his raucous, penetrating laugh.
我听到那沙哑又刺耳的笑声就能认出是人事部经理。

同义字词 loud, boisterous, coarse
反义字词 quiet, calm, silent
高分秘诀
▲ recognize v. 认出
▲ personnel manager 人事部经理
▲ penetrating adj. 刺耳的

1505. raze [rez] [raze] ☆☆★★★

v. 夷为平地, 消除 — The old skyscraper was razed to ground, and a new one was built.
那栋摩天大楼被完全拆掉了，并盖了一栋新大楼。

同义字词 demolish, topple, destroy, flatten
反义字词 stet, don't delete, remain, stay
高分秘诀
▲ skyscraper n. 摩天大楼
▲ be razed to ground 被完全拆除

1506. realization [ˌrɪələˈzeʃən] [re·al·i·za·tion] ☆☆★★★

n. 实现, 意识 — When he has grown up, he had a full realization of the importance of study. But it turned out late.
当他长大并充分体悟到学习的重要性时，已经太晚了。

同义字词	fulfillment, awareness, actualization
反义字词	not become true, unrealize
衍生字词	▲ realize v. 认识，明白 ▲ reality n. 现实，实际 ▲ realistic adj. 现实的，现实主义的 ▲ realism n. 写实主义
高分秘诀	▲ grow up 长大 ▲ have a full realization of sth. 充分体会领悟到某事 ▲ the importance of study 学习的重要性

1507. rear [rɪr] [rear] ☆★★★★

v. 培养，饲养	He rears all kinds of rare birds. 他饲养各种珍禽。
n. 后面	The hall is in the rear of the center building. 礼堂位于中央大楼的后面。
同义字词	raise, nurture, produce
反义字词	destroy, kill, ruin
衍生字词	▲ rearer n. 养育员，饲养员 ▲ bring up the rear 殿后，走在后面 ▲ rearmost adj. 最后的
高分秘诀	▲ all kinds of 各种各样的 ▲ rare birds 珍稀鸟类 ▲ center building 中央大楼

1508. rebel [rɪˋbɛl] [reb·el] ☆☆★★★

n. 叛徒	The hero spent two years as the prisoner of rebel soldiers in another city. 这位英雄被另一个城市的叛军抓走两年。
v. 谋反，叛逆	The colonists took up weapons to rebel against the British ruler in the end of the movie. 电影的结尾是殖民地的人民拿起武器反抗英国统治者。
同义字词	revolt, dissent, riot
反义字词	obey, comply, heed
衍生字词	▲ rebellion n. 谋反，叛乱 ▲ rebellious adj. 造反的，反叛的 ▲ rebeldom n. 反叛者；叛徒 ▲ rebel at the very idea of 想到……就有反感

rear ~ reception

高分秘诀
▲ prisoner n. 囚徒
▲ rebel soldiers 叛军
▲ rebel against 反抗

1509. rebuke [rɪˋbjuk] [re·buke] ☆☆★★★

v. 斥责，谴责
She rebuked him strongly for her son's negligence.
她严厉斥责他对她儿子的疏忽。

n. 指责，谴责
The desperate housewife accepted the rebuke silently, though she didn't have to.
这位绝望的家庭主妇默默接受责难，虽然她并不是非这样做不可。

同义字词　admonish, scold, reprimand, reprove

反义字词　praise, laud compliment

衍生字词
▲ rebukeful adj. 充满斥责的
▲ rebuker n. 指责者
▲ without rebuke 无可非议的

高分秘诀
▲ negligence n. 疏忽
▲ desperate adj. 绝望的

1510. recall [rɪˋkɔl] [re·call] ☆★★★★

v. 忆起，记忆
I can recall the features of the significant leader.
我回忆起伟大领袖人物的容貌。

n. 召回，唤回
A pleasant recall always brings you much happiness.
令人愉悦的回忆总是带给你快乐。

同义字词　remember, call back, recollect

衍生字词
▲ beyond recall 无法挽回的，无法追忆的
▲ recall from 撤回，召回

高分秘诀
▲ feature n. 特征，特色
▲ significant adj. 重要的，有重大意义的
▲ leader n. 领导，领袖

1511. reception [rɪˋsɛpʃən] [re·cep·tion] ★★★★★

n. 接待，招待会
Their company gave a reception to their new potential customer.
他们公司为有潜力的新客户举办了一个招待会。

| 同义字词 | entertainment, festivity, party |
| 衍生字词 | ▲ receptionist n. 招待员
▲ receptor n. 接收器，感受器
▲ receptive adj. 善于接受的 |

1512. recession [rɪˋsɛʃən] [re·ces·sion] ☆★★★★

n. 萧条时期,（经济）衰退

It is said that during the economic recession the big factory terminated a large number of workers.
据说在经济衰退时期，这家大工厂解雇了许多工人。

同义字词	depression, stagnation, recess
反义字词	prosperity, successfulness
衍生字词	▲ recess n. 休息，放假 v. 使暂停 ▲ recessionary adj.（经济）萧条的 ▲ recession cone 回收锥

1513. recipe [ˋrɛsəpɪ] [re·ci·pe] ☆★★★★

n. 食谱,诀窍

Mutton can substitute for pork in this recipe.
依照这个食谱，羊肉可代替猪肉。

同义字词	prescription, instructions
反义字词	method, way, scheme
衍生字词	▲ a recipe for living long 长寿秘诀 ▲ a recipe book 食谱
高分秘诀	▲ mutton n. 羊肉 ▲ substitute for 代替

1514. recipient [rɪˋsɪpɪənt] [re·cip·i·ent] ☆★★★★

n. 接受者,接收方

It is said that the recipients of prizes had their names printed in the latest paper.
据说获奖者名单登在最近的报纸上。

同义字词	receiver, beneficiary
反义字词	transmitter, sender, vector
衍生字词	▲ recipient cell 受体细胞 ▲ recipient dividend 股息领取人 ▲ recipient vessel 接收器
高分秘诀	▲ it is said that 据说 ▲ the recipients of prizes 获奖者名单

recognize ~ recognize

1515. reckless [ˈrɛklɪs] [reck·less] ☆★★★★

adj. 轻率的，鲁莽的

The careless driver is quite reckless of his own safety.
这个粗心的司机完全不顾自己的安全。

同义字词	devil-may-care, irresponsible, careless
反义字词	cautious, prudent, watchful
衍生字词	▲ recklessly adv. 轻率地，鲁莽地 ▲ recklessness n. 轻率，鲁莽 ▲ be reckless of 不注意

1516. reckon [ˈrɛkən] [reck·on] ☆★★★★

v. 计算，猜想

The readers reckon the book as one of the old poet's best works.
读者认为本书是这位古诗人的优秀作品之一。

| 同义字词 | compute, calculate, estimate |
| 衍生字词 | ▲ reckon among 算在……之内
▲ reckon for 对……负责
▲ reckon in 把……估计在内
▲ reckon on 依赖，依靠 |

1517. reclaim [rɪˈklem] [re·claim] ☆☆★★★

v. 开垦，回收利用，拿回

The old man always reclaims valuable materials from wastes to make a good deal.
老人总是从废物中回收有价值的材料做一笔好生意。

同义字词	rehabilitate, rejuvenate, regenerate
衍生字词	▲ reclaimable adj. 可改造的 ▲ reclaimed adj. 再生的，翻造的，收复的 ▲ past reclaim 不可救药的，无法改造的
高分秘诀	▲ valuable adj. 有价值的 ▲ material n. 材料 ▲ make a good deal 做一笔好生意

1518. recognize [ˈrɛkəɡˌnaɪz] [rec·og·nize] ★★★★★

v. 识别，辨认

At that instant the scared girl did not recognize the man that had kidnapped her.
那一瞬间，受惊吓的女孩没有认出绑架她的人。

衍生字词	▲ recognition **n.** 赞誉，承认
	▲ recognized **adj.** 公认的，经过证明的
	▲ recognizable **adj.** 可认出的，可识别的
高分秘诀	▲ at an instant 一瞬间
	▲ scared **adj.** 受惊吓的
	▲ kidnap **v.** 绑架

1519. recoil [rɪˋkɔɪl] [re·coil] ☆★★★★

v. 弹回，反冲	In most situation recoiling from death is natural. 在大多数情况下，害怕死亡是自然的一件事。
同义字词	rebound, resile, bounce, bound
衍生字词	▲ recoil-labeling **n.** 反冲标记
	▲ recoil-operated **adj.** 用后退力来动作的
	▲ recoil on 报应
高分秘诀	▲ in most situation 在大多数情况下
	▲ recoil from death 怕死

1520. recollection [ˌrɛkəˋlɛkʃən] [re·col·lec·tion] ☆★★★★

n. 回忆，记忆	That evening's party is one of my happiest recollections. 那天晚上的宴会是我记忆中最快乐的事情之一。
同义字词	memory, remembrance, recall
衍生字词	▲ beyond recollection 想不起，记不得
高分秘诀	▲ party **n.** 聚会，晚会
	▲ one of ……的其中一个
	▲ happiest recollection 最幸福的回忆

1521. recommend [ˌrɛkəˋmɛnd] [rec·om·mend] ★★★★★

v. 推荐，劝告	Can you recommend to the audience a good dictionary used for checking these questions? 你能推荐一本专门用来查询这些问题的好字典吗？
同义字词	suggest, advise, advocate, direct
衍生字词	▲ recommendation **n.** 推荐，介绍（信）
	▲ recommendable **adj.** 可推荐的
高分秘诀	▲ audience **n.** 观众
	▲ dictionary **n.** 字典

1522. recount [ˌriˋkaʊnt] [re·count] ☆★★★★

rectify ~ rectify

v. 叙述, 描写	To our surprise, the defeated candidate demanded a recount of the votes.
	令我们吃惊的是，落败的候选人要求重新验票。

同义字词　narrate, depict, describe

衍生字词
▲ recountal n. 详细叙述
▲ recount one's sins 述说某人的罪恶

高分秘诀
▲ to one's surprise 令某人吃惊的是
▲ candidate n. 候选人
▲ vote n. 选票

1523. recreation [ˌrɛkrɪˈeʃən] [rec·re·a·tion] ★★★★★

n. 消遣, 娱乐	I suggest that we had better take sufficient recreation to relax after work.
	我建议我们工作后，最好放松一下。

同义字词　amusement, entertainment, enjoyment

衍生字词　▲ recreational adj. 娱乐的

高分秘诀
▲ suggest v. 建议
▲ had better do sth. 最好做某事

1524. recruit [rɪˈkrut] [re·cruit] ☆★★★★

v. 征兵, 补充	It is lucky for him to come to the seaside to recruit.
	他很幸运能到海滨休养。
n. 新兵, 新手	Tim was conscripted last month, so he is a very raw recruit.
	吉姆在上个月被征召入伍，所以他是个新兵。

同义字词　enlist, enroll, draft, muster

衍生字词
▲ recruiter n. 新兵
▲ recruit one's health 恢复健康
▲ recruit oneself 休养

高分秘诀
▲ seaside n. 海边
▲ conscript v. 征召入伍
▲ raw recruit 新兵

1525. rectify [ˈrɛktəˌfaɪ] [rec·ti·fy] ☆★★★★

v. 矫正, 改正	It is necessary for us to rectify errors quickly when we found them.
	发现错误时，我们必须立即纠正。

同义字词	correct, amend, adjust
衍生字词	▲ rectify errors 改正错误
高分秘诀	▲ it is necessary for sb. to do sth. 某人去做某事很有必要
	▲ rectify errors 改正错误

1526. recur [rɪˋkɝ] [re·cur] ☆★★★★

v. 重现，再来

It is unfortunate for him that his fever recurred.
很不幸的是，他又感冒了。

同义字词	reappear, come again, repeat, return
衍生字词	▲ recurring adj. 往复的，再次发生的
	▲ recur to 重新提起，重新浮现
	▲ recurrence n. 复发，反复
	▲ recurrent adj. 经常发生的，周期性的
高分秘诀	▲ unfortunate adj. 不幸运的
	▲ fever n. 发烧

1527. recycle [rɪˋsaɪkl] [re·cy·cle] ☆★★★★

v. 重复使用，再利用

He always recycled old jokes which made us very boring.
他总是重复说老笑话，让我们感到很无聊。

衍生字词	▲ to recycle waste paper 反复使用废纸
	▲ recycled old jokes 老笑话重复说
高分秘诀	▲ recycled old jokes 老笑话重复说
	▲ boring adj. 无聊的

1528. refine [rɪˋfaɪn] [re·fine] ☆☆★★★

v. 精炼，精制

The author would like to refine on his work of five years ago.
作者想把他五年前的著作修改得更完美。

同义字词	purify, develop, improve, perfect
反义字词	worsen, aggravate, decline, exacerbate
衍生字词	▲ refined adj. 优雅的，精制的
	▲ refinement n. （言语、举止等的）文雅，精巧
高分秘诀	▲ author n. 作者
	▲ would like to do sth. 想要做某事

1529. reflection [rɪˋflɛkʃən] [reflec·tion] ☆★★★★

rectify ~ refreshing

n. 反映, 反射光, 深思, 反省
The naughty boy felt curious when he saw her own reflection in the mirror.
这个淘气的小男孩看到自己在镜子中的倒影，感到很好奇。

同义字词 expression, contemplation, manifestation, thoughtfulness

衍生字词
▲ reflectional **adj.** 反射的，反映的
▲ reflectionism **n.** 反映论
▲ reflectionless **adj.** 无倒影的
▲ on reflection 经再三思考
▲ without (due) reflection 轻率

高分秘诀
▲ naughty **adj.** 顽皮的，调皮的
▲ curious **adj.** 好奇的，奇怪的

1530. reform [rɪˋfɔrm] [re·form] ☆★★★★

n. 改革, 革新
The progressive party made a clamor for reform.
激进党强烈要求改革。

v. 改革, 革新
Our reform about traffic problems made an inexorable march of progress.
我们对于交通问题的改革取得了势不可挡的进展。

同义字词 betterment, improvement, improve

衍生字词
▲ reformer **n.** 改革家
▲ reformism **n.** 改革主义
▲ reformable **adj.** 可改革的

高分秘诀
▲ the progressive party 激进党
▲ traffic problems 交通问题
▲ inexorable **adj.** 不可阻挡的

1531. refreshing [rɪˋfrɛʃɪŋ] [re·fresh·ing] ☆☆★★★

adj. 提神的, 凉爽的
At a sudden, we get a refreshing cool breeze.
突然之间，我们感到一阵令人凉爽的微风。

同义字词 invigorating, energizing, brisk

反义字词 fainthearted, muzzy, low-spirited

衍生字词
▲ refreshment **n.** 茶点，提神之事物
▲ refreshingly **adv.** 耳目一新地
▲ refresh **v.** 使精力恢复，使精神振作

高分秘诀
▲ at a sudden 突然之间
▲ a refreshing cool breeze 使人感到凉爽的微风

1532. refrigerate [rɪˋfrɪdʒəˌret] [re·frig·er·ate]

v. 使冷却, 冷藏

The meat spoiled because we did not refrigerate it.
因为我们没有把它放到冰箱，这块肉坏了。

衍生字词
- ▲ refrigerator **n.** 冰箱，冷藏库
- ▲ refrigeration **n.** 冷藏，冷却
- ▲ refrigerant **n.** 制冷剂

高分秘诀
- ▲ spoil **v.** 变质，损坏

1533. refurbish [riˋfɝbɪʃ] [re·fur·bish] ☆☆★★★

v. 刷新, 再磨光

Some people like to refurbish an old legend.
有些人喜欢重编老故事。

同义字词
redecorate, polish, freshen up

衍生字词
- ▲ refurbishment **n.** 刷新，磨光
- ▲ refurbish an old car 整修一辆旧车

高分秘诀
- ▲ like to do sth. 喜欢做某事
- ▲ refurbish an old legend 故事新编

1534. refute [rɪˋfjut] [re·fute] ☆☆★★★

v. 反驳, 驳倒

I was able to refute the lawyer's argument to defend him.
我能反驳那个律师的论点来保护他。

同义字词
decline, disprove, argue, contradict

衍生字词
- ▲ refutable **adj.** 可驳倒的
- ▲ refuter **n.** 辩驳者
- ▲ refutation **n.** 反驳
- ▲ refute an opponent 驳倒对方

高分秘诀
- ▲ be able to 能够
- ▲ lawyer **n.** 律师
- ▲ defend 为……辩护

1535. regardless [rɪˋgɑrdlɪs] [re·gard·less] ★★★★★

adv. 不管, 不顾

The plucky girl is determined to do regardless of all consequences.
这个有毅力的女孩不顾一切后果，决心这样做。

同义字词
despite, whatever, notwithstanding

regulate ~ regulate

反义字词	simply, just, merely
衍生字词	▲ regardlessly adv. 不受注意地 ▲ regardlessness n. 不顾一切，不重视 ▲ regardless of 不管，不论
高分秘诀	▲ plucky adj. 勇敢的，坚决的 ▲ consequence n. 结果，后果

1536. regime [rɪˈʒim] [re·gime]   ☆★★★★

n. 政权，政体

It is said that the overthrow of the regime was followed by a period of anarchy.
据说政权被推翻后，有一段时期处于无政府状态。

同义字词	government, authorities, regimen
衍生字词	▲ regimentation n. 系统化
高分秘诀	▲ it is said that 据说…… ▲ the overthrow of the regime 政府被推翻 ▲ anarchy n. 混乱

1537. register [ˈrɛdʒɪstɚ] [reg·is·ter]   ★★★★★

v. 登记，注册

Though you are a famous statesman, you need to register at the hotel.
尽管你是个著名的政治人物，你依然要在饭店登记姓名。

n. 登记（表）

I've finished the most part of registering form.
我已经填好了大部分的注册资料表。

同义字词	record, enroll, enter, indicate, inscribe
衍生字词	▲ registerer n. 注册者 ▲ registerable adj. 注册的 ▲ (be) in register 对得齐 ▲ (be) on register 有嫌疑，被怀疑
高分秘诀	▲ statesman n. 政员 ▲ need to do sth. 需要做某事 ▲ accommodation n. 住宿 ▲ the condition of housing 住房条件

1538. regulate [ˈrɛgjəˌlet] [reg·u·late]   ☆★★★★

v. 管制，控制

The clock in our office is always slow; it needs to be regulated.
我们办公室的时钟总是比较慢，需要调准。

同义字词	direct, command, control
反义字词	uncontrol, out of control
衍生字词	▲ regulatory adj. 按规矩来的，规章的 ▲ regulation n. 规则，规章
高分秘诀	▲ slow adj. 缓慢的 ▲ office n. 办公室 ▲ need to 需要做某事

1539. rehabilitate [ˌrihəˈbɪləˌtet] [re·ha·bil·i·tate] ☆★★★★

v. 使康复，使复职

The government will plan to rehabilitate the run-down neighborhood.
政府计划重建这个没落的街区。

| 衍生字词 | ▲ rehabilitation n. 恢复，复员
▲ rehabilitative adj. 复原的，康复的
▲ rehabilitate oneself 恢复名誉 |
| 高分秘诀 | ▲ government n. 政府
▲ plan to do sth. 计划做某事
▲ run-down adj. 破旧的 |

1540. rehearse [rɪˈhɝs] [re·hearse] ★★★★★

v. 预演，排练

They found a speaker broken when they rehearsed.
他们在彩排时发现其中的一个喇叭坏掉了。

| 同义字词 | practice, drill, prepare, repeat |
| 衍生字词 | ▲ rehearsable adj. 预演的
▲ rehearser n. 排练者
▲ rehearse a play 排演一出戏 |

1541. reign [ren] [reign] ☆★★★★

n. 君主的统治

People will remember the tyrannies of the emperor reign.
人们不会忘记这位皇帝统治时期的暴行。

v. 统治，支配

We find with surprise that chaos reigns supreme in our new house.
我们惊讶地发现新房子竟然一团混乱。

| 同义字词 | sovereignty, rule, control |

reiterate ~ reiterate

衍生字词
- ▲ reigning adj. 统治的
- ▲ a reign of terror 恐怖统治
- ▲ the Reign of Terror 恐怖时期
- ▲ under the reign of 在……的统治下

高分秘诀
- ▲ remember v. 记得，牢记
- ▲ tyranny n. 暴行，专政
- ▲ emperor n. 皇帝，君主

1542. reimburse [ˌriɪmˈbɝs] [re·im·burse] ★★★★★

v. 偿还, 付还

We will reimburse you after a time limit of 14 days.
我们将会在十四天后退款。

同义字词
compensate, pay back, repay, recoup

衍生字词
- ▲ reimbursement n. （费用等的）偿还，报销
- ▲ reimburser n. 偿还者
- ▲ reimburse sb. for a loss 赔偿某人的损失

高分秘诀
- ▲ expense n. 花费，花销
- ▲ carrying luggage 运带行李

1543. reinforce [ˌriɪnˈfɔrs] [re·in·force] ☆★★★★

v. 加强, 增强

Public reaction will reinforce the effect of reformation.
大众的反应将会进一步增强改革的作用。

同义字词
strengthen, enhance, fortify, intensify

反义字词
enervate, impair, weaken

衍生字词
- ▲ reinforce a wall 给墙加固
- ▲ reinforced concrete 钢筋混凝土
- ▲ reinforce provisions 补充粮食

高分秘诀
- ▲ public reaction 社会反响
- ▲ the effect of ……的作用
- ▲ reformation n. 改革

1544. reiterate [riˈɪtəˌret] [re·it·er·ate] ☆★★★★

v. 重申, 反复说

Please be good enough to reiterate your point about this issue.
请重述您对于这件事的观点。

同义字词
repeat, recount, retell, review

衍生字词	▲ reiteration n. 重复
	▲ reiterate the rule 重申规则
高分秘诀	▲ reiterate one's point 重申某人的观点

1545. reject [rɪˋdʒɛkt] [re·ject] ★★★★

| v. 拒绝, 抵制 | The board of directors rejected my proposition.
董事会拒绝了我的提议。 |
| n. 废弃品 | Sometimes a tire that is a reject is useful too.
有时候废弃轮胎也很有用。 |

同义字词	turn down, refuse, deny
反义字词	adopt, approve, believe, consent to
衍生字词	▲ rejectee n. 遭拒绝者
	▲ rejecter n. 丢弃者
高分秘诀	▲ the board of directors 董事会
	▲ useful adj. 有用的

1546. rejuvenate [rɪˋdʒuvənet] [re·ju·ve·nate] ☆☆★★

| v. (使)返老还童, (使)恢复活力 | It will be benefit for you because the seaside air will rejuvenate you.
海边的空气会使你恢复活力, 对你好处多多。 |

同义字词	make young again, reinvigorate, refresh
衍生字词	▲ rejuvenation n. 更新
	▲ rejuvenate of capital 资本更新
	▲ rejuvenate head 回春点
高分秘诀	▲ benefit v. 好处, 益处
	▲ seaside n. 海滨, 海边

1547. relay [rɪˋle] [re·lay] ☆☆★★

| v. 传播, 转述 | The significant event was relayed all round the world.
这个重大的事件已向全世界实况转播。 |

同义字词	carry, deliver, hand on, impart
衍生字词	▲ to relay a broadcast 转播
	▲ work in relays 轮班工作
	▲ new relays of troops 新轮替的部队
高分秘诀	▲ significant event 重大事件
	▲ all round the world 全世界

reiterate ~ reliable

1548. release [rɪˋlis] [re·lease] ☆★★★★

v. 释放，发布	Please release your pressure after you get the lesson. 学到教训后，请舒缓自己的压力。
n. 释放，解除	The man concerned the case secured the release of the hostages. 关心这个案子的人已经设法使人质获释。
同义字词	give off, liberate, freedom, emancipation
反义字词	apprehend, arrest, imprison, seize
衍生字词	▲ on general release 能在所有影院上映的 ▲ release a prisoner 释放犯人
高分秘诀	▲ get the lesson 得到教训 ▲ concern **v.** 关心，担心

1549. relevant [ˋrɛləvənt] [rel·e·vant] ☆☆★★★

adj. 有关的，切题的	In this situation every common-sense notion about space, time, and speed becomes totally not relevant. 在这种情况下，关于空间、时间和速率的每一个常识性概念统统都不切题。
反义字词	improper, unfitting, unsuitable
衍生字词	▲ relevance **n.** 相关 ▲ nonrelevant **adj.** 非关联的，非相关的 ▲ irrelevant **adj.** 不相关的
高分秘诀	▲ in this situation 在这种情况下 ▲ common-sense **n.** 常识 ▲ notion **n.** 概念，观念

1550. reliable [rɪˋlaɪəbḷ] [re·li·a·ble] ☆★★★★

adj. 可靠的，可信赖的	The girl who was in charge of this section was totally not reliable, so she was given her marching orders. 负责这个部门的女孩完全不可靠，所以被解雇了。
同义字词	dependable, trustworthy
衍生字词	▲ reliant **adj.** 依靠的，信赖自己的 ▲ reliance **n.** 依靠 ▲ reliability **n.** 可靠性

高分秘诀	▲ in charge of 负责
	▲ section n. 区域，部门
	▲ totally adv. 完全地
	▲ march v. 进军

1551. relic [ˈrɛlɪk] [rel·ic] ☆☆★★★

n. 遗迹，纪念物

As we all knew this ruined bridge is a relic of the Civil War.
据我们所知，这座断桥是南北战争时期的遗迹。

同义字词	antique, remains, remembrance, souvenir
衍生字词	▲ unearthed relics 出土文物
	▲ old relic 老爷车
高分秘诀	▲ as we all knew 据我们所知
	▲ bridge n. 桥梁
	▲ civil war 美国南北战争，内战

1552. relieve [rɪˈliv] [re·lieve] ☆★★★★

v. 减轻，消除

This medicine will relieve your headache in some sense.
这种药将在一定程度上减轻你的头痛。

同义字词	assuage, alleviate
反义字词	intensify, compound, deepen, escalate
衍生字词	▲ relieved adj. 放心的
	▲ relieve oneself 使用洗手间，方便
	▲ relieve sb.'s mind 解除某人忧虑
	▲ relieve guard 换岗
高分秘诀	▲ headache n. 头疼
	▲ in some sense 在一定程度上

1553. reluctant [rɪˈlʌktənt] [re·luc·tant] ☆★★★★

adj. 不情愿的，勉强的

The child was reluctant to read the books.
这个孩子不愿意读书。

同义字词	unwilling, averse, disincline
反义字词	agreeable, compliant, consenting
衍生字词	▲ reluctantly adv. 不情愿地
	▲ reluctant assistance 勉强的协作
	▲ reluctant followers 胁从分子
高分秘诀	▲ be reluctant to do sth. 不情愿做某事

1554. remark [rɪˈmɑrk] [re·mark] ★★★★★

n. 评论, 注释
I accepted completely his remark on my article.
我完全接受他在我文章上的评论。

v. 评论, 谈及
The editor remarked that magazine was well written.
编辑评论那本杂志编得很好。

衍生字词
▲ remarkable **adj.** 显著的
▲ remarkably **adv.** 显著地, 引人注目地

高分秘诀
▲ completely **adv.** 完全地
▲ article **n.** 文章
▲ editor **n.** 编辑, 编者

1555. remedy [ˈrɛmədɪ] [re·me·dy] ☆★★★★

n. 药物
This kind of medicine is a good remedy for a cold.
这种药是治疗感冒的良药。

v. 治疗, 补救
This kind of medicine will remedy the illness.
这类药能够治这种病。

同义字词
drug, cure, fix, repair

衍生字词
▲ remediable **adj.** 可治疗的
▲ to remedy a fault 纠正错误
▲ be past remedy 无法补救的, 治不好的
▲ sovereign remedy 特效药, 万灵丹

高分秘诀
▲ a good remedy for a cold 治疗感冒的良药
▲ remedy the illness 治病

1556. remnant [ˈrɛmnənt] [rem·nant] ☆☆☆★★

n. 残余, 遗迹
The man with small mustache is suffering from some remnant feeling of disgrace.
留着小胡子的这个人还在为受到的耻辱感到苦恼。

同义字词
fossil, vestige, remains

衍生字词
▲ remnantal **adj.** 残余的, 剩余的
▲ the remnants of the feast 宴席的剩菜
▲ a remnant of the feudal times 封建残余

1557. remote [rɪˈmot] [re·mote] ☆★★★★

adj. 遥远的，偏僻的	You can't predict the remote future of yours. What you should do is to try your best to make preparation for a bright future. 你不能预测遥远的未来，你应该做的是尽力为美好的未来作准备。
同义字词	distant, far, hidden, isolated, removed
反义字词	at hand, close, imminent, near
衍生字词	▲ remote-effects n. 间接影响 ▲ remote-indication n. 远距离指示，遥测
高分秘诀	▲ the remote future 遥远的未来 ▲ try one's best to do sth. 尽力做某事

1558. renaissance [rəˋnesn̩s] [ren·ais·sance] ★★★★

n. 复活，文艺复兴	It is said that these are the cultural legacies of the Renaissance. 据说这些是文艺复兴时期的文化遗产。
同义字词	rebirth, revival, renewal
衍生字词	▲ Early Renaissance 文艺复兴初期的艺术风格 ▲ High Renaissance 文艺复兴时期盛期 ▲ Late Renaissance 文艺复兴后期
高分秘诀	▲ cultural legacies 文化遗产

1559. render [ˋrɛndɚ] [ren·der] ★★★★

v. 给予，提供	The lovely girl rendered the song beautifully. 可爱的女孩将这首歌演唱得很美。
同义字词	provide, allot, allow, give
衍生字词	▲ rendering n. 表现，描写 ▲ renderable adj. 给予的 ▲ renderer n. 提供的人 ▲ render oneself up to 投降 ▲ render up 祷告，放弃

1560. rendition [rɛnˋdɪʃən] [ren·di·tion] ★★★

n. 表演，演唱	People all agreed with that it is a gifted rendition of the aria. 人们都同意这是个极富天赋的咏叹调的演唱。
同义字词	performance, rendering

remote ~ repel

衍生字词
▲ chromatic rendition 彩色再现
▲ colour rendition 现色性
▲ contrast rendition 对比度再现
▲ detail rendition 细节重现

高分秘诀
▲ agree with 同意
▲ gifted adj. 有天赋的，有才华的
▲ aria n. 咏叹调

1561. renounce [rɪˋnaʊns] [re·nounce]   ☆☆★★★

v. 声明放弃，宣布断绝关系

He renounced his claim to the property after the accident.
意外后，他宣布正式放弃财产所有权。

同义字词
give up, abandon, deny, discard, disclaim

衍生字词
▲ renunciation n. 放弃
▲ renounce one's old habits 戒绝旧习惯
▲ renounce the world 退隐

高分秘诀
▲ claim v. 声称，断言
▲ property n. 财产，资产

1562. renovate [ˋrɛnəˌvet] [ren·o·vate]   ☆★★★★

v. 革新，修理

It is just a renovated old building. Don't take it for granted that it is completely new.
它只是整修翻新的建筑物，不要理所当然认为它是全新的。

同义字词
refurbish, renew, recondition, redo

衍生字词
▲ renovation n. 修复，整修
▲ renovator n. 革新者
▲ a renovated tyre 再生轮胎

高分秘诀
▲ building n. 建筑物，楼房
▲ take it for granted 想当然地认为
▲ completely adv. 完整的

1563. repel [rɪˋpɛl] [re·pel]   ☆★★★★

v. 击退，驱逐

In my opinion a country must have the will to repel any invader.
在我看来，一个国家必须有决心击退任何入侵者。

同义字词
repulse, beat back, resist

反义字词
captivate, charm, draw, fascinate

衍生字词	▲ repellence n. 击退，驱逐
	▲ repeller n. 击退的人
高分秘诀	▲ in one's opinion 在某人看来
	▲ invader n. 侵略者

1564. replace [rɪˋples] [re·place] ★★★★★

| v. 代替，取代，车换放回原处 | Computers have replaced typewriters.
电脑已经取代打字机。 |

同义字词	instead, in place of, rather than
反义字词	deduct, discard, dispose of
衍生字词	▲ replaceable adj. 可替换的
	▲ replacement n. 回归原位，更换
高分秘诀	▲ typewriter n. 打字机

1565. replenish [rɪˋplɛnɪʃ] [re·plen·ish] ☆★★★★

| v. 补充，把……再备足 | Please replenish a glass with wine to the honoured guest.
请再为这位贵客斟满一杯酒。 |

同义字词	refill, restock, furnish
衍生字词	▲ replenisher n. 补充者，充电器
	▲ replenishment n. 再斟满，充实
高分秘诀	▲ replenish a glass with wine 再斟满一杯酒

1566. replicate [ˋrɛplɪˌket] [re·pli·cate] ☆★★★★

| v. 复制 | He invited the unskilled worker to his laboratory to see if he could replicate the experiment.
他请这个不熟练的工人去试验室，并看看他是否能重新示范这个实验。 |

同义字词	copy, double, duplicate
衍生字词	▲ replicator n. 复制品
	▲ replication n. 复制
高分秘诀	▲ unskilled adj. 不熟练的
	▲ laboratory n. 实验室

1567. represent [ˌrɛprɪˋzɛnt] [re·pre·sent] ★★★★★

| v. 代表，描绘 | It is said that lions represent England.
据说狮子是英格兰的象征。 |

| 同义字词 | stand for, illustrate, depict |

replace ~ repute

衍生字词
- ▲ representation n. 表示，表现
- ▲ representative n. 代表

1568. repress [rɪˋprɛs] [re·press] ☆★★★★

v. 抑制，镇压

To our surprise, the famous writer's childhood was repressed and solitary.
令我们惊讶的是，这位名家有着压抑且孤独的童年。

同义字词: depress, restrain, squash, squelch

反义字词: agitate, excite, flame, instigate

衍生字词
- ▲ repressed adj. 被抑制的
- ▲ represser n. 压制者
- ▲ repressible adj. 压抑的
- ▲ repressive adj. 可镇压的

高分秘诀
- ▲ to one's surprise 令某人惊奇的是
- ▲ famous adj. 著名的，出名的

1569. repulse [rɪˋpʌls] [re·pulse] ☆☆★★★

v. 击退，拒绝

For some special reasons she repulsed his proposal.
因为某种特殊的原因，她拒绝他的求婚。

n. 击退

The poor girl's request for a donation met with a rude repulse.
可怜的女孩请求捐款，却遭到无礼的拒绝。

同义字词: repel, drive back

衍生字词
- ▲ meet with (a) repulse 被拒绝
- ▲ repulse an unreasonable request 拒绝不合理的要求

高分秘诀
- ▲ for some special reasons 因为某个特殊原因
- ▲ proposal n. 建议
- ▲ meet with (a) repulse 被拒绝

1570. repute [rɪˋpjut] [re·pute] ☆☆★★★

n. 名声

Take repute from me and my life is done.
若没有名誉，我也命在旦夕。

衍生字词
- ▲ reputed adj. 名誉好的，有……名气
- ▲ disrepute n. 坏名声，不光彩
- ▲ be in repute 有名望
- ▲ of repute 出名的

高分秘诀
- ▲ take sth. from 从……拿走
- ▲ my life is done 我的生命终结

1571. rescue [ˈrɛskju] [res·cue] ☆★★★★

v. 营救，救援
We had better think a good way to rescue them from prison.
我们最好想一个好办法把他们从监狱里救出来。

n. 营救，救援
Going to their rescue in an ambulance is a bit of a forlorn hope.
搭乘救护车去救他们的希望不大。

同义字词　save, salvage, retrieve

衍生字词
▲ rescuer **n.** 救援者，救星
▲ go to one's rescue 进行援救
▲ search and rescue 搜索和营救
▲ rescue party 援救队

高分秘诀
▲ had better do something 最好做某事
▲ a good way 好办法

1572. resemble [rɪˈzɛmbl] [re·sem·ble] ☆★★★★

v. 像，类似
He resembles his brother in appearance but not in character.
他和他兄弟外貌相似，但性格不同。

同义字词　be similar to, take after, look like

衍生字词
▲ resemblance **n.** 相似，酷肖
▲ resemblingly **adv.** 相像地，类似地
▲ resembler **n.** 类似的人

高分秘诀
▲ appearance **n.** 外貌，外观
▲ character **n.** 特点，特征

1573. resent [rɪˈzɛnt] [re·sent] ☆★★★★

v. 愤怒，怨恨
I bitterly resent his attempts to interfere in my private affairs.
我非常讨厌他企图干涉我的私事。

衍生字词
▲ resentful **adj.** 忿恨的，怨恨的
▲ resentingly **adv.** 愤恨地

高分秘诀
▲ interfere **v.** 干预
▲ private affairs 私事

1574. reserve [rɪˈzɝv] [re·serve] ★★★★★

v. 储备，预定
Thank you for your reserving a seat for me.
谢谢你为我预留一个座位。

同义字词	stock, conserve, keep
衍生字词	▲ be reserved to 留作……用 ▲ reservoir n. 水库，蓄水池 ▲ in reserve 备用的 ▲ without reserve 无保留地
高分秘诀	▲ thank you for doing sth. 谢谢你做某事 ▲ reserve a seat 预定一个座位

1575. reside [rɪˋzaɪd] [re·side] ☆★★★★

v. 居住, 定居	Jim and Meg reside at the same room hotel and meet each other surprisely. 吉姆和梅格住在同一间饭店，出其不意地碰见对方。
同义字词	dwell, live, inhabit
衍生字词	▲ resident n. 居民 ▲ residential adj. 住宅的 ▲ residence n. 居住，住处

1576. residue [ˋrɛzə͵dju] [re·si·due] ☆☆★★★

n. 剩余, 渣滓	It is said that a small residue is retained tenaciously by the surface. 据说少量的残留物会牢牢地留在表面。
同义字词	trace, remainder, remains
衍生字词	▲ residual adj. 剩余的，残留的 ▲ for the residue 至于其他 ▲ agricultural residue 农业残余物
高分秘诀	▲ retain v. 保持，保留 ▲ tenaciously adj. 牢固地

1577. resist [rɪˋzɪst] [re·sist] ★★★★★

v. 抵抗	Many young people could not resist the spiritual pollution of this kind. 很多年轻人不能抵制这种精神污染。
同义字词	withstand, act against, counteract, oppose
反义字词	comply, heed, listen to, mind, submit, yield
衍生字词	▲ resistant adj. 抵抗的，有抵抗力的 ▲ resistance n. 反抗，抵抗 ▲ irresistible adj. 不可抵抗的
高分秘诀	▲ spiritual pollution 精神污染

1578. resolve [rɪˋzɑlv] [re·solve] ☆★★★★

v. 解决，决心 — He is resolved to get a good job.
他决心要找到一个好工作。

同义字词	settle, solve, determine, decide
衍生字词	▲ resolute **adj.** 坚决的，毅然的 ▲ resolution **n.** 坚定，解析度 ▲ be resolved 兹决议，决议如下 ▲ keep one's resolve 坚持
高分秘诀	▲ keep one's resolve 坚持 ▲ get a good job 找到好工作

1579. resonance [ˋrɛzənəns] [re·so·nance] ☆★★★★

n. 回声，反响 — It is proved that resonance will occur again, but not so strong as before.
共振被证实会再次发生，但不如先前那么强烈。

同义字词	reverberation, plangency, vibrancy
衍生字词	▲ atomic resonance 原子共振 ▲ fission resonance 裂变反应共振
高分秘诀	▲ it is proved that 被证实的是…… ▲ occur **v.** 发生，出现

1580. resort [rɪˋzɔrt] [re·sort] ☆★★★★

n. 旅游胜地 — Next month the whole family will visit a resort in order to get some pleasure.
所有家庭成员将于下个月到旅游胜地放松一下。

v. 凭借，求助于 — Meeting such matter you should have resorts to your friends.
碰到这种事，你应该向朋友求助。

衍生字词	▲ to resort to force 诉诸武力 ▲ resort to all kinds of methods 采取一切办法
高分秘诀	▲ the whole family 一家人 ▲ in order to 为了 ▲ get some pleasure 娱乐一下

1581. respiration [͵rɛspəˋreʃən] [res·pi·ra·tion] ☆☆★★★

n. 呼吸，呼吸作用 — He needs to do an artificial respiration immediately.
他需要立即做人工呼吸。

resolve ~ retain

同义字词	breathing, inhaling, exhaling
反义字词	no breath, suffocate, stifle, choke
衍生字词	▲ respiratory adj. 呼吸的 ▲ artificial respiration 人工呼吸
高分秘诀	▲ need to do 需要做…… ▲ artificial respiration 人工呼吸 ▲ immediately adv. 立即，马上

1582. restore [rɪˋstor] [re·store] ☆★★★★

v. 使恢复, 修复　　After the trial he restored himself to his old post.
审判后，他恢复原职。

同义字词	reinstate, renovate, renew
衍生字词	▲ restoration n. 恢复，翻新 ▲ to restore stolen property 归还赃物
高分秘诀	▲ trial n. 审判，审理 ▲ restore one to his old post 使某人复职

1583. restrain [rɪˋstren] [re·strain] ☆★★★★

v. 克制, 抑制　　He couldn't restrain his curiosity to study this strange toy.
他抑制不住自己的好奇心研究这个奇怪的玩具。

同义字词	limit, inhibit, confine
反义字词	move, propel, stimulate, drive
衍生字词	▲ restrain n. 抑制，克制 ▲ unrestrained adj. 无限制的
高分秘诀	▲ curiosity n. 好奇心 ▲ study v. 学习，研究 ▲ strange toy 奇怪的玩具

1584. retain [rɪˋten] [re·tain] ☆★★★★

v. 保持, 保留　　She retains a clear memory of her school days.
她仍清晰记得学生时代的点滴。

同义字词	conserve, keep, preserve
反义字词	cease, depart, desert, discard
衍生字词	▲ retentive v. 保留的，有记忆的 ▲ retainable adj. 可保持的 ▲ eliminate the false and retain the true 去伪存真 ▲ retain one's presence of mind 镇定自若

1585. retool [ri`tul] [re·tool]

v. 将机械重新整备，重组

In the building industry, engineers have to retool frequently.
在建筑业中，工程师必须经常吸收新知并充实自己。

同义字词: reorganize, reconstitute, revise

高分秘诀:
▲ building industry 建筑业
▲ engineer **n.** 工程师
▲ frequently **adv.** 经常地，频繁地

1586. retract [rɪ`trækt] [re·tract]

v. 缩回，撤回

Since I had promised it, I could not retract.
既然我答应了，就不能食言。

同义字词: pull back, retreat, withdraw, cancel

衍生字词:
▲ retractable **adj.** 可缩进的
▲ retractile **adj.** 可缩回的

高分秘诀:
▲ since **conj.** 既然
▲ promise **v.** 允诺，答应

1587. retreat [rɪ`trit] [re·treat]

n. 消退，退缩

In this situation, it is beyond retreat.
在这种情况下，没有退缩的可能。

v. 撤退，退却

The enemy was forced to retreat because of consequence of failure.
敌人因为失败被迫撤退。

同义字词: receding, seclusion, secede

反义字词: move forward, proceed, progress

衍生字词:
▲ beat a retreat 避开，逃开
▲ retreative **adj.** 消退的，退却的
▲ be beyond retreat 没有后退的可能

高分秘诀:
▲ in this situation 在这种情况下
▲ be beyond retreat 没有后退的可能

1588. retrieve [rɪ`triv] [re·trieve]

v. 重新找回，取回

I should like to retrieve my bag which I left in the taxi.
我想找回我留在出租车上忘记带走的包。

同义字词	bring back, recover, regain
衍生字词	▲ retriever n. 能把猎物找回来的犬
高分秘诀	▲ taxi n. 出租车

1589. retrospect [ˈrɛtrəˌspɛkt] [re·tro·spect] ☆☆★★★

n. 回顾，回想

In retrospect the thing happened yesterday was a nightmare.
回想起来，昨天发生的事真是一场噩梦。

同义字词	review, reexamination, reminiscent
衍生字词	▲ retrospective adj. 回顾的，怀旧的 ▲ retrospection n. 回顾
高分秘诀	▲ in retrospect 回顾，回顾往事 ▲ nightmare n. 噩梦

1590. reveal [rɪˈvil] [re·veal] ★★★★★

v. 展现，揭露

Being an inspector, he never revealed his identity.
作为一个侦察人员，他从未暴露过自己的身份。

同义字词	expose, uncover, evidence
反义字词	camouflage, cover, hide
衍生字词	▲ revealer n. 展示者，揭露者 ▲ reveal itself 出现，呈现
高分秘诀	▲ inspector n. 侦察员 ▲ real one's identity 暴露自己的身份

1591. reverent [ˈrɛvərənt] [rev·er·ent] ☆☆★★★

adj. 恭敬的，虔敬的

He gave reverent attention to his talking.
他毕恭毕敬地听他讲话。

| 衍生字词 | ▲ reverently adv. 虔诚地
▲ irreverent adj. 不尊敬的
▲ irreverence n. 不尊敬 |
| 高分秘诀 | ▲ give reverent attention to 毕恭毕敬地听…… |

1592. reverse [rɪˈvɜs] [re·verse] ☆★★★★

v. 颠倒，翻转

Please reverse the positions of two desks.
请把两张桌子的位置交换一下。

n. 背面

The result was just the reverse of what I expected.
结果正好与我期望的相反。

adj. 相反的，倒转的	Please read the catalog reverse then I need to rearrange it. 请看看这张目录，先从最后看起，等一下我会重新整理。
同义字词	overturn, invert, contrary
反义字词	back up, regress, return, revert
衍生字词	▲ reversible adj. 可逆的，可翻转的 ▲ irreversible adj. 不能撤回的，不能取消的
高分秘诀	▲ expect v. 预料，期望

1593. revise [rɪˈvaɪz] [re·vise] ☆★★★★

v. 修改, 修订	The famous editor was revising what she had written in recent days. 这位名编辑当时正在修改她最近写的文字。
同义字词	amend, change, alter
衍生字词	▲ revision n. 修订，校订 ▲ reviser n. 校对员 ▲ revised and enlarged 修订增补的
高分秘诀	▲ editor n. 编辑 ▲ in recent days 最近

1594. revitalization [rɪˌvaɪtəlaɪˈzeʃən] [re·vi·ta·li·za·tion] ☆★★★★

n. 新生, 复兴	As a member, we have the duty to complete the revitalization of the organization. 作为一个会员，我们有责任振兴这个组织。
同义字词	rebirth, reinvigoration
衍生字词	▲ revive v. 使复活
高分秘诀	▲ have the duty to do 有使命去做……

1595. resuscitate [rɪˈsʌsəˌtet] [re·sus·ci·tate] ☆☆★★★

v. 使（某人或某物）苏醒	The profound doctors are studying a way to resuscitate a person who has been nearly drowned. 资深医生正在研究一种帮助溺水的人苏醒的方法。
同义字词	recover, renew, revive

revise ~ rhetoric

衍生字词	▲ resuscitative adj. 复苏的
高分秘诀	▲ profound adj. 知识渊博的
	▲ a way to 一种……的方法
	▲ drown v. 溺死

1596. revolt [rɪˋvolt] [re·volt] ☆★★★★

| n. 反抗，反叛 | The ruler convened his troops to put down the revolt of farmers.
统治者召集部队镇压农民的叛乱。 |
| v. 起义，反叛 | The workers revolted against their oppressors.
工人起义反抗压迫者。 |

同义字词	resist, rebel, offend, repel, revolutionize, riot
反义字词	comply, heed, listen to, mind, submit, yield
衍生字词	▲ in revolt （在）叛乱中
	▲ armed revolts 武装起义
	▲ raise a righteous revolt 起义
高分秘诀	▲ ruler n. 统治者
	▲ convene troops 召集军队
	▲ put down 镇压

1597. revolutionize [ˌrɛvəˋluʃənˌaɪz] [rev·o·lu·tion·ize] ☆☆★★★

| v. 在……方面发动革命 | Machines have revolutionized manual work.
机器的运用彻底改变了手工作业。 |

同义字词	completely change, dramatically change
反义字词	be conservative
衍生字词	▲ revolution n. 革命
	▲ revolutionary adj. 革命的
高分秘诀	▲ machine n. 机器
	▲ manual work 手工作业

1598. rhetoric [ˋrɛtərɪk] [rhet·o·ric] ☆★★★★

| n. 修辞，雄辩言辞 | Have you learned something about rhetoric in your college?
你在学校学习修辞学了吗？ |

| 同义字词 | grandiloquence, grandiosity, hot air |

衍生字词	▲ empty rhetoric 花言巧语，富有表现力的修辞
高分秘诀	▲ learn v. 学，学习
	▲ in one's college 在某人的大学时期

1599. rhythm [ˈrɪðəm] [rhy·thm] ☆★★★★

n. 节奏，韵律	The poetry has cadence or rhythm in most situations. 大多数情况下，诗歌有韵律或节奏。
同义字词	pattern, beat, tempo
衍生字词	▲ rhythmic adj. 有节奏的，有韵律的
	▲ rhythmless adj. 无韵律的
高分秘诀	▲ cadence n. 节奏，韵律
	▲ in most situations 在大多数情况下

1600. ridicule [ˈrɪdɪkjul] [ridi·cule] ☆★★★★

v. 嘲笑，嘲弄	Her sister poured ridicule on her boyfriend's idiot. 她姐姐嘲弄她的男友是白痴。
同义字词	mock, make fun of, scoff
反义字词	admire, adore, appreciate
衍生字词	▲ ridiculous adj. 荒唐的，可笑的
	▲ ridiculer n. 嘲笑者
	▲ lay oneself open to ridicule 使自己成为笑柄
高分秘诀	▲ pour ridicule on someone 尽情地嘲笑某人
	▲ idiot n. 傻子，笨蛋

1601. rigid [ˈrɪdʒɪd] [rig·id] ☆☆★★★

adj. 坚硬的，不易弯曲的	Habits have ossified into rigid dogma. 习惯已僵化为一成不变的教条。
同义字词	stiff, strict, severe
衍生字词	▲ rigidity n. 僵化，死板
	▲ rigid ideas 固执的看法

rhythm ~ rip

| 高分秘诀 | ▲ habit n. 习惯，习性
▲ dogma n. 教条，教义 |

1602. rigorous [ˈrɪgərəs] [rig·or·ous] ☆☆★★★

adj. 严格的，苛刻的	He makes a rigorous study of the animals in the area. 他对该地的动物进行完整缜密的研究。
同义字词	stringent, strict, hard
反义字词	undemanding, lax, relaxed
衍生字词	▲ rigor n. 严酷，严格，严厉 ▲ rigorously adv. 严格地，苛刻地
高分秘诀	▲ make a rigorous study of 对……做缜密的研究

1603. rinse [rɪns] [rinse] ☆☆★★★

v. 用清水冲洗，漱	I rinsed the clothes that I'm going to wear tomorrow. 我清洗了我明天要穿的衣服。
同义字词	gargle, rinsing, wash
衍生字词	▲ negative resist rinse 负光阻剂清洗剂 ▲ reclaim rinse 漂洗回收 ▲ spray rinse 喷淋洗涤
高分秘诀	▲ rinse the clothes 漂洗衣服 ▲ the next day 第二天

1604. riot [ˈraɪət] [ri·ot] ☆★★★★

n. 暴动，骚乱	His arrest touched off a riot. 他被捕后引起一阵骚动。
同义字词	commotion, rebellion
高分秘诀	▲ arrest v. 逮捕，拘留 ▲ touch off 引起，激起，触发

1605. rip [rɪp] [rip] ★★★★★

v. 撕，撕裂	They ripped us off in that country. 那个国家的人敲我们竹杠。
同义字词	tear, rend, break

衍生字词	▲ rip-roaring adj. 喧闹的，闹嚷嚷的
高分秘诀	▲ rip off 敲诈
	▲ country n. 国家，国土

1606. roam [rom] [roam]　　★★★★

v. 漫游，漫步	The couple roamed about in the beautiful avenue. 这对夫妻在漂亮的林荫大道上漫步。
同义字词	wander, ramble, stroll, meander
衍生字词	▲ roamer n. 漫步行走的人或动物
	▲ couple n. 夫妻，情侣
	▲ roam about 漫步于……

1607. roar [rɔr] [roar]　　★★★★

n. 吼，轰鸣	The roar of the traffic made us very annoyed. 往来车辆的喧闹声使我们很烦。
同义字词	bellow, rumble, boom
衍生字词	▲ roar one down 大声喊叫得使某人停止讲话
	▲ a roaring success 巨大的成功
高分秘诀	▲ the roar of the traffic 往来车辆的喧闹声
	▲ make someone annoyed 使某人烦闷

1608. roast [rost] [roast]　　★★★★

v. 烤，烘，嘲讽	The dogs and cats in the yard lie in the sun and roast. 院子里的狗狗和猫咪躺在太阳下取暖。
同义字词	bake, toast, laugh at
衍生字词	▲ roast-reaction n. 焙燃反应
	▲ donkey roast 盛大的节日集会或庆祝会
	▲ rule the roast 做主人，当家
高分秘诀	▲ yard n. 院子
	▲ lie in the sun and roast 躺在太阳下取暖

1609. robust [rə`bʌst] [ro·bust]　　★★★

| adj. 强壮的，健壮的 | A robust faith about love is not easy to be broken.
关于爱的坚定诺言不容易被打破。 |
| 同义字词 | strong, healthy, vigorous |

roam ~ rote

反义字词	dainty, fragile, frail, light	
衍生字词	▲ robust work 强体力劳动 ▲ robust coffee 浓咖啡	
高分秘诀	▲ a robust faith 坚定的诺言 ▲ be easy to do something 容易做某事	

1610. roost [rust] [roost] ☆☆★★★

n. 栖息处，鸟巢	Look! There is a fledgling in the roost of this tree. 看！这棵树上的鸟窝里有只雏鸟。
v. 栖息	It's Bobby's wife who really rules the roost in that family. 在鲍比家中，真正当家的是他的老婆。
同义字词	alight, perch, rest
衍生字词	▲ rooster n. 公鸡 ▲ come home to roost 得到报应 ▲ go to roost 上床睡觉
高分秘诀	▲ fledgling n. 雏鸟 ▲ rule the roost 当家，称雄

1611. rotate [`rotet] [ro·tate] ☆☆★★★

v. 轮流，（使）旋转	It is a nature rule that the earth rotates round the sun. 地球绕太阳转是个自然规律。
同义字词	alternate, turn, swirl
衍生字词	▲ rotate men in office 职员轮流值班 ▲ rotate crops 轮作农作物 ▲ rotational adj. 旋转的，轮流的 ▲ rotatory motion 旋转运动

1612. rote [rot] [rote] ☆☆★★★

n. 死记硬背，生搬硬套	The diligent boy recited the grammar by rote. 这个勤奋的男孩死背这个语法。
衍生字词	▲ rote learning 机械学习 ▲ learn by rote 由死记硬背来记忆
高分秘诀	▲ diligent adj. 勤奋的，勤勉的

1613. routine [ruˋtin] [rou·tine]   ☆★★★★

n. 常规, 惯例 — We must introduce some system into our office routine to constrain ourselves.
我们必须在日常公务中建立一些制度来约束自己。

adj. 常规的, 日常的 — It is our routine work to do a cleaning on Thursday afternoon.
周四下午大扫除是我们例行的工作。

同义字词: convention, habit, custom

衍生字词:
▲ routinely **adv.** 例行公事地
▲ routine-time **n.** 授课时间
▲ go into one's routine 说自己照例要说的话

高分秘诀:
▲ introduce **v.** 介绍
▲ system **n.** 系统, 体系

1614. rudimentary [ˌrudəˋmɛntəri] [ru·di·men·tary]   ☆☆★★★

adj. 基本的, 初步的 — I have only a rudimentary grasp of advanced Mathematics.
我对高等数学仅有初步的了解。

同义字词: primitive, unsophisticated, undeveloped

衍生字词:
▲ a rudimentary knowledge of anatomy 解剖学的基本知识
▲ have a rudimentary grasp of chemistry 化学初步知识

高分秘诀:
▲ have a rudimentary grasp of... ……的初步知识
▲ advanced Mathematics 高等数学

1615. rugged [ˋrʌgɪd] [rug·ged]   ☆☆★★★

adj. 高低不平的, 崎岖的 — The visitors who got lost walked on the rugged country road.
迷路的游客走在崎岖不平的乡村小路上。

同义字词: even, smooth, polished

衍生字词:
▲ rugged manners 粗犷而朴实的态度
▲ rugged honesty 率直

高分秘诀:
▲ get lost 迷路
▲ walk on the road 在路上走着

1616. ruin [ˋrʊɪn] [ru·in]   ★★★★★

v. 破坏, 毁灭 — He ruined his prospects by cheating in the exam.
他因考试作弊而断送前途。

routine ~ rustic

同义字词	destroy, devastate, exterminate
反义字词	renew, renovate, restore
衍生字词	▲ ruins n. 废墟，遗迹 ▲ in ruins 成为废墟 ▲ ruin oneself 毁掉自己
高分秘诀	▲ prospect n. 前途 ▲ cheat in the exam 在考试中作弊

1617. rumble [ˈrʌmbl] [rum·ble] ☆★★★★

v. 发出低沉的隆隆声	The thunder rumbled in the distance predicts the storm's coming. 远处雷声隆隆暗示暴风雨的来临。
n. 隆隆声	A rumble scared the little girl and made her begin to cry. 轰隆隆的响声把这个小女孩吓哭了。
同义字词	roar, growl, roll
高分秘诀	▲ thunder n. 雷声 ▲ in the distance 在远处 ▲ made sb. do something 使某人做某事

1618. rupture [ˈrʌptʃə] [rup·ture] ☆★★★★

n. 断裂，断绝	The rupture of a gas tank usually cause a smother to people in the house. 气罐的突然破裂往往造成屋内的人窒息。
v. 破裂，不和	He'll rupture a muscle if he goes on lifting the heavy things! 他要是继续抬重物的话，将会拉伤肌肉！
同义字词	break, burst, crack
衍生字词	▲ rupture a muscle 拉伤肌肉 ▲ rupture oneself 疝
高分秘诀	▲ gas tank 气罐 ▲ smother v. 窒息，透不过气来 ▲ rupture a muscle 拉伤肌肉 ▲ go on doing sth. 继续做某事

1619. rustic [ˈrʌstɪk] [rus·tic] ☆★★★★

| adj. 乡村的 | The girl is pretty and rustic when you look at her carefully.
当你仔细看这个女孩时，（你会发现）她其实是个漂亮的乡下女孩。 |

同义字词	rural, bucolic, countrified, plain, provincial
反义字词	citified, civic, metropolitan, municipal
衍生字词	▲ rusticity n. 乡村特点，乡村气息 ▲ rustic charm 质朴，田园般的魅力
高分秘诀	▲ carefully adv. 小心地，谨慎地

Ss 托福 TOEFL iBT

托福(TOEFL)的测验对象为母语为非英语的人
申请入学美加地区大学或研究所时，托福成绩单是必备文件之一。

- n. 名词
- v. 动词
- adj. 形容词
- adv. 副词
- prep. 介词
- art. 冠词
- pron. 代词
- aux. 助词
- conj. 连词

Ss 托福 TOEFL iBT

托福(TOEFL)的测验对象为母语为非英语的人
申请入学美加地区大学或研究所时,托福成绩单是必备文件之一。

1620. sacred [ˈsekrɪd] [sa·cred]   ☆☆★★

adj. 宗教的,祭祀的,神圣的	A promise is sacred. 承诺是神圣的。
高分秘诀	▲ make a promise 答应,允诺 ▲ hold a promise sacred 信守诺言

1621. saga [ˈsɑɡə] [sa·ga] ☆☆★★

n. 传说,冒险故事	Young Chloe's favorite movies are Twilight Saga. 小克柔依最喜欢的电影就是"暮光之城。"
同义字词	anecdote, epic, tale, yarn
高分秘诀	▲ biography n. 传记 ▲ Twilight Saga 暮光之城(小说,电影名称)

1622. salient [ˈselɪənt] [sa·li·ent] ☆☆★★

n. 凸角,突出部分	The salient points of my speech are summed up in this report. 这份报告概括了我演说的重点。
adj. 显著的,突出的	This program could be applied to the most of salient pole machines. 该程序适用于大多数常规结构的突极同步电机。

1623. saline [ˈselaɪn] [sa·line] ☆☆☆★★

n. 盐湖,盐井	Not even a grass grows in the saline. 盐田上寸草不生。
adj. 盐的,含盐分的	The nurse diluted the drug with saline water. 护士用生理盐水把药物稀释。

1624. sanctimonious [ˌsæŋktəˈmonɪəs] [sanc·ti·mo·ni·ous]

adj. 假装神圣的,伪装虔诚的	There is always a sanctimonious smile on his face. 他总是假仁假义地微笑。

sacred ~ sarcastic

衍生字词	▲ sanctimoniousness n. 伪善，道貌岸然
	▲ sanctimoniously adv. 伪善地
高分秘诀	▲ a sanctimonious smile 假仁假义的微笑
	▲ a sanctimonious remark 假仁假义的言词
	▲ a sanctimonious person 假仁假义的人
	▲ a sanctimonious letter 假仁假义的抗议信

1625. sanction [ˈsæŋkʃən] [sanc·tion] ☆★★★★

n. 核准, 约束力	The UN imposed economic sanctions against Iraq.
	联合国对伊拉克实施经济制裁。
v. 认可, 赞许	The law would not sanction his second marriage.
	法律不会承认他的第二次婚姻。
高分秘诀	▲ economic sanctions 经济制裁
	▲ legal sanction 法律制裁

1626. sanctuary [ˈsæŋktʃuˌɛrɪ] [sanc·tu·ar·y] ☆★★★★

n. 圣所, 避难所	It is a classic sanctuary in which the rationalist fancy may take refuge.
	这是一栋古典的圣殿，理性主义者可以在此受到庇护。
高分秘诀	▲ sanctum n. 圣地，密室
	▲ sanctity n. 神圣
	▲ rationalist n. 理性主义者
	▲ take refuge 避难
	▲ holy place 圣所，圣殿

1627. sanitary [ˈsænəˌtɛrɪ] [san·i·tar·y] ☆★★★★

adj. (有关)卫生的	He worked hard to improve the sanitary conditions of the slums.
	他努力工作以改善贫民窟的卫生条件。
同义字词	hygienic, prophylactic
高分秘诀	▲ slums n. 贫民窟
	▲ slum dog millionaire（电影）贫民百万富翁

1628. sarcastic [sɑrˈkæstɪk] [sar·cas·tic] ☆★★★★

adj. 讽刺的, 挖苦的	I felt completely squashed by her sarcastic comment.
	她对我冷嘲热讽，害我一句话都说不出来。

衍生字词	▲ satire n. 讽刺，讽刺文学
	▲ satirist n. 讽刺作家
	▲ satiric adj. 讽刺的，挖苦的
高分秘诀	▲ squash v. 硬塞，挤扁
	▲ comment n. 闲话，评论

1629. saturate [ˈsætʃəˌret] [sat·u·rate] ☆☆★★★

v. 浸透，使湿透	I went out in the rain and got saturated.
	我冒雨出门，浑身都湿透了。

1630. scale [skel] [scale] ☆★★★★

v. 攀登，向上	He learned to scale a rock face from his father.
	他向他父亲学习攀岩的技巧。

| 高分秘诀 | ▲ rock face 岩壁 |

1631. scan [skæn] [scan] ☆☆★★★

v. 扫描，审视	A fire lookout scanned the hills carefully.
	火警监视员仔细查看山区。

| 高分秘诀 | ▲ a fire lookout 火警监视员 |

1632. scapegoat [ˈskepˌgot] [scape·goat] ☆★★★★

n. 替罪羔羊，代人受过的人	The old curmudgeon found a new scapegoat and that let me out.
	那个老守财奴找到一个新的替罪羔羊，这样我就可以脱身了。

| 高分秘诀 | ▲ curmudgeon n. 脾气坏的人 |

1633. scarce [skɛrs] [scarce] ☆★★★★

adj. 缺乏的，稀有的	Economics is the study of how people choose to use scarce or limited productive resources.
	经济学是研究大家如何抉择，使用有限的生产性资源的学科。

| 同义字词 | rare, limited, barely |
| 高分秘诀 | ▲ productive resources 生产性资源 |

1634. scatter [ˈskætɚ] [scat·ter] ☆★★★★

n. 消散，散播	A scatter of applause reached him when he ended his speech.
	演讲结束时他听到稀稀落落的掌声。
v. 使分散，扩散	The crowd scattered when the police charged.
	当警察冲过来时，人群便散开了。

saturate ~ scour

同义字词　sprinkle, disseminate, spread

1635. scavenger [ˈskævɪndʒə] [scav·eng·er]　☆☆★★★

n. 清道夫, 清除剂　My cat is acting like a scavenger — she is constantly searching for food and when she finds it, she eats like a snake.
我的猫咪行为简直像清道夫，不断地在找食物，找到后像蛇般一口就吞下去。

同义字词　magpie, pack rat

1636. scent [sɛnt] [scent]　☆★★★★

n. 气味, 香味　The policemen easily picked up the scent of the murderer.
警察毫不费力地搜查到谋杀者的线索。

同义字词　odor, fragrance, perfume

1637. schedule [ˈskɛdʒʊl] [sched·ule]　★★★★★

n. 时间表, 计划表　The fog disrupted airline schedules.
这场大雾扰乱了航空公司的时刻表。

v. 预定, 安排　One of the scheduled events is a talk on flower arranging.
安排的活动中有一项是插花艺术讲座。

同义字词　timetable, agenda, arrange

1638. scotch [skɑtʃ] [scotch]　☆★★★★

v. 镇压, 粉碎　His arrival in the capital scotched reports that he was dead.
他抵达首都并粉碎了他已经死亡的传言。

adj. 苏格兰人的, 苏格兰语的　Anyway, there never was any one more Scotch in the world.
不管怎样，全世界没有人比他更像个苏格兰人。

衍生字词　▲ Scotch whisky 苏格兰威士忌
　　　　　▲ Have a Scotch! 喝一杯苏格兰威士忌！

1639. scour [skaʊr] [scour]　☆★★★★

v. 冲刷, 擦掉　The torrent scoured a gully down the hillside.
那急流顺山坡而下冲出一条水沟.

同义字词　scrub, rub, wear away

1640. scout [skaʊt] [scout]   ☆★★★★

| n. 侦察，侦察员 | He had a scout round to see what he could find.
他四处搜寻看看能找到些什么。 |

| v. 侦察 | They scouted around for some antiques to furnish their new apartment.
他们到处搜罗一些古董装饰新居。 |

同义字词　probe, hunt, search out

高分秘诀
▲ scoutmaster 童子军队长
▲ scout around/about 到处寻找某人／某物
▲ antique n. 古董，古玩 adj. 古代的，过时的
▲ a good scout 好人

1641. scramble [ˋskræmbl] [scram·ble]　☆★★★★

| v. 搅乱，攀登 | He was knocked down in the scramble, but he quickly picked himself up and dusted himself down.
他在争抢中被撞倒，但很快就站起来，并拍掉身上的灰尘。 |

同义字词　jumble, mix

衍生字词
▲ scrambled egg 炒蛋
▲ scrambler n. 爬行者，扰频器
▲ knock down 撞倒，击倒
▲ dust n. 灰尘

1642. scrap [skræp] [scrap]　☆★★★★

| n. 废料，残余物 | The scrap merchant has a machine which crushes cars.
那位贩卖废品的商人有个压碎汽车的机器。 |

| v. 将……作为废物，废弃 | It is high time that the old plane was scrapped.
这架旧飞机该报废了。 |

同义字词　garbage, litter, trash

衍生字词
▲ scrappy adj. 杂乱的，不完全的
▲ scrapper n. 好打架的人，拳击手
▲ crush v. 压碎，弄皱
▲ scratch... away/off 刮去……
▲ scratch paper 便条纸
▲ cover with 覆盖
▲ thorn n. 刺，荆棘

scout ~ seclude

1643. scrape [skrep] [scrape] ☆☆★★★

v. 刮，擦，擦去

I had scraped out a sticky saucepan.
我已经把锅垢刮掉了。

同义字词 brush, grade, gaze, pinch

高分秘诀
▲ saucepan **n.** 深底平锅
▲ sticky **adj.** 黏的，棘手的

1644. scratch [skrætʃ] [scratch] ☆★★★★

v. 挠，搔

Her hands were covered with scratches from the thorns.
她手上有很多被刺划伤的伤痕。

1645. scrupulous [ˈskrupjələs] [scru·pu·lous] ☆☆☆★★

adj. 小心谨慎的，细心的

His teaching style is scrupulous about every detail.
他的教学风格一丝不苟。

同义字词 fastidious, careful, meticulous

反义字词 unprincipled, unscrupulous

1646. sculpt [skʌlpt] [sculpt] ★★★★★

v. 雕刻，造型品

My teacher selected a particularly pleasing form from his sketches and then sculpts the intricate shape in wood or plastic.
我的老师从草稿图中选择一个特别令人满意的图形，然后用木头或塑胶雕塑出精巧复杂的形状。

同义字词 carve, model, shape, chisel

1647. seam [sim] [seam] ☆★★★★

n. 接缝，缝合线

The seam of her skirt ripped.
她裙子的接缝裂开了。

同义字词 crease, crinkle, furrow, line, wrinkle

1648. seclude [sɪˈklud] [se·clude] ☆★★★★

v. 使隔离，隔开

She secludes herself from the world to work in her study.
她与世隔绝，在书房埋头苦读。

| 同义字词 | isolate, separate, sequester |

高分秘诀
▲ seclusion n. 独处，隐居
▲ secluded adj. 很少有人去的或见的
▲ secludes oneself from the world 与世隔绝

1649. secondary [ˈsɛkənˌdɛrɪ] [se·con·dary] ☆★★★★

| adj. 中级的，次要的 | Such considerations are secondary to our main aim of improving efficiency.
对于我们提高效率的主要目的，这些想法都是次要的。 |

高分秘诀　▲ consideration n. 考虑的事，体贴，关心

1650. secrete [sɪˈkrit] [se·crete] ☆★★★★

| v. 分泌，使隐秘 | Saliva is secreted by glands in the mouth.
唾液是由口腔的唾液腺分泌出来的。 |

1651. secular [ˈsɛkjələ] [se·cu·lar] ☆★★★★

| adj. 世俗的，现世的 | We live in a secular age, and I'm a product of it.
我们生活在一个世俗的时代，我是这个时代的产物。 |

| 同义字词 | mundane, earthly, worldly |

衍生字词
▲ secularism n. 世俗主义
▲ secularist n. 世俗主义者
▲ secularize v. 世俗化

1652. secure [sɪˈkjʊr] [se·cure] ★★★★★

| v. 使安全，保卫 | It is necessary to secure our shop against the dangers of the robbery.
采取针对抢劫的防范措施是非常必要的。 |
| adj. 安全的，放心的 | Now my house is secure against burglary.
现在我的房子很安全，不必担心被盗窃。 |

| 同义字词 | attach, fasten, fix |

1653. sedentary [ˈsɛdn̩ˌtɛrɪ] [sed·en·tar·y] ☆☆★★★

| adj. 久坐的，土生的 | Sedentary habits often interfere with health.
长坐不动的习惯往往有害身体健康。 |

| 同义字词 | unmoving, motionless |

高分秘诀
▲ a sedentary worker 工作需要久坐的人
▲ lead a sedentary life 过着久坐不动的生活
▲ interfere with 干扰……，干涉……

secondary ~ sequence

1654. sediment ['sɛdəmənt] [se·di·ment] ☆☆★★★

n. 沉积物,沉淀物　As with all wines of premium quality, this wine may produce some sediment.
如所有优质葡萄酒一样,这款酒也存在少许沉淀物质。

1655. seduce [sɪ'djus] [se·duce] ☆★★★★

v. 诱惑,引诱　Higher salaries are seducing many students into industry.
在高薪利诱之下,许多学生进入产业界。

同义字词　tempt, entice, lure

1656. segregate ['sɛgrɪˌget] [seg·re·gate] ☆★★★★

v. 分离,隔离　Why should the handicapped be segregated from the able-bodied?
为什么要把伤残人士和身体健康的人分开?

衍生字词　▲ segregation **n.** 隔离
▲ a policy of racial segregation　种族隔离政策

1657. seismic ['saɪzmɪk] [seis·mic] ☆☆★★★

adj. 地震的,由地震引起的　Seismic sections show the response of the earth to seismic waves.
地震剖面是地壳对地震波的回应。

高分秘诀　▲ section **n.** 剖面,截面
▲ seismic waves　地震波

1658. sensible ['sɛnsəbl] [sen·si·ble] ☆★★★★

adj. 有感觉的,明智的　The seriously wounded soldier was temporarily speechless but still sensible.
那位受重伤的士兵暂时无法说话但仍有知觉。

同义字词　intelligent, logical, rational

高分秘诀　▲ seriously **adv.** 严重地
▲ speechless **adj.** 说不出话的

1659. sequence ['sikwəns] [se·quence] ☆★★★★

n. 序列,顺序　Historians deal with events in historical sequence.
历史学家按照历史上的先后顺序研究大事件。

同义字词　continuation, progression, series, succession

高分秘诀　▲ historian **n.** 历史学家
▲ in historical sequence　历史顺序

1660. serene [sə`rin] [se·rene] ☆★★★★

| adj. 宁静的,安详的 | In spite of the panic, she remained serene and in control.
尽管人心惶惶,她却泰然自若。 |

同义字词　calm, pacific, peaceful, quiet, tranquil, untroubled

高分秘诀　▲ in spite of 尽管
　　　　　▲ in control 在控制之下

1661. serrated [`sɛretɪd] [ser·rated] ☆☆★★★

| adj. 锯齿状的,有锯齿的 | He was cutting the vegetable with a knife with serrated blade.
他正在用一把锯齿刀切菜。 |

1662. sewerage [`soɔrɪdʒ] [sew·er·age]

| n. 排水设备,污水 | The acid waste waters are discharged into a sump or the sewerage system.
酸性废水被送往销毁池或污水系统。 |

高分秘诀　▲ acid adj. 酸的,酸性物质

1663. shatter [`ʃætɚ] [shat·ter] ☆☆★★★

| v. 打碎,粉碎 | This event shattered all my previous ideas.
这件事推翻了我以前的所有想法。 |

同义字词　break, destroy, fragment, smash

1664. shear [ʃɪr] [shear] ☆☆★★★

| v. 剪,修剪 | The assembly had been shorn of its legislative powers.
议会被剥夺立法权。 |

同义字词　cut, clip, crop, cut off

1665. shed [ʃɛd] [shed] ☆☆★★★

| v. 流出,放射 | This method can help students shed inhibitions.
这一方法能帮助学生去除顾虑。 |

同义字词　radiate, throw off, cast

1666. shield [`ʃild] [shield] ☆★★★★

| v. 庇护,保护
n. 盾 | She lied to the court to shield her boyfriend.
她对法庭说谎以保护她男友。 |

serene ~ sidle

| 同义字词 | protect, guard, defend, shelter |
| 高分秘诀 | ▲ court n. 法院，法庭 |

1667. shot [ʃɑt] [shot] ★★★★★

n. 射击，射门	A shot in which figures appear small against their background is a long shot. 人在画面中显得很小的镜头叫远景镜头。
同义字词	blastoff, snap, shooting
衍生字词	▲ shot (at...doing...) 试图……，设法…… ▲ a shot of vodka 一点伏特加 ▲ an action shot 连续镜头 ▲ a shotgun wedding 被迫举行的婚礼
高分秘诀	▲ long shot 远景镜头 ▲ figure n. 轮廓，图像

1668. shrink [ʃrɪŋk] [shrink] ★★★★★

| v. 收缩，缩小 | He did not shrink from the personal exertions required.
这个人对他应尽的个人努力不会畏缩不前。 |
| 高分秘诀 | ▲ personal exertions 个人努力 |

1669. shrivel [`ʃrɪvl] [shriv·el] ☆★★★★

| v. 枯萎，皱缩 | Their seed ripens, and soon they turn brown and shrivel up.
它们的种子熟透了，不久就会枯萎。 |
| 同义字词 | shrink, wither, wrinkle |

1670. shuffle [`ʃʌfl] [shuf·fle] ☆☆★★★

| v. 拖着走，搞乱 | Don't shuffle your own responsibility onto others.
不要把你的责任推诿给他人。 |

1671. sidle [`saɪdl] [si·dle] ☆☆★★★

| v. 侧身而行，悄悄地走 | He sidled past, trying to seem casual.
他悄悄地溜过去，装作漫不经心的样子。 |
| 高分秘诀 | ▲ casual adj. 漫不经心的，随便的 |

1672. sidestep [ˈsaɪdˌstɛp] [side·step] ☆★★★★

v. 横跨一步躲闪, 回避

The drunk sidesteps clumsily when the bull charged at him.
当公牛向这个醉汉冲过去的时候，他笨拙地躲到一边。

高分秘诀 ▲ clumsily **adv.** 笨拙地

1673. signify [ˈsɪgnəˌfaɪ] [sig·ni·fy] ☆☆★★★

v. 表示, 意味

He signified his approval with a smile.
他笑了笑表示赞成。

同义字词 denote, mean, indicate

1674. simulate [ˈsɪmjəˌlet] [sim·u·late] ☆☆★★★

v. 假装, 冒充

Many believe artificial soils do not simulate natural soils.
许多人相信人造土并不像天然土。

高分秘诀 ▲ artificial **adj.** 人造的，模拟的

1675. sinuous [ˈsɪnjuəs] [sin·u·ous] ☆☆★★★

adj. 蜿蜒的, 迂回的

We moved along the sinuous gravel road.
我们沿着这条蜿蜒曲折的碎石路前进。

高分秘诀 ▲ gravel road 碎石路

1676. skeptic [ˈskɛptɪk] [skep·tic] ☆★★★★

n. 无神论者, 怀疑论者

He is an ingrained skeptic.
他是一个天生多疑的人。

1677. skimp [skɪmp] [skimp] ☆☆★★★

v. 舍不得给, 节俭

We have to skimp on money to buy fuel.
我们不得不省钱去买燃料。

同义字词 scant, scrimp, stint

1678. skip [skɪp] [[skip] ★★★★★

v. 跳, 蹦

The button allows you to skip an entire set of related screens.
按此按钮可以跳过整个相关荧幕组。

sidestep ~ sluggish

1679. skyrocket [ˈskaɪˌrɑkɪt] [sky·rock·et] ☆☆★★★

v. 猛涨，突增

The price of materials is skyrocketing because of the inflation.
物价由于通货膨胀而猛增。

高分秘诀　▲ inflation **n.** 膨胀，通货膨胀

1680. slander [ˈslændɚ] [slan·der] ☆☆★★★

n. 诽谤，诽谤罪

It's a malignant slander to me.
这是对我恶意的诽谤。

v. 诽谤，诋毁

They slander us that we have stolen their corporate secrets.
他们诽谤我们窃取他们公司的机密。

同义字词　defamation, malign, defame, vilify

1681. slender [ˈslɛndɚ] [slen·der] ☆★★★★

adj. 苗条的，纤细的

She is a slender, graceful ballet-dancer.
她是一个苗条而动作优美的芭蕾舞演员。

同义字词　slim, thin, frail, slight

1682. slime [slaɪm] [slime] ☆★★★★

n. 黏土，黏液

Their skin produces a slime that helps to keep it moist.
它们的皮肤产生一种黏液，帮助保持皮肤湿润。

同义字词　mire, muck, mud, slush

1683. slothful [ˈsloθfəl] [sloth·ful] ☆★★★★

adj. 怠惰的，迟钝的，懒惰的

If we work hard, we will have a better life than the incompetent and slothful.
如果努力工作，我们的生活就会过得比无能者和懒惰虫好。

同义字词　lazy, sluggish, indolent

1684. sluggish [ˈslʌgɪʃ] [slug·gish] ☆☆★★★

adj. 偷懒的，迟钝的

Sluggish demand in the world's biggest market is the main reason for the abrupt reversal in Asia's fortunes.
全球最大市场的需求减缓导致亚洲经济突然下降。

同义字词　slow, lethargic, inactive

1685. slumber ['slʌmbɚ] [slum·ber] ☆☆★★★

n. 睡眠，沉睡状态

I need a deep slumber to help me forget the irritating things.
我需要沉沉地睡一觉，忘记不愉快的事。

[同义字词] sleep, doze, rest, snooze

1686. smother ['smʌðɚ] [smoth·er] ☆★★★★

v. 使窒息，闷住

The prisoner of war was smothered to death.
战俘因窒息致死。

[同义字词] prisoner of war 战俘

1687. smuggle ['smʌgl] [smug·gle] ☆★★★★

v. 偷运，私运

He was arrested for smuggling out currency.
他因私携货币出境而被捕。

[同义字词] contraband, illicit trade, owling

1688. snap [snæp] [snap] ☆★★★★

v. 咬，抓，突然折断

The dog snapped at the boy's ankles.
狗对准男孩的脚踝猛地咬下去。

[同义字词] break, crack, snatch, split

[衍生字词]
▲ snappish **adj.** 脾气暴躁的，爱生气的
▲ snappy **adj.** 精力充沛的，活蹦乱跳的
▲ snap at... 对……发飙
▲ snap... out 抢购……/迅速抓住……
▲ snap out of 迅速从……中恢复过来
▲ ankle **n.** 踝关节

1689. snippet ['snɪpɪt] [snip·pet] ☆★★★★

n. 片断，小碎片

On the bus I heard this interesting snippet of conversation.
我在公交车上听到这小段有趣的谈话。

[同义字词] piece, fragment

[衍生字词]
▲ splash water about 四处泼水
▲ splash down（尤指太空船）溅落
▲ splash out 心血来潮地或随意地花钱（于某事物上）

slumber ~ solitary

1690. snug [snʌg] [snug]
☆☆★★★

adj. 舒适的，整洁的
Everything in this villa is thriving and snug.
这栋别墅的一切都显得生机蓬勃并且井然有序。

同义字词　cozy, comfortable, homelike, warm

1691. sociable [ˈsoʃəbl] [so·cia·ble]
☆☆★★★

adj. 好交际的，友善的
Americans are sociable and gregarious.
美国人好交际且喜群居。

同义字词　gregarious, friendly, affable

1692. solder [ˈsɑdɚ] [sol·der]
☆☆★★★

v. 焊接，焊在一起
Two pieces of metals are soldered together with a high melting point.
用高熔点将两块金属焊在一起。

同义字词　weld, bind, cement, fasten

1693. solemn [ˈsɑləm] [sol·emn]
☆☆★★★

adj. 严肃的，庄严的
He was very solemn and refrained from talking.
他很严肃并且沉默寡言。

同义字词　serious, somber, sober

1694. solicit [səˈlɪsɪt] [so·lic·it]
☆☆★★★

v. 请求，乞求
Many beggars disposed to solicit this rich and generous man.
许多乞丐想向这个富有而大方的人乞讨。

同义字词　appeal, plead for, beg

1695. solidarity [ˌsɑləˈdærətɪ] [so·li·da·ri·ty]
☆☆★★★

n. 团结，团结一致
The student leaders declared they must show solidarity with the strikers.
学生领袖声称他们要与罢工工人团结一致。

同义字词　disunion, dissociation

1696. solitary [ˈsɑləˌtɛrɪ] [so·li·ta·ry]
☆☆★★★

adj. 孤独的，独居的
Far-flung solitary villages were on the mountainside.
偏远冷清的村落散落在山腰上。

|高分秘诀| isolated, alone, unaccompanied

1697. soluble [ˈsɑljəbl] [sol·u·ble] ☆☆★★★

adj. 溶解的，可以解决的

Tablets can be soluble in water easily.
药片在水中很容易溶解。

|同义字词| ▲ unsolvable **adj.** 不能解决的

1698. soothe [suð] [sooth] ☆★★★★

v. 使（某人情绪）平静，安慰

A bit of embrocation will soothe your bruised knee.
涂一点药剂可让你瘀青的膝部消肿。

|同义字词| quiet, alleviate, mitigate, relieve, calm

1699. sophisticated [səˈfɪstɪˌketɪd] [so·phis·ti·cat·ed] ☆★★★★

adj. 诡辩的

The astronauts used the sophisticated devices in spacecraft.
太空人在太空梭上使用最尖端的仪器。

|同义字词| intricate, complex, experienced

1700. soundproof [ˈsaʊndˌpruf] [sound·proof] ☆★★★★

adj. 隔音的

The government is making the standard for soundproof of civil building
政府正在制定住宅隔音标准。

|同义字词| impermeable to noise, insulative

1701. souvenir [ˈsuvəˌnɪr] [sou·ve·nir] ☆★★★★

n. 纪念品

He found a long white scar on his leg, his souvenir of battle.
我发现他腿上有一条长长的白色伤疤，那是战争留下的记号。

|衍生字词| ▲ a souvenir shop for tourists 旅游纪念品商店

1702. sovereign [ˈsɑvrɪn] [sov·er·eign] ☆★★★★

n. 君主

He was then the sovereign of England.
他那时是英国的君主。

adj. 独立自主的，至高无上的

For a brief time that country was a sovereign nation.
一个短暂的时间，那个国家曾是一个主权国家。

|高分秘诀| ▲ a brief time 一个短暂的时间。

soluble ~ spectacle

1703. spangle [ˈspæŋgl] [span·gle]   ☆☆★★★

n. 闪闪发光之物
A spangle used to ornament a dress or costume.
亮片是用来装饰衣服或服装的金属片。

v. 闪烁发光
Tiny shells was spangled on that woman's dress.
那个妇女的礼服上装饰着小贝壳。

> 同义字词　diamante, bespangle, sequin

1704. spanking [ˈspæŋkɪŋ] [spank·ing]   ☆★★★★

adj. 轻快的，敏捷的
He heard a horse approaching at a spanking trot.
他听到一匹马正疾步驰近。

> 同义字词　brisk, lively, merry, snappy

1705. sparse [spɑrs] [sparse]   ☆★★★★

adj. 稀疏的，薄的
The sparse applause did not do justice to the brilliant performance.
这样精彩的演出只获得稀稀落落的掌声并不公平。

> 同义字词　scarce, meager, scanty, thinly

1706. spawn [spɔn] [spawn]   ☆☆★★★

v. 产卵，大量产生
Many new housing estates have spawned everywhere in recent years.
近年来处处涌现新的住宅区。

> 高分秘诀　▲ estate **n.** 住宅区，土地

1707. specify [ˈspɛsəˌfaɪ] [spe·ci·fy]   ★★★★★

v. 具体指定，明确说明
The regulations specify that you may not take a phone in the examination.
规则中明确规定考试不可携带手机。

> 同义字词　detail, designate, define

1708. spectacle [ˈspɛktəkl] [spec·ta·cle]   ☆★★★★

n. 场面，奇观
The sunrise seen from high in the mountains was a tremendous spectacle.
从山上居高远望，日出景象蔚为奇观。

> 高分秘诀　▲ tremendous **adj.** 巨大的，精彩的

1709. spectrum ['spɛktrəm] [spec·trum] ☆★★★★

n. 谱, 光谱 — They could look at the spectra of the light the moons reflected.
他们可以观察到月亮反射的光谱。

衍生字词　▲ the sound spectrum 声谱

1710. speculate ['spɛkjəˌlet] [spec·u·late] ☆★★★★

v. 推测, 沉思 — I wouldn't like to speculate on the reasons for her resignation.
我不愿意猜测她辞职的原因。

同义字词　hypothesize, guess, ponder, consider

1711. spill [spɪl] [spill] ☆★★★★

v. 使溢出, 使散落 — He knocked the bucket over and all the water spilt out.
他撞翻了水桶，水全部流出来了。

衍生字词　▲ spill the beans 说溜嘴

1712. spine [spaɪn] [spine] ☆★★★★

n. 脊椎, 骨气 — He sustained an injury to his spine when he fell off his horse.
他从马上摔了下来，脊椎骨受伤了。

同义字词　backbone, acanthi, thorn, pricker

1713. spiral ['spaɪrəl] [spi·ral] ☆★★★★

adj. 螺旋形的, 盘旋的 — The spiral of rising oli prices and living cost is making our lives more difficult.
油价和物价的交替上升使我们的生活更加困难。

同义字词　rotary, curled, twist

1714. splash [splæʃ] [splash] ☆★★★★

v. 溅, 泼 — The spacecraft splashed down in the Pacific.
那艘太空船迫降在太平洋上。

高分秘诀　▲ spacecraft n. 航天器，太空船

spectrum ~ sprout

1715. spoil [spɔɪl] [spoil] ☆★★★★

v. 损坏, 宠坏

Don't spoil your appetite by eating sweets between meals.
不要在两顿饭之间吃糖果，以免坏了胃口。

1716. spontaneous [spɑnˋtenɪəs] [spon·ta·ne·ous] ☆★★★★

adj. 自发的, 无意识的

We all had a spontaneous gaiety of manner when we were young.
我们小时候都很天真愉快。

|同义字词| instinctive, natural, inherent

1717. spotlight [ˋspɑtˏlaɪt] [spot·light] ☆★★★★

v. 强调, 突出重点

The report has spotlighted real deprivation of the women's rights.
这篇报道披露了妇女权利被剥夺的真相。

|同义字词| highlight, stress, emphasize

1718. sprawl [sprɔl] [sprawl] ☆☆★★★

v. 散乱地延伸

Taipei's Shilin nightmarket is a very sprawl of aisles in a new multi-story complex.
台北的士林夜市是一个占地辽阔、道路四通八达的新建复合式夜市。

|同义字词| extend, stretch, spread, expand

1719. spray [spre] [spray] ☆★★★★

v. 喷洒, 喷涂

The broken glass sprayed over the refugees with from the explosion.
炸碎的玻璃喷溅到难民的身上。

|同义字词| sprinkle, spatter, splash

|高分秘诀|
▲ spray-gun 喷枪
▲ sprayer **n.** 喷雾者
▲ spray... on... 向……喷洒雾状……（液体）
▲ spray paint 喷雾颜料
▲ refugee **n.** 难民
▲ explosion **n.** 爆炸

1720. sprout [spraʊt] [sprout] ☆★★★★

v. 很快地成长, 使发芽

The tree is already sprouting leaves.
这棵树已发出新芽。

| 同义字词 | bud, burgeon, germinate, shoot up |

1721. spur [spɝ] [spur] ☆★★★★

| v. 刺激, 鞭策 | The manager found a spur to improve the efficiency of the worker. 经理找到提高工人效率的刺激动力。 |

| 同义字词 | stimulate, urge, goad, urge |

1722. squarely [ˈskwɛrlɪ] [square·ly] ☆☆★★★

| adv. 坚实地, 坚固地 | This recent tragedy has put the manufacturers of the drug squarely in the dock. 最近发生的这场不幸意外使药品厂商受到指控。 |

| 高分秘诀 | ▲ in the dock 在被告席上 |

1723. squirt [skwɝt] [squirt] ☆★★★★

| v. 喷出, 溅进 | The little girl squirted us with water with her water-pistol. 那个小姑娘用水枪向我们射水。 |

| 高分秘诀 | ▲ water-pistol 水枪 |

1724. stack [stæk] [stack] ☆★★★★

| v. 堆积, 堆满, 堆叠 | My room was stacked with old books and magazines. 我的房间堆满了旧书报。 |

1725. stagger [ˈstæɡɚ] [stag·ger] ☆★★★★

| v. 蹒跚, 摇晃 | The unexpected blow did not stagger his resolution. 这个意外的打击并没有动摇他的决心。 |

| 高分秘诀 | ▲ resolution n. 决心, 决定 |

1726. stagnant [ˈstæɡnənt] [stag·nant] ☆☆★★★

| adj. 停滞的, 迟钝的 | Water lying stagnant in ponds and ditches is very smelly. 池塘和水沟中的死水味道很臭。 |

| 高分秘诀 | ▲ ditch 沟, 管道 |

1727. sustain [sə'sten] [sus·tain] ☆★★★★

v. 支撑，供养

The foundations were not strong enough to sustain the weight of the house.
这片地基不够牢固，无法承受房屋的重量。

同义字词 ▲ foundation 地基，基础，基金会

1728. stalk [stɔk] [stalk] ☆★★★★

v. 跟踪，蔓延

The infatuated fan stalked the celebrity.
那位疯狂的粉丝跟踪这位名人。

同义字词 follow, chase, hunt, search, seek

1729. stamina ['stæmənə] [stam·i·na] ☆★★★★

n. 毅力，精力

It's remarkable that a 90-year-old man has the stamina he had!
一个九十岁的人还有他那样的毅力，真是非比寻常！

高分秘诀 ▲ remarkable adj. 引人注意的，非凡的

1730. staple ['stepl] [sta·ple] ☆★★★★

n. 主要产品，日常必需品

Don't forget staples like sugar and salt when you go to the shops.
你去商店时，不要忘记购买盐和糖之类的必需品。

v. 把……分级，装订

The letter was stapled to the other documents in the file.
把这封信与卷宗的其他文件钉在一起。

同义字词 basic part, basic elements, attach, bind

1731. stardom ['stardəm] [star·dom] ☆★★★★

n. 演员的身份，演员们

His meteoric rise to stardom made him a failure at last.
他的迅速蹿红最终使他一败涂地。

高分秘诀 ▲ meteoric adj. 流星的，昙花一现的

1732. stark [stark] [stark] ☆☆★★★

adj. 严酷的，荒凉的

His actions were in stark contrast to his words.
他的行动与他的话语构成鲜明的对比。

adv. 完全，简直

He came out of the bathroom stark irritated.
他非常愤怒地走了出来。

高分秘诀 ▲ in stark contrast 形成鲜明对比

1733. stash [stæʃ] [stash] ☆☆★★★

v. 藏起来
Not only has Hong Kong's merchandise trade surplus narrowed, but investment income from Hong Kong's stash of foreign reserves has also dropped.
不仅是香港商品贸易的盈余缩水，香港巨额的外汇储备投资收入也在减少。

同义字词 cache, hoard, lay away

1734. stationary [ˈsteʃənˌɛrɪ] [sta·tion·ar·y] ☆★★★★

adj. 不动的，常备军的
Such batteries are already in use, but mainly in stationary applications.
这种电池已被使用，主要应用于静止设备中。

同义字词 fixed, motionless, static, immobile, steady

1735. statistic [stəˈtɪstɪk] [sta·tis·tic] ☆★★★★

n. 统计量，统计数值
Dou you have you any statistics that would support your dissertation?
你有任何统计资料可以支持你的论文吗？

高分秘诀 ▲ dissertation **n.** 论文，专题

1736. statue [ˈstætʃu] [stat·ue] ☆★★★★

n. 雕像，塑像
The Statue of Liberty is a symbol of independence, democracy and freedom.
自由女神像是独立、民主和自由的象征。

高分秘诀 ▲ The Statue of Liberty 自由女神像

1737. stature [ˈstætʃə] [stat·ure] ☆☆★★★

n. 身高，声望
I can endure the false stature, but never the false personality.
我能容忍身材是假的，但是不能容忍虚伪的个性。

同义字词 ▲ endure **v.** 忍受，容忍

1738. statute [ˈstætʃut] [stat·ute] ☆☆★★★

n. 法令，法规
The country's statutes forbade them from holding high office.
国家章程禁止他们担任高级公职。

同义字词 decree, enactment, law, legislation

▲ statutory **adj.** 法定的，法规的
▲ statutorily **adv.** 根据法律条文
▲ statute-book 成文法典，法令全书

1739. steadfast [ˈstɛdˌfæst] [stead·fast]

adj. 坚定的，固定的
His loyalty and support was steadfast, and I was sure of myself.
我深信他对我的忠诚和支持始终不渝。

同义字词 unwavering, constant, resolute

1740. steer [stɪr] [steer]

v. 驾驶，指导
He tried to steer military appropriations through the Congress.
他试图通过国会操纵军款。

同义字词 conduct, direct, guide, regulate

1741. stellar [ˈstɛlɚ] [stel·lar]

adj. 星的，显著的
Astronomers have found that many stellar objects contain hydrogen atoms.
天文学家们已经发现，许多星体上含有氢原子。

1742. sterile [ˈstɛrəl] [ster·ile]

adj. 贫瘠的，不育的
Scientific experiment proved it a sterile debate.
科学实验证明这是一个毫无结果的辩论。

1743. stern [stɝn] [stern]

adj. 苛刻的，严厉的
The police are planning sterner measures to combat crime.
警方正在制订更严厉的措施打击犯罪活动。

高分秘诀 ▲ combat **v.** 战斗，斗争

1744. stifle [ˈstaɪfl] [sti·fle]

v. 使窒息，扼杀
I hate the stifle atmosphere of the royal court and the restrictive rules.
我讨厌皇室中令人窒息的气氛和繁文缛节。

1745. stimulate [ˈstɪmjəˌlet] [stim·u·late]

v. 刺激，激发
An adverse economic forecast will stimulate people to take some action.
不利的经济预报将会刺激人们采取行动。

| 高分秘诀 | ▲ adverse adj. 不利的，有害的 |

1746. sting [stɪŋ] [sting] ☆★★★★

v. 刺，刺痛	Their taunts stung him to action. 他们的冷嘲热讽激怒他采取行动。
同义字词	puncture, prink, inflame
衍生字词	▲ stinger n. 刺 ▲ sting... for... 向……索取……高价 ▲ sting... into... 激怒……，惹恼或冒犯…… ▲ taunt n. 辱，嘲弄

1747. stipend [ˈstaɪpɛnd] [sti·pend]

n. 津贴，奖学金	We hope to be awarded a stipend for further research. 我们希望能被给予进一步研究的费用。
同义字词	allowance, pension

1748. stipulate [ˈstɪpjəˌlet] [stip·u·late] ☆★★★★

v. 规定，约定	He stipulated payment in advance. 他规定预先付款。
高分秘诀	▲ in advance 预先，事先

1749. stitch [stɪtʃ] [stitch] ☆★★★★

v. 缝，固定	She picked up her embroidery and started stitching. 她拿起针线工具开始刺绣。

1750. stocky [ˈstɑkɪ] [stock·y] ☆☆★★★

adj. 矮而结实的，粗壮的	His stocky figure was moving constantly, instructing and exhorting. 他结实的身影不断来回走动，一边发号施令，一边替他们打气。
同义字词	solid, stout, chubby, sturdy

1751. stout [staʊt] [stout] ☆☆★★★

adj. 结实的，勇敢坚定的	This man was vaunting to a stout farmer the excellence of his shoes. 这个人正在向一位身体结实的农夫吹嘘鞋子的优点。

1752. strain [stren] [strain] ☆☆★★★

- **n.** 过度的疲劳，紧张
  Her speech continued in the same dismal strain.
  她以悲伤的语调接着往下叙述。
- **v.** 拉紧，劳累
  The teenagers strain at the leash to escape from the parental control.
  青少年极力想要摆脱父母的控制。

1753. stratum [ˈstretəm] [stra·tum] ☆☆★★★

- **n.** 地层，社会阶层
  Tramps are in a low stratum of society.
  流浪汉处于社会阶级的下层。

1754. strenuous [ˈstrɛnjuəs] [stren·u·ous] ☆★★★★

- **adj.** 奋发的，繁重的
  Because of the bad weather, we have to make a strenuous itinerary.
  因为恶劣的天气，我们得再规划艰难的旅行路线。

  同义字词　arduous, intense, laborious

1755. stretch [strɛtʃ] [stretch] ★★★★★

- **v.** 伸展，伸长
  He woke up, yawned and stretched.
  他一觉醒来，边打呵欠边伸懒腰。

1756. stride [straɪd] [stride] ☆★★★★

- **n.** 大步，一跨步
  He has made enormous strides in his maths this term.
  他本学期数学大有进步。

1757. striking [ˈstraɪkɪŋ] [strik·ing] ★★★★★

- **adj.** 醒目的，打击的
  There is a striking contrast between the two interpretations.
  这两种解释截然不同。

  同义字词　dramatic, outstanding, remarkable

1758. stringent [ˈstrɪndʒənt] [strin·gent] ☆★★★★

- **adj.** 迫切的，严厉的
  The government will take stringent austerity measures.
  政府将制定严格的紧缩措施。

  同义字词　strict, rigorous, severe

1759. strip [strɪp] [strip] ☆★★★★

v. 脱衣，剥夺 The bandits stripped him of all his money.
强盗把他的钱抢光了。

衍生字词 ▲ strip cartoon 连环漫画

1760. strive [straɪv] [strive] ☆★★★★

v. 努力，奋斗 You must understand that and strive against oppression in your life.
你必须懂得这一点并在生活中反抗压迫。

同义字词 endeavor, struggle, fight, battle

1761. stroke [strok] [stroke] ☆★★★★

n. 中风，打击 Various strokes of misfortune led to his ruin.
接二连三的打击让他一蹶不振。

v. 击打，奉承； She stroked the ball cleverly to pass the ball to her opponent.
她巧妙的一击将球打过对手。

1762. stubborn [ˈstʌbən] [stub·born] ☆☆★★★

adj. 倔强的，顽固的 The conservatives show stubborn resistance to change.
保守的人对改革采取顽抗态度。

同义字词 obdurate, headstrong, obstinate, tenacious

衍生字词 ▲ stubbornness **n.** 倔强，顽强
▲ stubborn as a mule 倔强的像头驴
▲ conservative **adj.** 保守的
▲ resistance **n.** 反抗，抵制

1763. stumble [ˈstʌmbl] [stum·ble] ☆★★★★

v. 绊倒，失足 The boy stumbled through his recitation.
这男孩结结巴巴地背诵。

同义字词 falter, flounder, stagger, tumble

衍生字词 ▲ stumble over... （说话、演奏等）出错
▲ stumbling-block 绊脚石
▲ recitation **n.** 背诵，详述

strip ~ submit

1764. stun [stʌn] [stun]

v. 使晕倒, 使惊吓 — I was stunned by the new revelation.
这一新发现使我感到很震惊。

1765. stunt [stʌnt] [stunt]

n. 特技, 噱头, 惊险动作 — Climbing up Taipei 101 was a fine publicity stunt.
攀爬台北101大楼是非常棒的宣传花招。

v. 阻碍成长, 表演特技 — Inadequate food can stunt a child's development.
食物不足会影响儿童的发育。

衍生字词 ▲ stunt man 替身演员

1766. sturdy [ˈstɝdɪ] [stur·dy]

adj. 强健的, 坚固的, 坚决的 — The containers on ships must be stacked, so they should be sturdy in construction.
船上的集装箱必须叠放, 所以应该建造得够坚固。

1767. subduct [səbˈdʌkt] [sub·duct]

v. 减去, 除去 — The continental crust began to subduct beneath the ocean.
大陆地壳开始向海洋俯冲。

1768. subject [ˈsʌbdʒɪkt] [sub·ject]

n. 题目, 主题 — How many subjects are you choosing this semester?
这学期你选几门课程?

v. 使隶属, 使受到 — She was repeatedly subjected to torture.
她不断受到折磨。

1769. submerge [səbˈmɝdʒ] [sub·merge]

v. 沉没, 淹没 — The main argument was submerged in a mass of tedious detail.
大量单调乏味的细节掩盖了主要论点。

1770. submit [səbˈmɪt] [sub·mit]

v. 使服从, 提交 — Counsel for the defence submitted that his client was clearly innocent.
被告的律师辩称其委托人显然是无辜的。

1771. subside [səbˈsaɪd] [sub·side] ☆☆★★★

v. 退落,消失

This place will subside into a sleepy and closed city.
这个地方将衰退成一个死气沉沉、封闭的小城。

[同义字词] die down, appease, mitigate

1772. subsidiary [səbˈsɪdɪˌɛrɪ] [sub·sid·i·ar·y] ☆☆★★★

n. 子公司,附属机构

Our subsidiary is famous for its firm and uncompromising practices in corporate governance.
我们的子公司以廉洁及严谨的作风闻名。

adj. 辅助的,附属的

Rural area handwork subsidiary business is destroyed, the peasant family income decreased.
农村手工业受到摧残,农家收入因而减少。

[同义字词] branch, accessory, adjunct, ancillary
[反义字词] main, important
[衍生字词] ▲ subsidiary money 辅币
▲ subsidiary account 辅助账户
[高分秘诀] ▲ uncompromising **adj.** 不让步的,不妥协的

1773. subsidize [ˈsʌbsəˌdaɪz] [sub·si·dize] ☆★★★★

v. 给予补助金,贿赂

The United States wants to subsidize their armed forces in perpetuity.
美国永久资助他们的军队。

[同义字词] finance, fund
[衍生字词] ▲ subsidy **n.** 补助金,津贴
[高分秘诀] ▲ armed forces 武装部队
▲ perpetuity **n.** 永恒,永久

1774. subsist [səbˈsɪst] [sub·sist] ☆★★★★

v. 生存,存在

We need sufficient wage to subsist a family comfortably.
我们需要能使生活富足的工资。

[同义字词] exist, live, survive
[衍生字词] ▲ subsistence **n.** 生计,存活
▲ sufficient **adj.** 足够的,充分的
▲ subsistence crop 自给作物
▲ subsistence level 勉强糊口的生活水准

subside ~ subtle

1775. substantial [səb`stænʃəl] [sub·stan·tial] ★★★★

adj. 可观的，坚固的
The executives suspected that the figure was substantial.
总裁估计这些数字相当可观。

同义字词： large, significant, sturdy, solid, firm

衍生字词：
▲ substantially **adv.** 相当多地，大大地
▲ substance **n.** 物质，实质

高分秘诀： ▲ executive **n.** 主管，行政官

1776. substantiate [səb`stænʃɪ,et] [sub·stan·ti·ate] ★★★★

v. 使实体化，证实
Do you have any proof to substantiate your alibi?
你有证据表明当时不在犯罪现场吗？

衍生字词：
▲ substantive **adj.** 独立存在的，直接的
▲ substantively **adv.** 实质上
▲ unsubstantiated **adj.** 未被证实的
▲ substantiation **n.** 实体化，证明

高分秘诀： ▲ alibi **n.** 不在场证明

1777. substitute [`sʌbstə,tjut] [sub·sti·tute] ★★★★

v. 代替，取代
Life imprisonment is a better substitute for the death penalty sentence.
无期徒刑是一种代替死刑的比较好的刑罚。

同义字词： ▲ substitute bench 替补席

1778. subterranean [,sʌbtə`renɪən] [sub·ter·ra·ne·an] ★★★★

adj. 地下的，秘密的
This insect grasps a target with its multiple subterranean tentacles.
这只昆虫利用它的秘密触角抓住目标。

衍生字词： ▲ subterranean water 地下水

1779. subtle [`sʌtl] [sub·tle] ★★★

adj. 微妙的，不可思议的
There is just a subtle distinction between the two pictures.
这两幅画之间只存在着细微的差别。

同义字词： slight, delicate, tricky

1780. subtract [səb`trækt] [sub·tract] ☆★★★★

v. 减去，减少

Tom did not hesitate to subtract terms with literal coefficients.
汤姆毫不迟疑地进行文字系数项的相减。

同义字词　reduce, deduct, discount

1781. subversive [səb`vɝsɪv] [sub·ver·sive] ☆☆★★★

adj. 颠覆性的，破坏性的

The new and radical experiments were considered subversive to other countries.
对其他国家来说，这个颠覆性的实验有破坏作用。

1782. succinct [sək`sɪŋkt] [suc·cinct] ☆☆★★★

adj. 简洁的，紧身的

The criminal commenced a succinct but clear narrative of all that occurred during the night.
犯人就夜里发生的事简单而清楚地一一交代。

1783. succumb [sə`kʌm] [suc·cumb] ☆☆★★★

v. 屈服，死

It is easy for youngsters to succumb to temptation.
青少年很容易屈服于诱惑。

1784. sue [su] [sue] ★★★★★

v. 控告，请愿

She sued the company for racial discrimination.
她以种族歧视为由对公司提出告诉。

高分秘诀　▲ racial discrimination 种族歧视

1785. sumptuous [`sʌmptʃuəs] [`sump·tu·ous] ★★★★★

adj. 奢侈的，华丽的

We were ushered into a sumptuous private mansion.
我们被领进一间豪华餐厅。

高分秘诀　▲ usher **n.** 迎宾员

1786. superb [su`pɝb] [su·perb] ★★★★★

adj. 堂皇的，宏伟的

This athlete turned in a superb performance to win the decathlon.
这个运动员在十项全能比赛中表现得十分出色。

高分秘诀　▲ decathlon **n.** 十项运动（体育比赛）

1787. superficial ['supə'fɪʃəl] [su·per·fi·cial]

adj. 表面的, 肤浅的

This manager was always promiscuous and superficial.
这个经理总是随便又肤浅。

1788. superintendent [ˌsupərɪn'tɛndənt] [su·per·in·tend·ent]

n. 监督人, 负责人

John was soon promoted to the post of superintendent of Foreign Trade.
约翰很快就被提拔为对外贸易总监。

1789. superior [sə'pɪrɪə] [su·pe·ri·or]

n. 上司, 长官

Their country won the battle because they are superior in numbers.
他们国家赢得战争的胜利是因为人数众多。

1790. supervise ['supəvaɪz] [su·per·vise]

v. 监督, 指导

The secretary was asked to supervise the refurbishing.
这位秘书被派去监督整修工作。

同义字词 administer, direct, govern, regulate

1791. supplant [sə'plænt] [sup·plant]

v. 排挤掉, 代替

Maybe TV and computers would supplant the time with others, but cyberchats don't improve social skills.
电视和电脑或许可以取代与他人相处的时光，但是网上聊天并不能提高社交技巧。

高分秘诀 ▲ cyberchat 网上聊天

1792. supple ['sʌpl] [sup·ple]

adj. 柔软的, 灵活的

The patient's abdomen is supple without organomegaly.
这个病人的腹部是柔软的，并无脏器肿大。

高分秘诀 ▲ organomegaly **n.** 器官肿大症

1793. supplement ['sʌpləmənt] [sup·ple·ment]

v. 增补, 补充

Foreign investment is a major supplement to the finance of our country.
外资是我们国家财政的重要补充。

n. 增补, 补充

I got a part-time job to supplement the family expenses.
我找了一份兼职工作以补充家庭开销。

1794. suppress [sə`prɛs] [sup·press] ☆★★★★

v. 镇压，查禁

The revolt was suppressed by the police in a few hours.
叛乱在几小时之内就被警方镇压了。

同义字词　restrain, control, repress, restrict

1795. supreme [sə`prim] [su·preme] ☆★★★★

adj. 至高的，终极的

India will challenge Japan's supreme place in the field of electronics.
印度将挑战日本在电子学领域中的领先地位。

1796. surcharge [`sɝ͵tʃɑrdʒ] [sur·charge] ☆★★★★

n. 装载过多，附加税

The surcharge may change the composition of our country's trade deficit.
附加税可能会改变我国贸易赤字的组成结构。

衍生字词
▲ import surcharge 进口附加税
▲ exchange surcharge 汇兑附加税
▲ bunker surcharge 燃油附加税

高分秘诀
▲ composition n. 构成，成分，创作
▲ deficit n. 赤字，亏空

1797. surge [sɝdʒ] [surge] ☆★★★★

n. 汹涌，澎湃

The blazing magma was surging in the volcano.
炽热的岩浆正从我们的身边奔腾而过。

同义字词　outburst, eruption, stream

衍生字词
▲ surge wave 水击波，涌波
▲ storm surge 风暴潮
▲ surge tank 平衡水箱

高分秘诀
▲ blazing adj. 燃烧的，炫目的
▲ magma n. 岩浆

1798. surmount [sə`maʊnt] [sur·mount] ☆★★★★

v. 战胜，克服

Most of these obstacles in our task can be surmounted.
我们任务中的大多数困难都是可以克服的。

同义字词　overcome, conquer, climb

1799. surpass [sə`pæs] [sur·pass]

v. 超越，胜过

We will surpass our predecessors, and future generations will certainly surpass us.
我们要突破前人，后人也必然会突破我们。

[同义字词] exceed, outrun, surmount

1800. surplus [`sɝpləs] [sur·plus]

n. 剩余，盈余

This luxury necklace is surplus to requirements.
这款奢华的项链供过于求。

adj. 过剩的，剩余的

The surplus labour force in China's rural areas will exceed 200 million.
中国农村剩余劳动力将超过两亿。

[衍生字词]
▲ free surplus 自由盈余
▲ surplus reserve 盈余储备
▲ capital surplus 公积金

1801. survive [sə`vaɪv] [sur·vive]

v. 存活，（物）耐久

You need to be tough to survive in the jungle.
要在丛林中活下来就要有坚忍不拔的意志。

[同义字词] endure, tolerate, outlive

1802. susceptible [sə`sɛptəbl] [sus·cep·ti·ble]

adj. 易被感动的

He was highly susceptible to flattery.
他听几句好话就感到飘飘然。

1803. suspend [sə`spɛnd] [sus·pend]

v. 吊，中止

The Ministry of Foreign Affairs decided to suspend negotiation.
外交部决定中止谈判。

1804. suspense [sə`spɛns] [sus·pense]

n. 悬疑，焦虑

Our next strategic move was still in suspense.
我们的下一个战略行动还悬而未决。

1805. sustain [sə`sten] [sus·tain]

v. 支撑，维持

A permanent state of cold war has sustained for many years.
冷战状态已经持续很多年。

1806. sustenance [ˈsʌstənəns] [sus·te·nance] ☆★★★★

n. 食物，生计

In rudderless despair, he began to search for ideological sustenance.
在失去航向的绝望中，他开始寻找思想上的寄托。

衍生字词
▲ rudderless **adj.** 无指导者的
▲ lack of sustenance 缺乏营养
▲ excess sustenance 营养过剩

1807. swallow [ˈswɑlo] [swal·low] ☆★★★★

v. 吞下，咽下

He flatters her outrageously, and she swallows it whole.
他极力奉承她，而她竟以为那完全是由衷之言。

n. 燕子，吞咽

One swallow does not make a summer.
一燕难成夏。

高分秘诀 ▲ outrageously **adj.** 异常地，残暴地

1808. swamp [swɑmp] [swamp] ☆★★★★

n. 沼泽，湿地

The heavy rain has turned the small garden into a swamp.
大雨使这小花园变成了一块沼泽地。

v. 淹没，浸没

I've been swamped with mediation this year.
今年我一直忙于调解。

1809. swarm [swɔrm] [swarm] ☆★★★★

n. 蜂群，一大群

At last a swarm settled in a hive.
终于有一群蜜蜂落进蜂巢。

v. 分群，被挤满

The sea was swarming with submarines.
海中有许多潜水艇。

同义字词 throng, flock, crowd, cram, crowd

1810. sway [swe] [sway] ☆☆★★★

v. 摇动，摇摆

She swayed her waist seductively as she danced.
她跳舞时诱人地摆动着纤腰。

高分秘诀 ▲ seductively **adv.** 诱惑地，勾引地

1811. swell [swɛl] [swell] ☆★★★★

v. 增大，肿胀

The murmur in the office swelled into a roar.
办公室的窃窃私语变成了一片喧哗。

adj. 很棒的，一流的，漂亮的；	What a swell advice! 多好的建议！
高分秘诀	▲ murmur v. 小声抱怨，窃窃私语

1812. swift [swɪft] [swift] ☆★★★★

adj. 迅速的，敏捷的	He was swift to condemn the violence/in condemning the violence. 他立即谴责那种暴力行为。
同义字词	quick, rapid, nimble

1813. symbiosis [ˌsɪmbaɪˈosɪs] [sym·bi·o·sis] ☆☆★★★

n. 共生，合作关系	There is no other team with the privilege to have such a deep symbiosis with a football genius. 从没有任何球队与一位足球天才保持如此特殊深切的依附关系。
衍生字词	▲ symbiotic adj. 共栖的，共生的 ▲ symbiotical adj. 共生现象的

1814. symmetry [ˈsɪmɪtrɪ] [sym·me·try] ☆★★★★

n. 对称，调和	The need to incorporate a picture will ruin the perfect symmetry. 加上一张图片将会破坏完全对称。
高分秘诀	▲ incorporate v. 加上，把……合并

1815. synchronize [ˈsɪŋkrənaɪz] [syn·chro·nize] ☆☆★★★

v. 同步，同时发生	If you want to synchronize this folder, run this wizard again. 如果你想同步处理档案夹，请再次运用这个向导程序。
同义字词	contemporise, sync, synchronise

1816. synonymous [sɪˈnɑnəməs] [syn·on·y·mous] ☆★★★★

adj. 同义字的，同义的	In those days botany was virtually synonymous with herbalism. 植物学和本草学在那个时候实际上是同义的。
同义字词	similar, identical, equivalent

1817. synthesize [ˈsɪnθəˌsaɪz] [syn·the·size] ☆★★★★

v. 综合，合成	He synthesized old and new ideas to form a new theory. 他将新旧想法融合成一个新理论。
衍生字词	▲ photosynthesis n. 光合作用 ▲ synthetic fabrics 合成织物

Tt 托福 TOEFL iBT

托福(TOEFL)的测验对象为母语为非英语的人
申请入学美加地区大学或研究所时，托福成绩单是必备文件之一。

- n. 名词
- v. 动词
- adj. 形容词
- adv. 副词
- prep. 介词
- art. 冠词
- pron. 代词
- aux. 助词
- conj. 连词

Tt 托福 TOEFL iBT

托福(TOEFL)的测验对象为母语为非英语的人
申请入学美加地区大学或研究所时，托福成绩单是必备文件之一。

1818. tableland [ˈtebḷˌlænd] [table·land]   ☆☆☆★★

n. 高原

A beautiful poem said that night slowly reached the tableland.
一首小诗中说："夜，缓缓来到高原。"

衍生字词
- ▲ table **n.** 桌子，台子
- ▲ land **n.** 陆地，陆上，土地
- ▲ coral tableland 珊瑚丘
- ▲ loess tableland 黄土原

1819. tactics [ˈtæktɪks] [tac·tics] ★★★★★

n. 战术，策略

As we all know an army commander must be skilled in tactics.
大家都知道身为一名军事指挥官必须精通战术。

衍生字词
- ▲ blitz tactics 闪电战术
- ▲ customary tactics 惯用伎俩
- ▲ infiltration tactics 渗透战术
- ▲ partisan tactics 游击战术

高分秘诀
- ▲ as we all know 众所周知
- ▲ army commander 军队指挥官
- ▲ be skilled in... 精通……

1820. tactile [ˈtæktl] [tac·tile] ☆★★★★

adj. 触觉的，可触觉的

Some insects have quick tactile sense.
有些昆虫具有灵敏的触觉。

反义字词 imperceptible, pretersensual, unperceivable

1821. tag [tæg] [tag] ☆★★★★

v. 给……加标签，附加

You should tag your name on your suitcase.
你应该在行李箱上标示你的名字。

n. 标签，货签

Have you put tags on your belongings?
你在自己的东西上贴上标签了吗?

tableland ~ tardy

| 高分秘诀 | ▲ put tags on 把标签贴于……
▲ belonging n. 附属物，附件 |

1822. taint [tent] [taint] ☆★★★★

n. 污点, 瑕疵	It is said that moral taint has spread among young people. 据说道德败坏的趋势在年轻人之间蔓延。
v. 污染, 玷污	The meat was tainted because it is smelly. 这块肉坏了，因为它发出难闻的气味。
同义字词	stain, blot, spot, tarnish, contaminate
衍生字词	▲ taintless adj. 未感染的，纯洁的 ▲ clover taint （牛奶的）三叶草味 ▲ fishy taint 鱼腥似的腐坏 ▲ surface taint （奶油）表面腐坏 ▲ moral taint 道德败坏
高分秘诀	▲ spread v. 蔓延，散布 ▲ smelly adj. 发出难闻的气味，发臭的

1823. tally [ˈtælɪ] [tal·ly] ☆☆★★★

v. 符合, 吻合	Your account tallies with hers. 你的账目和她的相符。
n. 记录, 记账	Don't forget to keep a careful tally of what you spend in dealing with this issue. 别忘了仔细记下处理这件事的开支账目。
高分秘诀	▲ keep a careful tally of 仔细记下 ▲ deal with 处理

1824. tap [tæp] [tap] ☆☆★★★

| v. 开发, 利用 | We have enormous reserves of coal still waiting to be tapped.
我们有大量的矿藏等待开发。 |
| n. 敲, 水龙头 | He gave a tap at the microphone before singing.
他在唱歌前先轻叩一下扩音器。 |

1825. tardy [ˈtɑrdɪ] [tar·dy] ☆★★★★

| adj. 迟到的, 缓慢的 | Tim is always tardy for school.
吉姆上学老是迟到。 |
| 同义字词 | late, delayed, slow |

衍生字词
- ▲ tardiness n. 迟到，缓慢
- ▲ tardily adv. 缓慢地，拖拉地
- ▲ tardy arrival 来迟
- ▲ make a tardy appearance 迟到
- ▲ a tardy amendment 为时已晚的补救
- ▲ a tardy consent 勉强的答应
- ▲ be tardy for... 做……迟到

1826. tariff [ˈtærɪf] [tar·iff] ☆★★★★

n. 关税，价目表
There is a very high tariff on smoke.
烟类的税率很高。

衍生字词
- ▲ tariffing n. 制定运价表
- ▲ tariffless adj. 无关税的
- ▲ smoke n. 烟
- ▲ tariff-free 免税（的）
- ▲ tariff-walled 关税壁垒的
- ▲ agreement tariff 关税协定，协定关税
- ▲ high tariff on... ……的高税收

1827. tarnish [ˈtɑrnɪʃ] [tar·nish] ☆★★★★

n. 晦暗，污点
The criminal wanted to remove the tarnish from his file.
这个犯人想删去他档案上的污点。

v. 使失去光泽，玷污
It is said that Tom's bad behaviour has tarnished the good name of the school.
据说是汤姆的行为不轨败坏了学校的声誉。

1828. tectonics [tɛkˈtɑnɪks] [tec·ton·ics]   ☆☆☆★★

n. [地]构造地质学
It is known to us that plate tectonics are now almost universally accepted.
如今板块构造学几乎被普遍接受。

衍生字词
- ▲ plate tectonics 板块构造
- ▲ gravity tectonics 重力构造
- ▲ new global tectonics 新全球构造地质学
- ▲ raft tectonics 漂浮构造
- ▲ sedimentary tectonics 沉积构造

tariff ~ tentacle

1829. tedium ['tidɪəm] [te·di·um] ☆★★★★

n. 单调乏味

The two hours of being locked in the dark room is the unrelieved tedium for me.
被关在黑屋的两个小时对我来说烦闷难耐。

| 同义字词 | drudgery, boredom, tediousness |

1830. temperate ['tɛmprɪt] [tem·per·ate] ☆★★★★

adj. （气候等）温和的，有节制的

It's Tony's not temperate remarks got him into trouble.
托尼的言语肆无忌惮，惹出了麻烦。

| 反义字词 | intemperate, excessive, unrestrained |

1831. temporary ['tɛmpəˌrɛrɪ] [tem·po·rar·y] ☆★★★★

adj. 短暂的，暂时的

They just reached a temporary agreement about this big accident.
他们就这件大事达成了一项临时协议。

| 衍生字词 | ▲ temporary punishment 有期徒刑
▲ temporary workers 临时工 |
| 高分秘诀 | ▲ temporarily **adv.** 临时
▲ temporary pleasure 一时的快乐
▲ reach a temporary agreement 达成一个暂时的协定 |

1832. tempt [tɛmpt] [tempt] ☆★★★★

v. 诱使

My brother's friend tempted him to rob the bank.
我弟弟的朋友竟怂恿他去抢银行。

| 同义字词 | entice, allure, attract, seduce, appeal |

1833. tensile ['tɛnsl] [ten·sile] ☆★★★★

adj. 可拉长的，可伸长的

I found the rope has a strong tensile strength.
我发现这条绳子的抗拉强度很强。

1834. tentacle ['tɛntəkl] [ten·ta·cle] ☆★★★★

n. 触角，触须

It is a fact that many molluscs have tentacles.
事实证明很多软体动物都有触角。

| 高分秘诀 | ▲ mollusc **n.** 软体动物 |

1835. terminal [ˈtɝmənl] [ter·mi·nal]

adj. 末端的，极限的
The machine has reached its terminal speed and can run faster no longer.
这个机器的速度已达到极限，无法运转更快。

n. 总站，终点站
When the bus reaches its terminal, please inform me.
汽车到终点站时请通知我。

衍生字词　▲ bus terminal　公共汽车终点站

1836. terminology [ˌtɝməˈnɑlədʒɪ] [ter·mi·nol·o·gy]

n. 用词，术语
Don't argue about it now. It is only a chemical terminology.
不要为它而争论不休，它只是一个化学术语。

衍生字词
▲ accounting terminology　会计术语
▲ chemical terminology　化学术语

高分秘诀
▲ argue about...　为……而争论
▲ chemical terminology　化学术语
▲ kinship terminology　亲属术语
▲ organic terminology　有机术语

1837. terrain [ˈtɛren] [ter·rain]

n. 地势，地形
He had made a detailed study of the terrain about western district.
他对西部地区地形作了缜密的研究。

同义字词　land, landform, topography

1838. terrify [ˈtɛrəˌfaɪ] [ter·ri·fy]

v. 使恐怖，使惊吓
People and animals were terrified by the storm.
人们和动物被那场暴风雨吓坏了。

1839. testify [ˈtɛstəˌfaɪ] [tes·ti·fy]

v. 作证，证明
He will not testify against his own sister.
他不会出庭作对自己妹妹不利的证词。

高分秘诀　▲ testify against...　作不利于……的证明

1840. thaw [θɔ] [thaw]

n. 解冻
It's a common phenomenon the spring thaw can cause flooding.
春暖融化解冻引起洪水泛滥，是一个常见的现象。

terminal ~ thorough

| v. 融化, 融解 | Spring is coming because a thaw is setting in.
春天快到了，因为江河渐渐解冻。 |

衍生字词　thawer n. 解冻装置

1841. theft [θɛft] [theft]　☆☆★★★

| n. 偷窃 | As soon as he discovered the theft of her money, he went to the police.
他一发现钱被偷，就报警了。 |

衍生字词　▲ theft insurance 盗窃保险

1842. theoretical [ˌθiəˋrɛtɪk!] [theo·re·ti·cal]　☆★★★★

| adj. 理论上的 | Getting the sense of happiness is a theoretical matter as well as a practical one.
获得幸福不仅是个实用问题，也是个理论问题。 |

同义字词　academic, theoretic, abstract

1843. thermal [ˋθɝm!] [ther·mal]　☆★★★★

| adj. 热的, 热量的 | This thermal underwear is in a high quality.
这件保暖内衣品质很好。 |

高分秘诀
▲ non-thermal 非热能的
▲ thermal underwear 保暖内衣
▲ in a good quality 品质很好
▲ thermal capacity 热容量
▲ thermal circulation 热循环
▲ thermal conductivity 热传导性
▲ thermal cross-overs 热交点
▲ thermal detector 热检波器
▲ thermal infrared radiation 热红外线
▲ thermal pollution 热污染（高温废液或气体对环境产生的不利影响）
▲ thermal radiometer 热辐射计
▲ thermal scanner 热扫描器

1844. thorny [ˋθɔrnɪ] [thorn·y]

| adj. 有刺的, 痛苦的 | He devoted much to the thorny road to peace.
他为通往和平的荆棘之路做出了很多贡献。 |

1845. thorough [ˋθɝo] [thor·ough]　★★★★★

| adj. 完全的, 彻底的 | They made a thorough search for the lost purse, but didn't find it.
他们仔细寻找过那只遗失的钱包，可是没有找到。 |

| 高分秘诀 | ▲ make a thorough search 做一个彻底的搜查 |

1846. thoughtful [ˋθɔtfəl] [thought·ful] ★★★★★

| adj. 体贴的,考虑周到的 | He is in a thoughtful and solemn mien.
他一副若有所思而又严肃的表情。 |

1847. threaten [ˋθrɛtn̩] [threat·en] ★★★★★

| v. 威胁,可能来临 | By this time the fire was beginning to threaten people in the house.
这个时候,火势已开始凶猛地威胁屋内人们的安危。 |

| 反义字词 | secure, ensure, make safe |

1848. threshold [ˋθrɛʃhold] [thresh·old] ☆★★★★

| n. 开始,开端 | It is no doubt that the treaty will be the threshold of lasting peace.
毫无疑问,这个条约将成为持久和平的开端。 |

同义字词	entrance, beginning, doorway, gateway, portal, inlet
反义字词	outlet, egress, exit
衍生字词	▲ at the threshold of... 在……的开始 ▲ cross someone's threshold 走进某人家里 ▲ cross the threshold 跨进门内 ▲ on the threshold 在门口 ▲ on the threshold of... 在……的开头 ▲ stumble at [on] the threshold （事情）刚一着手就搞砸

1849. thrifty [ˋθrɪftɪ] [thrift·y] ☆★★★★

| adj. 节省的,节俭的 | My wife is a very thrifty housekeeper.
我的妻子是一个很勤俭的管家。 |

| 同义字词 | economical, frugal, sparing |
| 反义字词 | wasteful, uneconomical, luxurious |

1850. thrive [θraɪv] [thrive] ☆★★★★

| v. 繁荣,兴旺 | I always believe that a business cannot thrive without good management.
我相信好的经营管理是兴旺的基础。 |

thoughtful ~ topography

1851. thrust [θrʌst] [thrust] ☆☆★★★

n. 推力, 冲
The man jumped back to avoid another thrust of the knife.
他往后跳以躲避另一把刀的戳刺。

v. 插入, 用力刺
The old lady thrust herself through the crowd to find her pet dog.
老妇人挤过人群寻找她的宠物狗。

[同义字词] push, drive, pierce, prick

[衍生字词]
▲ thrust oneself forward 出风头
▲ thrust... upon... 将……强加于……
▲ a home thrust 打中要害的一击
▲ rapier thrust 巧妙的讽刺，犀利的言辞

[高分秘诀]
▲ jump back 跳到后面去
▲ thrust... through ……挤过
▲ the crowd 人群
▲ pet dog 宠物狗

1852. tint [tɪnt] [tint] ☆☆★★★

v. 给……着色, 染
How about you give a tint to the picture drawn by him?
你为他画的这幅画着色怎么样？

n. 色彩, 浅色
This music takes on a tint of sorrow.
这首曲子有一抹淡淡的忧愁。

[衍生字词] tint-tool n. 雕刻工具

1853. tolerate [ˈtɑləˌret] [tol·er·ate] ☆★★★★

v. 忍受, 容许
The teacher cannot tolerate talking with each other on the class.
老师不容许课堂上大家彼此交谈。

[同义字词] endure, put up with, withstand, stand

1854. topography [təˈpɑgrəfɪ] [to·pog·ra·phy] ☆☆★★★

n. 地形, 地形学
He is an expert who is skilled in topography.
他是精通地形学的专家。

[衍生字词]
▲ topographical adj. 地形学的
▲ accretion topography 加积地形
▲ aged topography 成年地形
▲ autogenetic topography 自成地形
▲ baric topography 气压地形

高分秘诀 ▲ be skilled in 精通

1855. torpor [ˈtɔrpə] [tor·por]

n. 迟钝，不活泼

I don't know why my boyfriend was falling into the state of comatose torpor.
我不知道我男友为什么陷入这种昏睡的状态。

衍生字词 ▲ deep torpor 深度麻痹状态
▲ a state of comatose torpor 昏睡无感觉的一种状态

1856. torrent [ˈtɔrənt] [tor·rent]

n. 连发，迸发

Our troop were proceeding through torrents of rain.
我们部队在倾盆大雨中前进。

衍生字词 ▲ torrential rain 暴雨，大雨

1857. tortuous [ˈtɔrtʃuəs] [tor·tu·ous]

adj. 曲折的，转弯抹角的

It's the tortuous plots that absorbed the audience's attention.
这些曲折的剧情吸引了观众的注意。

1858. tournament [ˈtɜnəmənt] [tour·na·ment]

n. 比赛，锦标赛

I've heard the news that the tournament is open to amateurs as well as professionals.
我听说这次比赛不仅职业运动员可以参加，业余运动员也可以。

衍生字词 ▲ open tournament 公开赛
▲ consolation tournament 安慰赛

1859. toxic [ˈtɑksɪk] [tox·ic]

adj. 有毒的，中毒的

Mr. Smith, can you tell me the symptoms of the toxic hepatitis?
史密斯先生，你能告诉我中毒性肝炎的症状吗？

高分秘诀 ▲ toxic hepatitis 中毒性肝炎

1860. trail [trel] [trail]

n. 踪迹，小路

It didn't take much time for the dog to find the trail of the goat.
猎犬没花多少时间就发现了山羊的踪迹。

v. 追踪

The singer's long skirt trailed along behind her.
这位歌手的长裙拖曳在身后。

torpor ~ transform

1861. tragedy [ˈtrædʒɪdɪ] [trag·e·dy] ☆★★★★

n. 悲剧, 灾难　　The recent tragedy in Japen brings world together.
近日发生在日本的灾难将世界联系在了一起。

1862. trait [tret] [trait] ☆☆★★★

n. 特征, 特性　　His responsibility is one of his good traits.
责任心强是他的特点之一。

1863. trample [ˈtræmpl] [tram·ple] ☆☆★★★

v. 踩踏, 蹂躏　　There is a notice says "Don't trample on the grass."
布告上说"禁止践踏草地"。

1864. tranquil [ˈtræŋkwɪl] [tran·quil] ☆★★★★

adj. 宁静的, 安静的　　When she got the terrible news, she was as tranquil as if nothing had happened.
当她知道这个消息时,她那副悠闲的样子就像什么事也没发生似的。

1865. transaction [trænˈzækʃən] [trans·ac·tion] ☆★★★★

n. 交易, 办理　　Buying a house is an important transaction for most people.
买房子对大多数人来讲都是件重要的事。

　　同义字词　　deal, business
　　衍生字词　　▲ hole-and-corner transactions 秘密的交易, 偷偷摸摸的交易
　　　　　　　▲ bargaining transaction 买卖交易
　　　　　　　▲ bilateral transaction 双边直接交易

1866. transcend [trænˈsɛnd] [tran·scend] ☆☆★★★

v. 超出, 超越　　It is a truth that we can't transcend the limitations of the ego in some sense.
在一定程度上我们无法超越自我的局限性,这是一个真理。

1867. transform [trænsˈfɔrm] [trans·form] ☆★★★★

v. (使)变形, 改观　　Success and wealth transformed his value of life.
成功和财富改变了他的生活价值观。

1868. transition [træn`zɪʃən] [tran·si·tion] ☆★★★★

n. 转变,过渡

I think nothing can affect her, let alone such a sudden transition.
我认为什么都影响不了她,更何况这样的一个突然变化。

高分秘诀
▲ let alone 更不用说
▲ sudden transition 突然变化

1869. translucent [træns`lusn̩t] [trans·lu·cent] ☆★★★★

adj. 半透明的,清楚易懂的

The lavatory windows of my house are made of translucent glass.
我家的洗手间窗户是用半透明玻璃做成的。

1870. transmit [træns`mɪt] [trans·mit] ☆★★★★

v. 传送,传播

The scientist analyzed it and found that this infection was transmitted by mosquitoes.
这位科学家通过分析得出结论,这种传染病是由蚊子传播的。

衍生字词
▲ neurotransmitter **n.** [生化] 神经传递素

1871. transmute [træns`mjut] [trans·mute] ☆★★★★

v. 使变化,使改变

The scientist made the energy transmute into matter.
科学家使能量变成物质。

衍生字词
▲ transmutable **adj.** 可改变的

1872. transparent [træns`pɛrənt] [trans·par·ent] ☆★★★★

adj. 透明的,显而易见的

Today the hostess dressed a transparent silk blouse.
今天女主人身穿一件轻薄透明的丝绸衬衣。

衍生字词
transparent colour 透明色料;

1873. transplant [træns`plænt] [trans·plant] ☆★★★★

v. 移植,移居

I know nothing about the heart transplant; to me it's a wonderful thing.
我对心脏移植一无所知,对我来讲它是一件神奇的事。

高分秘诀
▲ heart transplant 心脏移植

1874. trap [træp] [trap] ☆★★★★

v. 捕捉,困住

How many goats have you trapped in your special trap this week?
这个星期你用特制的捕兽器捉到多少只山羊?

transition ~ tributary

n. 圈套，陷阱   The zebra fell into the trap and couldn't get out from it.
斑马掉入了陷阱，无法自己挣脱。

> 同义字词   catch, entomb, snare

1875. treacherous [ˈtrɛtʃərəs] [treach·er·ous] ☆☆★★★

adj. 不可靠的，有暗藏的危险的   If my memory serves me right, I often had treacherous actions in my childhood.
如果没记错的话，我小时候常有叛逆行为。

1876. tread [trɛd] [tread]

v. 踏，践踏   She said politely, "I am sorry that I trod on your toes."
她礼貌地说道："我踩到你的脚，对不起。"

> 衍生字词
> ▲ treadmill **n.** 踏车，跑步机
> ▲ tread on air 得意洋洋，手舞足蹈
> ▲ tread on... toes 激怒……，伤……的心
> ▲ tread water （游泳时）踩水

1877. treason [ˈtrizn̩] [trea·son] ☆☆★★★

n. 叛逆，叛国   It's quite common for a chancellor to be degraded for treason.
大臣因叛国罪被贬职很常见。

1878. trove [trov] [trove] ☆☆★★★

n. 被发现的东西，收藏的东西   I know that this museum housed a priceless treasure trove.
我知道该博物馆存放着一件无价之宝。

1879. trespass [ˈtrɛspəs] [tres·pass]

v. 侵犯，闯入私人领地   Have you noticed the sign on the board "No trespassing"?
你没注意到牌子上写的"不准擅自闯入！"吗？

1880. trial [ˈtraɪəl] [tri·al] ☆★★★★

n. 实验，审讯   The man was on trial for robbery.
此人因抢劫而受审。

1881. tributary [ˈtrɪbjəˌtɛrɪ] [trib·u·tar·y] ☆★★★★

adj. 辅助的，支流的   I only know that it is a tributary state of Britain.
我只知道它是英国的附属国。

| n. 支流，分支 | It is a tributary of that big river.
这是那条大河的支流。 |

高分秘诀 ▲ a tributary state 附属国
▲ Britain n. 不列颠，英国

1882. trigger [ˈtrɪɡə] [trig·ger]　☆★★★★

| v. 引发，引起 | The man accidentally triggered his rifle, and killed his lover.
男人无意中扣发了步枪的扳机，误杀了他的爱人。 |

1883. trilogy [ˈtrɪlədʒɪ] [tril·o·gy]　☆★★★★

| n. 三部曲 | Claire just finished reading J.R.R. Tolkien's "The Lord of the Ring" trilogy.
克莱尔刚看完托尔金的《魔戒》三部曲。 |

1884. trim [trɪm] [trim]　☆★★★★

| v. 修剪，整饬 | How often should I trim my hair if I'm planning on letting it grow back long?
如果想留长发到背，我该多久修一次头发呢？ |
| adj. 整齐的，整洁的 | He arranged the house to keep it trim.
他整理房间以保持整洁。 |

1885. triumph [ˈtraɪəmf] [tri·umph]　☆★★★★

| n. 胜利 | He achieved great triumphs in this battle.
他在这场战斗中大获全胜。 |
| v. 获得胜利，成功 | Our team triumphed over theirs in the tournament.
这次锦标赛中我们这队赢了他们那一队。 |

1886. trivial [ˈtrɪvɪəl] [triv·i·al]

| adj. 微不足道的，琐碎的 | Don't trouble with the trivial thing.
不要为这种小事自寻烦恼。 |

1887. tumble [ˈtʌmbl] [tum·ble]　☆☆★★★

| v. 翻滚 | She tumbled down the stairs suddenly and got hurt.
她突然滚下楼梯受伤了。 |
| n. 摔倒，坠落 | He had a nasty tumble when he trod on the sticky floor.
当他踩上黏黏的地板时，他重重地摔了一跤。 |

trigger ~ tycoon

高分秘诀　▲ tumble down the stairs 跌下楼梯

1888. turbulent [ˈtɝbjələnt] [tur·bu·lent] ☆★★★★

adj. 吵闹的，狂暴的
She tried to calm her turbulent thoughts and recollect her attention.
她试图冷静下来并重新集中注意力。

1889. turnpike [ˈtɝnˌpaɪk] [turn·pike] ☆★★★★

n. 公路，高速公路
You have no choice but to pay a toll to drive on a turnpike.
在高速公路上开车必须缴通行费。

1890. tutor [ˈtjutɚ] [tu·tor] ★★★★★

v. 当……的家庭教师
For extra money, she tutors on weekends in her university.
为了多赚些钱，大学时期她在周末当家教。

n. 家庭教师
Her parents employed a tutor to teach her French.
她父母请一位家教教她学法语。

1891. twine [twaɪn] [twine] ☆★★★★

v. 搓，织，编饰
I saw him twined his arms round and seemed to be thinking something.
我看他两臂抱胸，好像在思考着什么。

n. 麻线，细绳
She tied the parcel with twine.
她用细绳捆包裹。

1892. twist [twɪst] [twist] ☆★★★★

n. 扭曲，拧
He told us a story with a quirky twist.
他告诉我们一个高潮迭起的故事。

v. 转动，歪曲
According to the instruction, you have to twist the knob clockwise.
按照说明书，你要按顺时针方向转动旋钮。

同义字词　circle, curve, swivel, turn, wheel, wind

1893. tycoon [taɪˈkun] [ty·coon] ☆☆★★★

n. 大企业家，大亨
His uncle is a tycoon of textile business.
他的叔叔是棉纺织品的商业巨头。

同义字词　magnate, entrepreneur, baron

1894. typify [ˈtɪpəˌfaɪ] [typ·i·fy] ☆★★★★

v. 代表，为……之典型	My sister typifies the bored housewife, she seldom going out for fun, just staying at home. 我姐姐是典型的家庭主妇，宅在家很少出门玩乐。
同义字词	represent, characterize

1895. tyrannical [taɪˈrænɪkl] [tyr·an·ni·cal] ☆★★★★

adj. 暴虐的，残暴的	He is a tyrannical emperor in history. 他在历史上是一个残暴的皇帝。
同义字词	dictatorial, domineering, authoritarian

Uu 托福 TOEFL iBT

托福(TOEFL)的测验对象为母语为非英语的人
申请入学美加地区大学或研究所时,托福成绩单是必备文件之一。

- n. 名词
- v. 动词
- adj. 形容词
- adv. 副词
- prep. 介词
- art. 冠词
- pron. 代词
- aux. 助词
- conj. 连词

Uu 托福 TOEFL iBT

托福(TOEFL)的测验对象为母语为非英语的人
申请入学美加地区大学或研究所时，托福成绩单是必备文件之一。

1896. ultimate [ˋʌltəmɪt] [ul·ti·mate] ☆★★★★

adj. 最终的，最后的　What was your ultimate goal for doing this?
你做这件事的最终目的是什么？

高分秘诀　▲ ultimate goal 最终目标

1897. ultrasonic [͵ʌltrəˋsɑnɪk] [ul·tra·son·ic] ☆★★★★

adj. 超音速的，超声(波)的　These planes travel at ultrasonic speeds in the sky.
这些飞机以超音速的速度在天空飞行。

1898. ultraviolet [͵ʌltrəˋvaɪəlɪt] [ul·tra·vi·o·let] ☆★★★★

adj. 紫外线的　There is a kind of material called ultraviolet rays.
有一种物质被叫作紫外线。

衍生字词　▲ ultraviolet lamp 紫外线灯
▲ roentgen rays n. X射线，伦琴射线

1899. unanimity [͵junəˋnɪmətɪ] [u·na·nim·i·ty] ☆☆★★★

n. 全体一致，一致同意　Our discussions about the housing bulit led to plenary unanimity.
我们讨论关于建房子的事情取得了完全一致的意见。

同义字词　concord, consensus, harmony

1900. unbridled [ʌnˋbraɪdld] [un·bri·dled] ☆☆★★★

adj. 放纵的，无约束的　I was amazed at the gang of robbers' unbridled glee.
那些盗贼兴高采烈的情绪真让我吃惊。

1901. undergo [͵ʌndəˋgo] [un·der·go] ☆★★★★

v. 经历，遭受　The old man underwent a lot of in his youth age.
老人在青年时期有许多坎坷的经历。

同义字词　experience, suffer, endure, go through

1902. undergraduate [ˌʌndəˈgrædʒuɪt] [un·der·gradu·ate]

n. (尚未取得学位的)大学生

A few years ago, Science of Business Administration is the most popular subject for undergraduate.
几年之前，工商管理学是大学本科生最欢迎的课程。

高分秘诀 ▲ Science of Business Administration 工商管理学

1903. underlying [ˌʌndəˈlaɪɪŋ] [un·der·ly·ing]

adj. 基础的，潜在的

The underlying danger of the judicial case is very serious.
司法案件隐含的危机十分严肃。

同义字词 fundamental, elementary

1904. undermine [ˌʌndəˈmaɪn] [un·der·mine]

v. 渐渐破坏，暗地破坏

Illness undermined the robust man's strength.
疾病逐渐削弱这个壮汉的力气。

同义字词 weaken, impair, destroy, sabotage

1905. underscore [ˌʌndəˈskor] [un·der·score]

v. 画线于……下，强调

She underscored the most import points.
她在最重要的重点下划线。

同义字词 emphasize, stress, underline

1906. undertake [ˌʌndəˈtek] [un·der·take]

v. 从事，承担

I want you to undertake all the responsibility of this operation.
我要你承担这个手术的所有责任。

同义字词 take on, embark on, assume

1907. unearth [ʌnˈɝθ] [un·earth]

v. 发觉，挖出

The reporter had unearthed some intimacy about the strange man.
记者挖出一些关于他的隐私。

反义字词 cover, keep in secret

1908. uniform [ˈjunəˌfɔrm] [u·ni·form]

n. 制服

Students wear a distinctive uniform in this school.
这所学校的学生们穿着特制的校服。

| 同义字词 | homogeneous, consistent, unanimous, standardized |

1909. unique [juˋnik] [u·nique] ☆★★★★

adj. 独一无二的，独特的

Humans are unique among mammals in several repects.
就哺乳类动物观点而言人类是非常特别的一群。

| 同义字词 | peerless, unmatched, unrivaled |

1910. unity [ˋjunətɪ] [u·ni·ty] ☆★★★★

n. 结合，一致

It is said that they maintained only formal unity.
据说他们只在表面上保持一致。

同义字词	cohesion, harmony, integrity
反义字词	non-uniform, disunion, discrepancy
衍生字词	▲ unity element 单位元素
	▲ unity feedback 单位回馈，全回馈
	▲ unit cost 单位成本
	▲ unit price 单价
	▲ unit pricing 单位订价法
	▲ unit trust 单位信托投资公司
	▲ universal disk format 通用碟片格式
	▲ universal donor 全适型供血者
	▲ universal joint 万向接头
	▲ universal time 格林尼治标准时间

1911. unpalatable [ʌnˋpælətəbl] [un·pal·at·able] ☆★★★★

adj. 味道差的，不好吃的

The camel meat was particularly unpalatable.
这骆驼肉特别难吃。

1912. unravel [ʌnˋrævl] [un·rav·el] ☆☆★★★

v. 弄清楚（秘密），拆开

The experts unraveled a mystery of the tumulus.
专家们已揭开这个古墓之谜。

| 同义字词 | discover, solve, work out, unwind, untangle |

1913. unsubstantiated [ˌʌnsəbˋstænʃɪˌetɪd] [un·substan·ti·ated] ☆★★★★

adj. 未经证实的

He points out that it is a dangerous, absurd, and totally unsubstantiated accusation.
他指出这是一个危险的、荒诞的、完全没有根据的指控。

unique ~ uphold

| 同义字词 | unverified, unverified, uncorroborated |

1914. unwieldy [ʌnˋwildɪ] [un·wieldy] ☆☆★★★

| adj. 笨拙的，笨重的 | People worked in the government have unwieldy political power.
在政府机关工作的人可以行使巨大的政治权力。 |
| 同义字词 | cumbersome, unmanageable, bulky |

1915. upgrade [ˋʌpˋgred] [up·grade] ☆★★★★

v. 使升级，提升	The reason for their upgrading the land is to improve it with new luxurious house. 他们提高土地等级的原因是为了建造新豪宅。
同义字词	improve, advance, elevate
反义字词	downgrade, breakfast, demote
衍生字词	▲ upgrade fever 升级热（一种拼命想拥有最新、最快、最强的硬体和软体的盲目欲望。） ▲ grade crossing 铁路交叉道，平交道 ▲ grade point average （美国学生各科成绩的）平均分数，总平均 ▲ grade school 小学

1916. upheaval [ʌpˋhivl] [up·heav·al] ☆★★★★

n. 剧变，大动荡	The three terrorists caught up in the embassy upheaval. 这三个恐怖分子卷入大使馆的动乱。
同义字词	a violent disturbance, outburst, turmoil
衍生字词	▲ campus upheaval 大学学潮 ▲ currency upheaval 货币动荡 ▲ economic upheaval 经济震荡 ▲ secular upheaval 长期缓升

1917. uphold [ʌpˋhold] [up·hold] ☆★★★★

| v. 维护，支持，保持 | The public upheld our innovation.
公众支持我们的革新。 |
| 同义字词 | support, preserve, maintain |

衍生字词	▲ in support of 支持，拥护
	▲ support group 摇滚音乐会的配角乐团
	▲ support level 支撑水准
	▲ support stocking 弹性袜
	▲ support the weak and restrain the powerful 扶弱抑强
	▲ public access （特别区域、文件阅读范围等的）向公众开放
	▲ public access channel （电视台为团体特辟的非营利的）向公众开放频道
	▲ public address system 扩音装置，有线广播，公共喊话系统
	▲ public affairs 公众事务
	▲ public bar （酒馆中设施较简单的）公众酒吧
	▲ public company 公开招股公司
	▲ public convenience （英）公共厕所
	▲ public corporation 公开招股公司，市政局
	▲ public defender （政府等为无钱聘律师的被告指聘的）公设辩护律师
	▲ public domain 公有土地，权利消失状态
	▲ Public Domain Software （电脑）公用领域软件，共享软件
	▲ public expenditure 公用事业费用，市政开支
	▲ public footpath （英）公用道路
	▲ public funding （英）投资公债
	▲ public gallery （会议的）旁听席
	▲ public health 公共卫生
	▲ public holiday 国定假日
	▲ public house 旅舍或酒馆
	▲ public housing 公共住房（政府为穷人造的住宅或公寓）

1918. uproot [ʌpˋrut] [up·root] ☆☆★★

v. 连根拔起，拔除	Gales uprooted trees and made a big turmoil. 大风将树连根拔起，造成混乱。

1919. urban [ˋɝbən] [ur·ban] ☆★★★

adj. 城市的	That the quality of urban living has been damaged by excessive noise levels. 城市生活的品质已被过度的噪声破坏。

uproot ~ utopian

衍生字词
- ▲ urban decay 城市衰落，城市衰败
- ▲ urban forest 城市森林
- ▲ urban legend（往往含有幽默、恐怖，或教训意味的）来源不明、缺少或无证据，但自然地以各种形式出现的当代故事或传说
- ▲ urban myth 都市神话（指许多人都相信的发生在某人身上的稀奇故事）
- ▲ urban sprawl 城市扩张，都市向郊区扩张的现象
- ▲ urban tribe 城市族群

1920. urge [ɝdʒ] [urge] ☆★★★★

v. 催促，恳求
Your progress will urge him to work hard.
你的进步会促进他努力学习。

n. 冲动，强烈愿望
He has an urge to become a famous botanist.
他非常希望成为著名的植物学家。

高分秘诀
▲ botanist **n.** 植物学家

1921. usher [ˈʌʃɚ] [ush·er] ☆☆☆★★

n. 引座员，迎宾员
The usher stood at the door giving out programs.
招待员站在门口分发节目单。

v. 引领陪同
She ushered the guests into the room.
她把客人引进屋子中。

1922. utility [juˈtɪlətɪ] [u·til·i·ty] ★★★★★

n. 公共事业，如水电、煤气等（费用）
Does the monthly rent include any utilities?
月租金有包括水电煤气费吗？

同义字词
something useful, public service

1923. utopian [juˈtopɪən] [u·to·pi·an] ☆☆☆★★

adj. 乌托邦式的，空想的
This is a kind of utopian novels.
这是乌托邦小说的一种。

衍生字词
- ▲ Utopia **n.** 乌托邦（理想中美好的社会）
- ▲ dystopian **adj.** 反面乌托邦的，反面假想国的

1924. utter [`ˈʌtɚ`] [ut·ter] ☆★★★★

v. 作声, 发表	After she got anger with her husband she didn't utter a word all night. 她对丈夫发怒后，整夜一言不发。
adj. 全然的, 完全的	He was in utter despair about this issue. 他对这件事完全绝望。

MEMO

Vv 托福 TOEFL iBT

托福(TOEFL)的测验对象为母语为非英语的人
申请入学美加地区大学或研究所时,托福成绩单是必备文件之一。

- n. 名词
- v. 动词
- adj. 形容词
- adv. 副词
- prep. 介词
- art. 冠词
- pron. 代词
- aux. 助词
- conj. 连词

Vv 托福 TOEFL iBT

托福(TOEFL)的测验对象为母语为非英语的人
申请入学美加地区大学或研究所时，托福成绩单是必备文件之一。

1925. vacant [ˋvekənt] [va·cant]   ★★★★★

adj. 空的，未被占用的	The position remains vacant.
	那职位仍旧空着。
同义字词	empty, uninhabited, absence, emptiness
衍生字词	▲ vacancy n. 空白，空缺 ▲ vacant position 空位 ▲ vacant space 未用空间 ▲ vacancy area 空地区域 ▲ vacant lot 空地 ▲ vacant possession 空屋

1926. vacate [ˋveket] [va·cate] ☆★★★★

v. 腾出，空出	There is rule that guests were asked to vacate their rooms before 12:00.
	按规定，房客被要求在中午十二点以前退房。
同义字词	depart, leave, empty, annul, revoke, repeal
衍生字词	▲ vacation n. 度假，休假 ▲ vacation club account 零存整取度假储蓄 ▲ vacation pay 假期工资 ▲ vacation school 讲习会，短期暑修学校 ▲ vacation rental 度假租借，假日租借
高分秘诀	▲ vacate someone's room 腾出某人的房间

1927. vaccinate [ˋvæksɪn͵et] [vac·ci·nate] ☆★★★★

v. 进行预防接种	Doctors vaccinate the children so that they don't catch smallpox.
	为了预防小朋友得天花，医生为他们打预防针。
衍生字词	▲ vaccine n. 疫苗 ▲ vaccinator n. 种痘，预防接种

1928. vague [veɡ] [vague]

adj. 模糊的，含糊的 — Through the window screening I could just make out a vague figure.
透过窗纱，我只能看见一个模糊的人影。

1929. valid [ˈvælɪd] [val·id]

adj. 有效的，正确的 — Do you have valid reasons for your postponing?
你延迟有正当理由吗？

同义字词: authentic, sound, logical

1930. vanish [ˈvænɪʃ] [van·ish]

v. 消失，灭绝 — In fact, many types of animals have now vanished from the earth.
事实上，很多种类的动物现在已从地球上绝迹了。

1931. vaporize [ˈvepəˌraɪz] [va·por·ize]

v. （使）蒸发，使气化 — It is a common sense that water vaporizes when it boils.
水煮开时变成蒸汽，这是一个常识。

1932. variable [ˈvɛrɪəbl] [var·i·a·ble]

n. 变数 — Have you taken all the variables into account in your study?
你的研究中，有没有把所有的可变因素都考虑进去？

adj. 变化的，可变的 — The variable weather made me get a serious cold.
这种多变的天气让我得了重感冒。

同义字词: factor, differed, diversified, diverse, assorted

1933. varnish [ˈvɑrnɪʃ] [var·nish]

v. 涂上清漆，修饰 — In normal situation varnished furniture has a gloss.
正常的情况下，上漆的家具表面光滑。

n. 清漆，光泽面 — The varnish of the desk was slightly chipped.
桌子上光泽的表面被磨掉一点点。

同义字词: lacquer, cover, glaze, paint, color

1934. vegetation [ˌvɛdʒəˈteʃən] [veg·e·ta·tion]

n. 植物，草木 — The variety of the vegetation turned to be worse than we expected.
植物的多样性比我们期望的少了。

同义字词　plants, flora, growth, botony

1935. vehicle [ˋviɪkl] [ve·hi·cle]

n. 交通工具，车辆　No vehicles are permitted into.
禁止任何车辆进入。

衍生字词　▲ vehicle registration 车辆登记

1936. veil [vel] [veil]

v. 隐藏，遮蔽　Please use a cloth veil your face.
请用块布遮住脸。

n. 面纱　The beautiful princess dropped her veil and exposed her pretty face.
这个公主摘下面纱，露出漂亮的脸蛋。

1937. venerable [ˋvɛnərəbl] [ven·er·a·ble]

adj. 值得尊敬的，庄严的　My grandma is a venerable and roseate old man.
我的奶奶是一个德高望重的乐观老人。

同义字词　revered, honored, dignified, majestic

1938. venom [ˋvɛnəm] [ven·om]

n. （蛇的）毒液　The miserable girl retold the story with venom in her voice.
这可怜的女孩怨恨地把她的经历又讲述了一遍。

同义字词　poison, spite, malice, bitterness

1939. ventilate [ˏvɛntlˋet] [ven·ti·late]

v. 使通风，公开讨论　We had to ventilate the carriage by opening windows in an intense cold day.
即便天寒地冻，我们仍不得不开窗使车厢内空气流通。

1940. venture [ˋvɛntʃɚ] [ven·ture]

n. 冒险（事业），投机活动　It is a rewarding business venture.
这是个有利可图的商业投机活动。

v. 冒险，敢于　Venture a small fish to catch a great one.
放长线钓大鱼。

反义字词　▲ play for safety 不冒风险
　　　　　▲ security investment 安全投资

vehicle ~ vertical

1941. verify [ˈvɛrəˌfaɪ] [ver·i·fy] ★★★★★

v. 证明，证实
The facts mentioned just now verified his misdeed.
刚才提到的事实都证明了他的罪行。

同义字词　confirm, prove, certify, validate

1942. versatile [ˈvɝsətl] [ver·sa·tile] ☆★★★★

adj. 多才多艺的，通用的
She is a versatile person in her team and she usually gives performance to the public.
她是一个多才多艺的人，经常公开演出。

同义字词　talented, skilled, competent

1943. converse [kənˈvɝs] [con·verse] ★★★★★

v. 谈话，交谈
It is difficult to converse with such a stubborn person.
和如此固执的人交谈真是困难。

n. 谈话，交谈
You should give her a converse immediately.
你应该立即和她谈一下。

adj. 相反的，颠倒的
You can consider it from its converse aspect.
你可以从反面观点思考一下。

反义字词　same, conversation, talking

1944. vertebrate [ˈvɝtəˌbret] [ver·te·brate] ☆★★★★

n. 脊椎动物
Generally speaking, fishes, birds, and some mammals are vertebrates.
大致上，鱼、鸟和人类都是脊椎动物。

衍生字词　vertebrate fauna 脊椎动物区系

1945. vertical [ˈvɝtɪkl] [ver·ti·cal] ☆★★★★

adj. 垂直的，竖直的
It is said that ape as the ancestor of human beings in vertical walking.
据说人类的远祖猿猴是直立行走的。

同义字词　upright, perpendicular, erect, standing

衍生字词
▲ vertical trade 纵向贸易，南北贸易
▲ vertical assistance 垂直援助
▲ vertical ascent 垂直上升
▲ vertical circle 垂直圈
▲ vertical dance 垂直舞蹈（结合芭蕾舞和攀岩的特殊表演艺术，由美国加州的Project Bandaloop团体首创）

▲ vertical integration 垂直整合
▲ vertical job-loading 垂直工作增加
▲ vertical proliferation （核子武器的）纵向扩散
▲ vertical tasting 同一种葡萄酒不同年份产品的试喝

1946. vestige [ˈvɛstɪdʒ] [ves·tige] ☆☆★★

n. 痕迹, 遗迹　　There is not a vestige of lying in what he says.
他所说的没有一句是假话。

衍生字词　without a vestige of clothing 一丝不挂

1947. veto [ˈvito] [ve·to] ☆☆★★

n. 否决, 否决权　Teachers put a veto on our lating for school.
老师不允许我们上学迟到。

衍生字词　▲ veto in detail 部分否决（权）
　　　　　▲ veto power 否决权

1948. viable [ˈvaɪəbl] [vi·a·ble] ☆★★★

adj. 可行的, 切实　The sketch is apparently viable in finding the
可行的　　　　buried treasure.
从表面看起来，寻找宝藏时使用这个草图是可行的。

衍生字词　▲ viable yeast 活酵母

1949. vibrant [ˈvaɪbrənt] [vi·brant] ☆★★★

adj. 活泼的, 生气　The city is vibrant with life.
勃勃的　　　这座城市活力十足。

同义字词　active, energetic, lively, vivacious

1950. vigilance [ˈvɪdʒələns] [vig·i·lance] ☆☆★★

n. 警戒, 警惕　　In spite of vigilance the prisoner escaped from jail.
尽管警戒森严，那个犯人还是成功越狱了。

同义字词　watchfulness, alertness, caution

1951. vigorous [ˈvɪɡərəs] [vig·or·ous] ☆★★★

adj. 健壮的, 精力　The old professor is still vigorous and lively even
旺盛的　　　in his 90s.
即使已经九十多岁，老教授依然精力充沛。

同义字词　robust, strong, energetic, mighty

vestige ~ vulnerable

1952. violent [ˈvaɪələnt] [vi·o·lent] ☆★★★★

adj. 暴力引起的，暴烈的

They laid violent hands on the convict in the camp.
他们对在集中营的囚犯施以暴力。

同义字词 turbulent, strong, powerful

1953. viscous [ˈvɪskəs] [vis·cous] ☆★★★★

adj. 黏滞的，黏性的

Generally speaking gases are much less viscous than liquids.
大致说来，气体的黏滞性小于液体。

同义字词 gelatinous, sticky, gluey, viscid

1954. vital [ˈvaɪtl] [vi·tal] ☆★★★★

adj. 极重要的，致命的

This business is of vital importance to us.
这个生意对我们来说非常重要。

同义字词 essential, crucial, important, animate, alive

1955. volatile [ˈvɑlətl] [vol·a·tile] ☆★★★★

adj. 挥发性的，易变的

Her volatile emotions is out of our imagination.
她喜怒无常的情绪超出我们的想象。

1956. voluntary [ˈvɑlənˌtɛrɪ] [vol·un·tar·y] ☆★★★★

adj. 自愿的，志愿的

We are voluntary to donate the blood for the hospital without charge.
我们自愿捐血给这家医院。

反义字词 accidental, compulsory, involuntary

1957. voracious [voˈreʃəs] [vo·ra·cious] ☆☆★★★

adj. 狼吞虎咽的，贪吃的

She's a voracious reader of all kinds of wisdom stories.
她对任何智慧小故事都百看不厌。

高分秘诀 ▲ voracious reader 百读不厌的读者

1958. vulnerable [ˈvʌlnərəbl] [vul·ner·a·ble] ☆★★★★

adj. 易受攻击的，脆弱的

He volunteered to protect his girlfriend as she looked so vulnerable.
他的女朋友看起来很脆弱，令他想保护她。

同义字词 defenseless, susceptible

Ww 托福 TOEFL iBT

托福(TOEFL)的测验对象为母语为非英语的人
申请入学美加地区大学或研究所时，托福成绩单是必备文件之一。

- n. 名词
- v. 动词
- adj. 形容词
- adv. 副词
- prep. 介词
- art. 冠词
- pron. 代词
- aux. 助词
- conj. 连词

Ww 托福 TOEFL iBT

托福(TOEFL)的测验对象为母语为非英语的人
申请入学美加地区大学或研究所时，托福成绩单是必备文件之一。

1959. wade [wed] [wade] ☆★★★★

| v. 涉水，费力行走 | Our troop waded out into the long river.
我们的军队一路涉水经过这条长河流。 |

高分秘诀　▲ troop n. 军队，部队

1960. waive [wev] [waive] ☆★★★★

| v. 放弃，免除 | It is not wise to waive the claim.
放弃索赔是不明智的。 |

1961. walkout [ˋwɔkˏaut] [walk·out] ☆★★★★

| n. 罢工，离去 | Factory workers in our city staged a walkout to protest for pension.
我们城市的工厂工人为了争取合理的养老金而发起罢工。 |

高分秘诀　▲ pension n. 养老金，退休金

1962. wane [wen] [wane] ☆☆★★★

| v. 减少，衰落 | His strength was on the wane before his death.
他临死前体力越来越虚弱。 |

同义字词　decline, dwindle, diminish

1963. ward [wɔrd] [ward] ☆★★★★

| n. 病房，区 | The patient lay quietly on his bed in the medical ward.
病人安静地躺在内科病房的床上。 |
| v. 监护，守护 | The boxer quickly used a fist to ward off the blow.
这位拳击手迅速用拳头挡开这一击。 |

衍生字词　▲ ward in chancery 受英国大法官监护的未成年人

wade ~ weather

1964. ware [wɛr] [ware] ☆☆★★★

n. 陶器,货品

It was the heyday of lacquer ware in the Han Dynasty.
汉朝是陶器的鼎盛时期。

[同义字词] pottery, tool, implements

1965. warrant [ˋwɔrənt] [war·rant] ☆★★★★

v. 保证,担保

Our manager will warrant me an honest and reliable fellow.
我们经理可以保证我是一个诚实可靠的人。

n. 授权证,许可证

This is a warrant for success.
这是一个成功的保证。

1966. warrior [ˋwɔrɪə] [war·ri·or] ☆★★★★

n. 战士,勇士

I showed my respect for ancient warriors when I watched the costume film.
当我看史诗电影时,我对古代的战士充满敬意。

[同义字词] fighter, combatant, soldier

1967. wary [ˋwɛrɪ] [war·y] ☆★★★★

adj. 小心翼翼的,机警小心的

He is very wary of flattering people.
他对拍马屁者心存戒心。

1968. waxy [ˋwæksɪ] [wax·y] ☆☆★★★

adj. 苍白的,光滑的

This crystal is shinning with a waxy luster.
这块水晶闪烁着蜡样的光泽。

1969. weather [ˋwɛðə] [weath·er] ★★★★★

v. 风化,挨过

Rocks outside the house must be preserved or else they will weather.
房子外面的石头一定要妥善保存,不然会风化。

n. 天气,气象

If there is good weather tomorrow, I will go shopping with mom.
如果明天是好天气的话,我将会和妈妈一起去购物。

1970. weave [wiv] [weave] ☆★★★★

v. 迂回行进, 组合 — He is weaving his way through a crowd to chase his girlfriend.
他在人群中穿梭, 追赶女友。

同义字词 cloth making, knit, interlace, meader, waver

1971. weep [wip] [weep]

v. 哭泣, 流血 — Don't weep for the tribulation you went through.
不要为你所经历的苦难而哭泣。

1972. weird [wɪrd] [weird] ★★★★★

adj. 怪诞的, 奇异的 — She has some weird ideas to verify her theory.
她使用一些怪念头证明她的理论。

衍生字词 ▲ weird sisters （希腊神话）命运三女神

1973. weld [wɛld] [weld] ☆☆★★★

v. 焊接, 熔接 — It is said that the mechanism of improving the toughness of the weld is the finer grain size and the lower hardness of the weld.
据说焊缝韧性改善的原理是因为近缝区晶粒细化和硬度降低。

同义字词 bind, cement, join, solder, unite

1974. whim [wɪm] [whim] ☆☆★★★

n. 随意, 一时兴致 — He spoiled his children and indulges their every whim.
他溺爱自己的孩子，并且满足他们的任何要求。

同义字词 fancy, caprice, impulse, notion

1975. whisk [wɪsk] [whisk] ☆★★★★

v. 挥, 甩（某物） — The general's horse stood whisking its tail.
将军的马站着挥动着尾巴。

n. 掸, 拂（如马尾巴的摆动） — The horse brushed off the flies with a whisk of its tail.
那匹马尾巴一甩拂走苍蝇。

1976. whittle [`wɪt]] [whit·tle] ☆☆★★★

v. 削, 削减 — The government are trying to whittle down our burden.
政府正在着手减轻我们的负担。

高分秘诀 ▲ whittle down 消减

1977. wholesale [`holˌsel] [whole·sale] ☆★★★★

| adj. 批发的，大规模的 | Recreation is provided in the resort by wholesale.
这个休闲胜地为人们提供大量消遣娱乐。 |
| v. 批发 | They wholesale the skirts at $20 each.
他们以每件二十美元的批发价出售这些裙子。 |

1978. wholesome [`holsəm] [whole·some] ☆★★★★

| adj. 有益健康的 | Bitter pills may have wholesome effects.
良药苦口。 |
| 同义字词 | healthful, beneficial, sound |

1979. wipe [waɪp] [wipe] ☆★★★★

v. 擦，拭	She went on weeping, occasionally wiping at her face with a towel. 她继续哭着，偶尔用毛巾擦一下脸。
n. 擦，拭	You had better give your boy's nose a good wipe before performance. 演出前，你最好把孩子的鼻子擦干净。
同义字词	rub, stroke, clean, sweep

1980. withdraw [wɪð`drɔ] [with·draw] ☆★★★★

| v. 撤退，撤销 | He withdrew from the race for some special reason.
他因为某些特殊原因退出比赛。 |
| 同义字词 | retreat, depart, revoke, retract |

1981. wither [`wɪðɚ] [with·er] ☆★★★★

| v. (使)枯萎，凋谢 | The lilacs in the garden withered because there was no water.
花园的丁香因缺水而枯死。 |
| 同义字词 | shrivel, shrink, wilt |

1982. withstand [wɪð`stænd] [with·stand] ☆★★★★

| v. 承受，抵住 | Generally speaking a politician must be able to withstand public criticism.
一般来说，政治人物必须经得起公众的批评。 |

1983. witness [ˈwɪtnɪs] [wit·ness] ☆★★★★

v. 目击，为……作证	I witnessed the fierce murder. 我目睹了这起残忍的凶杀案。
n. 证人，证词	Let the witness be sworn in. 让证人宣誓作证。

衍生字词
- ▲ bear witness to 证明
- ▲ witness box （英）证人席
- ▲ witness stand 法庭中的证人席
- ▲ swear off 发誓戒除
- ▲ swear like a trooper 破口大骂
- ▲ swear to secrecy （使某人）发誓保密

1984. wrap [ræp] [wrap] ☆★★★★

v. 裹，包，捆	Please wrap the corpse of the stray dog with a piece of clean cloth. 请用一块干净的布把那只流浪狗的尸体包起来。

同义字词 enclose, cover, surround

1985. wreck [rɛk] [wreck] ☆★★★★

n. 失事，失事的残骸	The wreck of the ship blocked the entrance to the harbour. 那艘船的残骸堵塞了港口。
v. 毁坏某物，失事	It is said that the fire wrecked the museum. 据说那场大火把博物馆烧毁了。

同义字词 destruction, ruins, sink, destroy, demolish

1986. wrestle [ˈrɛsl] [wres·tle] ☆★★★★

v. 搏斗，摔跤	He taught his students how to wrestle with their opponents. 他教导学生如何和对手摔跤。

1987. wring [rɪŋ] [wring] ☆★★★★

v. 绞，绞掉	The robber shouted, "I'll wring your neck if you don't behave!" 强盗大喊："你敢乱来，我就拧断你的脖子！"

同义字词 twist, squeeze, wrest

witness ~ wrinkle

1988. wrinkle [`rɪŋkl] [wrin·kle]   ☆★★★★

| **n.** 皱纹，褶皱 | She reconciled her dress to try to remove all the wrinkles.
她熨她的裙子，想把褶皱熨平。 |
| **v.** 起皱纹 | You can buy this kind of cloth because it won't wrinkle.
你可以买这种布料，因为它不会起皱。 |

| 同义字词 | furrow, crease, fold |
| 高分秘诀 | ▲ remove from 移动，搬开，调动
▲ remove to 搬家，迁移
▲ remove the cloth 食后撤席
▲ dress up 穿上盛装，装扮
▲ dress circle（剧场）特别座，特等席
▲ dress coat 燕尾服，礼服
▲ dress down 整饬（皮革），梳刷（马毛），叱责
▲ dress rehearsal （戏剧正式上演以前的）彩排，总排演
▲ dress shirt 男子于正式场合穿的衬衫
▲ dress uniform 军礼服
▲ dress-down Fridays 便服日，上班时不用穿制服的日子
▲ dressed-up 穿上盛装的，精心打扮的
▲ dressing gown （英）晨袍，浴衣
▲ dressing room 更衣室，化妆室
▲ dressing table 梳妆台，镜台
▲ dressing-up （孩子们的）化妆游戏
▲ dressing-down 斥责，打
▲ cloth cap 布帽
▲ cloth yard 量布尺，布码尺 |

Yy 托福 TOEFL iBT

托福(TOEFL)的测验对象为母语为非英语的人
申请入学美加地区大学或研究所时，托福成绩单是必备文件之一。

- n. 名词
- v. 动词
- adj. 形容词
- adv. 副词
- prep. 介词
- art. 冠词
- pron. 代词
- aux. 助词
- conj. 连词

托福(TOEFL)的测验对象为母语为非英语的人
申请入学美加地区大学或研究所时,托福成绩单是必备文件之一。

1989. yarn [jɑrn] [yarn] ☆☆☆★★

n. 纱, 纱线　　The girl knits a beautiful hat from yarn.
　　　　　　　那女孩用纱线织一顶漂亮的帽子。

1990. yawn [jɔn] [yawn] ☆★★★★

n. 呵欠　　　His yawns revealed he kept working for so long time.
　　　　　　　呵欠连天说明他已经工作太久了。

v. 打呵欠　　The little boy stopped crying and yawned then fell asleep.
　　　　　　　小男孩停止哭泣,打呵欠睡着了。

1991. yelp [jɛlp] [yelp] ☆☆☆★★

n. 叫吠, 叫喊声　The little girl gave a little yelp and had a blackout.
　　　　　　　小女孩尖叫一声跑开了。

v. 叫吠, 叫喊　His eyes got plucked out in the battle and he yelped in pain.
　　　　　　　战斗中他的眼睛被刺瞎了,让他痛得直叫。

1992. yield [jild] [yield] ☆★★★★

v. 生产, 屈服　The team will never yield to its opponent.
　　　　　　　这个队伍永远不会向对手屈服。

n. 产量, 收益　The new measures have helped raise farm yields steadily.
　　　　　　　新措施有助于农业产量的稳定提升。

　　同义字词　output, income, defer, surrender

1993. yolk [jok] [yolk] ☆☆★★★

n. 蛋黄　　　In western countries, people use egg yolk as the emulsifying agent in salad dressing.
　　　　　　　在西方国家,调味沙拉酱料时习惯用蛋黄作乳化剂。

Zz 托福 TOEFL iBT

托福(TOEFL)的测验对象为母语为非英语的人
申请入学美加地区大学或研究所时,托福成绩单是必备文件之一。

- n. 名词
- v. 动词
- adj. 形容词
- adv. 副词
- prep. 介词
- art. 冠词
- pron. 代词
- aux. 助词
- conj. 连词

Zz 托福 TOEFL iBT

托福(TOEFL)的测验对象为母语为非英语的人
申请入学美加地区大学或研究所时，托福成绩单是必备文件之一。

1994. zealous [ˈzɛləs] [zeal·ous] ☆☆★★★

| adj. 热心的，狂热的 | He showed his zealous passion to Radical Party.
他对激进党表现出狂热的激情。 |

反义字词　indifferent, disinterested, impersonal

1995. zenith [ˈzinɪθ] [ze·nith] ☆☆☆★★

| n. 顶点，顶峰 | To be the champion of Olympic Games was the zenith of his glory.
获得奥运冠军使是他的辉煌极盛期。 |

衍生字词　▲ zenith distance 天顶角距

1996. zigzag [ˈzɪgzæg] [zig·zag] ☆☆★★★

adj. 曲折的	We walked along a zigzag road to get the top of the mountain. 我们沿着一条曲折的路到达山顶。
n. Z字形，小径	A zigzag is in front of us when we have crossed the creek. 当我们穿过这条小溪时，一条Z字形的小路出现在我们前面。
v. 弯弯曲曲地走路，曲折地前进	The drunken man zigzagged down the road. 那醉鬼东倒西歪地沿路走去。

衍生字词　▲ zigzag fastening 交错连接，参差紧固

1997. zone [zon] [zone] ★★★★★

| n. 区域，地带 | A lot of foods were parachuted into the earthquake zone.
很多食物已空投到地震灾区。 |

同义字词　region, district

zealous ~ zone

版权专有　侵权必究

图书在版编目（CIP）数据

新托福核心单词速记 / 蒋志榆著. —北京：北京理工大学出版社，2019.8
ISBN 978-7-5682-4162-5

Ⅰ．①新… Ⅱ．①蒋… Ⅲ．① TOEFL－词汇－自学参考资料 Ⅳ．① H313.1

中国版本图书馆 CIP 数据核字（2017）第 134962 号

北京市版权局著作权合同登记号图字：01-2016-2910
简体中文版由我识出版社有限公司授权出版发行
躺着背单字 TOEFL iBT 托福，蒋志榆 著，2011 年，初版
ISBN：9789866163159

出版发行 /	北京理工大学出版社有限责任公司
社　　址 /	北京市海淀区中关村南大街 5 号
邮　　编 /	100081
电　　话 /	（010）68914775（总编室）
	（010）82562903（教材售后服务热线）
	（010）68948351（其他图书服务热线）
网　　址 /	http://www.bitpress.com.cn
经　　销 /	全国各地新华书店
印　　刷 /	定州启航印刷有限公司
开　　本 /	710 毫米 × 1000 毫米　1/32
印　　张 /	17.25
字　　数 /	480 千字
版　　次 /	2019 年 8 月第 1 版　2019 年 8 月第 1 次印刷
定　　价 /	49.00 元

责任编辑 /	武丽娟
文案编辑 /	武丽娟
责任校对 /	杜　枝
责任印制 /	李　洋

图书出现印装质量问题，请拨打售后服务热线，本社负责调换